The Story of
NORWICH

Iconic buildings of Norwich: the castle and cathedral as depicted on the cover of R.H. Mottram's Assault on Norwich.

The Story of NORWICH

Frank Meeres

Phillimore

2011

Published by
PHILLIMORE & CO. LTD
Healey House, Andover, Hampshire

ISBN 978 1 86077 713 4

Printed and bound in Malta

Manufacturing managed by
Jellyfish Solutions Ltd

Contents

List of Illustrations

Frontis: Iconic buildings of Norwich.

Colour plates, between pp.168-9

ONE

The Beginnings

The popular view of Norwich is that it is flat, but this is far from true, as anyone knows who has walked up Gas Hill, or from King Street up to Ber Street. Sylas Neville, looking from Thorpe in 1771, noted that 'Norwich is most irregularly built. The situation of some streets is high, but the greater part very low.' Norwich originated at the lowest point where the river on which it stands, the Wensum, could be crossed as it bends between two ridges of high land, the Ber Street ridge (now dominated by the Norman castle) and Thorpe Heights. Its topography and boundaries were also determined by the small rivers that run down from the hills into the Wensum; these streams, known locally as cockeys, still exist but all of them are now covered over.[1]

Norwich did not develop as a town until Saxon times, but people have settled in the area for many thousands of years, and new finds are continually coming to light. The relatively few finds from the Palaeolithic era (before 10,000 B.C.) include several hand axes at Carrow, and another one turned up at Morse's Rose Garden in Eaton in 1943. When the Jarrold Stand was built at Norwich City football ground in 2002, the site of a sandy island in the river was discovered, to which flint had been brought and worked in Palaeolithic times; thus one of the city's most recent – and most used – structures stands on one of the earliest sites of occupation in Norwich.[2]

A few signs of settlement along the river in the Mesolithic period have been found, mainly in the form of flint tools, such as the blade found at the corner of Cowgate and Magdalen Street in 1974. There are a greater number of finds from the later Neolithic and early Bronze Age periods. Work in 2002 on the former Bussey's Garage site, between Quayside and Palace Street, produced not only flints but also post-holes of a building of this period, and another rectangular structure was discovered at the Oaks in Harvey Lane in 1999.

A Neolithic settlement has been found at Eaton Heath, with a radio-carbon date of about 4000 B.C. In addition to the normal post-holes, a group of mysterious shafts were also found, 21 in all, each some eight yards deep. It is not absolutely certain that they were man-made: Rodney Castleden suggests they could be natural solution pipes into which Neolithic occupation material has fallen, but Paul Ashbee thought that the shafts were holes for huge posts. In his eyes, the site was an artificial sacred grove.[3]

Lying in the valley across the river from Norwich is an important religious centre – Arminghall Henge. Discovered as a result of aerial photography by Wing-Commander Insall in 1929, it stood on a promontory above the meeting place of the waters Tas and Yare. It consists now of a horseshoe of eight holes that once contained huge timber posts, each over a yard across and sunk into the ground to a depth of well over two yards; each post must have weighed about seven tons. Charcoal from these posts has been given a date of about 3000 B.C. We can only guess what the structure looked like. Perhaps the posts had lintels on top, like a wooden version of Stonehenge; possibly each was a tall carved totem pole, or perhaps they were connected to form some type of tower. It was surrounded by ditches, and the entrance faced south-west: mid-winter sunset. The henge, whose postholes are today preserved in concrete, is close to several burial mounds; one not far away was cut into when the southern bypass was built, revealing the site of a very early individual burial. Careful analysis of stains in the soil showed that someone had been buried in a wooden coffin in the third millennium B.C.[4]

There is considerable evidence of Bronze Age settlement (about 2500-800 B.C.). In 1979 the Norfolk Archaeological Unit excavated a site at Bowthorpe, only recently brought within the city boundary for a new housing estate, which air photography had shown as a circular crop mark. It turned out to be the remnant of a Bronze Age barrow, radiocarbon-dated to about 2000 B.C. Here, too, the archaeologists were able to detect that there had once been a burial in a wooden coffin. Signs of 11 more graves were found around the edge of the barrow; the best-preserved of these contained a body resting on a hay-filled pillow in a coffin made of oak planks. A thousand years later, the barrow was once more used for a burial but customs had changed: the ashes were found of a cremated body covered by a large urn. Two round burial mounds, of an original group of four, survive on Eaton golf course. In central Norwich, evidence has been found in recent years of possible dwellings along a stream whose site is now occupied by Pigg Lane, and of possible barrows on the hill behind, at Ber Street and the Forum. Brian Ayers suggests that 'the hills and valleys of central Norwich would have lent themselves to the development of a prehistoric ritual landscape with monuments occupying summits and 'false crests''.[5]

Bronze tools and weapons have been found all over the area, such as an arrow head found in 1979 at what is now Anglia Television. Rescue archaeology along the route of the southern bypass revealed a fine Iron Age longhouse not far from the later Roman town at Caistor St Edmund. The greatest treasure of the period now to be seen in Norwich does not come from the city but from Snettisham in the north-west of the county:

1 *The Jarrold Stand at Carrow Road, on the site of a Neolithic island.*

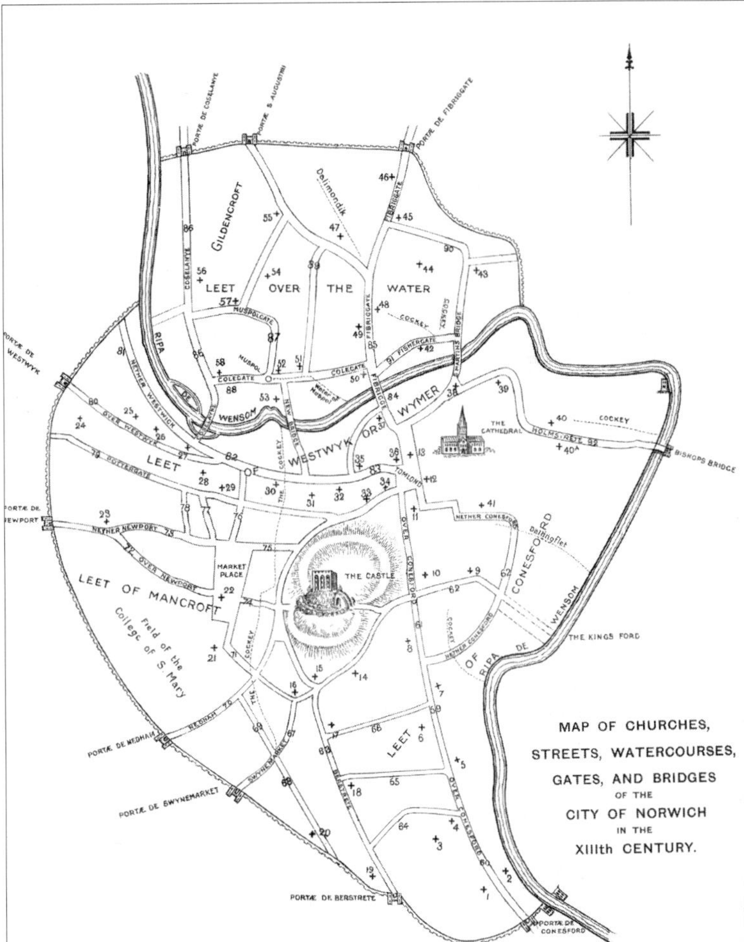

2 *The streams of Norwich, which still run beneath the streets.*

a collection of magnificent torcs or necklaces. These demonstrate the wealth of some of the area's inhabitants in the Iron Age period, which is the date of our first named inhabitant, and the first of very many strong women from the area: Boudica, famed for her struggle against the Roman Empire.

In A.D. 43, when the Romans invaded Britain, Norfolk was a part of the kingdom of the Iceni, under Prasutagus, who became a client king of the Romans. When he died, he left the Roman emperor co-heir to the kingdom along with his two daughters. The Romans treated the Iceni as defeated enemies and the girls were raped, which prompted the rebellion led by Boudica. The Iceni spread devastation in Colchester, London and St Albans before their eventual defeat. Roman writers disagree about Boudica's fate. Tacitus says that she took poison, but Dio Cassius says that she died from disease, and tantalisingly adds that the British gave her a rich burial; any such grave has yet to be discovered.[6]

The 'new town' of *Venta Icenorum* ('market place of the Iceni') was probably founded soon after Boudica's revolt; two miles south of the present city, the Roman town at Caistor, with its imposing town walls, is well worth a visit. The street pattern was probably laid out in about A.D. 70, with the main buildings – market place, public hall, baths – erected in the second century. The market place adjoined the town hall, leading to this intriguing comment from archaeologist John Davies: 'We may compare the appearance of these prominent Roman buildings with the current arrangements of Norwich market and City Hall, from where civic dignitaries look out from their splendid offices across the assembled awnings of the market stalls covering the large piazza below.' There was also an amphitheatre, the Roman equivalent of Norwich city football stadium, of which nothing visible remains beyond a slight dip in the surface 90 yards south of the walls.[7]

3 *Palace Plain in the 1960s, with Bussey's Garage on the left.*

The town was beside the river Tas, then navigable by barges up to this point; as late as 1728, Norfolk antiquarian John Kirkpatrick thought he saw 'ringbolts in the walls, whereto ships were fastened', but, if he was correct in his interpretation, these have long disappeared. The story of the town is not one of peaceful and uninterrupted progress. The forum was at one time destroyed by fire and remained derelict for half a century before being rebuilt on a much smaller scale. The third-century walls that we see today actually enclose an area only half that of the original town, another sign of decline.

It is possible that the association of the Norwich area with the production of wool goes all the way back to Roman times. There is a fourth-century reference to the Roman army being supplied with cloth from a state-run weaving mill at '*Venta*'. This could well be Caistor, but could refer instead to one of the two other towns in Roman Britain called *Venta*: Winchester and Caerwent.[8]

The Roman town at Caistor existed long before any town was established at Norwich itself; when Norwich was built, Caistor was used as a place from which to gather stone for its new buildings, especially for the cathedral. This gave rise to a local saying, 'Caistor was a town when Norwich was none: Norwich was built with Caistor's stone.'

Although there was no Roman town at Norwich, it was at a crossing point of two Roman roads. One ran east-west from a port at Brundall, entering the city near present-day Pilling Park and running down Gas Hill, across the river where Bishop Bridge now stands and through a causeway in the marshland of what is now the Cathedral Close. It continued along the line now made up of Tombland Alley, Prince's Street, St Benedict's and the Dereham Road, and then, running westward across the county, eventually reached the Fen Causeway, providing a connection with the Midlands. Although the road's origins must have been forgotten, much of it remained a right of way, for example in the churchyard of St George Tombland. Ayers, following an idea of Alan Carter, has suggested the intriguing possibility that Tombland Alley represents perhaps a deliberate symbolic 'remembrance' of the Roman road. The other road ran north-south, connecting Caistor with the Roman industrial site at Brampton near Aylsham; it ran up Long John Hill and along Ber Street, crossing the other Roman road near the present *Hog and Armour* public house.[9]

There would have been farmsteads and fields where the city now stands, almost entirely obliterated by later urban growth. Malcolm Atkin suggested a farmstead in the St Augustine's area, pottery of Roman date having been found near Magdalen Street, and Romano-British field systems and a possible farm were discovered in 2003 at the Chapelfield site. There have been other finds in the Yare valley at Eaton and in the Wensum valley at Lakenham and Earlham, probably also farmsteads. Two rich Roman burials were discovered at Stanley Avenue in Thorpe in 1950; one included three coins of Nero. Two skeletons found under Woodlands Park off Dereham Road in 1861 were probably of the third or fourth century A.D. Pottery fragments and Roman coins have been found all across the city, but these of course could have been dropped years or even centuries later.[10]

Early Saxon Norwich

As the Roman Empire fell apart, the Saxons invaded; however, they probably did not slaughter the British but slowly merged with them. Three Saxon cemeteries very close to Caistor show that people continued to live there long after the Romans had left, either within the walls or around the site of the Roman town, perhaps right through to the ninth century.[11]

Some place-names of early Saxon Norwich are still used today in the city. The name *Coslany* is one: the last two elements of the word may imply 'long island'. Coslany was indeed an island in medieval times, with bridges to both the south and the north. As late as 1391, Nicholas Edgefield was paying the city rents for the 'bitemay' in the river in Coslany; Hudson and Tingey define this as 'an island forming part of the river bank'. The first element 'cos' was taken by Alan Carter, whose archaeological work in the 1970s provided many new insights into the city's history, to mean 'pigs'; perhaps pigs were farmed on the island, or it could have been, as he suggested, an insulting term for the inhabitants. However, Sandred and Lindstrom take the 'lan' element in the name to mean the course of a river through meadowland, and think that 'Cos' could well be a personal name. Little evidence has been found of early Saxon settlement in Coslany, excavation having shown instead large-scale iron working as late as the 10th century.[12]

4 *Tombland Alley, preserving the site of a Roman road.*

The name 'Westwick', the western settlement, is also still used, being first found in documents in the 12th century; the form of the name suggests it originated before 850. The name 'Conesford' means 'king's ford', the second element being English and the first element Danish. It has come to be used for the area at the southern end of King Street, but it seems the ford was the crossing by the Romans already mentioned, and so actually at the northern end. Where Anglia Square now stands was once a wood called Mereholt, which means 'Boundary Wood', and it perhaps marked the northern limit of the early Saxon settlement; there was a pagan Saxon cemetery at Eade Road, above the city and close to the Roman road.[13]

It was once thought that a settlement might have existed on the hill south of the river, at the area later known as Needham (meaning poor meadow or poor homestead); however, archaeological work on the Castle Mall failed to find any sign of it. The pattern seems to be one of gradual growth along the gravel terraces on both sides of the river rather than separate villages that later coalesced. Recent work has uncovered more evidence of Saxon Norwich. A dig at Fishergate in 2005 uncovered Ipswich ware and a small hoard containing sceats – mid-Saxon pennies – one of them a forgery! Evidence of structures was found – post-holes and a pit – probably indicating a small trading settlement. North of the river, a series of holes, perhaps a mid-Saxon building, were found two yards down at St Saviour's Lane in 2011.[14]

'Viking' Norwich

Scandinavian forces conquered the east of England after they defeated King Edmund in 869. This is traditionally said to have been at Hoxne, although a few authorities think it was at Hellesdon north of Norwich; the most likely spot of all is a meadow called Hellesdon in Bradfield St Clare, close to Bury St Edmunds. Edmund was killed after the battle, and a medieval representation of his martyrdom can be still be seen in Norwich, carved in the stone spandrel of the west door of St Lawrence church. He is shown being struck by many arrows; the wolf which, according to the legend, guarded his head is also portrayed.

The Scandinavians were not just raiders, but had come to stay; the Treaty of Wedmore of 878 restricted them to the east of England, including Norfolk and Norwich. The signs they left of their presence include several city place-names. Most well known is the street ending '-gate', as in Fishergate, Cowgate, Colegate and Pottergate; this does not refer to an opening but is the Scandinavian word 'gata', meaning street. Pottergate and Fishergate relate to the occupations practised on them; the curve of Fishergate was once thought to represent the ancient riverbank, but Ayers has suggested that it curves to a bridging point over a small creek, which ran inland close to the present St Edmund's church, where small boats were moored.

Two other Scandinavian words in street names are Ber Street, Ber meaning 'ridge', and also nearby Finkelgate. Finkel could mean 'crooked' or, as Sue Margeson suggested, it could come from the Scandinavian word for 'cuddles' and be the Viking equivalent of a later Norwich street name 'Whores' Alley'. If so, the street had already come to assume an urban function it has not entirely relinquished today.[15]

Left: 5 *The murder of St Edmund, above the west door of St Lawrence.*
Below left: 6 *Moray Smith's proposed Viking image for a pub in Sprowston.*

The principal Viking settlement was north of the river, probably centred around the church of St Clement, a popular church dedication among Danes (as in the well-known St Clement Danes in London). Other churches north of the river paid a portion of their tithes to St Clement centuries later, indicating that they had been carved out of the original parish as the number of inhabitants grew.

7 *St Clement's church, the minster church on the north bank.*

In the early 10th century, the settlement was defended by a bank and ditch. The western side of this ran along St George's Street, with Calvert Street preserving the line of a passage inside the defences. It is not clear where the eastern boundary lay: the curve of Cowgate may be a relic of it, or it could have been along Peacock Street instead, especially probable as the Dalymond stream would then have formed a natural eastern defence for the settlement.

Finds in the city from the period of Viking occupation include a cross shaft with Scandinavian-style decoration found on the site of St Vedast church at Rose Lane, which is now on display in the Castle Museum.

'Anglo-Scandinavian' Norwich

The Scandinavians in East Anglia were defeated by the English armies of King Edward the Elder in A.D. 917. However, this did not lead to the restoration of an independent kingdom of East Anglia; instead, it became part of the kingdom of the west Saxons. The Scandinavians did not all leave, of course; the city clearly still had a large Scandinavian presence. One proof of this is the dedication of two churches in the city to Olaf, king and later patron saint of Norway. Olaf died in battle in 1030, becoming regarded as a saint almost at once, so the dedications indicate a strong Scandinavian presence in Norwich even at this date. Brian Ayers suggests that the term 'Anglo-Scandinavian Norwich' best sums up this period of the city's history.

Recent excavations are revealing more information about Anglo-Scandinavian Norwich. In 1992-3 excavations at the Franciscan friary site discovered a die that could have been used in the making of coins; the work also revealed the only definite late ninth- or early 10th-century building yet found in Norwich. A Viking gold ingot, and evidence of gold making, was found at the site of the Millennium Library. Ayers comments, 'the unexpected discovery of evidence for tenth-century gold working – in the form of a small ingot and fragments of a crucible on the site of the Millennium Building in 1999 – is of interest, not because it indicates gold-working in the pre-Conquest period (it would be astonishing if there were none) but because the activity was undertaken at a location remote from the known centre of urban settlement, presumably to reduce risk of fire and minimise interference'.[16]

The word 'Northwic' appears for the first time in the reign of Edward's son, Athelstan, who was king between 925 and 939. It occurs not on a document as such, but on coins; one can be seen in the Castle Museum. This means there must have been a mint in Norwich making the coins, which in itself proves that the town was already of some importance – mints were only set up in 'burhs', the essential features of which were fortifications and a market. The very name 'wic' means trading place. It could have been called Northwic because it was the northern wic in East Anglia (in contrast to a southern 'wic' now called Ipswich). Alternatively, it could simply have been the 'wic' north of the river, as opposed to the area already mentioned called Westwick west of the river; majority opinion now favours the latter theory.

There was probably a mid-10th-century bridge where Fyebridge now stands. W.H. Hudson saw massive timbers when the sewers were being constructed at the end of the 19th century, and the associated pottery found was of that date.

The earliest known document to mention Norwich is in the *Book of Ely*, written for the monastic house of Ely, probably in the 980s (but surviving only in a 12th-century copy). The Abbot of Ely wanted to buy land in Cambridge, and he was informed that 'Cambridge, Norwich, Ipswich and Thetford were of such liberty and dignity that if anyone bought land there he did not need witnesses'. This document shows that Norwich was one of four settlements in East Anglia regarded as a 'civilised' place rather than a frontier town, one where law and order prevailed, and where the Abbot could be confident of keeping hold of any property he purchased.[17]

The second earliest document tells a much more dramatic story, and shows how Viking attacks had started up again at the end of the 10th century, with drastic results. The source is the *Anglo-Saxon Chronicle*. In the year 1004 we are told: 'Here Swein came with his fleet to Norwich and completely ravaged and burnt down the town.' King Swein was avenging Vikings who had been massacred in England on the orders of King Ethelred in 1002. Edith Henderson, writer of a brilliant child's history of Norwich in about 1918, imagined the scene:

> Norwich suffered terribly from the cruelty of Swein and his warriors. They came to the little fishing town here at the foot of the hills of the Yare estuary: and when they sailed away, the red flames were leaping from the homesteads, spreading from hut to hut, filling all the sky with a fierce, red glare.[18]

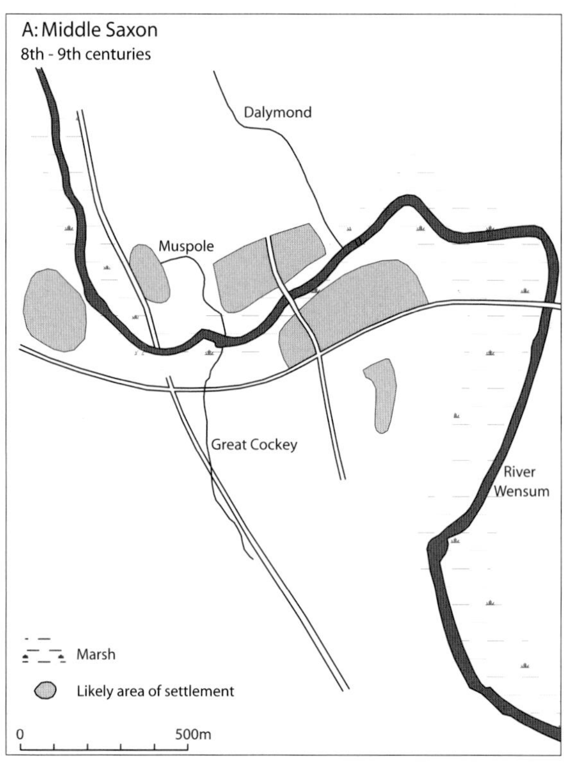

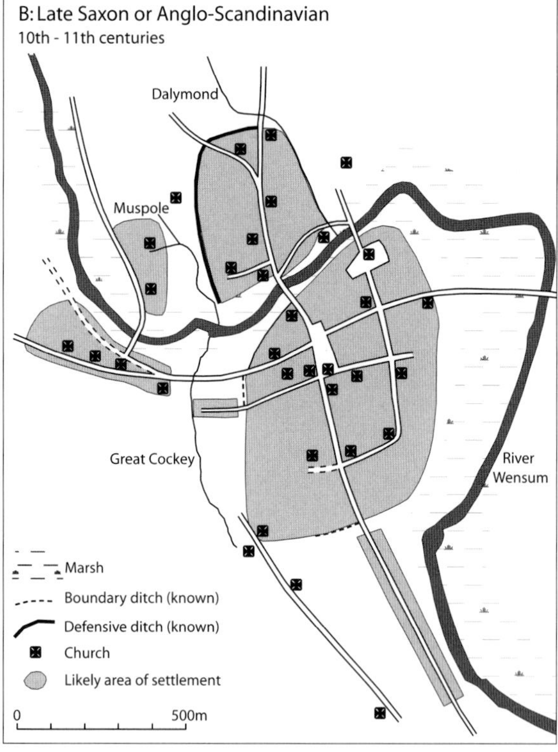

8 *Mid Saxon and Anglo-Scandinavian Norwich.*

Two churches on Magdalen Street long preserved the memory of a great fire in their names – St Mary Unbent (unburnt) and St Margaret Incombusto (in the burnt area). The implication is that the churches stood in a sea of devastation; this could well be a recollection of the 1004 fire, but fire was such a common destroyer of medieval towns that certainty is impossible.

In 1013 the whole of eastern England surrendered to Swein, and King Ethelred fled abroad. Swein died later in the year, but his son Canute eventually won the entire kingdom for himself. He was very much king of the North Sea, ruling over Denmark and, from 1028, Norway as well; the Viking chronicler Ottar the Black, court poet to King Olaf, says, 'Canute is the foremost sovereign under heaven.' Ottar mentions an incident, perhaps the 1004 attack or perhaps, as Sue Margeson suggests, in 1016, an event she describes as 'one of the last Viking raids'. Addressing Canute, Ottar says, 'Gracious giver of mighty gifts, you made mail-coats red in Norwich … you pressed on, blunting swords upon weapons; they could not defend their strongholds when you attacked'. So our third reference to Norwich, like the second, is a record of battle.[19]

Canute was much more than a Viking raider. He secured his place in the line of English kings by marrying the widow of his predecessor, Ethelred the Unready, and devised a code of law based on those of earlier Anglo-Saxon kings. Under Canute, as under Athelstan three generations earlier, money was minted in Norwich; over three hundred pre-Conquest coins are known (compared, however, with three times as many from Lincoln and from York). In the time of Canute, England was part of an empire centred on the North Sea, which was a highway for trade and travel rather than a barrier. Towns on or near the east coast must have benefited enormously from this in the same way towns on the west coast gained from the development of trade with America five centuries later.[20]

Boats landed goods on the south side of the river near St Martin at Palace Plain: wicker mats were placed along the bank, onto which the boats were dragged. There may well have been a market beside by the river, but the main market of Anglo-Scandinavian Norwich was the large open space now called Tombland. Larger than the present space, it has been encroached by the cathedral on one side and St George Tombland on the other. Here imported and locally made goods were traded, such as the pottery that gave Pottergate its name. The name Tombland has nothing to do with tombs, deriving from a Danish word meaning 'empty' or 'open' space. The earliest written evidence for it is in about 1250, so it may not have been its original name. This was the heart of the Norfolk town; even today, the main roads in Norwich like Magdalen Street and King Street lead to Tombland rather than the present market place. At the southern end was the palace of the Earl of East Anglia, balanced by that of the Bishop at the north (where the *Maid's Head* now stands).

It appears that the area north of the river declined in the early 11th century, perhaps because of the damage caused by the fire, in contrast to the south bank, where a partly planned town, with a pattern of rectangular streets and churches at the junctions, grew up around Tombland, bounded by the river to the north, the Great Cockey to the west, and marshy ground to the east. Heather Wallis made excavations on the Cinema City site between 2003 and 2006, finding evidence of settlement in the Anglo-Scandinavian and early Norman periods, including pottery making. In the courtyard a ditch was discovered, running north-south, and another was found in excavations at Steppings Lane; these could be the two ends of the defensive works, although they are not on the same scale. Thus the town was in effect two settlements, one on each bank, connected by the bridge; Ayers describes it as a double burh. The fourth written mention of pre-Conquest Norwich is in a Saxon will which has been dated to 1035-8, which merely mentions a house plot in Norwich.[21]

Pre-Conquest Norwich was producing pottery (the street called Pottergate then continued down Lobster Lane and Bedford Street), and evidence of one kiln, last fired about 1010, was found in the 1980s after Hovell's basket shop burnt down. Other products were being made from bone and leather. Trading routes existed with Norway, importing schist for whetstones, while pottery was imported from Rhineland, the Low Countries and northern France. There was some suburban development along St Benedict's, extending from the probable pre-Conquest foundation of St Gregory across the Great Cockey, and perhaps also southwards along King Street.

Anglo-Scandinavian buildings have recently been revealed by major work for Castle Mall and at the Franciscan friary site, and evidence of a two-roomed building was found at a Palace Street dig in 2006. The Franciscan friary site cuts across the 11th-century roads of the Anglo-Scandinavian planned town; the site is itself now cut by the Victorian Prince of Wales Road.

What was life in Anglo-Scandinavian Norwich like? The fact that part of the town was destroyed for the castle made the excavations of the Castle Mall site especially exciting. The work took place between 1987 and 1991 and showed little evidence of settlement before the 10th century. Finds showed several types of building, including some used for grain storage and others for industrial processes such as pottery manufacture. DNA research on one young male, who died some time between 930 and 1050 A.D., has shown a gene identified as Romani, the earliest recorded in Britain and five centuries earlier than the Romani people were thought to have first arrived here. Burials discovered in the Castle Mall area include several of Scandinavian people: pre-Conquest Norwich was clearly a cosmopolitan society, with people moving along the trade routes between different countries.

A church, described on p.12, was excavated at the Anglia Television site in 1979, and a large number of skeletons were recovered from the churchyard. Some 130 pre-Conquest burials were found, half of them children. Of the adults, 40 were male and just 20 female. This may have been because the whole of the graveyard could not be excavated; perhaps some areas were reserved for males and some for females. The age of death could be calculated: 46 per cent of the men and 67 per cent of the women survived to an age of between 35 and 45; very few people lived beyond this age.[22]

The lives of these people were hard, and their torsos and arms show signs of heavy labour. Several suffered from rickets and nine had a bone condition which gave them continuous pain behind their eyes. These diseases suggest their diet was inadequate, and providing supplies to such a large town would certainly have required fairly sophisticated organisation. Roberta Gilchrist has estimated that a town of 10,000 people in 1050 A.D. would consume in one year 1,750 sheep, 1,250 cows and 1,000 pigs. It would require almost two million pounds of grain for bread, and a further 200,000 pounds for beer. Waste would need to be organised, too; such a town would have produced almost a million gallons of human urine and over 700,000 tonnes of human excrement each year.[23]

The Christian Church

Some of the citizens of the later Roman empire were certainly Christian, and the Saxons would have found it an established religion, at least among the elite. During the late fifth and sixth centuries England seems to have largely lapsed back into paganism.

Bede says that the first seat of the bishopric of East Anglia was set up by Felix in the mid-seventh century at a place called 'Dommoc'. A Burgundian, Felix was bishop from 630 until his death in 647; his see has traditionally been thought to be at Dunwich, but more recent scholars have suggested Felixstowe as a more likely site. The bishopric was divided in 673, the northern part being given its centre at Elmham. The identity of this Elmham is not certain:; some people think it was South Elmham in Suffolk, but North Elmham seems more probable. Pope Gregory recommended that Christian churches be built at places already used by pagans as places of worship; a possible example in the city is St Michael at Plea as fragments of a cremation urn were found in the churchyard. Because of the Danish occupation, the bishopric lapsed in the ninth and early 10th centuries. After the Christian Saxons re-established their authority, the two centres of the diocese were at Hoxne and at North Elmham.[24]

It is not known which was the first church to be established in Norwich. Both St Gregory and St Clement can be described as 'minster' churches, from which later churches developed as the built-up area expanded. As we have seen, nearby churches paid some part of their tithes to St Clement, and the same applies to St Gregory, which is very close to the Roman crossroads previously mentioned. Two pre-Conquest churches – St Mary and Christchurch – are named in the will of Sifflaed, our fifth – and final – pre-Domesday document to mention Norwich. Unfortunately the date of this will is not known, but it must be some time between 990 and 1066. There were between 25 and 40 churches by 1066, six of them being given names in the Domesday Book: All Saints, Lawrence, Martin (at Palace), Michael (on Tombland), Simon and Jude, and Sepulchre. Churches of the Anglo-Scandinavian period in the Tombland area south of the river are commonly on street corners, implying a degree of urban planning, as already suggested.[25]

The east wall of St Martin at Palace church shows what is regarded as a pre-Conquest feature: the Barnack limestone of its corners are arranged in the style known as long-and-short work. Excavation in 1986/7 found evidence of earlier timber buildings on the alignment of the street rather than on that of the later, larger church we see now, which was erected in the 11th century. The finding of a fragment of grave-cover made in Lindsey in Lincolnshire is evidence of trade and wealth: someone could afford to bring it here. According to Domesday Book the richest church in Norwich was that of St Michael Tombland. This stood on the site of the present public lavatories in Tombland, and when they were being dug in 1878, a cross made of walrus ivory was discovered, which Ayers called 'the finest piece of art known from pre-Conquest Norwich'. It belongs to the Victoria and Albert Museum in London, and is currently on loan to Norwich Castle Museum.[26]

9 *St Martin at Palace, showing 'Saxon-style' long-and-short work.*

The discovery of the church underneath what is now Anglia Television shows how inadequate our written sources are – there was nothing to suggest its existence. It is also important because it can be dated fairly exactly: we know that the buildings in this area were cleared to make way for the Norman castle. There appear to have been three stages of development of the church, the final one being of a nave 26 by 16 feet, with a chancel 10 feet square. There was a font, which replaced an earlier baptistery. The building, like its predecessors, was made of wood, like the small wooden churches still to be seen in some Scandinavian villages. This is the kind of building in which our ancestors worshipped in Anglo-Scandinavian Norwich.

One Saxon resident of the Norwich area, according to legend, was Walstan, who became a popular saint in the area. The legend is that he was the son of a king, born at Blythburgh, but renounced his wealth, giving away his clothes and working as a simple farm labourer near Taverham. His parents travelled around looking for him, and issued a proclamation about their lost son. Walstan's employer saw it and went to him, but he died very soon after. He was buried at Bawburgh by the Bishop of Norwich and his monks, and healing miracles occurred at his grave. Much of this is unhistorical, as he is supposed to have died in about 1016, at which date there were no kings in Blythburgh and no bishop or monks in Norwich. Yet the legend was believed by everybody in Norfolk in the Middle Ages – a local farm labourer became a saint much loved among the peasantry. Even today two images of him can be seen in Norwich, on the font now in St Julian and on the screen from St James Pockthorpe, now in St Mary Magdalen on Silver Road.

Then came the Norman Conquest and the shape of Norwich was forever changed.

TWO

Norwich in the Middle Ages

The Normans invaded England in 1066, beating the English at Hastings and killing their king, Harold – who had Norwich connections as he had been Earl of East Anglia between 1045 and 1053. It is debatable how much the change of rulers affected ordinary people, as many aspects of daily life would have gone on much as they did before. Some features in city churches commonly said to be of 'Saxon' style were almost certainly built after the Conquest, such as the belfry openings in St Mary Coslany tower, as the stone with which they are constructed is from Caen. All the surviving round towers of the city's churches were probably constructed in the Norman period. The west wall of the cathedral cloister has double-splayed windows, another feature traditionally associated with the pre-Conquest period, but it must have been constructed three decades after 1066.

However, there is no doubt that Norwich was greatly affected by the Conquest, the urban landscape being transformed by two iconic buildings, the castle and the cathedral, and by the establishment of the New Borough around a new market place – still in use almost a thousand years later. It was also greatly affected by a dramatic event occurring less than a decade after the Conquest: the rebellion of Earl Ralph Guader.

King William gave the earldom, city and castle of Norwich to Ralph in 1071. Ralph was a Breton on his father's side with a Welsh mother. He married Emma, the daughter of William Fitz Osbern and sister of Roger, Earl of Hereford, in 1075. According to the *Anglo-Saxon Chronicle*, the wedding feast was celebrated in Norwich, although John of Worcester says it was in Exning. Many Saxon nobles were present, including Roger and also Waltheof, Earl of Northumberland. At the feast, Roger persuaded them to join in a conspiracy against William, who was in Normandy at the time. William of Malmesbury does not say where the feast occurred, but notes that 'their reason was entirely clouded by drunkenness'.

Next day, Earl Waltheof changed his mind and went to Lanfranc, the Archbishop of Canterbury, who was guardian of the kingdom. On Lanfranc's advice, he sailed over to Normandy and told the king about the planned rebellion. Meanwhile Odo, Bishop of Bayeux, and Jeffrey, Bishop of Coutances, raised an army loyal to the king. They forced Ralph back into his castle in Norwich, from where he took ship, either to raise help from Denmark or to escape to Brittany. Emma was left to defend the castle, which she apparently did for three months, another of the strong women Norwich has seen over the centuries – Ralph Mottram calls her 'heroic Emma'. When finally forced to surrender, she was allowed to follow her husband to Brittany.[1]

At Christmas, the king himself came to Norwich and punished those who supported Ralph, some being banished and others having their eyes gouged out. The next year (1076), he pursued Ralph into Brittany and besieged him in his castle at Dol. However, Philip, the King of France, came to Ralph's support and William was forced to withdraw. Ralph and Emma were left unpunished; both later joined the first crusade and both died in about 1096 before reaching Jerusalem.

It is not clear to what extent the rebellion was led by Englishmen, as F.M. Stenton thought, or by men from Brittany. Ralph himself can be seen as either a Breton or an Englishman. The *Anglo-Saxon Chronicle* thought that Ralph was the son of an Englishman from Norfolk, but Archbishop Lanfranc calls him 'Breton dung'; in contrast Breton documents also describe him as an Englishman. There was a strong Breton presence in early medieval Norwich, shown in the dedication of one church to the Breton saint Winwaloy.

At Christmas in 1085, King William decided to make a great survey of England and this was completed by autumn 1086. This is the well-known Domesday Book. The section for Norwich is the first detailed account of the city, showing what it was like just before the Conquest and 20 years after it. It states that before 1066 there were some 1,320 burgesses in Norwich. By 1086, some 22 had fled to Beccles and another 12 elsewhere – 'those fleeing and others remaining have been utterly devastated partly because of Earl R[alph]'s forfeitures, partly because of fires, partly because of the king's tax, partly by Waleran'. (Waleran was a royal officer, who was dead by 1076; his son held land in Norfolk in 1086.) There were 190 empty buildings in 1086. The construction of the castle also made a huge hole in the old town, as 88 buildings were cleared away for it. It had already been proposed to move the site of the bishopric from Thetford to Norwich; the entry mentions 14 buildings given by King William 'for the principal seat of the bishopric'. The castle and cathedral are described later in this chapter.[2]

The death of King William in 1087 led to further trouble. After Ralph's treachery, Roger Bigot had been appointed constable of Norwich Castle and king's bailiff. Roger was one of many Frenchmen who supported the claim to the throne of William's eldest son, Robert, rather than the younger son, William Rufus. Rufus was supported by many, including Losinga and almost all the bishops, and the rebellion was defeated. Bigot was driven

Left: 10 *The round tower at St Mary Coslany, with its 'Saxon-style' windows, made with stone from Caen. This photograph was taken in 1907.*

Below left: 11 *Norwich Cathedral, with its Norman tower and 15th-century spire.*

from his own castle, to which, however, he was soon readmitted, and his family continued as the king's officials for several generations. Afterwards there was a half-century of relative calm, and record-keeping improved. In the first surviving pipe roll, that for 1130, the sheriff of Norfolk paid £25 as the aid, or tax, for Norwich; 100 shillings were excused so the total tax expected was £30.

It was probably in 1158, just four years into his reign, that Norwich was granted its first charter by Henry II. Like many early documents, it is not dated and historians have to use detective work to establish when it was written. The clues are the names of the witnesses and the known movements of the king. If the historians are right, the charter must have been written between April and August 1158. It does not grant any specific rights, merely confirming to the citizens of Norwich the customs and liberties they had enjoyed in the time of Henry's grandfather, Henry I.[3]

In 1163 King Henry granted Norwich to Hugh Bigot. When Prince Henry, the king's eldest son, rebelled in France, Hugh supported the son against the father, and in 1173 Hugh landed in England with an army of Fleming soldiers. He expected the people of Norwich to support him, but they remained loyal to their king and he was forced to attack his own town. Once he had captured it, on 18 June 1174, he burnt it in revenge and held the richest citizens to ransom. The king raised an army against Hugh, who surrendered without a fight; soon after he went to the Holy Land, where he died. Most of the Flemings were weavers and had their eyes on English wool, and after the war was over some stayed on in England, so that as early as the 12th century two of the main themes of Norwich history were already established: the importance of wool and weaving, and the close links with the Low Countries.[4]

12 *The charter of Richard I, 1194.*

King Henry died in 1189 and was succeeded by Richard, known to history as the Lionheart. It was he who in 1194 gave to Norwich the charter from which the foundation of the city is normally dated, although like many such charters it may well just have formally recognised the already existing situation. It granted that the citizens of Norwich were to choose their own ruler, or reeve, each year so that the courts and assemblies were headed by men of the citizens' own choosing and not by the king's appointees. The citizens now held the city at a fixed rent or farm of £108 per year, which they paid directly to the king's exchequer and not through the sheriff of Norfolk.[5]

Norwich has always regarded this as the key charter in its history. In 1443 they argued that it was this document that gave the citizens their franchises; centuries later, in 1994, the city celebrated 800 years of self-government. Edith Henderson knew the importance of the charter:

> That charter is perhaps the most precious document that we have in Norwich, for it is the first real grant of our freedom … It is just a small strip of parchment with some writing in Latin on it. To see it you would scarcely think that it could have meant so very much to many generations of Norwich people.[6]

The charter was confirmed in almost identical terms by King John when he succeeded to the throne. He became involved in civil war with his barons; Roger Bigot, the constable of Norwich, took the side of the rebel barons and Norwich Castle was seized by the king. One of Roger's grandsons was held hostage by John during the civil war, first at Norwich and later at Sandwich. The Bishop of Norwich remained loyal to the king, who sent him to raise an army in the king's French domains to destroy the barons. The bishop did this, but most of the soldiers were drowned during a storm while crossing over from the Continent. King Louis of France landed in support of the barons in 1216, and John slowly retreated before him.[7]

John died in October 1216 and was succeeded by his child-son, Henry III. Louis eventually returned to France, and Norwich was returned to Roger Bigot. In 1228 the citizens petitioned Henry for a new charter, which he granted them. It was largely identical with those of Richard and John but with an extra paragraph ordering that everyone resident in the city should pay royal taxes, and not just citizens. He granted Norwich two further charters, the last when he visited Norwich in 1256.

In 1266 the city was once more plundered by enemies. The so-called 'disinherited barons' had been living in hiding on the Isle of Ely after supporting Simon de Montfort against Henry III. (Simon and his followers were defeated by the king's army at the battle of Evesham in 1265; Simon was killed in the battle and his supporters had their lands confiscated.) These barons raided Norwich, killing many citizens and carrying others away with them for ransom. One man killed by the barons on 16 December 1266 was Ralph, servant of William Payn, or so nine persons swore on oath to the city court in 1268.

In 1272 long-running quarrels between the people of Norwich and the cathedral priory came to a head, leading to a riot described by Christopher Harper-Bill as 'one of the most violent assaults on a religious institution in medieval England'. The riots are described from the monks' viewpoint in Bartholomew Cotton's *Chronicle,* which naturally blames the townsmen, and from that of the citizens, blaming the prior and monks, in the *Liber de Antiquis Legibus* by various chroniclers.[8]

About the time of the feast of Holy Trinity (19 June), there was trouble around a jousting post on Tombland. It was a violent incident – some of the townsmen died – and two priory men were taken by the authorities. The prior strengthened his defences by sending to Yarmouth for reinforcements; three boatloads of men came upriver, armed with crossbows and bows and arrows. Trouble flared again about 10 or 11 August, when the priory shut its gates but some of its men broke out, robbing a merchant named Alfred le Cutler and helping themselves to wine from a tavern run by Hugh le Bromham. On the next day the citizens attacked the priory, firing flaming arrows across Tombland from the top of the tower of St George's church, while the prior's men responded from the bell tower or clocher near the (later) Erpingham Gate. The Yarmouth men also burnt down three houses beside the Franciscan friary across St Faith's Lane. The clocher burnt down – apparently by accident, the defenders having left a fire there unattended. The cathedral itself was set on fire, while the townspeople – led by a woman – set fire to St Ethelbert's Gate and obtained entry, robbing the buildings and killing some of the defenders. Many buildings were burnt, including St Ethelbert's church, the nearby almonry and some stables.

Cotton says that the whole of the cathedral was consumed except for the chapel of St Mary (at the eastern end, so furthest away from the trouble); this is an obvious exaggeration as most of the Norman building still survives today. The monks claimed that many documents were destroyed in the fire, and it is true that only one account roll of the cathedral officials survives from before this date. Thirteen of the prior's men were killed. The city blamed the riot on the Yarmouth men – 'evildoers ... clearly acting contrary to the king's peace', while Cotton blamed the citizens who, even after the monks had fled, 'continued their burning, killing and plundering for three days'.

Henry III was actually not far away, attending a Parliament at Bury St Edmunds. He arrived in Norwich on 14 September and restored order. By the time he left on 27 September, it is said that 34 men had been dragged to their deaths behind carts, others hanged, drawn and quartered, and the woman who attacked the gates burnt alive. Twelve other men forfeited their possessions. On the cathedral side, the prior resigned. The king himself died soon after, and the final peace agreement was made under his successor, Edward I. It rather optimistically ordered that all parties were to be 'real friends', as well as punishing the citizens, who were to pay the priory 500 marks a year for six years for repairs, and also to give them a pix, or cup, worth £100. A party of the chief citizens had to travel to the Pope in Rome and obtain his pardon. New gates and entrances were to be made; the Ethelbert Gate still bears evidence of the attack. The vertical line of freestone inside the arch marks the former inner end of the gateway, which was extended after the riot. The pinkness of these stones reflects their exposure to the extreme heat of the fire of 1272 – that unnamed Norwich woman has left her mark to this day. The cloisters were destroyed, or at least damaged, in the riot, and were gradually rebuilt over the next 150 years.[9]

Peace was restored; Edward I came to Norwich with his wife and many nobles to enthrone William Middleton as bishop in 1278. In 1285 he granted the city a charter confirming those of his predecessors, and in 1295 he issued a second charter, which gave to the citizens the area called Newgate (roughly corresponding to the present Surrey Street). This had been previously claimed by the cathedral priory, and an extra £10 was added to the city's fee farm rent for the privilege of undisputed possession. Half a century later, in 1345, there was another expansion of the city's authority. Edward III granted the land lying in the outer bailey of the castle to the city in return for a further small increase in the fee farm rent. This was well worth paying as the bailey had become a haunt of evildoers outside the city's jurisdiction; the line of the present Opie Street leading from it was one of the red light districts, being known, even in documents issued by the cathedral, as 'Gropecunt Lane' in the Middle Ages, and shown on maps as late as the 18th century as 'Whores' Alley'.

13 *Norwich cathedral cloisters, the east walk, drawn by John Adey Repton.*

Relations between the city and the Crown were not always untroubled. In December 1372, the city assembly received an order to build a barge for the navy, for which they raised a rate; in April of the following year the assembly book refers to 'the imprisonment of those rebelling and refusing to pay the tax assessed upon them for causing the barge to be made'. However, in 1430 the city received royal praise for the speed with which it paid its contribution to the wars against France.

The last major disturbance to the peace of the medieval city came in 1381: the Peasants' Revolt. People in many parts of England rebelled against the imposition of poll tax. The revolt in the Norwich area was led by Geoffrey Litester or Lister, a dyer from Felmingham near North Walsham. A large number of people, mainly peasants, gathered just outside the city on Mousehold Heath – a popular place for protest movements over the centuries, as we shall see.

Different chroniclers have different stories of what happened, reflecting their own bias. The rebels wanted Sir Robert de Salle to lead them; he refused and, as he tried to get on his horse, the mob seized him. Froissart says he died nobly, killing 12 of the rebels before he fell, but other chronicles say he was captured by the rebels and then executed by them. Thomas of Walsingham says he was knocked on the head by one of his own serfs.

Norwich's richer citizens then went to Lister and offered him money to keep out of the city, but he entered it anyway. According to Norwich's first published historian, Francis Blomefield, he was not without urban supporters, entering the city 'with a great throng of citizens that had joined him', and they demolished the houses of lawyers and nobles. They raided Salle's house – his chattels were later assessed as worth £200 – and beheaded one justice of the peace, Reginald Eccles. Lister established himself in Norwich Castle and forced four captured knights, Stephen de Hales, Lord Scales, William de Morley and John de Brewes, to be his food tasters and to serve him at meals. He sent men to Carrow priory to seize their documents, which were brought back to the city and publicly burned in the market place. Eventually, according to Walsingham, he sent Morley and Brewes to the king, with 'a large sum of money which they had taken from the citizens of Norwich on the pretext of saving the town from slaughter, fire and plunder'. They were hoping for a pardon but it was too late: vengeance was on its way in the form of Henry Despencer, known to history as 'the fighting bishop of Norwich'.

14 *The arms of England (three lions), East Anglia (three crowns) and Norwich (lion and castle), on the east wall of St Andrew's church.*

Despencer was at his manor at Burleigh near Oakham when news of the revolt reached him. He at once marched towards Norwich, gathering supporters and scattering rebels as he went. Walsingham describes him as 'dressed as a knight, wearing an iron helm and a solid hauberk impregnable

to arrows as he wielded a real two-edged sword'. The rebels retreated and were beaten in battle at North Walsham. Lister was found hiding in a nearby cornfield, and was immediately sentenced to be hanged, drawn and quartered. The bishop now took on a more pastoral role, hearing his confession and walking with him to the gallows. His quarters were put on display in various places in Norfolk, and his goods forfeited to the king; his stock in trade at Felmingham was valued at 33 shillings. The size of the rebel 'army' can be seen from the fact that Henry Lomynour identified over 600 men whom he accused of attacking his house in Norwich; over a third came from north-east Norfolk and they were not all peasants as they included constables and merchants.[10]

John of Gaunt visited Norwich at Easter in 1389, and every freeman was ordered to turn out in his honour. Ten years later the city declared for his son Henry, as Henry IV; as a result, when he did become king in 1399, he favoured the city with a charter confirming all previous ones. In 1404 he gave a new charter to the city, which took Norwich out of the control of county officials by making it a county in its own right – a privilege already granted to Bristol, York and Newcastle. The bailiff was replaced by two sheriffs, and a mayor was appointed, who, along with four 'probi homines' (honest men), exercised the office of justice of the peace. The first mayor of the city was William Appleyard, who lived in the house now the Bridewell Museum; he was mayor for the first three years of the new system, and held the office a further three times later. The great and little wards established in 1404 remained the basic units of government for well over 400 years. Keith Lilley comments, 'With incorporation in 1404, the previous institutions that made up Norwich's urban government were regularised, as if a common roof had been found for a massive and irregular building.'[11]

The 1404 charter did not define the city's boundaries and there were many disputes over the next century between the city and the lay and religious lords who owned the surrounding villages. It was also unclear about how the city was to be governed: it said that an advisory body was to be created of 24 men but did not say if city officials were to be chosen by the 24 or by all the freemen. The differences were submitted to Sir Thomas Erpingham, who arranged a 'Composition' in 1415. This recommended a Common Council of 60 members elected annually by the citizens, and a Mayor's Council of 24 who could do nothing without the consent of the Common Council.

In 1417 Henry V (who two years earlier had fought at Agincourt, with Erpingham as the leader of his archers) gave the city a new charter that confirmed the charters of his father, Henry IV, and the new 'Composition'. The mayor and one of the sheriffs were to be elected by all the freemen. The common council consisted of 60 people – all male, of course

– elected every year in Passion Week; they had to live within the ward for which they were elected. Although, in theory, a new set of people could be chosen each year, in reality there was a fair degree of continuity. The mayor was required to call the councilmen together with the aldermen at least four times a year, but they usually met far more frequently. The council ratified decisions made by the aldermen, and elected officials such as the clavors (literally 'key-holders', who looked after the city's cash).[12]

The aldermen, mayor (one of the aldermen) and two sheriffs formed a body of 26 men with the real power in the city. The 24 aldermen, six from each ward, were to be elected by the freemen. What gave city government its continuity was the fact that, once elected, an alderman served for life. In some other boroughs, the aldermen acquired the right to choose for themselves who was to fill a vacancy, and so became a 'self-perpetuating oligarchy'. This never happened in Norwich; its aldermen were always elected by the freemen of the ward they represented. The mayor was elected on 1 May and took up his office in June; both occasions were marked by ceremony and feasting. The procedure was that the councilmen and aldermen met together and chose two aldermen who had formerly been sheriff. The aldermen and sheriffs then voted by secret ballot which of the two men was to become the next mayor. These arrangements continued, with only a few minor changes, until 1834.

There were inevitable disputes about these rules in the decades that followed. In 1433 a group of citizens accused the outgoing mayor, Thomas Wetherby, an alderman for Conesford ward, and his friends of trying to choose their own man to succeed him in office. Wetherby walked out and the assembly chose its own candidate, but they were not sure if the election was valid in the absence of Wetherby, who was still the mayor. The assembly then banned Wetherby and his supporters from holding offices. They were restored to the freedom in 1436 and this led to further trouble in the 1437 mayoral election, when a group of citizens forcibly prevented Wetherby and his men from taking part. He was associated with the cathedral priory and the Duke of Suffolk, two of the city's opponents. Central government had predicted trouble and sent a bishop and a justice to supervise the election. Trouble continued for over a week, with a city hospital being attacked on 8 May. The city's liberties were revoked and the king appointed a warden to administer the city. He chose John Welles, a London alderman and grocer with Norwich connections, having been born in the city. The city's liberties were taken into the king's hands for two years.

In 1442 a dispute between the city and the abbot of St Benet's, another clerical enemy, was decided against the city. This led directly to the incident known as Gladman's Insurrection in 1443. The city claimed later that it was not a riot but a 'disport' or entertainment, with John Gladman riding through the city dressed as Christmas. This was done every year on Shrove Tuesday – but Shrove Tuesday in 1443 was on 5 March and this event took place on 25 January! An inquest into the event presents a different picture, claiming the authorities planned 'a common insurrection and disturbance'. Gladman, they said, rode like a crowned king with a sceptre and sword

15 *St George conquers the dragon; glass by King and Co. for Holy Trinity church, Heigham.*

before him, and with 24 supporters all on horseback. They gathered up 3,000 followers and tried to attack the priory, piling wood against the gates of the Close. The city kept the city gates closed from 28 January to 4 February, keeping out not only their enemy the Duke of Norfolk but also the Earl of Oxford, who had been sent by the king to restore order. However, the riot was very different to 1272: no one was killed and when punishment was imposed no one was hanged. The city received a fine of £2,000 with further fines on individuals totalling £1,500; the collective fine was later reduced to 1,000 marks (£666 6s. 8d.). Its liberties were withdrawn once more, remaining in the king's hands until 1447.

There was further trouble between the cathedral and city authorities on Palm Sunday, 5 April 1506. The gaol keeper and the sergeant at mace of the city arrested a William Herryes for a felony, and tried to take him to the guildhall gaol. The prior, Robert Catton, with three other monks and about two dozen citizens, assembled with swords and knives and rescued Herryes. Thomas Large, one of the city sheriffs, managed to get Herryes back into custody but the prior and his men then attacked the sheriff himself, the prior saying, 'in the mother tongue': 'Shirreve thowe shalt not have this prisoner, thowe hast no thing a doo with hym, not so hardy in thy hede to medell with hym'. One of the monks, Nicholas Bewfeld, caught the sheriff by his cloak, tearing it, and Herryes was able to break free; he was taken off by the monks and their supporters to the sanctuary of the cathedral priory.

Guilds, St George – and the dragon

Guilds were organisations with a religious and often also a social purpose; they would meet to celebrate their particular saint, and some would also offer a weekly pittance to members who fell on hard times. There were almost twenty in medieval Norwich, some related to specific trades such as the guilds for tailors, barbers, saddlers or peltyers (skinners) – the latter naturally adopted St William (see p.30) as their patron. About half made provision for members in poverty, usually between seven and 14 pence a week. One guild was called the 'Poor Man's Guild', formed to maintain the 'poor church' of St Augustine, and only able to give three pence a week to members in need.[13]

The most important of the guilds was that of St George, which the guild returns tell us was founded in 1385. Each member subscribed a farthing a week. In the case of a member falling into poverty, that person would be given eight pence a week, but the main intention was to raise money for an image of St George. The guild held services on St George's feast day – April 23. If that day fell within a week of Easter the event was put off until early in May, so as not to clash with the religious events surrounding Easter, which were of great importance in the medieval calendar. The services were held in Norwich Cathedral, where there was an altar dedicated to St George just below the high altar.

The earliest surviving records date from about 1420, but earlier local historians, such as Benjamin Mackerell, writing in the 18th century, could look at older ones; he saw guild records for 1408 that referred to George and to the dragon. Guild orders for that year provided for two new jackets of fustian and red buckram to be bought for the 'henchmen' (attendants upon George in the procession), who also had a man to carry the sword. The 1408 orders also stated that the figure of George was to 'go in procession and make a conflict with the dragon'. We do not know what this early dragon looked like; it may not yet have assumed the form familiar to us as Snap. An account roll of 1420/1 records that a new dragon was made in this year, costing 9s. 4d. John Diggard was paid four pence for playing in it, so this dragon was clearly a fabricated figure to be operated by a man inside its body. Two shillings was spent on the hire of horses for George and his companions. In 1428 Diggard was paid extra to store the dragon, presumably in his house, and in the 1430s it was Thomas Diggard who bore the dragon, so perhaps the role of dragon bearing had early become a family tradition.

16 *The 'Erpingham window', formerly on a house in World's End Lane.*

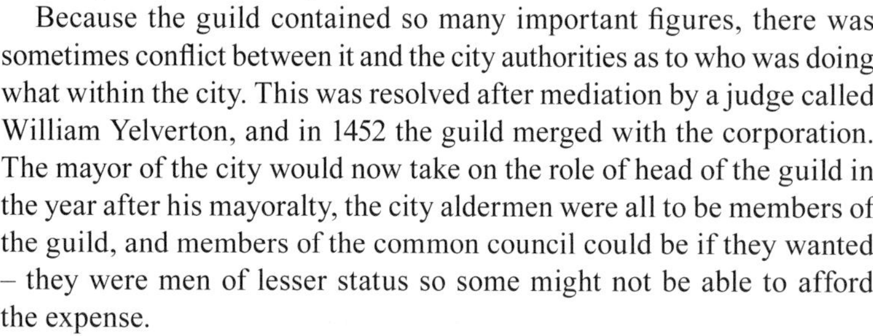

Because the guild contained so many important figures, there was sometimes conflict between it and the city authorities as to who was doing what within the city. This was resolved after mediation by a judge called William Yelverton, and in 1452 the guild merged with the corporation. The mayor of the city would now take on the role of head of the guild in the year after his mayoralty, the city aldermen were all to be members of the guild, and members of the common council could be if they wanted – they were men of lesser status so some might not be able to afford the expense.

There was a major new development in the procession at some time in the early 16th century. In a document of 1532, a female companion for George called Margaret is mentioned for the first time. No doubt she was Margaret of Antioch, in whose legend a dragon is prominent; she can be seen emerging from one in a wooden carving in St Helen's church. This was an early recognition of a role for women, to be played by a sister of the guild as the George was by a brother. She, too, rode on horseback, and wore a costume decorated with jewels.

The role of the dragon-bearer also developed. In 1429 2s. 4d. was paid to Diggard instead of the usual four pence for 'playing in the dragon with gonne [gun] powder'; presumably the extra two shillings were 'danger money'. The venture does not seem to have been repeated. By 1500, the dragon-bearer was being paid 12 pence. In 1522 gloves were provided for *two* players in the dragon, and the accounts note, 'the player in Dragon and his man paid twelve pence'. Twenty years later, this had risen to two shillings. As we have seen, George was a much more noble figure, riding a horse and in fine garb: not surprisingly, he was receiving a much larger sum – 20 shillings in 1543. The Margaret figure, in contrast, does not appear to have been paid.

17 *St George and St Michael (with wings) and their dragons, shown on a font now in St Julian's church.*

Many members of such a guild were very wealthy – including men like Sir Thomas Erpingham and Robert Toppes – but some people were supported by its charitable side, most spectacularly William Welles, a mercer and alderman, who lost his aldermancy after illness in 1494 and became dependent upon the guild.

The Cathedral

Norwich Cathedral is perhaps the finest Romanesque building in England – if only because later bishops did not have the money to alter the work of its founder. This founder was Herbert Losinga, who had been brought up as a monk at Fecamp monastery in Normandy and became prior there, later becoming prior of Ramsey Abbey in the Fens. He created a scandal when he paid William II a large sum of money to be made Bishop of East Anglia, and to have his father made abbot at Winchester, thus committing the sin known as simony. He later went to the Pope to obtain absolution, and moved the bishopric from Thetford (where it only been for about twenty years) to Norwich. The *Chronicles of Stephen* record:

> [Losinga] bought for a great sum a large part of the town of Norwich and, having torn down houses and levelled the ground for a great space, built in an excellent position on the river Yare a most beautiful church called the Holy Trinity.

There was already a church called Holy Trinity on the site and part of the grid plan of the late Saxon town was destroyed to make way for the new building, which in fact lies directly on the line of the Roman road mentioned earlier. Work began in 1096, commencing at the east end as is usual in a church. Limestone was brought from Caen in Normandy, as is well known, and also from Barnack in Northamptonshire. Rubble core for the walls was collected locally and includes Roman bricks from Caistor. The church was built rapidly for such an enormous undertaking, with Herbert constantly urging on the monks in his letters:

> The work drags on and in providing material you show no enthusiasm. Behold the servants of the king and mine are really earnest in the works allotted to them. They gather stones, carry them to the spot … You meanwhile are asleep with folded arms … failing in your duty through a paltry love of ease.[14]

Three small roundel paintings on an arch within the cathedral survive to tell Herbert's story. The first shows Herbert handing over money, the second his absolution, the third the new cathedral that he is building. Thought to date from about 1190, this is the first known representation of the cathedral.

When Herbert died in 1116, the eastern arm of the church and the first few bays of the nave had been completed. The work was continued in much the same style by his successor, Bishop Eborard, who brought it to completion by the time of his retirement in 1145. The cathedral had taken half a century to complete, an amazing achievement considering the primitive building methods of the time. There was a serious fire in the cathedral in 1171; the bishop of the time, William Turbe, sat outside the west door begging for money for the repairs.

Later building programmes have not taken away the feeling of that original masterwork, especially within the nave. The greatest change has been at roof level, where the original wooden roof has been replaced with stone vaulting, the carved bosses of which are another of the great glories of Norwich. Those in the cloister, a total of 394 bosses on religious and secular themes, are the earliest. They are also the easiest to see as those in the main building are so high up. The largest sequence on one subject is that telling the story of the Book of Revelation in 102 bosses in the south and west walks. The cathedral account rolls tell us that an illuminated copy of this work was purchased to provide the inspiration. A good place to appreciate the carvings is at the south-west corner. Looking up at the carved stone bosses, one can see the face of a man peeping through leaves, known as a Green Man. We know who carved this face in the stone: a Dutch immigrant named Brice, who in 1416 was paid 4s. 8d. for his work.

There is a curious figure in the eastern walk, which Eric Fernie has described as that of a defecating man:

> whoever was in charge of the iconography of the bosses saw nothing incongruous in juxtaposing scenes of the greatest Christian solemnity with representations of folk-tales, musicians, grotesques, and worse, which may be one of the most important things these carvings can communicate about the attitudes of the society which made and used them. One boss in particular indicates the extremes to which the nature of things could go. The figure on the boss above the doorway to the slype represents a naked man with thick, ungainly limbs clinging to the ridge rib, and twisting violently apparently in order to be able to defecate into the void beneath him, visiting his attentions on those passing through the arch below ... one suspects a straightforward delight in the obscene.[15]

The nave of the cathedral has over 250 ceiling bosses telling the Bible story from the Creation to the Last Judgement in lively images reflecting contemporary life. In the Red Sea scene, Pharaoh is dressed as a medieval king and has been thrown from a typical Norfolk cart. In the Last Supper scene there is a plate on the table with two large fish on it, such as might have been bought in Norwich market.[16]

The present spire is not part of the original building, but the fourth one to top the Norman tower. The first was destroyed in the riot of 1272; the second blew down in 1361 or 1362, damaging the presbytery; and the third collapsed after being struck by lightning in 1463. The present spire was then built by Bishop Goldwell. It is really constructed of brick, with a very thin cladding of stone, and at 315 feet is the second tallest in England after Salisbury Cathedral. Like the square shape of the castle keep, the cathedral spire is a key icon of the city, featuring for generations on Norwich Union publicity and the direct ancestor of the attenuated yellow triangle in the logo of Aviva today.

The damage to the presbytery when the second spire fell meant that the eastern arm of the cathedral had to be rebuilt. This was done largely at the cost of Bishop Despencer and was carried out in the style of the day, with large windows and flying buttresses outside. It harmonises wonderfully with Losinga's work of 250 years earlier on which it stands. There were statues on the heads of the flying buttresses as there are today, but these are now 19th-century replacements.

Losinga's cathedral had a round east end, mirroring the very unusual circular eastern chapels. It was replaced by a Gothic Lady Chapel built by Bishop Walter Suffield in the middle of the 13th century; the entrance can be seen inside the cathedral, and its eastern end is marked by the low wall outside. The building was allowed to decay after the Reformation, and the present eastern chapel was built in the 20th century as a war memorial. Bishop William Alnwick rebuilt the west entrance to the cathedral, and his arms are above the doorway. He also left money to rebuild the great west window (the glass itself is 19th-century).

The cathedral was built as the centre of a Benedictine priory, staffed by about sixty monks and following a rule based on that of Fecamp, where Losinga had previously been prior. The monks rose at 2.30 in the morning in winter (earlier in summer) for services and reading until the service of prime was said at daylight. Much of the morning was spent in prayer or reading, with an interlude for washing. Evidence of these activities can still be seen in the cloister where there are book cupboards and washing facilities (with modern statues). The groups of nine small holes that can be seen in a few places in the cloister benches were carved by novices playing games of marbles, showing that not everyone took their vocation with complete seriousness. The monks then met in the Chapter House for discussion; this was the first time in the day when they were permitted to talk. Their main meal was eaten at about 2 p.m., in silence while one of their number read passages from the Bible. The afternoon was taken up with work, followed by prayers and a service at about 7 p.m., before going to bed.

Although there were only 60 monks, there were many more mouths to feed: the records show up to 250 people eating there each day. These were guests and also servants and workmen, who combined to make the monastery the richest institution and the largest employer in the medieval city. The yearly revenue was about £2,200 in the early 14th century, which contrasts with the city itself, whose revenue never exceeded £270 a year even in the 15th century. The cathedral priory was indeed the Aviva of its day.

The buildings of the Close reflect its role as a Benedictine monastic house. There are three main entrances. The Ethelbert Gate was rebuilt at the citizens' expense after the 1272 riots. The passage is a very early example of a lierne vault, that is with extra rib vaults springing from another rib rather than from the main springers or the central boss. The outside of the gate is decorated in a pattern of limestone and cut squared flints that was to become a characteristic of East Anglia.

The Water Gate, loosely known as Pull's Ferry (really the adjoining house), is 15th-century. A canal ran under it and up to the Lower Close, and this was used to bring the stone for the cathedral to the site. The stone was purchased in Normandy, loaded onto ships to travel across the Channel and transferred to smaller barges for the journey up the Wensum and along the short canal. Documents record boys being paid a few halfpennies to move the stone to the builder's yard beside the cathedral, although larger loads needed men with carts.

The Erpingham Gate was built by, or as a memorial to, Sir Thomas Erpingham. It has two rows of statues, the outer of female saints and the inner of 12 men, probably the apostles. The kneeling figure of Sir Thomas was not originally intended for the niche where it is now, its legs having been chopped to fit it in the space; perhaps it originally came from a chantry chapel over his tomb in the cathedral. A fourth gate is that in St Martin at Palace Plain – not to the cathedral but to the Bishop's Palace. It was built by Alnwick; the repeated letter 'M' with a crown over it is a symbol for the Virgin Mary, to whom he was especially devoted. The carving of a bishop in the vault of the gate may be a portrait of Alnwick himself. The basement of the structure was once the Bishop's prison.[17]

The chapel between the Erpingham Gate and the west front of the cathedral, now used by Norwich School, was built by Bishop John Salmon in about 1316. The undercroft was used as a charnel house, where bones were moved out of the city's overcrowded churchyards and stored in a heap. Prayers were said by the monks for the souls of the dead in general, as individuals were, of course, unidentifiable. This was common medieval practice. When the charnel house became full, the bones were taken out and burnt, the resultant bone fire giving us our present word 'bonfire'.

Other buildings in the Close have gone, including most of the living quarters of the monks. Their sites have been cleverly adapted in recent years; the present restaurant is where the monks had their refectory or dining room, and the newly built hostry where people are invited into the cathedral is on the site of the medieval guest quarters, even embracing the original entrance arch. The fourth side, the eastern one, was taken up by the monks' dormitory; this has not been replaced. The Chapter House was on this side, and the three bays marking its entrance can be seen in the cloister, but the building itself disappeared in the 16th century.

The Lower Close preserves many of the working buildings typical of a medieval monastery or large manor house. The long building on the north side was the granary, while the 17th-century buildings at the eastern end are on the site of the bakery and brewery. The Victorian houses on the south side mark the site of the swan pit, while the 18th-century buildings are built around the church of St Mary in the Marsh, the wall of which makes up the spine of the building.

The Upper Close contained the almonry, with its barns and almoner's house, as an important function of a monastic house was to provide for the poor. Although monastic houses were often criticised, the scale of charitable giving was impressive: the prior gave to the poor in the almonry over 10,000 loaves a year, as well as giving money to beggars at the gate, lepers, and prisoners in the castle for whom food was provided. About 10 per cent of the monastic house's income went to charity.

The cathedral had a fine library, although many books given by the founder were destroyed in the 1272 fire. The replacement was augmented by the bequest of Adam Easton, a monk at Norwich Cathedral born in the village after which he is named, who went to Oxford University at the priory's expense and rose through the church's hierarchy to become a Cardinal in 1382. This involved living in Rome, and the life of a Cardinal was rather different than it is today: at one stage he was not only deposed but tortured on the command of the Pope before being restored to his office. Easton died in Rome in 1397. He left his books to Norwich cathedral priory, and they finally arrived, packed in six barrels, some ten years after his death. At least five of the books survive, although none in Norwich.[18]

At the other end of the Upper Close, marked now only by a plaque, was the belfry, known locally as the clocher. Burnt down in 1272, it was replaced on a massive scale – over 36ft square – between 1299 and 1307. After the Reformation, it was no longer used and no doubt provided a useful source of building stone. An infirmary was an essential part of any monastic house, and that at Norwich survived until the 19th century. A painting by John Crome shows it being demolished, and some piers still survive in the car park.

The Castle and the New Borough

The Norman castle made it possible for the new rulers of Norwich to dominate the native inhabitants. The tower would originally have had a wooden building on top while the earth settled down. The mound had to be extended but was not given sufficient time for settling, and this weakness explains the cracks in the castle walls.

We have seen that Emma defended the castle against an army in 1075, but the castle she defended was nothing like the castle we see today. It is not absolutely certain that it was even on the same site; Sandy Heslop has suggested that it could have been the fortified tower now part of the Bishop's Palace in the Close.

The Norman castle is one of the greatest buildings in England of its – or any other – period. Heslop calls it 'architecturally the most ambitious secular building in western Europe'.[19] It had three elements: the bailey, the mound and the keep. The bailey or castle fee was an enormous area covering the later Castle Market, now the Castle Mall shopping centre, Castle Meadow and extending down to the beginning of the Prince of Wales Road. Its outline can be made out in physical features today such as the sudden steepening in the road by the Crown Bank building. Back of the Inns is where the Great Cockey runs, then an open stream which acted as a natural moat on the west side of the castle bailey. The edge of the royal liberty was marked by plaques bearing the royal arms mounted on posts.

The mound was once even larger than it is today as successive widenings of Castle Meadow have cut into one side of it; N.G.J. Pounds calculated that it would have taken 30,000 man-days to construct. The keep on the mound was built of a core of flint, originally with a facing of Caen limestone. It is 93ft by 108ft, and 70ft high. Some masons worked on both the cathedral and the castle, as is shown by masons' marks that can still be seen; for example, some in the east of the cathedral match those in the basement of the castle keep. In the 1840s, the Caen stone was replaced almost entirely with a new facing of Bath limestone (you can still see the original stone in a small figure on the south front). This may have changed the colour of the building as seen from a distance – in the Middle Ages it was known as 'la blanchefleur' (the white flower). The ground floor, used for storage, was not faced with stone as it is now, and its dark flint walls emphasised the grandeur of the limestone facing of the royal apartments above.

18 *Representation of the castle by Nick Arber, showing the size of the baileys and outworks.*

However, the pattern of buttresses and arches of the keep – and it is a pattern – is unchanged and can be appreciated by a look at its four sides. The south side is the most regular, based on a medieval measurement known as the perch (16ft 6ins). The spaces between the buttresses are a perch in length and each buttress is one third of a perch wide. The west side, although facing the market place, is actually the back of the building; the latrines are on this side. If you stand on the mound outside the keep you can see where the chutes come down. There was also a small emergency exit from the first floor on this side, at the right-hand corner as you look at it, with a set of wooden steps bending round the corner. The north side is very like the south but with a vital difference – there is an extra buttress, put in to strengthen this wall after a large crack appeared as it was being built. The east side is the front of the castle. There are stone steps leading up to the tower defending the main door, generally known as Bigot's tower. You can still walk up these stairs, now inside the Museum; the flat part halfway up was originally the site of a drawbridge that could be raised as a further defence. At the top, the main entrance has some stunning original carvings not to be missed, including a kneeling knight and a winged horse.

The castle was probably complete when Henry I spent Christmas here in 1121, as is recorded in the *Anglo-Saxon Chronicle*, but the inside of the castle keep was very different to today. Where the balcony now runs around the wall was then the floor of the main apartments, and the large open arches now dominating the interior were then a solid wall. The main rooms were the Great Hall, the royal chamber, and the chapel with an ante-chapel next to it. On the west side were two service rooms and the latrines, and these and the chapel in the south-east corner are the two most obvious features from the medieval interior today.

Earl Ralph used the lands he held west of the new castle to form a new borough, which at its formation had 36 French and six English burgesses. The older parts of the town suffered as a result of Ralph's rebellion, but the new borough flourished; in 1086, it had 41 French burgesses among its residents. The market place was moved from Tombland to the site the present market occupies. The Norman market was larger, however, stretching from the present Guildhall to St Stephen's church. Tenements along the market place would have their frontages facing the Market and

stretch a long way back from it, a pattern which could be seen on the west side until the 20th century, when it was obliterated by the building of City Hall. It can still clearly be seen on the east side, where long narrow blocks of land run from the market place to the Great Cockey, now covered over by the street called Back of the Inns.

The church of St Peter Mancroft was in the centre of the market, as St Michael had been at Tombland. Newcomers to Norwich sometimes think the church is named after a saint called St Peter Mancroft, but the dedication is to St Peter and the location is Mancroft. It used to be thought that this originated from the words Magna Crofta, meaning 'great field', but Brian Ayers has shown that the real derivation is from (Ger)maene Crofta, meaning 'common land'. Archaeologists have found evidence of some earlier industrial activity in this area, but much of it was open field before the New Borough was established. Ayers notes the curious alignment of St Peter's Street, suggesting that it may have derived its distinctive 'reverse S' shape from developing on the headland of former open field. In this way, a street preserved the skeleton of a field that disappeared a millennium ago; the pattern was lost when the whole area was redesigned for the new City Hall in 1938.[20]

The French and English inhabitants of Norwich soon merged into one community, a characteristic of the city over the centuries. Richard of Devizes wrote in about 1190 that 'in Durham, Norwich and Lincoln you will hear scarcely any speaking Romance [French].' Paradoxically, by the later Middle Ages, the French language was the fashionable tongue of the gentry whatever their origin, and although Erpingham fought against the French, his wife's will is written in that language, as are those of many of her upper-class contemporaries.[21]

The Jewish Community

The chronicler William of Malmesbury says that Jews first came to England with William the Conqueror, and there is no evidence for an earlier Jewish community in Norwich. The name Isaac first occurs in the names of the Frenchmen living in the New Borough. The Jewish community was not large, perhaps numbering 200 people at its height and declining to 50 or 60 in the decades before the final expulsion from England in 1290. The majority lived between the castle and Haymarket, and this area was known to contemporaries as 'the Jewry'; one reason was that the Jews might retreat into the castle bailey for royal protection when they were threatened.

Many people shop in Gentleman's Walk and White Lion Street today, but few realise they are on the site of a synagogue which was at the heart of the medieval Jewish community and played a significant part in Norwich life for perhaps two centuries. The Jews had a variety of occupations – we know of references in title deeds and similar documents to several physicians, such as Isaac who lived on Saddlegate. Another – Solomon – had an herb garden, the earliest known reference in England to a private herb garden according to V.D. Lipman. Others were tradesmen, including cheesemongers, wine merchants and a fishmonger. At least one was also a poet – Meir ben Elijah, known as Meir of Norwich.[22]

Although most Jews lived within this area, it was never compulsory to do so and the most famous of medieval Jewish families lived in King Street, on the site later known as the Music House, and now Wensum Lodge. The undercroft or cellar is the only surviving part of the house traditionally associated with Jurnet the Jew, but in fact owned by Jurnet's son Isaac, and by Isaac's descendants. The first known owner was John Curry, who sold it to Isaac in about 1225; Isaac obtained a licence to create a quay by the river here. Isaac died 10 years later, in 1235, and the property was divided between his two sons, Moses and Samuel, with a further subdivision when Moses died in 1240. Some parts soon passed out of Jewish hands; the house itself was owned by Simon le Paumer by 1266, and possibly a decade earlier. The earliest part of the house, at right angles to the street, was constructed in the early 12th century, and its five-bay undercroft still survives. In about 1175, the house was extended southwards along the street, but only the lower section of two vaults and part of one of the piers of this aisled hall exist today. A brick undercroft was built in the 14th or 15th century.

19 *The Music House; the house of Isaac the Jew is the left-hand section.*

Without the Jewish community, many of the greatest medieval buildings could not have been built: as Christians were forbidden to lend money at interest, it was only Jews who could provide the funding necessary for large-scale projects. They were involved with Norwich cathedral; a charter survives relating to money owed by the prior of Norwich cathedral to Isaac, son of Jurnet. The charter is dated in the year 4978 of the Jewish calendar, which corresponds to 1218 in Christian-style dating. We know from a mason's mark that at least one of the masons who worked at Isaac's house also worked on the cathedral infirmary, so that the links were obviously close – and fruitful for Norwich.[23]

On 24 March 1144, the mutilated body of a 12-year-old boy was found on Mousehold Heath. It was identified as that of William, who had been an apprentice to a skinner, but was apparently enticed away from home by a man offering him work as a cook. His mother was naturally distraught and ran through the town screaming aloud. Somehow, perhaps because the body was found on Easter Saturday, the rumour spread that William had been murdered by Jews in a form of mock crucifixion. William was buried in the monks' cemetery at the cathedral. Apparent miracles at the grave led to his being moved first into the Chapter House and then into the cathedral itself.

The story was written up by a Norwich monk, Thomas of Monmouth, but the cult was never strong outside East Anglia; its significance is that it was the first known example of an accusation of ritual murder by Jews at Easter. Sadly, there were to be many examples of this ridiculous charge over the following centuries, some extremists even believing Jews conspired to choose a town somewhere in Europe each year to carry out the ritual murder. James Campbell wrote; 'it is of sharp interest in the history of Europe because it marks the point in which the deadly lie of Jewish ritual murder comes to the surface'.[24]

It does not seem that there was persecution of the Norwich Jewish community immediately after the murder of William. Half a century later, in 1190, there was an outbreak of violence, probably as a result of crusading fervour stirred up by King Richard, and the constable of the Tower of London rendered accounts for £28 7s. 2d. on the chattels of Norwich Jews who were killed at this time. There were further disturbances in Norwich in the 1230s after an allegation that a Christian boy had been forcibly circumcised by some members of the Jewish community.

In answer to Pope Gregory's renewed condemnation of usury, Edward I in 1275 forbade Jews to lend money at interest. In July 1290, writs were sent to all sheriffs ordering that every Jew must leave England by November that year, on pain of death. They were to be provided with safe passage across the Channel and could take money and personal property with them, but their house and lands passed to the king, no doubt a reason behind his action. Jews could stay if they converted to Christianity, and three women from Norwich are known to have done this, living in the House of Converts in London after doing so. The synagogue itself and some of the houses in Norwich owned by Jews appear to have been destroyed by fire. In the late 19th century, when the basement of the Curat House in White Lion Street was being rebuilt, fragments were found of stone columns,

20 *Reconstruction drawing of the Jewish area of Norwich, and its synagogue, by J.P. Chaplin.*

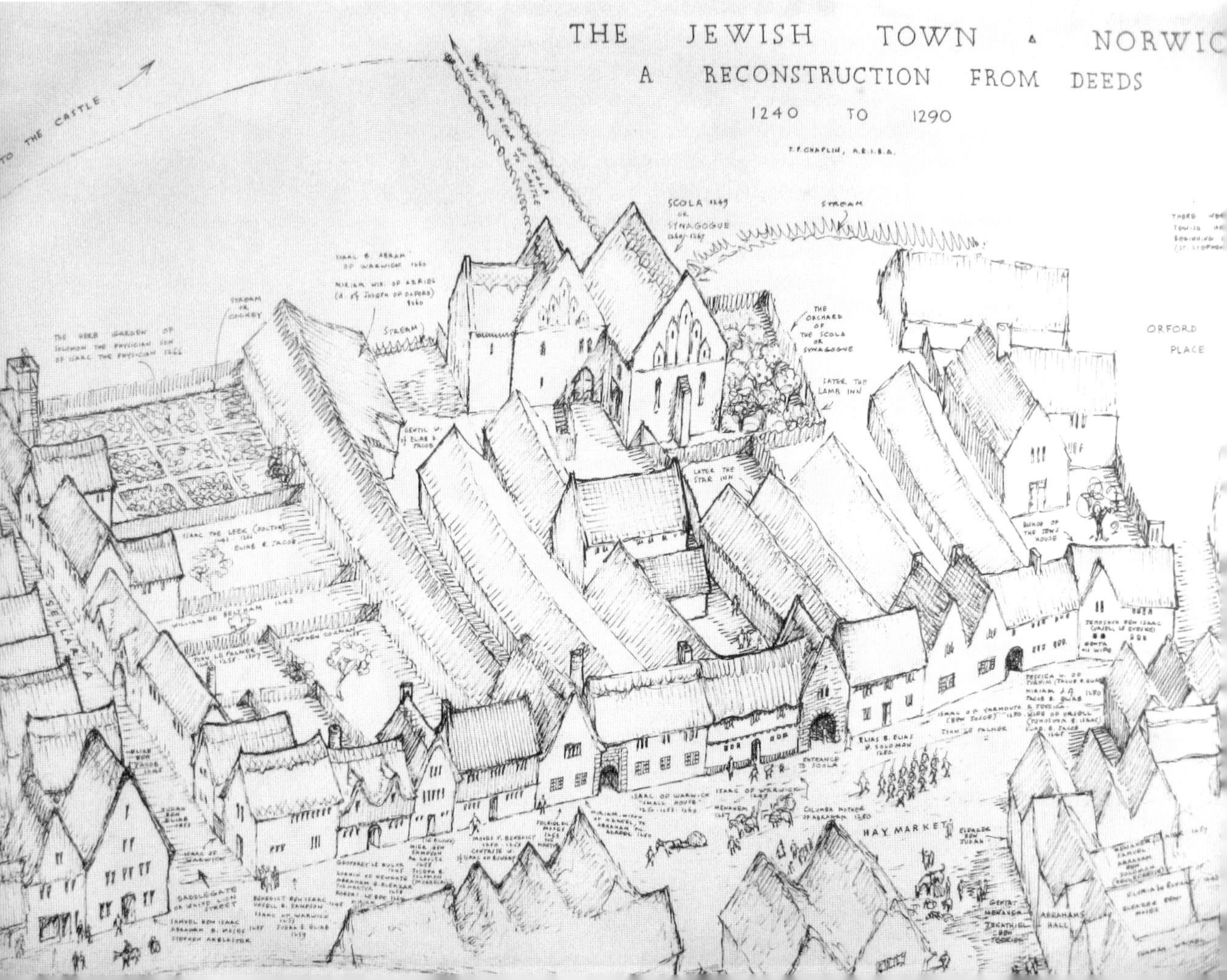

glass and pottery, as well as a layer of burnt material. Some bones were disturbed during this work, and there have been rumours ever since of the house being haunted by a Jewish rabbi.[25]

Religious Life

There was one female religious house in Norwich, the priory at Carrow (although the building was later known as 'Carrow Abbey', it was never an abbey). The cartulary for Carrow no longer survives but was seen by the antiquarian Thomas Tanner in the 18th century; one entry said that the priory was founded in 1146 by Seyna and Lescelina, sisters at the Hospital of St Mary and St John in Norwich. A charter of King Stephen gave the nuns 25 shillings worth of land; this is undated but was probably written about 1136. It seems probable that the priory developed out of an otherwise unknown earlier hospital on a different site.

As befits a royal foundation, it had a large church, at 195ft in length the longest in the city apart from the cathedral, and a fair part of the eastern end still survives. Local gentry tended to place their unmarried daughters in a nunnery, and in 1229 a papal bull ordered that local lords stop trying to force Carrow to receive more inmates than it could maintain. Many of the nuns naturally came from Norwich and Norfolk families, such as Joan and Agnes, the two daughters of Oliver Wyth, who were nuns there at the time of their father's death in 1291, and Margaret Folcard, only daughter of John Folcard, citizen and alderman of Norwich, who was a nun at Carrow in the 1460s. Jane Scrope took refuge at Carrow after her father, John Wyndham, was executed for treason in 1502. She had a pet sparrow, which was unfortunately eaten by the priory cat, Gib, the incident being recorded in a poem by John Skelton, the rector of Diss.[26]

The priory was just outside the city walls but it was not clear whether or not it was legally within the city, and this led to a bizarre dispute in 1415. A man called William Koc was murdered in the fields of Lakenham by a gang of men armed with spades. His widow, Margery, raised the hue and cry, and neighbouring villages were searched but the men could not be found. This was because they were in Carrow priory; the prioress, Editha, was presumably claiming the right to try them as the fields in question were within her jurisdiction. The city disagreed, and she and another nun spent some time in Norwich Castle prison accused of being, in effect, murderers, as they were sheltering the criminals. Various courts pondered the rights and wrongs of the case and in 1418 it was decided that the prioress was not guilty of the charge – but also that Carrow was in the city of Norwich.

The religious life of the city was revolutionised in the 13th century with the arrival of groups of friars. Friars were established in the late 12th century as a reaction to the wealth and power of the older religious orders, and represented a new approach to religion. Unlike monks and nuns, whose prime role was prayer within their monastic house, the friars' role was among the poor: preaching, hearing confessions, burying the dead. Whereas monks and nuns lived from the income of their large estates, the friars, in the beginning, had no estates, and at first did not even own their churches. Friars were mendicants: they lived by begging and were as confrontational in medieval Norwich as beggars in the 21st century city.

Six orders of friars came to Norwich in the following century; two were fairly short-lived but the other four lasted about three centuries, until the Reformation. The first two groups to arrive were the Franciscans, or Grey Friars, and the Dominicans, or Black Friars, both of whom came to the city in 1226. The Franciscan house was at the top of the present Prince of Wales Road and John de Gelham gave the Dominicans the parish church and rectory of St John the Baptist on the corner of Calvert Street and Colegate. By 1275, six adjoining properties, several of them gardens, had been given to the Dominicans by Norwich landowners, and there were further gifts over the next 25 years, until they owned a large block of land along the north of Colegate to Golden Dog Lane. Access to the river was very important for the friars. In 1275 Richard of Norwich gave them an estate on the south side of Colegate extending to the Wensum; it was presumably not satisfactory, as in 1290 they exchanged it with Roger of Pentney for part of another property slightly further to the east, where they established their riverside facilities. The Dominicans claimed the site was still not what they wanted, as the difficult approach to the site made it perilous for those who wanted to attend their church.

At the same time, another group, the Friars Penitential, established themselves beside Elm Hill. They were never a large order and were one of the victims of a decision made at the Council of Lyons in 1275 that only the four large orders could take in new members; the other orders gradually disappeared as their members died off. By 1307 there was only one friar in the Elm Hill friary, and he was 'broken with age and nearly blind'. The Dominicans petitioned both king and Pope for permission to take over the site, and were permitted to do so, the Pope insisting that they care for the last friar of the Penitential order. They proceeded to buy up the land south of the friary over the next 20 years, enabling them to build a much larger church and, of equal importance, to have a preaching yard in the heart of the city. This is the origin of the open space known today as St Andrew's Plain; before the Dominicans came, there were houses along the north side of Princes Street opposite St Andrew's church. This process has been researched by Margot Tillyard, using the city court rolls. Many of the blocks of property passed through the hands of a man called William But before the Friars purchased them; it is not known if he was an agent acting for the friars, or whether he was working for himself, buying up properties that he knew the friars would need and then selling them off for a profit. Two parts of the buildings of the old order can still be seen, the crypt, now a coffee house (its vaulting is later), and the church, later used by the Dominicans as theirs, and now known as Becket's Chapel. Standing in Elm Hill looking at the buildings, one can see the contrast between the small church of the Friars' Penitential and the enormous church of their successors, the Dominicans.[27]

The old church was on the north side of Elm Hill but as the Dominicans enlarged the site they were able to divert the street around their new building, which explains the sharp bend of Elm Hill today. The church was badly damaged by fire in 1413, although some of its eastern arm survived, including the huge east window. When they moved across the river to their second site, they put a hermit in charge of the old buildings, and continued to maintain divine services in the church of St John. Now they retreated there while rebuilding their church on the same scale, but with added grandeur. A relative of Sir Thomas Erpingham was a friar there at the time, and the Erpingham family contributed to the cost of the new church, recording their generosity by having the family coat of arms placed between the windows of the clerestory.

21 *Becket's chapel, the church of the Penitential friars and later the library of the Dominican friars.*

The other two successful friaries were the Augustinian, or Austin, friars on King Street and the Carmelites, or White Friars, north of what is now Whitefriars Bridge. The Carmelite friars developed out of a group of hermits living on Mount Carmel in Palestine. The house in Norwich was founded by Philip, son of Warin (known in some documents as Philip de Cowgate), in 1256, and his deed of gift of property in Cowgate is recorded in the city'S Book of Pleas. The site was excavated in 2002, revealing that the church was very close to the river, with a cloister 100ft square to its north; the church was rebuilt on a larger scale in the mid-15th century. They had a notable library including books on astronomical and astrological themes. The Austin friars were the last to appear, arriving in King Street probably in 1289; Bartholomew de Acre, a Norwich merchant, left them a messuage in 1290.

The size of the friary churches can be estimated from the writings of William Worcester, who paced out the dimensions of major Norwich buildings in about 1480. He tells us that the nave of the White Friars church was 46 paces long and 36 paces wide. This can be compared with a still-standing building, St Andrew's Hall, where Worcester measured the nave as 75 paces long and 41 paces wide, making the White Friars nave a good deal shorter but only a little less wide than that building – a true preaching church. His steps also showed that the Franciscan friary church was almost as large at the Blackfriars building.

Friars placed a great emphasis on learning as an aid to their preaching role, and the Dominican and Franciscan friaries were colleges for students from all over Europe, the medieval equivalents of today's University of East Anglia. The Austin friary had a large library paid for by a bequest of Margaret Wetherby, widow of Thomas Wetherby, the troublesome alderman, in 1458. Friars, like monks, might rise to become bishops (such as Thomas de Colby, a Norwich Carmelite friar who became Bishop of Waterford and Lismore in 1399) and even popes.

The story, or legend, of Peter of Candia illustrates this. Supposedly, he was an orphan born in Crete in about 1339. A 'homeless beggar-boy in a Cretan city, knowing neither parents nor relations', he was brought up in a Franciscan friary on the island. He joined the order himself, firstly in Padua and later coming to the Norwich Franciscan friary. He went on to study at Cambridge University, and later lectured at universities throughout Europe; in 1402 he became Archbishop of Milan. This was at a time when there were two rival popes. A council met in 1408

to sort this out, deposing both the rival popes and electing Peter as the new one. He took the name Alexander V, but the other two popes both refused to resign, so that for a time there were three popes. Alexander was recognised by England, and by several other countries; he showed his interest in England by issuing a formal condemnation of the teachings of John Wycliffe. He died in Bologna in the following year so suddenly that there were rumours he had been poisoned by one of his rivals. He is officially regarded as an 'anti-pope', but some authorities prefer to call him a 'Conciliar Pope' as he was elected by a council of the church. He is the only pope with a direct link to Norwich.[28]

Almost half the people living in Norwich who left wills between 1370 and 1532 left money to the city friaries, usually to all four of them; many also wanted to be buried in a friary churchyard. Some of the bequests were large: when William, Lord Morley, was buried in the Norwich Augustinian friary, his mortuary was his best horse and he also gave the friary his 'principal complete vestment' and a cloth of gold embroidered with the 'heads of ladies'. The same house was given 100 marks by Joan Fransham in 1422, while Thomas Kerdiston left it the sum of 300 marks, a silver cross and a pair of silver basins. In fact, the friars soon became the victims of their own success: as more and more people left them money, the old ideals of poverty inevitably faded away, as shown in the grandeur of a building like The Halls.

The chapel of St Mary in the Fields was established just before 1248 by John le Brun, originally as a hospital but very soon becoming a college of canons. Six chantries were founded, the canons saying masses for the souls of the deceased; one chantry was that of the Appleyard family. The institution was built around a cloister, whose basic shape is preserved in the buildings of today's Assembly House. The fourth side was made up by a very big church, so large that the city assembly met there before the Guildhall was built, but nothing survives of this building.

22 *The Dominican friary, better known today as St Andrew's Hall.*

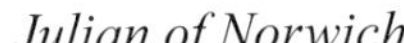

Julian of Norwich

The *Showings of Divine Love* by Julian of Norwich is an extremely important book of mystic devotion; the *Cambridge Medieval History* calls the author the first English woman of letters. Almost nothing is known of her life apart from the information it contains about her. Julian says that her revelation came on 8 May 1373 when she was aged 30 years 'and a half', so she was presumably born between October and December 1342. At another point she says that she has been meditating upon her revelation for 20 years minus three months, which takes us to February 1393. There are three other indications. Margery Kempe says that she had visited Julian in Norwich but gives no date; most authorities say 1412 or 1413 but this is only a guess, and it could have been a good deal earlier, say between 1400 and 1410. The Short Text of Julian's book has an introduction which seems to imply she was still living in 1413, at which time she would have been 71 years old. Finally, there are a small number of wills making bequests that appear to refer to Julian. A will made in March 1394 by Roger Reed, rector of St Michael Coslany, left two shillings to 'Julian anchorite'. Another will, made in November 1415 by John Plumpton, a Norwich citizen, left 40 pence to the anchoress in the church of St Julian, as well as 12 pence each to her current (unnamed) maid and to a former maid named Alice. Julian is also mentioned in a will of 1416. Many years later, a will of 1443 mentions an anchorite named Julian; on the basis of this will both Blomefield and the modern memorial in her cell assume she lived to be about one hundred, but it is very likely that this refers to another anchorite who had taken over the cell and was also named Julian.

Some of her thinking seems very modern, but this is because it is timeless. She was able to write of God, 'As truly as God is our father, so just as truly he is our mother.' She even writes of Jesus: 'The mother can give her child to suck her milk, but our precious Mother Jesus can feed us with himself, and does, most courteously and most tenderly, with the blessed sacrament, which is the precious food of true life.' Her optimism is reflected in her most famous words:

> And in this he showed me something small, no bigger than a hazel-nut, lying in the palm of my hand, and I perceived that it was round as any ball. I looked at it and thought: What can this be? And I was given this general answer: It is everything which was made. I was amazed that it could last, for I thought that it was so little that it could suddenly fall into nothing. And I was answered in my understanding: It lasts and always will, because God loves it; and thus everything has being through the love of God.[29]

23 *Julian as represented in the 20th-century glass at Holy Trinity, Heigham.*

Julian was not the only anchorite or anchoress in medieval Norwich: references are known to at least fifty between the mid-13th century and the Reformation (only 13 anchorites are known to have lived in London during this period). Some of the earliest wills mentioning anchorites include those of John Bonde, who left a few pence to five anchorites in about 1248; William de Dunwich, who left six pence to every anchorite in Norwich in 1272; and Oliver Wyth of Yarmouth, who left money to named city anchorites, Lady Margery at St George Colegate, Lady Ela and her companion, and to unnamed anchorites in Norwich, Bracondale and Trowse in 1291. Some were attached to churches, others lived on or by bridges and gates where they no doubt had functions of cleaning and maintenance and of raising money for minor repairs. The cells of anchorites were often built so that the occupant could see the high altar of the church; the 'squint' through which this was done can still be seen on the north wall of what is now Blackfriars' Hall.[30]

24 *Julian, a modern statue on the west front of the Anglican Cathedral.*

Anchorites would offer spiritual advice; Margery Kempe travelled from Lynn specifically to ask Julian if the visions she (Margery) was experiencing were genuine. The two women spent several days together, and Julian offered her reassurance and advice, telling her that 'patience is necessary to you, for in that you shall keep your soul'.

An important figure contemporary with Julian was Richard of Caister, vicar at St Stephen's between 1402 and 1409. Known as 'the good vicar', he had a reputation for sanctity, and miracles of healing were reputed to happen at his grave, which was visited by pilgrims including Margery Kempe. Pilgrims were a common feature in the medieval scene: Heather Wallis mentions fragments of stone moulds for mass-produced pilgrim souvenirs discovered on the Cinema City site.[31]

The parish churches

There is a well-known saying that Norwich has a church for every Sunday in the year – and a pub for every day! There were indeed more churches in Norwich than in any city north of the Alps, as Brian Ayers has pointed out. Nicholas Groves calculates a total of 63 churches in the medieval city, though not all functioning at the same time. There were well over fifty in the early Middle Ages, with a decline later, accelerated by the effects of the Black Death. St Matthew on Bishopgate was abandoned at that time, and, according to James Campbell, St Margaret Newbridge, St Winwaloy, St Michael in Conesford and St Olave Pitt Street 'certainly or probably went out of use in the generation after the plague'. The reasons for the number of churches are not entirely clear, but it seems pre-Conquest towns tend to have lots of relatively small churches, while post-Conquest ones are more likely to have just one large dominant church. Groves has put forward the intriguing idea that it was not the number of churches itself that mattered as much as the number of dedications: people wanted to honour a large number of saints by dedicating a church to them.[32]

Norwich is fortunate in having a large collection of late medieval wills; between 1370 and 1532, the wills of over 1,500 lay people and 300 clerics survive. These documents, which have been analysed in depth by Norman Tanner, tell us what people thought at the time of their impending death. Broadly, there seems to have been a gradual move over the centuries from giving to monastic houses to leaving money to one's own parish church. Almost every testator left money to their local parish church, most asking to be buried there. Some left money for specific building work and these can help the dating of the fabric; in 1479, William Blackdam left 10 marks towards painting the rood screen in St James Pockthorpe, which has the image of St Walstan referred to earlier, and is now in the church of St Mary Magdalen. In this way, we can know the names of some of the citizens who contributed to the wonderful heritage of Norwich's surviving medieval churches. Much has been lost, of course, such as the church of St Mary in the Fields, with its rood screen, for which Henry Bachcroft left the very large sum of £40.[33]

Popular religion in these churches was a much more sensuous experience than it is today. A good place to appreciate this is in St Gregory's, looking at the wall paintings, especially that of St George and the dragon, an underrated city treasure. Pevsner and Wilson describe these paintings as perhaps the finest late medieval wall paintings in the country after those in Eton College chapel. All wall spaces would have been painted like this, and now-empty niches, inside and outside of churches, would have been filled with statues of the Virgin Mary and the saints. Every church had a screen across the chancel in front of the altar, with a loft above on which the priest would stand at certain services, so that he would be close to images of St John and the Virgin Mary, gazing up at a painting or sculpture of the crucified Christ.

25 *St Peter Southgate, as drawn by John Kirkpatrick. The church was demolished in 1812.*

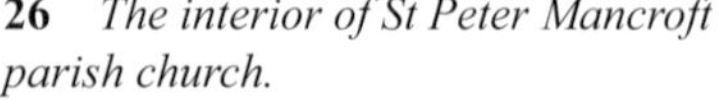

Every Norwich-born child would have been baptised in their local parish church and some fine medieval fonts do survive, such as that at St Peter Parmentergate, with two wild men and two wild women against the stem; that from All Saints, now in St Julian, with St George and St Michael standing over their respective dragons; and that at St John de Sepulchre with some very fine lions. Groves says of this: 'the maker has had fun carving the lions: they are exceptionally smug!' A wonderful image of medieval piety can be found in the spandrel of St Peter Parmentergate, where an unnamed woman holds a rosary (the carving is a Victorian replacement of the original).[34]

Some dramatic scenes must have taken place in these parish churches, for example at St Peter Hungate in 1466, where the body of John Paston lay for several days on its journey from London to its final resting place at Bromholme:

> a solemn dirige was sung there by Friars of the four Orders, and a gathering of 38 priests, 39 boys in surplices, and 26 clerks sang and prayed for the dead man's soul. Not only these, but the prioress of Carrow, followed by her maid, an anchoress from her lonely cell, as well as 23 sisters from Norman's Hospital, attended this service. Four torch-bearers stood about the corpse while the bells of S. Peter's and S. Stephen's churches tolled for the dead.[35]

26 *The interior of St Peter Mancroft parish church.*

Two retables (sets of paintings from altars) now in the cathedral illustrate the high quality of art in Norwich churches. One, of five panels, was always in the cathedral, probably paid for by Bishop Despencer and other notables as a thanks-offering for the suppression of the Peasants' Revolt. The other consists of three panels from a retable formerly at

St Michael at Plea. Joan Evans suggests that the retables may have been painted by the de Ocle family, Thomas and Richard both being known as painters in the city.

Upkeep of the chancel of a parish church was usually the responsibility of the rector, and the nave that of the parishioners, so that the two may now seem very different in date and style. However, it is a characteristic of late medieval churches in East Anglia to have no structural difference between nave and chapel, creating what Francis Bond called 'a great oblong aisled chapel … "Tudor lanterns" with a large window in every bay of the aisles, and two in every bay of the clerestory, and a great east window'. St Andrew, St Peter Mancroft and St Stephen are magnificent examples. St Peter Mancroft was pulled down in 1390 and the new church was completed in 1455, its building coinciding with that of the Guildhall across the market place. Joan Evans says: 'with its vast uniform aisle windows and its architecture dominated by oblong rectangles, [it] sets the note for the late Perpendicular East Anglian churches that are to come'.[36]

The names of those leaving bequests to rebuild St Andrew are listed in Table I, and show the progress of the building, while St Stephen is the latest of all the 'medieval' churches in the city, the nave and chancel being reconstructed in the first half of the 16th century. As it has a great west window as well, the tower was placed to the north-west rather than the west to allow this. The original tower appears to have been in the usual place at the west end, but the present tower rises from the north porch and was not built until 1601. The date used to be recorded upon it in letters of iron, but these were removed in 1960.[37]

Several Norwich churches have passages under their chancels, such as at St Gregory and St Peter Mancroft, and others have them beneath their towers, as at St John Maddermarket. Some of these may reflect the need to preserve rights of way in the crowded city, but their main function was

Table I: *Bequests to St Andrew's church, from Norwich wills.*

Year	Name	Bequest
1386	Bartholomew Appleyard	£20 to roof the church with lead
1467	John Drolle	£20 to new south porch, and bequest to paint perke [the roodscreen]
1478	Robert Hooker	20 pence to emend chapel of BVM in steeple
1483	Elizabeth Sayer	Reparation of chapel in steeple
1486	Thomas Buckenham	£6 to building of steeple and of the church
1496	Alice Gilbert	Bequest for reparation and making up of the tower
1499	John Reynold	£6. 13s. 4d. to making window
1499	Annabel King	20 shillings for 'making of a newe churche'
1500	ROYAL LICENCE	TO REBUILD CHANCEL AND LENGTHEN BY ONE FOOT
1502	William Nobbs	5 marks to 'new making'
1502	Margaret Dilham	8 marks to 'new bildyng'
1504	Katherine Bewfield	36s. 8d. to building church
1508	Anne Jeckis	6s. 8d. to 'beldyng of ye church'
1508	Robert Gardner	£10 to glazing north aisle, and bequest to make the perke in the 'myddes', to match the old work on both sides
1509	William Boucher	10 marks to glazing window
1522	John Smart	20 pence to Our Lady's chapel in steeple

One mark is 6s. 8d.

Source: *Paul Cattermole and Simon Cotton, 'Medieval Parish Church Building in Norfolk', in* Norfolk Archaeology, *vol. 38 (1983), p.257.*

for religious processions. There is still a niche over that at St Gregory where there would have been a statue.

From the 15th century, radical religious ideas, such as dislike of images and denial of the special role of priests, spread among some in Norfolk. Known loosely as Lollards, these people risked their lives by having these beliefs and a number were burnt at Lollards' Pit, outside Bishop Bridge. The city archives record the expenses of burning three 'eretycs' there in 1427-8. Two cartloads of wood were bought from the market to burn William White. William Waddon (other sources say his first name was actually John) and Hugh Pye were burned together; the wood was brought to the Pit by John Jekkes, faggots were supplied by John Excetre, and 'two logs to which the said eretics were bound' came from Edmund Snetisham. White had been tried at a diocesan synod, and was supposed to have opposed the friars, describing them as 'pseudo-prophets, mendacious masters, deceiving the people, introducing sects of perdition and blaspheming the way of truth'. However, execution was uncommon: 60 men and women were tried for heresy in Norwich diocese between 1428 and 1431, but none were sentenced to death, the usual punishments being flogging and penance. Only two of these 'lollards' were actually from Norwich: Thomas Wade, a city tailor, and Johanna, the wife of John Weston.[38]

27 *A processional way under the tower of St John Maddermarket.*

There was also a great deal of superstitious belief, and signs and portents were taken very seriously. In 1274, according to notes made by John Kirkpatrick, 'on St Nicholas' Eve [5 December] were great earthquakes, lightning and thunder, with a huge dragon and a blazing star'. In modern days, we would probably think first of unidentified flying objects rather than dragons, as did a man who saw unexplained lights above the University of East Anglia in November 1994 – perhaps the difference is merely one of the terminology of the times.[39]

Trade and Industry

Specific information on how livings were made in the early Middle Ages is very sparse. A French chronicler says that the reason the Flemings took Norwich in 1174 was that the men of the city 'for the most part were weavers, they knew not how to bear arms in knightly wise'. Central taxation records (the Pipe Rolls) mentions Norwich men trading in dyed cloth in 1202, and that of 1204 includes Norwich in a list of sea ports. The city had a traditional obligation to provide 24 herring pies to the king each year, a custom that continued until 1806 and reflects the importance of the fishing trade. An agreement survives from 1286 between the Norwich authorities and six merchants of Amiens and Corbeil in France dealing in woad, 'ashes' and weld. Woad is a blue dye which is also used as a fixative for other dyes; weld was cultivated for its yellow dye; the ashes were perhaps carbonate of soda used as the alkali in dyeing. Nicholas le Mouner may well have been one of these merchants; described as 'of Amiens', he purchased a house in Fyebridge in 1287, and appears to have lived there with his wife and family until his death in about 1330.[40]

Our knowledge of the life of the city is far greater after 1285, as from this date the city court rolls survive. These record changes in property ownership and for the first time give the names of large numbers of people living in Norwich. The rolls were used by the Norwich Survey to recreate the ownership of every property in the city between 1285 and 1341, an amazing piece of work, initiated by Helen Sutermeister, that took 12 years to complete.

Serena Kelly has used the records to look at occupations in the period 1285 to 1311; these are not always given in the documents but she has identified almost a thousand people whose employment is known. The largest groups were ecclesiastics of various kinds; there were 247 of these, over a quarter of those named, reflecting that these are mainly property owners. The others included 173 leather workers, 144 textile workers, 97 merchants, 60 metal workers and 43 bakers. The figures suggest a wide range of occupations, Norwich not yet having developed its specialisation in textiles.[41]

As Serena Kelly's figures make clear, the leather industry before 1300 was as important as the textile industry. The story of St William records that in about 1140, at the age of eight, he was apprenticed to a skinner; indeed he is England's first known apprentice. His biographer, writing just a few years later, sees nothing unusual in his becoming an apprentice at what seems to us such an early age. As Keith Wrightson says, at the age of seven or eight boys and girls 'had become part of the productive life of their families'. A 1291 Norwich apprenticeship indenture, between John, son of Gerard le Specer, and Hubert, son of William de Tibenham of Yarmouth, is the earliest known outside London. Hubert was to remain in the service of John for six years as his apprentice; he would obey John's orders, keep his secrets, guard his goods and warn him of impending damage. In return, John taught him his business as a spicer and provided him with suitable food and clothing.[42]

28 *The chapel of St William on Mousehold Heath, shown on a 16th-century map.*

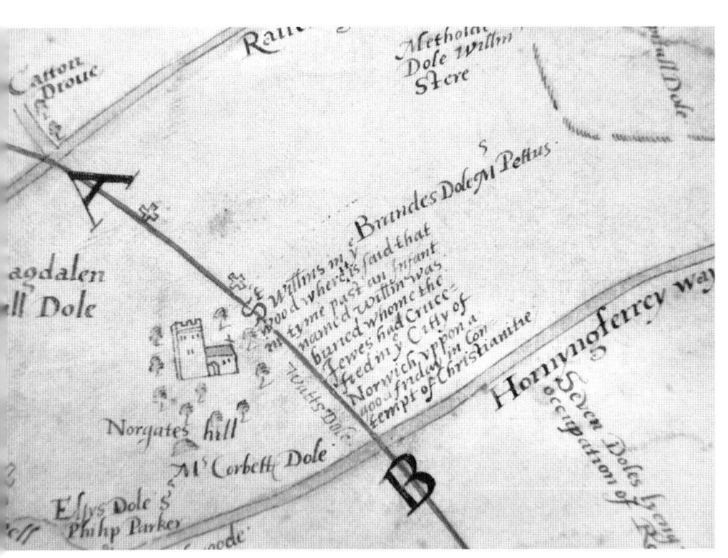

There was a large sheep population in Norfolk from at least the time of Domesday Book. By the late 13th century, Norfolk weavers had developed a lightweight cloth called worsted which was in demand throughout England and was also exported; worsted weavers are found in Norwich by 1329. The first known documentary evidence to worsted is in 1295, when it was already known in Dublin. In the same year, three Flemings – Bernard Pylat, Nicholas de Lo and John Waterbal – are known from Flemish archives to have been engaged with Norwich drapers, and English-made cloth was shipped to Holland and Zeeland both by merchants from those countries and by Norwich merchants. In later years, dornyx weaving also flourished, the earliest known reference in Norwich being in 1493. This originated in

Doornijk, now called Tournai, and produced a fabric suitable for beds and hangings generally woven in colours on the loom.

Trade in general was the lifeblood of the city. Formal letters relating to debt surviving on Yarmouth borough court rolls from 1290 to 1309 include references to trade with Norwich in iron, ginger, oysters, and tanning services. The types of goods being imported can be shown from a 14th-century disaster. On 19 October 1343, a boat loaded with people and goods coming upstream from Yarmouth to Norwich sank at Cantley in a sudden squall (Norfolk people would call it 'a roger'), and 40 people were drowned. The city had jurisdiction over the river as far as Hardley Cross, so the matter came before a Norwich inquest jury. The sinking was blamed on the rain, the strong wind and the overloading of the boat, which was filled with sea coal, salt, barrels of iron from Sweden, wood from Riga, onions and herrings. Another import was brick, and it is thought that the bricks used to make the undercroft of Bartholomew Appleyard's house (now the Bridewell Museum) in about 1370 came from Zeeland.[43]

There are many indications of the strong trading links between Norwich and Europe, and Elizabeth Rutledge has collated a number of these references. In 1317, five Brabant merchants had cloth worth £210 confiscated in Norwich. John Kempe came to Norwich from Flanders before 1331 to teach his system of weaving; he is probably to be identified with the John Kempe de Gaunt (Ghent) listed in the St Peter Mancroft tithing roll. Striped cloth seized in Yarmouth in the 1330s was imported from Flanders and belonged to Norwich merchants. In 1333 the ship *Nicholas*, bound for Hamburg, was driven off course to Bremen, and Roger de Blakeney of Norwich complained that he had lost woollen and worsted cloth, coverlets, silk garments and other articles including silver spoons, armour and wooden chests. Four Norwich merchants – William Hemstede, John Austin, Thomas Ritser and John Reinier – were involved in a legal dispute in Middleburgh in 1421, while in the same town some 46 years later another Norwich merchant, Richard Hart, claimed to have lost £20 because his agent there was slow to claim the money off a local merchant who had since died. John Asger, who was mayor of Norwich in 1426, is described on his brass in St Lawrence's as 'once a merchant of Bruges', and he was there when he was chosen as mayor, an entry in the city assembly books recording that the expenses of travelling to fetch him back were to be paid by the community.[44]

Another aspect of the role of Norwich as a port was shown in 1338 when Edward III was organising his first great expedition against France. For this 885 archers from 15 English counties and 700 men from North Wales were sent to Norwich to embark from Yarmouth. There was a delay before the fleet sailed, which caused some of the men to mutiny, but they were soon pacified. An important city like Norwich naturally furnished many men for military service, which was compulsory for all adult males. Their names and equipment are listed in its muster rolls; those for Conesford and Ber Street in 1355 list their armour and weapons 'as vividly as if marching before the eyes of the reader'. The weapons were swords and the armour jackets and helmets, but a decade later two Mancroft men, Adam de Poringland and John Spicer, each had 'a gunne with powder'. A century later, all the men had to possess a bow and a sheaf of arrows.[45]

The main 'road' to medieval Norwich was the river, the central trading area in the city having moved downstream since the Conquest to the quays or staithes off King Street, such as St Julian's staithe and St Olave's staithe. The surviving building that best represents this aspect of Norwich is Dragon Hall, beside the Wensum in King Street. However, James Campbell highlights a significant change from the second half of the 15th century onwards, with the increasing importance of road transport. Much of the cloth – even that being exported to the Continent – was going by road to London rather than by river to Yarmouth. The journey to the capital was not without its dangers: Margaret Paston's aunt refused to carry cash to London 'for fear of robbing. For it is said here that goeth many thieves betwixt this [city] and London.' Margaret herself, when she asked her son for some malmsey wine, told him to have it wound in canvas to prevent the carriers broaching it, as she had known this to happen before.[46]

There was a circuit of large fairs which traders would attend. A merchant from Bordeaux sold some wine to men from Norwich at the fair at Boston in 1273. He failed to get his money, so he searched for them in Boston and Norwich in the following year; he finally caught up with them at the fair at St Ives (Huntingdonshire) in May 1275 and was able to bring them to justice.[47]

Most of the trade was on a more local level, with the city supplying the needs of very many surrounding villages. Entries for this may be found in manorial accounts; for example, in 1378 the lord of the manor of Forncett bought in Norwich 20 boards of imported timber for windows. Carrying services by peasants on Norwich and Ely cathedral manors often include taking produce to and from the city.

Two early 14th-century cases relating to the market place involve traders from country villages. In 1307 Peter Monk bought a horse for eight shillings in Norwich market from Andrew Friday. As the horse was worth 20 shillings, Monk was suspicious and it turned out that Friday had stolen it from a neighbour in his home town of Raveningham three days earlier. However, evidence was produced that Friday was insane:

> They [the jurors] say that he is a lunatic and in the waning of the moon he becomes insane ... They say that 15 days before the theft Andrew cut down all the trees at his home in Raveningham and planted them in the ground.

Because of his mental state, Friday was taken back to the castle to await the king's pardon.[48]

Another case relating to the market came up two years later, in May 1309. A man named Geoffrey de Stanford de Crostwyght was taken for trying to sell a pair of socks in Norwich market place. This sounds harmless but it appears someone had recognised the socks as belonging to a man called Brice, who had been murdered in Tunstead (we are not told what it was about the socks that made them so identifiable). Geoffrey had to stay in gaol until March 1311 when the jury decided that, although he had the socks, he had not committed the murder, and after waiting almost two years in the castle prison, he was set free.[49]

The market was regulated by the leet courts and later by the city authorities through the mayor's court. Dealers were grouped according to their wares – the drapers in one spot, the fishmongers in another, etc. There was an apothecary shop, where herbs could be bought, by the late 13th century, as well as rows of shops of cordwainers (shoemakers) and spicers. According to Hudson and Tingey, the present Weavers' Lane was the Cobblers' Row of the medieval market place. From 1271, two groups of leatherworkers were told to keep to separate parts of the market to avoid fraud; they were the cordwainers, producing a better type of shoe, and those who used inferior leather from sheepskin ('bazan'). In 1320 Roger Brown of Norwich was among a group of traders whose shoes were confiscated in London because they were made of a mixture of bazan and cordwain.[50]

Some markets were held elsewhere: cattle, sheep, poultry and cheese were sold on the south side of St Peter Mancroft, now called Haymarket; horses were sold on Rampant Horse Street from at least the 13th century, according to title deeds (*Rampant Horse* is the name of an inn). Pigs were sold on All Saints' Green until the time of Edward I, when this market was moved to Hog Hill (now Orford Hill) and All Saints' Green was used for the timber market.

One of the markets is preserved in the name Maddermarket, madder being a plant used for dyeing. In 1438 Thomas Stevenesson, a Boston merchant, bought 12 bales of madder in Norwich from a merchant there, Thomas Skowe. He paid the very large sum of £42 for the madder, and when he was taking three of the bales by cart to Boston, he was just three miles out of Norwich when another Norwich merchant, Thomas Elys, stopped him and seized the cart and the madder. Stevenesson, not surprisingly, brought a case against Elys at the Norwich Assembly, but the end result is not known. No doubt there was a dispute between the men about payments, but it shows the kind of trade that went on in East Anglia in the later Middle Ages.[51]

Hudson and Tingey compiled a list of trades and occupations mentioned in city records in the last half of the 13th century. There are about 150, including some highly specialised skills such as bell-founder, goldsmith and parchment dealer, as well as surgeons and apothecaries. Such trades would be serving not just Norwich but the inhabitants of villages and market towns throughout east Norfolk and north-east Suffolk. Bell-founding continued into the 15th century as the services on offer in the city expanded to include further specialities like glass-making and the making of monumental brasses. The most well-known of the bell-founders are the Brassyer or Brasier family, whose monuments can be seen in St Stephen's church. One of their bells, thought to date from about 1490, was in the tower of St Julian's when it was bombed in the Second World War; the bell survived and can be seen today in the reconstructed tower.

Richard Brasier also made bells for Suffolk churches such as Mildenhall and Stansfield.[52]

Women could not sit on the council but they could have trades. Helen de Moundeforde, for example, describes herself as a glazier in her will of 1458. In the list of city freemen between 1317 and 1603, as printed by Walter Rye, there are just three females out of about 6,250 names: Petronilla de Bokenham in 1366, Isabella de Weston in 1367 and Elizabeth Baret in 1445-6. Another, missed by Rye, was Anselna, the daughter of Philip of Bawburgh, who took up the freedom in 1338. Elizabeth Baret was a single woman and enrolled as a worsted weaver, but we do not know the occupation or marital status of the other three. When the city began enrolling women as honorary freemen in the 20th century, the authorities thought they were breaking new ground, but these names show they were echoing events of many centuries ago.[53]

Brewing was, of course, an important activity from earliest times. Flemings brought to England the drink we now think of as the most English of all – beer. In the Middle Ages, English people drank ale – made from malted barley, water and yeast. In Europe it became the practice to use hops as well to produce beer; this was stronger and also kept better. Norwich, with its Dutch connections, led the way: Richard Somer is recorded as selling 'Flemish ale' in the late 13th century, the first documentary evidence for the sale of beer anywhere in Britain. It was being imported by the 1370s, mainly by Europeans, and began to be brewed in the city by the 1430s, at first principally by Dutchmen; lists of 'aliens' record one Dutch beer brewer in 1440. Despite a city order of 1471 forbidding the use of hops as 'unwholesome for manne's body', beer-brewing gradually became a major industry in the city.

Ale was brewed on a smaller scale and usually, although not invariably, by women – there are 286 brewers in the city in the leet rolls of 1288-9, declining to 208 a century later, about 80 per cent of whom were married women. The unmarried women are a fascinating group of people in themselves; there were 46 of these in 1288-9. Thirty-one are identified by name alone, nine are described as widows, two as concubines of clerics(!), and one who may have supported herself by prostitution as well as brewing. The final two are described as lodgers, and Judith Bennett identified them as probably of a class of itinerant brewing women she has found from other cities. The other brewing women often show up year after year, Margery de Brundall appearing as a brewer for a quarter of a century. In York such women very occasionally entered the freedom of the city, but there is no example of this in Norwich.[54]

Two public houses, the *Adam and Eve* and the *Maid's Head*, are rivals for the claim of oldest pub in Norwich. The *Adam and Eve* is said to date from 1249 and to be connected with the nearby Cathedral Priory or Great Hospital. The *Maid's Head* is known from the Paston letters in the mid-15th century, but is probably much older: a man stole goods from an innkeeper on Cook Row, the old name for Wensum Street, in 1289.

River fishing was a source of food, though many fish sales were of salt fish brought up from Yarmouth. Church rules forbade the eating of meat on many days in the year, including the whole of Lent, so there was an enormous demand. There was a fish house in St George Tombland parish, and the importance of shellfish is indicated by the discovery in 1963 of a layer of oyster shells 18 inches thick beneath the site of the *New Star* inn on Quayside. As we have seen, the city controlled the river down to Hardley Cross; the stream was divided into 19 sections called 'setts', each of which was leased out to fishermen. The importance of conserving fish stocks has been an issue for at least 600 years, and the five rules laid down by the city assembly on 13 September 1382 could have emanated from Brussels today:

1. No one can use a seyne or dragge net between 29 September and 1 August.
2. No net of this kind was to have a stone hanging from it of a greater weight than two pounds.
3. No one can fish in the river with any kind of net in the last two weeks of April and the first two weeks of May, except only with draglamms [drag nets].
4. Everyone may fish with lamms [nets into which fish are driven by beating the water] until 8 September, and at no other time of the year.
5. No one is allowed to fish in the river with leaps, trimmers or bownets at any time of year.

Norwich was an important centre for the herring trade in the early Middle Ages. Leicester Abbey bought fish from Norwich in 1286, and in that year no less than nine distant monasteries were reported for not appearing before the justices in connection with land they owned in Norwich for the purchase of fish, including four Cistercian monastic houses with property in King Street. However, all four had closed by the mid-14th century, probably sourcing their product closer to home.[55]

A city like Norwich attracts many incomers, especially young people in search of economic and social opportunities. These people would come from all over Norfolk and beyond. In theory you were supposed to pay a fine called chevage before leaving the country manor in which you lived. On the manor of Forncett, to take one example, 22 people paid to move into Norwich between 1400 and 1575.[56]

However, many other people naturally voted with their feet and simply left their manors, as a legal case involving people from Costessey demonstrates. In 1313 the king issued a writ concerning 18 people currently living in Norwich who, it was claimed, were really tenants of the manor of Costessy, and had moved to the city without permission from the lord. Fourteen, including the only two women in the list (Alice and Sibilla la Fevre) seem to have submitted, presumably paying a fine to the lord. However, four of the men resisted, claiming that they had become citizens of Norwich. William de Colton had been in the city for 60 years and William Fiz for 30, and two brothers, Henry and John Tobyn, had actually been born in the city – it was their father, called sometimes Robert Tobyn and sometimes Robert de Hegham, who had left the manor. Some also had charters concerning their claims in Norwich: William de Colton (also called William Mounford in the document) had been granted permission by King Edward to enclose and build on two plots he owned in Needle Row, while Robert Tobyn had a royal charter granting him property that had belonged to Isaac, the son of Deulacres, which had passed to the Crown on the expulsion of the Jews. The charters were the key, and the cases of Colton and the Tobyn brothers were allowed, whereas that of Fiz was referred to a jury – 30 years away from the manor were not necessarily enough to escape the clutches of its lord. The final outcome of his case is not known.[57]

While people from all over the county came to Norwich to trade, by the 15th century the richest elements of city society were looking to London. The letters of Margaret Paston illustrate this, frequently requesting items from her husband there. In November 1452, she asked for two dozen trenchers 'for I can none get in this town', and also a pound of a preserve made of quinces 'for the air is not wholesome in this town'. In April 1453, she asked him for a necklace: 'When the Queen was here, I borrowed my cousin Elizabeth Clere's device, for I durst not for shame go with my beads amongst so many fresh gentlewomen as were here at that time'. Her husband does not seem to have been quick to respond, as she was making the same request nine months later.

Everyone worked six days a week, having leisure only on Sundays and on the various religious festivals and saints' days through the year. In 1422 it was ordered that no one should open a stall or shop in the city on a Sunday, except for cooks, brewers and taverners. Work usually stopped at 4 p.m. on Saturdays and on the days before feast days. In 1490 the shoemakers claimed their labourers were 'greatly disposed to riot and idleness' during the early part of the week, and worked late in the evening on Saturdays and the days before festivals to make up; as a result they did not get up in time for divine service!

The carter for the Great Hospital, John Dernell, was taking two or three holidays every month in addition to Sundays in the early 14th century. His accounts survive for seven months in 1417, giving us a unique insight into labouring life. As well as working for the Hospital, he took on private commissions. Much of his time was spent carting muck, but he also carried clay to spread on the hospital's fields. Its farm at the Lathes was only just outside the city, north of St Augustine's churchyard, and included the Gildencroft, a dramatic reminder of how small the built-up area of the city was. Once he collected a load of thatch landed at Bishop's Bridge, and on one occasion took a millstone from the city staithe to Costessey. Occasionally he journeyed as far as Erpingham, once carrying a large log to Sir Thomas Erpingham there, returning with a load of peas and hay for the hospital.[58]

Civic Buildings

The city was enclosed with a bank and ditch in 1253, and in 1288 the prioress of Carrow and Robert Gerveys of Bracondale (spelt Brakendenne in the original) were prosecuted for letting their pigs and sheep feed in the city ditches. The first murage grant for a masonry wall was made in 1297, but the building programme took a very long time. The city walls and gates as known to later centuries were completed in 1343, mainly through the generosity of one citizen, Richard Spynk. They form two arcs, the one on the south extending from the river at Carrow to the river at New Mills, the northern arc extending from the river near St Martin at Oak to the river at Barrack Street. The walls were about 12 feet high with battlements. Towers and walls are made of flint bedded with lime mortar, with brick arches. It has been suggested that the brick was added to strengthen the wall against artillery about 40 years later, but Alan Carter was sure it was part of the original fabric. Ayers describes how the walls were built:

> the city wall was built in courses of flint which, because of the large quantities of mortar necessary, had to be erected in 'lifts', each lift being shuttered and allowed to set before the next lift was added. It is often possible to detect such 'lifts' in the surviving stretches of wall.

This is a feature well worth looking for in any large area of flint, whether a church wall or tower, or the wall between Tombland and the cathedral.[59]

The city agreed to release Spynk from all tolls and dues because of his generosity in completing the walls and furnishing them with espringolds (catapults) and other weapons of war. The two boom towers at Carrow were built at the same time; Spynk's charter of 1343 mentions 'two great chains of good Spanish iron across the river … so that no barge or boat might come in or depart without leave nor against the will of those who have to govern the city'. As this suggests, the function of the walls was not just military defence: controlling the number of ways in and out of the

29 *Conesford (King Street) Gate, as drawn by the antiquary John Kirkpatrick.*

30 *Reconstruction drawing by Tom Griffiths of Norwich in the 1340s, giving a good sense of the two arcs of the walls.*

31 *'Norwich's front door'; St Stephen's Gate, as portrayed by Moray Smith.*

city made it easier to regulate traffic and made sure the appropriate tolls were paid.[60]

The city built the Tolhouse in the market place and the Murage Loft nearby soon after the restoration of its liberties following the 1272 riots, probably as 'an attempt to restore some element of civic pride in the city following on from its loss of respectability and rights'. Katherine Colne hung herself with a girdle in the Tolhouse building in 1274. The Murage Loft had shops on its ground floor; in 1378-9, butchers and fishmongers assembled in the Loft to swear that 'all kinds of flesh and fish' would be sold on the common stalls and nowhere else. Kirpatrick identifies the Murage Loft as being the 'Chamber of Receipt' where a new covering for the exchequer table was bought, also in 1378-9.

Towards the end of the 14th century, the city began to acquire property in the market place, and could then order all traders to use their stalls. The common staithe was bought in 1379, part was freehold and the other part was on a 600-year lease from Wendling Abbey. The new common staithe was purchased in the following year. These staithes were off King Street, well downstream of the old city quay at Fyebridge, which appears to have been used mainly for landing shellfish (see p.46). All ships and boats were to be loaded and unloaded at the common staithes – and, of course, had to pay tolls to the city. A list of dues gives an idea of the very wide range of goods passing through, including iron from Spain, herrings from Sweden, oak boards from Riga, skins, cloth, wine, timber, copper, fruit, nuts, woad and madder, to name just a few examples.[61]

The city also purchased a block of buildings between the market, Pottergate, Dove Street and Lower Goat Lane. Part of the property was formerly an inn and seems to have continued as such; from 1409 it is called the *Common Inn*. By an Act of 1404, all merchants had to house with hosts assigned to them by the city authorities, and no doubt traders visiting Norwich stayed at this inn. The northern part of the property became the Worsted Seld, the only place in the city where weavers from the countryside could sell their produce.

City revenue was spent on a wide range of projects. Cow Tower was rebuilt in 1399. Formerly known as the Dungeon Tower, it is made entirely of brick upon a stone plinth and was originally about 50 feet high. It was used as a tollhouse by the priory, and then as the priory's prison, and was later sold to the Great Hospital. The Master of the Hospital granted it to the city in 1378 and it was then repaired; accounts survive among the city archives for the purchase of several thousand new bricks. Robert Snape was hired to make the 12 'shot-holes', being paid nine pence for each one.

32 *Bishop's Bridge, the only surviving medieval bridge in Norwich.*

33 *Bishop's Bridge, with its gate.*

Bishop's Bridge is the only surviving medieval bridge in the city. It is mentioned in an agreement of 1331 between the priory and the city: the prior was permitted to build houses on the bridge itself and along both banks of the river, but must allow the citizens access to the river beside the bridge for their horses, and to bring hay, rushes, turves 'and other necessaries' to shore. The bridge was maintained by the priory until 1393 when it was handed over to the city. The bridge had a gate on it, whose outer limits are marked by the semi-circular projections on the parapet wall. When work was being done on the bridge in 1998, a portion of the gate wall over six feet high was uncovered on its south side.

The 1404 charter led to a wave of building projects in Norwich, reflecting civic pride in the city's new status. The largest of the city projects was the Guildhall, begun in 1407 on the site of the old Tolhouse, the brick undercroft of which can still be seen underneath it. It is by far the largest building of its kind outside London, and its position adjoining the market is significant: 'such municipal buildings, often grand and imposing in nature, served to remind those traders (and others) who congregated in the market places of towns that they were under the watchful eye of the municipality'. Many local men supplied the materials, some free of charge – William Appleyard gave a 'great tree', which cost two shillings to transport.[62]

One surviving account roll describes the expenses of the building work; it dates from 1411-13 when the building must have been almost complete as half of the £100 spent is on lead for the roof. Additions were made throughout the century and major repairs were needed when the roof of the mayor's courtroom collapsed in 1511. Some 15th-century glass still survives, now gathered together in the windows at the east end of the Council Chamber. Other works included the Market Cross, over 70 feet high, built in 1409, as well as rebuilding the Murage Loft in 1411 and constructing the New Mills in 1429.

One of the masons working on the Guildhall was John Marwe, who worked on the building for 68 days in 1410-11, receiving the normal mason's rate of six pence a day, with an extra four pence a day for his labourers. In 1432 he was hired to rebuild the quay at Conesford, for which he was paid £53 6s. 8d. in four equal instalments and also given a Christmas present of cloth to make himself a gown. As this suggests, property bought by the city had to be maintained and improved. In 1426-7 a capstan was installed at the Common Staithe, and money was spent both on repairing the old sign, of a peacock, at the *Common Inn*, and on painting a new peacock sign; William Hervy was the painter.

Housing and Diet

Very few medieval houses survive in Norwich; those that do are mainly those of the wealthy. There are no illustrations or written descriptions of houses, so we are dependent on archaeological evidence and hints from documentary sources. Few houses were of stone, though there may have been more than was previously thought. Between the Norman Conquest and 1330 there are about twenty written references to stone houses; one worth seeing is the undercroft of Wensum Lodge, the house of Isaac the Jew. Others are only known from written sources, such as a stone house on Tombland known as 'le Heybothe', which must have been large as in 1283 it included three shops. In 1285 Nicholas de Ingham and his wife Gundreda gave their stone house in Fybridgegate to their son Walter.

34 *Norwich Guildhall, the largest outside London.*

Archaeologists have uncovered some evidence of stone houses not known from written sources. The most impressive, apart from the Music House, was discovered by excavation in 1981 and is now preserved under the Court Buildings by the river. There were others; the Millennium Library excavations revealed the existence of two stone houses, almost completely grubbed out, while another was discovered opposite Dragon Hall in excavations in 2000.

Leet court records give a few details about city houses, and in 1263, there is a description of a relatively upmarket house. Katherine, the widow of Stephen Justice, accused eight people of breaking into her house on 22 November while her late husband's body was laid out on a bier; the intruders were accused of doing damage, robbery and burning the corpse. The house was on Fyebridge Street in St Clement parish and stood around a courtyard. The principal room was the hall, where meals were taken and the men of the household slept. The private chamber was reached through the hall, and was where the most precious possessions of the house were kept and probably where the women slept.

The case may have centred on a private grudge, as did another case in the following year, which also clearly illustrates the dangers of fire in the medieval city. William de Eblaster and other men burnt down the house of John de Ballaya by setting fire to its gate. To make sure they were successful, they first went to the three nearest parish churches of

35 *Dragon Hall, showroom of Robert Toppes.*

36 *Dragon Hall: the dragon spandrel.*

St Peter Parmentergate, St Vedast and St Cuthbert, cutting the ropes of each church's bells and stealing the clappers. They did this to prevent any passerby who saw the fire trying to raise the alarm by ringing the church bells, the normal way of calling attention. In 1288 Robert Scott was reported to be in the habit of climbing by night over the outer walls of houses and then breaking *through* their inner walls, so they were presumably made only of wattle and daub.[63]

A flood in Norwich is said by a Bury chronicler to have done more harm to the city than either the raid of the disinherited barons or the depredations of royal officials after the riots of 1272. According to the *Chronicle* of the Norwich monk Bartholomew Cotton, a flood in the city in 1290 'overturned some houses and bore them along', so they cannot have been very solid constructions.

Although the area inside the walls of the city was so big that large parts of it were not built up, suburbs were developing just outside the city as early as the mid-13th century; there are references to 'suburbs of Norwich' in cathedral deeds of 1250 and 1261. A deed of 1295 mentions a lime kiln in the suburb of Norwich outside Conesford Gate, perhaps an ancestor of the large pit now known as Bracondale Grove, and there was a suburb outside Westwick in 1297, the earliest reference to development on what is now the Dereham Road.

One of the most revealing excavations was that conducted in Alms Lane, north of the river, by Malcolm Atkin in 1976. It appears that the area was used until the 13th century as a quarry and rubbish dump, and was then occupied by ironworks and breweries. The site began to be built up from about 1300, originally by single-storey dwellings and then by two-storeyed clay-wall houses. After about 1500, the houses were rebuilt in flint and brick, with timber-framed first floors. Delicate analysis of tiny bones has given us a picture of the diet of the inhabitants, which included much fish, as we have seen, but also meat: aside from fish bones, some 22,686 fragments of animal bone were recovered. These were mainly cattle, with a smaller quantity of pig bone. One rabbit bone was found from the 12th or 13th century. Rabbits were probably introduced to England in Norman times, and clearly caught on – rabbit bones became common from the late 13th century. Many bird bones were also found, mostly fowl and geese, probably raised on the site.[64]

South of the river, on Pottergate, archaeologists working in 1974 uncovered a 187ft-long frontage destroyed by fire, probably the great fire of 1507 described on p.67. After its destruction, the site was undisturbed for 150 years. Many kitchen artefacts were found, indicating increasing material wealth in the early 16th century. They included metal cooking vessels, pottery storage vessels and jugs, some made locally and others of a style imported in massive quantities from the end of the 15th century. These were houses of a higher status than at Alms Lane, 'heated perhaps by stoves, as fragments of stove-tiles were recognised, the earliest evidence in England for the use of closed stoves'.[65]

37 *Strangers' Hall, a merchant's house and now a museum.*

Some later medieval houses survive, such as the Bridewell, originally a private house built in about 1370 for the Appleyard family, who later supplied Norwich with its first mayor. The long wall of knapped flint has impressed generations of visitors; Celia Fiennes was here in 1698, writing,

> a wall made of flints that are headed very finely and cut so exactly square and even, to shutt in one to another, that the whole wall is made without cement at all they say, but it appears to be very little if any mortar, it looks very smoothe shining and black.

It is still impressive. Another merchant's house is that of Strangers' Hall, a house of many periods around a mid-15th-century hall built for William Barley. Both these houses can be visited as they are now museums. A rather different property is Dragon Hall, with a stunning seven-bay first floor, featuring the dragon that gives the house its name carved in the

38 *A Norwich undercroft, in use as a café.*

beams of the ceiling. This was the 88ft-long showroom of the merchant Robert Top or Toppes, who bought it in 1450 and used it to display the wares brought into the city along the adjacent river; he traded extensively with the Low Countries. This was not the first building on the site – it has been occupied since at least the 11th century – and Toppes probably adapted the building rather than built it. The house has a 14th-century doorframe with a 15th-century surround, while the timbers of the roof have been dated to the 1420s by dendrochronology. All three of these buildings have cellars, known as undercrofts: brick-built level and fire-proof platforms, originally with timber-framed houses above. More than eighty of these exist in the city, probably built in the 15th century; many are now underneath much later houses.[66]

Another building with a specialised use is the house now called the *Britons' Arms*. It has a medieval doorway facing the churchyard of St Peter Hungate, and is timber-framed. Each room has a fireplace, like a series of 'bedsits'. It was probably a beguinage, a group of religiously minded women living together. These groups are known in Europe, but are not well recorded in Norwich. Blomefield, writing in the 18th century, says there was such a group living north of St Peter Hungate churchyard. It is not known what his source was for this information, but his description exactly fits this house.[67]

In the early Middle Ages, houses were using massive quantities of peat for fuel, brought into the city by boat. The cathedral priory alone was using up to 400,000 turves of peat every year. Among his many bequests, William of Dunwich left 10 shillings to buy turves for the poor in 1272. In the house of Katherine of Norwich in 1336-7, faggots were used for brewing, turf for cooking and logs for heating the hall and chamber. By the end of the Middle Ages, peat was no longer so easily accessible and people turned to wood or coal. The peat pits were flooded as sea levels rose, and this is how the Norfolk Broads came into being. Eventually it was forgotten that the Broads were man-made: Thomas Browne, writing in the 17th century, assumed that they were natural. Although some Victorian antiquarians such as Samuel Woodward suggested they were artificial, their true nature was only revealed in the 1950s by Joyce Lambert and her colleagues, using a combination of archaeological and documentary evidence – and with practical help from the writer Marietta Pallis, who was digging a lake at Hickling to create an island in the shape of a double-headed eagle![68]

Norwich, like every medieval city, wrestled with problems of water supply and waste disposal, and the smells would probably be the most striking difference between medieval Norwich and the modern city. The river and the cockeys were much used, both for drinking and for carrying away waste products. The toilet arrangements of the Norman house under the present court buildings consisted of a garderobe or shaft, the bottom of which was open to the river, which washed the waste away. There were also wells, including a common well in the centre of the city, just north of White Lion Street. Uncovered in 1888, it was reported to be 50 feet deep and 'lined at the bottom with great stone like a church'. Other wells included one in the New Borough, in which the skeletons of several women and children were found, perhaps intended to poison the water supply, if the well was in use, or alternatively as a place of concealment if it was no longer being worked. Simon, son of Laurence of Shotesham, died when he fell into a pit from which he was drawing water with a pitcher and cord in 1272. In 1279 Thomas Dust was let down into a well he was making or repairing in a Norwich courtyard, but he fell out of the bucket and died of the foul air at the bottom of the well.

39 *The Great Hospital: roof of the Eagle Ward.*

Pits and ponds supplied water or became convenient places to get rid of waste matter, the incorrect disposal of which could lead to fines, as it does today. There was a pool called Muspool in front of St George Colegate church, which gives its name to Muspole Street, and several other pools. In 1289 William le Skinner was fined for throwing the bodies of cats (presumably the waste product of his skinning business) into a pit called Lothmere, on what is now Bethel Street; this pit survived into the 18th century. In 1375 Adam de Hindringham, a barber, was fined because he was 'wont constantly to lay his muck in the king's highway through the whole year and likewise his carts by day and by night to the great nuisance of the neighbours and of all that gather there, whereby the said way is always deeply and foully encumbered'. In 1391 John Wake, dyer, was fined because he was 'wont to throw ashes, paste and many other things issuing out of his craft into the king's river, to the blocking of the river'.

In March 1380 it was ordered that no one should carry any muck by boat, subject to heavy fines: 20 shillings for the first offence, 40 shillings for the second and for the third a 60 shilling fine and loss of citizenship – draconian penalties indeed. At the same time, it was ordered that anyone who had allowed rubbish to pile up in the market place or elsewhere must have it removed by 24 June or face a penalty of 40 pence a day until it was removed.[69]

The city issued regulations for cleaning the river from at least 1367, when John de Gnateshalle and William Staloun were elected to supervise the work. In 1422 every able-bodied person was ordered to labour at cleaning the river – or pay four pence a day for a substitute labourer. Orders were made for paving streets from at least 1426-7.

There were occasional attempts by the authorities to light parts of the city from the 14th century, relying on the individual householder. In December 1437 those householders who could afford it were told to hang a lantern or 'sconce' every evening between Christmas and Epiphany (6 January), and in 1453 it was ordered that these lights should be provided from 5 p.m. to 9 p.m.[70]

Health

The first 'hospital' in the city would have been at the cathedral as it was a duty of Benedictine monks to care for the poor and the sick; there was also an infirmary for the sick among the monks themselves. The cathedral also established the Hospital of St Paul, often known as Norman's

40 *Cloister of the Great Hospital.*

Hospital after its first master, in the early 12th century. The hospital supported up to 20 poor and frail people until they either died or were well enough to make way for others. It was also intended to house poor travellers overnight and provide an evening meal and bread for their journey. Unusually it also admitted sick pregnant women – it was the only hospital in the city to cater for pregnant women and nursing mothers. The hospital was run by 'sisters', not nuns but poor women themselves in need of alms. It seems to have been a popular local institution – about one third of the people in the city making wills between 1370 and 1532 left it something, some a few pence and others household items like bedding or furniture.[71]

41 *Musical manuscript from the medieval Great Hospital, reused as a wrapper. The importance of the Hospital's archive has been recognised by UNESCO.*

The largest of the hospitals was the Great Hospital, still functioning today on its original site in Bishopgate after well over seven centuries of service. It was founded in 1249 by Bishop Walter de Suffield. The hospital originally had a small chapel, but in 1270 it was given the parochial rights of the nearby church of St Helen; the monks demolished the church and greatly enlarged their chapel to serve both the poor and the parishioners. Because of this, the hospital is often known as St Helen's, but in fact the original dedication was to St Giles and other saints.

Towards the end of the 14th century, the present tower and chancel were built. The panels of the ceiling are painted with eagles, said to commemorate the visit to Norwich in 1383 of King Richard II and his young wife, Anne of Bohemia, a lady who appears to have caused as much of a stir as would Princess Diana in the later 20th century. One sign of Anne's modernity is that she was apparently the first person anyone in Norwich had ever seen riding side-saddle! Some people object that they are not double-headed eagles, but Carole Rawcliffe points out that the insignia of the Empire was the single-headed eagle at the time, only becoming double at a later date. A double-headed eagle can be seen in the stone frieze on the west wall of St Andrew's church.[72]

The role of the hospital was not to cure, but to care for the dying, both physically and – much more importantly – spiritually, by preparing their way into the next world; the beds of the sick were placed to allow the patients to see and hear the services in the church.

There were several other small hospitals in the city, really almshouses. All were religious institutions apart from Ivy Hall or Hildebrande's Hospital, on King Street not far from the present Normandie Tower. It was founded at the beginning of the 13th century by a wealthy Norwich merchant, Hildebrand the mercer, as a hostel for 'poor people wanting lodging'. It was never large, but bequests were sometimes made by local people, such as Emma Sewy or Swey, who asked to be buried there in her will of 1458 and also left money for the chapel to be decorated with broad Flanders tiles.[73]

Another group of small 'hospitals' were the leper houses around the edges of the city, the best-preserved being that on the Sprowston Road. This was presumably to isolate the infected before they entered Norwich, but there may have been deeper reasons; Roberta Gilchrist suggests it was both to 'remind travellers of the piety of charitable patrons' and to 'assert the corporate identity of a town through the maintenance and protection of its boundaries'. The leper houses do not form a complete ring; surprisingly there was none to the east on the road to Great Yarmouth. This may have been for a practical reason, as the contagion was thought to spread on the wind, which generally blows from the east, but there may have been a symbolic reason to face the setting sun as well. Whatever the truth of this idea, it draws attention to the fact that the medieval city would be much more attuned to the natural rhythms of day and night, winter and summer, than is the present-day city.[74]

In the later Middle Ages, as leprosy became less common, the hospitals may have taken in other sick people as well. Although they were intended for the poor, the wealthy could also catch the disease. In 1448 Henry Wells left money for a new chapel at the Magdalen Street hospital, where he lived, and he describes himself as a leper and his executors as 'leprosos'. A relative of his, Richard Wells, was also a leper and he, too, had sufficient property to make a will. In 1456 one of the cathedral monks, Richard de Walsham, contracted leprosy and, despite the attention of the best doctors and physicians, there was no cure. He was not sent to one of the hospitals; instead, provision was made for him to lead a solitary life in a specially built house in the grounds of the monastic cell at St Leonard's.[75]

Norwich has several claims to fame in medical history, according to Anthony Batty-Shaw: the Norwich city archives contain the first known reference in England to a barber, and the second earliest to a surgeon. The barber was John Belton, mentioned in a document of 1163; the surgeon was Ralph de Morley. Morley had a house in King Street mentioned in a deed of 1288, and he also occurs in the cathedral account rolls for 1313-14, when he was paid for attending sick monks.[76]

The Black Death

The Black Death of 1349 had an enormous effect on the city; a reasonable guess is that half the population died in about three months. However, as there were no records kept of individual deaths, we can never have an exact figure. The great 18th-century historian Francis Blomefield looked at the city archives and found this 'evidence' in the Norwich Mayor's Book: 'In 1348, Jan 1, the plague broke out in this city, from which time, to the first of July following, as our historians assure us, there died no less than 57,104 (or more rightly as others have it, 57,374) persons, in this city only, besides religious and beggars.' He also quotes the Norwich Book of Pleas: 'In the year of Our Lord 1349, God Almighty visited mankind with a deadly plague which began in the south parts of the world ... it was believed, that there was not a greater number of souls destroyed by the flood in the days of Noah, than died by this plague.' In fact, this quotation from the Book of Pleas is not meant to describe Norwich in particular; it is a copy of a chronicle written in Louth Abbey in Lincolnshire, and copied word for word into the Norwich book. The actual figure Blomefield quotes comes from a list of events in the Mayor's Book, but this book was not even bought by the city until 1526, so it is no sense contemporary evidence.[77]

42 *Death comes for the Bishop; glass in St Andrew's church.*

One evidence of mortality is the number of men invited to take up the freedom of the city in and after 1349. Penny Dunn says:

> The largest number of entrants for any year in the history of the Old Free Book, is recorded in 1349-50, when 120 men paid to join the Norwich franchise. In the previous year only twenty-one individuals had taken up the privilege and it seems that immigrants from outside Norwich were mostly responsible for the gradual provision of new citizens in the months following the loss of so many leading residents.[78]

Seventeen new freemen were registered on the Translation of St Edward, 13 October 1349, and 70 on the Saturday after the Feast of the Circumcision, 3 January 1350. About sixty have names indicating the place from which they come, and these embrace a large number of Norfolk villages, especially along the Yare valley and the areas around Wroxham, Dereham and Swaffham. Some are very local such as 'John de Bracondale, mercer', while only two have names definitely suggesting they came from outside Norfolk: Semannus of Beccles, only 20 miles from Norwich, and Thomas of Leighton Buzzard. There is one man from further afield among the 28 new freemen in the following year, Simon de Almannia, but almost all the losses among city trades appear to have been made up by recruiting from within the county.

There was a high turnover of clergymen in Norwich in the plague months, but the situation is complicated because not all new appointments appear in the bishop's register. Phyllis Pobst says that 20 parishes in the city, and possibly 24, were *donatives* – preferment was made to these by the patrons, without presentation to the bishop, so these would not be recorded in the diocesan records. About half the parishes in Norwich that appear in the registers appointed new incumbents in the second half of 1349 – two of them made two appointments. For comparison, in the same period in the previous year there was not a single new appointment to a Norwich parish, so clearly something unusual was happening.[79]

Deaths in the monastic houses also show the effects of the Black Death. There were no less than four new appointments to the six positions of prebend at the College of Saint Mary in the Fields in July 1349, and one of these was himself replaced in October, clear evidence of a high mortality rate in this college. There are traditions that all, or almost all, the friars in the Dominican and Franciscan friaries died, not surprising if they were fulfilling their duties among the poor.[80]

Norwich Cathedral also suffered: there is evidence that there were about 65 monks in 1348, half of whom died in the plague. These figures are based on the St Leonard's cell account rolls; the cell paid a small sum as pocket-money to each monk – Saunders says that the figure dropped to 37. The cathedral officials appear not to have succumbed at such a rate: Saunders points out that nine of the 10 lived through the Black Death, the only exception being Ralph de Swanton. Nevertheless, the accounts do reveal evidence of crisis, recording that building work on the cloisters came to a sudden end on 25 June 1349; the stone was sold and the remaining cash divided between the officials for safekeeping. Tradition says that the north-west corner had been reached and that the mouldings in the arches here – made of wood, not stone – are temporary ones put in at the time of the Black Death and never replaced.[81]

43 *Wooden bay of the cathedral cloister walk.*

Actions taken by the city in the 20 years after the Black Death show that the crisis was still ongoing. An assembly order of 19 November 1354 reads:

> Whereas great injuries and dangers so often have happened before this time in the City of Norwich and still happen from day to day in so much as boars, sows and pigs before this time and still go vagrant by day and night without a keeper in the said city, whereby divers persons and children have thus been hurt by boars, children killed and eaten and others buried exhumed, and others maimed, and many persons of the said city have received great injuries as wrecking of houses, destruction of gardens of divers persons by such kind of pigs upon which great complaint is often brought before the said bailiffs and community imploring them for remedy on the misfortunes, dangers and injuries which have been done to them.

The assembly ordered that pigs were to be kept in their enclosures, and any pig found going at large without a keeper could freely be killed. Every pig owner could let their animal out each Saturday from noon in order to clean their sties. Similar measures were applied to dogs wandering in the city, but certain dogs such as greyhounds, spaniels and dogs used for sports were excepted. An order of 12 June 1368, recorded in the Old Free Book, allowed the church of St Peter Mancroft to enlarge its cemetery to take in part of the market place. The property consists of two lanes and a piece of vacant land; Hudson and Tingey suggest that the current pathway through the churchyard marks its original boundary before its 14th-century extension.[82]

Once established, the plague frequently re-occurred, especially in the summer months. In September 1471 John Paston wrote to his son, 'I fear there is great death in Norwich', and in 1479 he wrote from the city 'the people dyeth sore in Norwich', and thought of departing to the country.

44 *A 19th-century illustration of Norwich Castle as a prison.*

Crime and Punishment

Law and order was controlled by a whole series of local and national courts depending on the location and nature of the crime and also the status of the criminal. In the period immediately after the Conquest there were probably separate courts to deal with the English and the French, but this distinction disappeared long before the earliest surviving court records, those for the leet courts. These dealt with minor offences; more serious cases were reserved for visiting royal justices.

Such a large city needed subdivisions. There were originally four leets, Wymer, Westwick, Mancroft and Coslany, and in 1223 they were divided into sub-leets for the purpose of exercising legal jurisdiction. Parts of the city were not controlled by it and so not included – the castle, the Cathedral Close and St Paul's parish (which was part of the priory fee). All adult males (aged 12 or over) had to be in a tithing, a group of people living in the same street, with mutual responsibility before the law: if one committed a crime and then ran away, the other members of the tithing were held responsible for the crime. Every year the sheriff took a view of frankpledge to make sure that every adult male was enrolled in a tithing. From the later 12th century, the view was accompanied by a report, or presentment, of any offences committed since the previous view. One man from each tithing (called the Chief or Capital Pledge) made the presentments on behalf of his group, and offenders were punished with fines. In theory, this jurisdiction belonged to the king, but it was granted to boroughs at a very early date; in Norwich, the view of frankpledge probably passed to the citizens under the 1194 charter.[83]

The surviving records include a tithing roll from the leet of Mancroft and Needham; many names are crossed through and others added as people moved or died and were replaced by other names. Elizabeth Rutledge used the roll to estimate the population of Norwich, as it should list all males in the leet aged 12 and over. By comparing the names with deeds and other sources, she has shown it to have been drawn up about 1311 and kept up to date until 1333. There are 860 names for 1311, rising to 1,513 in 1333; she doubled the figures to allow for adult women, then added a further 45 per cent to allow for children under twelve. This works out at 2,494 for 1311, and 4,388 for 1333. This is one of the four leets, so multiplying this by four gives roughly 10,000 for 1311, and just over 17,000 for 1333.

However, thanks to the reconstruction of the city from the enrolled deeds, Mrs Rutledge can introduce a further refinement. By 1340 Norwich had 1,870 habitable properties, and the proportion of these in the ward in question was 19 per cent. If the leet population is only 19 per cent of the city's total population, then the total population would be 23,095 people. Add religious people, the people in the liberties of the Prior of Norwich and the castle fee, evaders, and floating population, and we get a population of at least 25,000 in 1333, having risen from 17,000 in 1311.[84]

These figures have gradually won acceptance, and led to an increased respect for the organisation involved in a medieval city like Norwich. James Masschaele writes:

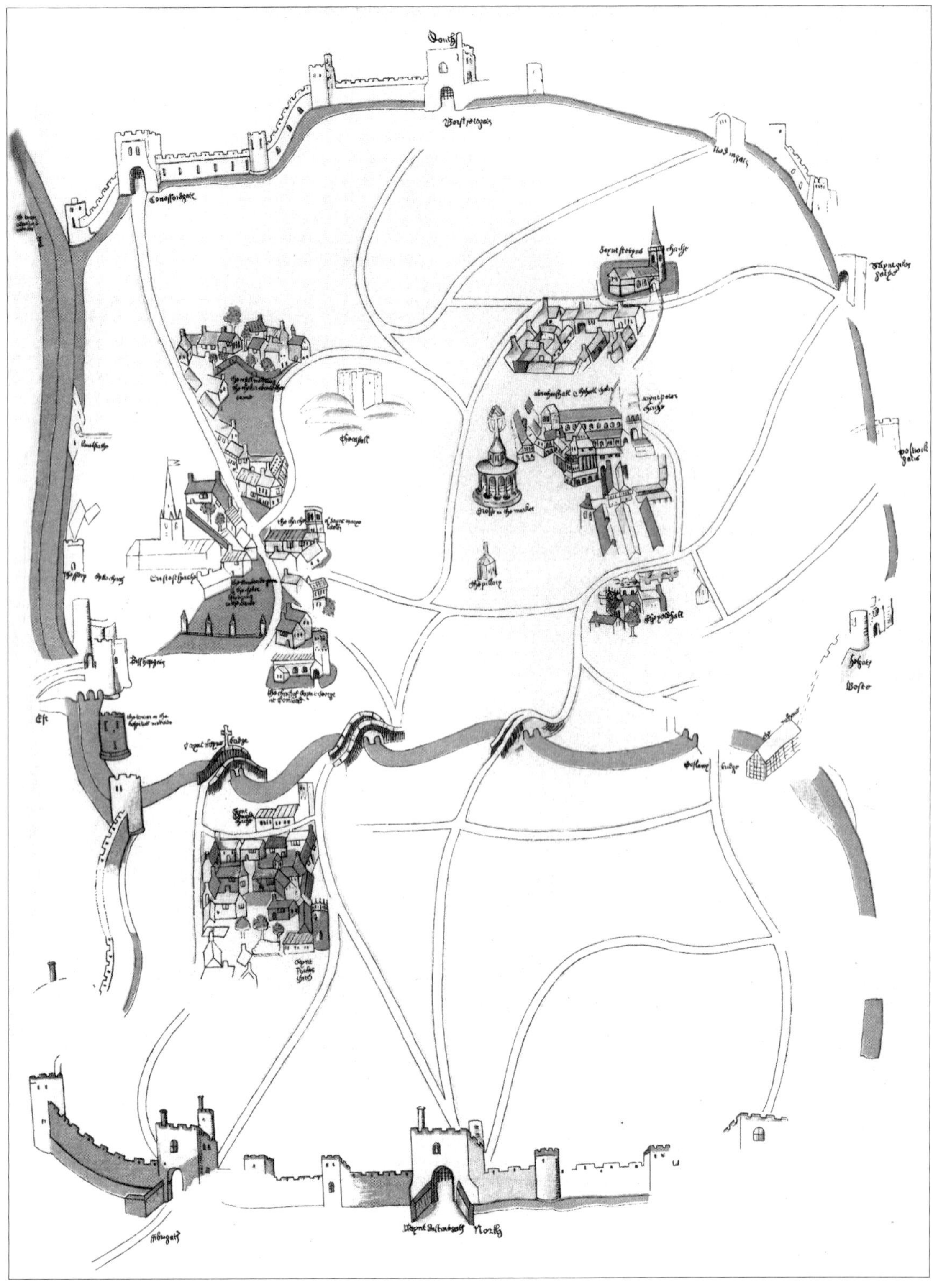
Crosse in the market
the pillory

45 *The Norwich Sanctuary map of 1541, the first map of the city.*

> In recent years, population estimates for London and Norwich before the Plague have been drastically revised upwards – London to around 80,000 and Norwich to 25,000 – and it may very well be that similar revision will be needed in other towns. Such population densities could only be achieved by means of an active trade in victuals between town and country.

Ayers agrees that the population was at least 25,000 and could have been as high as 30,000: 'such numbers in the Middle Ages implied a great city indeed and it is small wonder that Norwich was a complex organisation, tied together by its bridges and churches and surrounded by its extensive city wall'.[85]

Records for the Norwich leet court survive from 1288. The petty crimes punished give many insights into the life of the city in the late 13th century:

> Ralph Perconal found and keeps a plank cast up by the river and has not delivered it to the Bailiffs … Henry de Cawnbys is a thief and they hold him in suspicion and say that he is against the peace and clothes himself well and nobody knows what from and he is always roving about at night. The anchorite of All Saints has stopped up the Cockey so that no one can pass by there … Roger de Beumund has an extremely noxious muck heap … All the men of Sprowston sell sausages and puddings and knowingly buy measly pigs and they sell in Norwich market the aforesaid sausages and pigs, unfit for human bodies … John Janne bought from Alan de Catton eight drowned sheep and sold them for good meat.[86]

The leet court lost its importance after the 1404 charter when the new sheriffs began holding Tourns, at which presentments were made from the new wards, the successors of the leets. During the 15th century, the magisterial powers of the aldermen evolved into the mayor's court, which took over the responsibility for punishing minor crimes. It could also exercise a paternal care in domestic incidents, as a case in 1439 demonstrates. Henry Mayster beat his wife Joan so severely that the blood flowed 'to her ankles' and threw her out of the house; the mayor's court provided accommodation for Joan until a settlement could be reached.[87]

The case of Walter Eghe in 1286 shows that there could easily be disputes about the administration of justice. Eghe was indicted by the city leet for being caught in possession of cloth stolen from the house of Richard de la Hoe, and other larcenies. Two days later, he was brought before the city bailiffs and the commonalty in the Tolhouse (where the Guildhall now stands). He was questioned about the theft and found guilty, whereupon he was taken outside and hanged. However, this job was bungled, and when he was cut down and taken to the church of St George Tombland, he revived! He could hardly be dragged from the sacred edifice, so he remained inside with men from the four neighbouring parishes keeping watch. The stalemate lasted for 15 days until Eghe managed to escape and run across Tombland into the cathedral priory, a place of sanctuary in which he remained until he was granted a royal pardon.

The king clearly thought the city authorities were in the wrong; they were asked by what right they had hanged Walter, when he had not been caught in the act and they had heard no man's suit against him. He did not dispute their right to exercise capital punishment as such, but thought they had not followed the proper procedures. He took the matter seriously, taking the liberties of the city into his own hands, where they remained until they were restored by the next Parliament.[88]

The most serious crimes were reserved for royal justices, who would periodically visit the city from the late 12th century. The only punishment issued by the justices was death, usually by hanging. Many of the executions took place at Magdalen Gates, the bodies being thrown into pits at the nearby churchyard of St Margaret Combust, with their hands still tied behind their backs, and the church was sometimes known as 'St Margaret where the hanged men are buried'. Although people were not usually imprisoned as a punishment after trial, they might be held for months in the castle gaol waiting for the judges to come to the city and hear their cases.

Conditions there were awful, as the case of Richard Sapling demonstrates. He came before the king's justices in August 1308 and produced a parchment which had the royal seal attached but was completely unreadable. He claimed that it was a charter of pardon which he had been given by King Edward at Carlisle in January 1307. He had been kept in the north tower of Norwich Castle over the winter, where he was exposed to the elements and conditions were so bad that 'during that time his charter was in water except for the case of the seal.' The court had faith in the record keeping of central government, and ordered the chancery rolls be searched and a transcript made. They were too optimistic; Sapling came before the court again in May 1309 but the transcript had not appeared and he was returned once more to the castle.[89]

Another case reflecting conditions in the castle was that of John Bonde in 1310. In court, Bonde claimed that he had been forced into confessing a crime and naming an accomplice 'through various tortures, beating and starvation which were carried out in the lowest room of the gaol'. However, after considering the case, the authorities decided that his confession had been made voluntarily and not under torture, and Bonde was hanged.[90]

Another sad case is recorded only in a graffito scratched on a stone in the castle, written in French and dating from the 12th century:

> Bartholomew
> Truly wrongfully
> And without reason
> I am shut in this
> prison

People who were clerics could claim benefit of clergy and be tried by church rather than civil courts. In 1314 Hugh Tynile was accused of being involved in the murder of his own father, John; the actual murderer, John of Happing, was hanged, but Hugh told the court that he was a clerk and he was handed over to the Bishop for trial. The question of the age of criminal responsibility was also a consideration. In 1316 three people – Richard Crobyn, Robert le Heyward and Robert Gerard – were found guilty of stealing malt from the house of Thomas Sparwe in Norwich. Crobyn and Heyward were hanged, but, although the jury were convinced Gerard was involved, he was only 11 years old and was therefore acquitted.

An intermediate legal process was established after 1361 when local justices of the peace were allowed to try felonies and trespasses. In 1363 they were ordered to hold the courts four times a year, hence the name, court of Quarter Sessions. Norwich courts were held in the Guildhall.

As the Eghe case showed, there was a right of sanctuary: a criminal could hide in a church and not be taken by the authorities. They did not escape scot-free, of course: they had to abjure the realm, that is leave the country, usually by a named port to which they were escorted, and if found in England afterwards could be hanged without any further trial. In 1267 William de Fot sought sanctuary in St Gregory's church. He had stolen goods at Hempstead and been imprisoned at Yarmouth, from where he had escaped. He abjured the kingdom and was told to leave through the port of Sandwich. In 1268 William de Runham took sanctuary in St Cuthbert's after committing a murder; a watch was set on the church, but he escaped and disappeared. In the following year, Adam Spindelschanke took refuge in St Swithin's; acknowledging that he had forged the king's seal, he abjured the realm. In 1310 Adam Waterman was found in Yarmouth after he had abjured the realm in St Peter Hungate; he was hanged.

The person claiming sanctuary was supposed to leave within 40 days, but it was not clear what would happen if he did not, as a case at St Mary Unbrent in 1464 demonstrates. Thomas White, alias Blundell, took sanctuary in the churchyard after murdering John Cook. He refused to abjure the realm and, after the 40 days were up, a proclamation was issued in the city that no one was to give him any food. However, church authorities, including the prior of the cathedral and the Bishop of Norwich, claimed it was their duty to spend alms on feeding him in order to preserve ecclesiastical privileges. The recorder noted that these questions were very difficult and ambiguous in law, and sought further legal advice; we do not know how the matter concluded. The number of places where criminals could find sanctuary was limited by an Act of 1540, important for Norwich as it led to the production of the first ever map of the city. Sanctuary for criminals was finally abolished in 1623.

Education and Culture

The image of a schoolmaster caning a boy across his knee is a common one in carvings of the Middle Ages; there is one on a misericord in Norwich Cathedral, appropriate as the three medieval schools in the city – all for boys – were associated with the cathedral. One was a school for people wanting to become monks, known as the cloister school; the founder, Bishop Herbert, was especially interested in the education of boys, as his letters reveal.[91]

A second school was the Almonry School, intended for the education of poor boys. In 1408 when John Hancock was master, there were about two dozen boys at the school, who were taught grammar and song. The third school was the Episcopal School, the ancestor of Norwich Grammar School. The Lateran Council of 1179 ordered all cathedrals to provide a master to teach their clerks and poor scholars, and later it was ordered that the masters be given a benefice, so that they could afford to teach without charging their pupils. The school was situated in Holme Street, very close to where the *Adam and Eve* now stands. John Hancock was appointed master in 1403, and he seems to have taken the salary and hired others to do the teaching, while he continued to teach at the almonry school. He was also rector of St Mary in the Marsh and a very wealthy man, giving money for the rebuilding programme of the cathedral cloisters. Hancock committed suicide in the 1430s, and the enormous sum of £100 in cash was found in his possession, the ownership of which became the subject of yet another dispute between priory and city.[92]

Literacy among Norwich people became more common in later centuries; bone pens have been found on sites in the city from the 14th century. The guild of St Katherine included both literate and illiterate members – and women were found in both categories. Its rules required that 'every brother and sister that is lettered' should say the placebo and dirige for a dead member of the guild. However, 'every brother and sister that be nought lettered' need only say the paternoster and Ave Maria, as these would be so familiar that they could be said without recourse to a written text. A legal case in 1454 involving the bell-maker Richard Brasier illustrates the advantages of literacy. The churchwardens of Stansfield thought they had an agreement with him to cast a bell for them – and to replace it free of charge if the first was not satisfactory. He had drawn up the written agreement himself and had left out this clause – and when they asked for the replacement, he refused to make the second bell for them.

There must have been some teaching of girls at Carrow Priory although no record of it survives, and no doubt there was informal teaching from many of the ecclesiastics in the city. One of the most moving documents about the city is the will of Thomas Salter, who died in London in 1558. He made a bequest to the sisters of the Hospital of St Paul in Norwich. The reason for his bequest was that 'a verie good devoute sister of the said house … was the first creature that taught me to know the letters in my book'. Her name was Katherine Peckham and she had taught him his letters 72 years earlier, that is in about 1486. This old man's fond memory gives us an insight into informal education in the medieval city.[93]

THREE

Tudor and Stuart Norwich

The Tudor period began in 1485, when Richard III was killed at the Battle of Bosworth and his conqueror, Henry VII, succeeded to the throne. The new king visited Norwich at Christmas in 1485, and the city made him a handsome present of £40. Gifts had also to be provided for the many nobles who came with him – entertaining royalty continued to be a costly business. The king then went on to Walsingham on pilgrimage.[1]

In the early 16th century, the city was devastated by fire. Blomefield says there was one in 1505 and two more in 1507. The first of the 1507 fires began on 25 April and lasted for four days, starting near the *Popinjay* inn on Tombland and spreading into St Andrew's and into 15 parishes south of the river; it also spread across the river into St George Colegate. The second fire, according to the chronicler Holinshed, started on 4 June, originating in the house of a French surgeon named Peter Johnson in the parish of St George Colegate. In all, 718 houses were destroyed in the fires. The cathedral almoner's account shows the economic effect: rent from houses that had brought in £5 a year before the fires brought in just 33 shillings in 1505, because 'many tenements are burnt'; after the 1507 fires the rents received from the same properties shrank further, to just 19s. 4d.

Disputes between the city and the cathedral that had lasted for hundreds of years were finally resolved after arbitration by Cardinal Wolsey, which began when he first came to Norwich in 1517; the agreement is dated 26 August 1524. The priory surrendered their rights over their Norwich estates and their Pentecost Fair to the city in return for a one-off payment of 500 marks. The priory also gave the city their estate on the Newmarket Road known as the Town Close estate, described as 80 acres of land with an extra strip of land all around it six feet wide for a ditch and hedge; Wolsey himself paid for the draining and hedging. In return, the city gave up claims on the cathedral precinct, Holme Street, and on

Ratton Row on Tombland; they were held to be in the county of Norfolk and the hundred of Blofield. These arrangements were confirmed by royal charters in October 1524 and June 1525.

The Tudor period was a time of great changes in the religious landscape of the city, as of the whole country. Monasteries, friaries, chantries and other religious institutions were all abolished within a few years, their estates being taken over by the Crown, which then gave, or more commonly sold, them to lay proprietors. The monasteries dissolved included Norwich cathedral, which ceased to be run as a Benedictine priory but continued as a cathedral. It is this continuity that meant the medieval archive has survived, one of the richest for any monastic house in the country.

The continuity is shown in the fact that the last prior and 21 monks remained as the cathedral staff, but now formed a dean, six prebendaries and 16 minor canons. Only three of the former monks were not included in the new foundation and only one new man was brought in, a monk from Thetford. The new foundation took over the estates of the former priory. Norwich was the first of the monastic cathedrals to be 'changed', as it was known, and the Crown later decided it had been too generous. In 1547 the previous settlement was declared to be invalid, on the grounds that the Bishop of Norwich (as successor to the founder, Herbert Losinga) had not given his consent. The estate was once more surrendered to the Crown, and this time it was not all given back to the Dean and Chapter; some estates, such as those at Hemsby, were retained in the hands of the Crown and later sold off for its profit. The cathedral staff were celibate and lived in common; the real change came when Church of England priests were allowed to marry (apart from during the brief interlude of the reign of Queen Mary). This led to the canons ceasing to live in common and building individual houses for themselves and their families. It was this that gradually altered the Close from a medieval monastic house to the area of fine private houses that we see today.[2]

46 *Plan of Tombland and the area around the Cathedral Close in the 17th century. The* Popinjay, *where the fire of 1507 started, is shown in Rotten Row.*

Carrow priory had been dissolved, along with the smaller monastic houses throughout England, in 1536; there were only 13 nuns there at the time of its dissolution. The prioress, Cicely Suffield, was given a pension of £8 a year, the other nuns receiving lesser amounts. The property was granted by the Crown to the Shelton family, who thus became the first lay owners; in later centuries it passed to the Martineau and Colman families.[3]

The four friaries in the city were also dissolved, or bullied into surrender. Their last few years were ones of great uncertainty; the Dominican friary was forced to sell its bells, one being bought by St Andrew's parish church just across the road. In 1538 the Carmelite friars almost became the victims of a spectacular fraud, when a man called John Pratt called there, saying he had come from the Duke of Norfolk to suppress the house. However, the prior saw through him and had him brought before the mayor's court, where he confessed to fraud. He paid for his deception by being nailed by the ears to the pillory in Norwich market place; when it was time to release him, this was done by simply lopping off his ears, a not uncommon punishment in Tudor Norwich.

47 *Elm Hill, rebuilt after the great fires of 1507.*

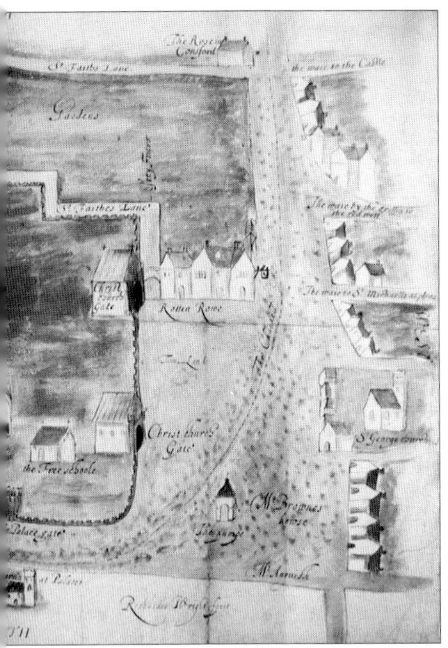

Each friary occupied a large space, and these have had an important effect on the landscape of the city. The Dominican friary was purchased by the city, which paid £81 for the two sites in June 1540. In 1544 the king asked for a further £152 for the lead roof – which in fact had specifically been included in the first purchase. However, even at a total cost of £233, the city had acquired a great bargain. The nave of the church was soon converted into an assembly hall, the chancel becoming a municipal chapel. The site north of the river was rented out for various purposes, the central portion becoming known as 'the Great Garden'.

The Franciscan friary site was granted to the Duke of Norfolk in 1539, and within a year the church was destroyed. Some of the floor tiles were re-used at St Andrew's Hall, and 42 spars from the church roof were used to repair the roof of Blackfriars' Hall. The city bought the site in 1559. The property of the White Friars was bought by John Spencer. On his death in 1561, his executors sold it to William Gilderne. The city considered buying this site as well, appointing surveyors 'to talke with William Gilderne for the purchase of the White Fryers to the use of the cittie', but nothing came of it. An arch, once thought to be part of an anchorite cell but probably part of the church itself, survives, as does some of the cloister vaulting. The 'Arminghall arch', taken from the friary after the Dissolution to a farmhouse in the village that gives it its present name, is now in the court building across the river from its original location. The final friary site, that of the Austin friars, was acquired by Sir John Godsalve.

The chapel of St Mary in the Fields was also dissolved and was granted to the last prior, Miles Spencer, who turned it into his private house. It later passed to the Hobart family and eventually became the city's Assembly House, discussed on p.146. The hospitals were also dissolved, several being taken over by the city, as we shall see.

Kett's Rebellion

There was a crisis in the city's affairs in the summer of 1549: Kett's Rebellion. On 6 and 7 July, there was unrest in Wymondham following festivities there, and the next day a small group of peasants began pulling down the fences of newly enclosed fields. A lawyer, John Flowerdew, bribed the men to attack the fences of a local enemy of his, a tanner and small landowner called Robert Kett. Somehow Kett managed to make himself the leader of the band, and after he had destroyed some of his own fences himself, they destroyed Flowerdew's fences and then marched towards Norwich, gathering more discontented countrymen to their side. The original protest was against changes in farming practice: the small farmer was being pushed off his land so that it could be enclosed for sheep, the great money-maker in 16th-century farming. Lords were also trying to enclose the village commons for the same reason, depriving the cottage holders of their common rights.

The city closed its gates to the protesters, so they skirted round it to the north and eventually camped on Mousehold Heath. An almost contemporary account records:

> [The Earl] of Surrey had built a faire and sumptuous house, wch had beneath it ye maine river running betwixt ye City, and hath on ye east and south ye wood and a little village called Thorpe, but on ye east and north Moushold Heath, which containeth in length and bredth more than six miles. Here they placed ye Chambers (&, as it were,) tents of their furies and lurking in those thicke woods, as dogs in their kennells, they violated all lawes of God and men. Moreover they entered ye goodly house and in places thereof left ye marks of their Villanies.
>
> And now whatsoever of ye vilest and basest of ye people were in any place, these came running thither, & all the dregs and filth of ye people of Norfolke joined themselves to this Campe, besides a great number out of Suffolke, also of men dwelling in other places and Countries, by ye ringing of Bells and firing of Beacons, came flocking thither. Moreover, they add one mischiefe to another, for this so horrible villany & desire (seldome heard of) of destroying all things: they cover with a certain shew of counterfeit holiness, for they get unto them a certain Minister of the City, whom they appoint to say prayers Morning and Evening. Furthermore, they endeavour to ioine to ye society of these outrages, men anyway excellent for Religion and Doctrine, and for vertue and innocence of life commendable, among whom was Robert Watson, preacher, Thomas Cod, maior of Norwich, Thomas Aldrich of Mangreen, a man while he lived beloved of all men. These three because they refused to be bound to their wicked agreements, & treacherous covenants, against their wills they constrained to be present at all their consultations, & to take upon them ye administration of all things, wth Kett, ye Chiefe Rebel.[4]

There were perhaps 16,000 to 20,000 (the later indictments against the Ketts give the higher figure) people camped on the Heath in a peaceful protest for about seven weeks from 12 July. The camp was centred on a large tree, known by them as the Oak of Reformation; this was further south than Mousehold Heath as we know it today, being approximately where the water tower on the Thorpe ridge now stands. From here the rebels held services, administered justice and even appointed governors in 25 hundreds in Norfolk and Suffolk; there were several other camps on open land in the two counties. Financial support was supplied by local parishes; for example, North Elmham churchwardens' accounts record that the men from this parish at the camp were being paid three pence a day for maintenance, and also record the payments for the delivery of food and beer for the camp.

48 *Robert Kett administers justice at the Oak of Reformation.*

Kett's rebellion occurred at the same time as a rebellion in south-west England, but it was very different in character. The Western Rebellion was about religious changes such as the abolition of the monasteries and the destruction of images in churches. The Norfolk rebels were not really interested in religion; the 29 articles of complaint they drew up were almost all concerned with economic issues, especially directed against overbearing manorial lords, including the famous statement: WE PRAY THAT ALL BOND MEN MAY BE MADE FREE.

The rebels were mainly countrymen but they did attract the support of the poorer people of Norwich too; Blomefield says, 'the scum of the city ... were on the rebels' side'. On 21 July, the rebels were offered a

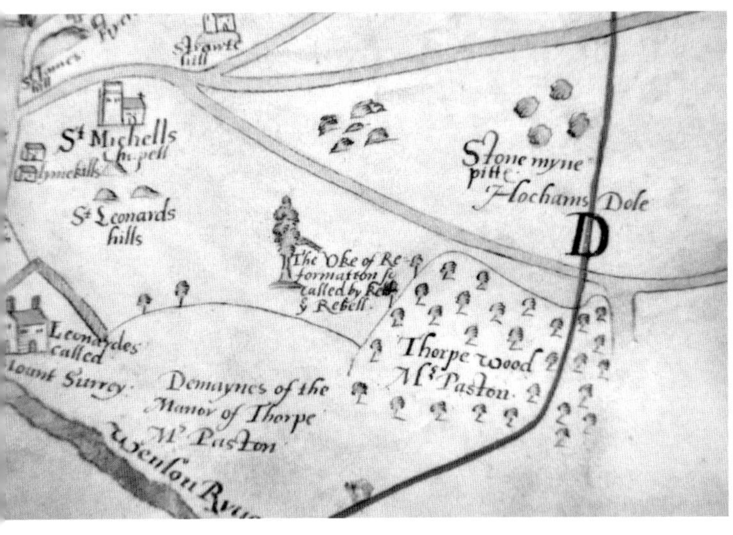

49 *Kett's Oak shown on a 1580s map.*

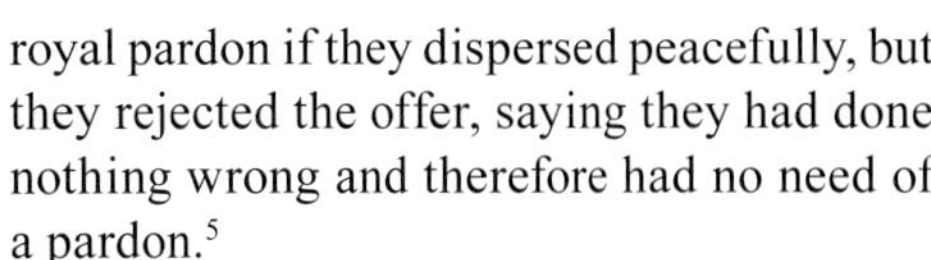

royal pardon if they dispersed peacefully, but they rejected the offer, saying they had done nothing wrong and therefore had no need of a pardon.[5]

The government was now committed to battle. On 1 August 1549 an army, led by the Marquis of Northampton, reached the city and fought the rebels in a battle centred in the Bishopgate area. Although the rebels lost about 140 men to the Marquis's 50, they forced the government forces to leave the city. Casualties included Edward, Lord Sheffield, who was on horseback but came to grief when his horse 'founded' in a ditch. Supposedly killed by a local butcher named Fulke, Sheffield was among 36 casualties of the battle buried in the graveyard of St Martin at Palace nearby. A plaque marks the approximate spot where he fell – and his ghost is supposed to haunt the area still.

Many of the leading citizens fled the city with the retreating army, leaving the city in the hands of the rebels. Blomefield quotes another contemporary chronicle:

> all the houses in Holmestrete were consumed with fire on both sides thereof, with St Giles' hospital … and divers other buildings in many places were burnt; had not the clouds by God's special providence commiserated the city's calamity, and melting into tears, quenched the flames, the whole city had been laid in ashes.

Nicholas Shaxton, master of the Great Hospital, was among those who fled; the chaplain, John Fysher, was forced to beg on behalf of his 40 poor residents. Norwich people responded generously, giving in cash and also in kind – in the first three weeks of August gifts included two barrels of beer, six gallons of ale, loaves, cheeses and salted fish.[6]

Meanwhile, the government acted. An army of 12,000 Englishmen and 1,200 Swiss mercenaries was already in the field, commanded by the Duke of Warwick and raised to fight the Scots. This army was diverted to Norwich, arriving on 24 August, with further reinforcements arriving two days later. Rebels and soldiers clashed in the streets, and about 320 people were killed. Rebels caught by Warwick were summarily hanged on the Market Cross and left to rot. The city had to spend 3s. 9d. on burying the bodies – and a further three pence on repairing the city ladder, which had broken under the strain of being used in so many hangings.

On 24 August the rebels were forced back up to Mousehold, from where they attacked the city with some guns from Warwick's army whose commanders had been captured after losing their way in the narrow lanes of the city. They mounted them on the hill above Bishop Bridge, from where they battered down the top of Cow Tower; its present jagged top is supposed to have been caused by this attack. The St Martin at Palace

register records the burials on 26 August of George Hastings and an unnamed gentleman, three gunners of Captain Durries – and of six people killed in these skirmishes who were buried in the garden of a Mr Spence off Holme Street. The rebels continued to raid the city, and on 25 August, they destroyed the granaries on the Common Staithe. The city paid two men to carry the city crome there: a long pole with a hook on the end, it was mainly used to pull weeds from ditches, but also to pull burning thatch from a roof to save a building.

The rebels were in a secure position on the steep hill above the town, but they chose to give up this camp and move to a place called Dussindale. They did this because of a traditional prophecy:

> The country gnoffes [peasants] Hob, Dick and Hick
> With clubs and clouted shoon [shoes]
> Shall fill the vale
> Of Dussin's Dale
> With slaughtered bodies soon.

Like so many prophecies, this was tragically ambiguous: the rebels assumed that they, the gnoffes, would slaughter their enemies there, but it was the trained army of Warwick that was victorious, and perhaps 3,000 of the rebels' bodies that filled Dussindale. It is not certain where this battle took place. City authorities have assumed it was east of the city and named a modern housing estate in its honour. However, all the chronicles say that the rebels moved north, not east, and the indictments against the Ketts say the battle took place in Sprowston and Thorpe. John Kirkpatrick concluded that the battle most probably took place at the valley on Mousehold Heath, now known as the Long Valley. This is now wooded, but the trees have only grown up because the Heath is no longer grazed by animals; it would have been open heathland in Kett's time. Kett himself fled the scene, and he was captured in a barn at Swannington.

Many rebels were executed immediately, while Robert Kett and his brother William were taken to London for trial. Inevitably they were sentenced to death, and were hanged on 7 December, William from Wymondham church tower and Robert from Norwich Castle, where his decomposing body hung in chains over the winter, a grim warning to the disaffected. Some people looked back on Kett's camp as a golden time; there are several cases of people accused of expressing their support for Kett in casual conversation in Norwich over the next few years.

The battle took place on 27 August, and the city authorities were so delighted at Warwick's victory (even though they made a loss of 30 shillings selling off bread they had bought for the soldiers) that they declared that from that time 27 August was to be a day of holiday and celebration forever – has this resolution ever been formally repealed? All official records speak of Kett's followers as 'rabble' or 'scum', but gradually

Above: 50 *Kett the local hero: a statue planned for the Castle Mound in the 1940s, drawing by Colman Green.*

official attitudes have changed, and in 1949 there was a serious proposal to erect a statue in honour of Kett on Norwich Castle mound to celebrate the 400th anniversary of the 'Rebellion'. If we were to commemorate 27 August today it might be not as the victorious day Kett the rebel was defeated, but as the day that a peaceful mass protest by the people of Norfolk was forcibly broken up by central government.

In 1556 a new charter was granted to the city by Philip and Mary. This was the first of the royal charters to define the boundaries of the city, and it included all the areas beyond the walls that it had been claiming for centuries. The boundary, which remained unchanged until the 20th century, was marked by crosses at key points, and one, much restored, can be seen by the Sweetbriar, Drayton and Boundary Road junction.[7]

This solved one of the city's problems, how to deal with people living outside the city. People thought that those living in the suburbs were taking advantage of what the city had to offer, but not contributing to it. In May 1549, people complained to the city assembly that masons, reeders and others served their apprenticeships in the city but then worked in the country, while the Assembly Book of 1553 noted that 'many evil disposed persons' lived in the city until they became freemen, and then moved out into the surrounding countryside, coming back in to buy or sell goods. It was ordered that these people, despite being freemen, could only trade in the city on the same terms as 'foreigners', and not enjoy the privileges of those who actually lived in the city.[8]

The 'Strangers' in Norwich

In the 1560s, the area we now think of as the Low Countries was occupied by Catholic Spain, and its governor, the Duke of Alba, persecuted Protestants living there. England, as a leading Protestant country, welcomed these fellow religionists into the country. In 1565 a royal letter patent invited 30 named master weavers to bring their 'families' (which would include servants and apprentices) to Norwich. Most were Dutch speakers, the others French speakers, also known as Walloons. The names of the 24 Dutch Masters were:

John Powells
George van Exham
John Garrett
Peter Janson
John de Rhrode
John Mychelles
Christian Vrinde
Gilberde Vijscheers
John Bruninge
George Vramboute
Romaine Debecke
Frauncis Trian
Francis Mysedome
John Looten
Adrian van Dorte
Peter Frenin alias van Brughe
Pascall Clarebote
Thomas Bateman
Jozhm Pottilberghe
Mychel Dosanytte
Frauncis Dedecre
John Goose
Lewis Spillebote
Wyll'm Steene

The names of the six Walloon Masters were:

Robert Goddarte
Noe le Turcke
Ipolite Barbe
John Dumince
John Karsye
Peter Waolls

Opposite: 51 *Robert Kett in bronze, on the Norwich City Hall doors.*

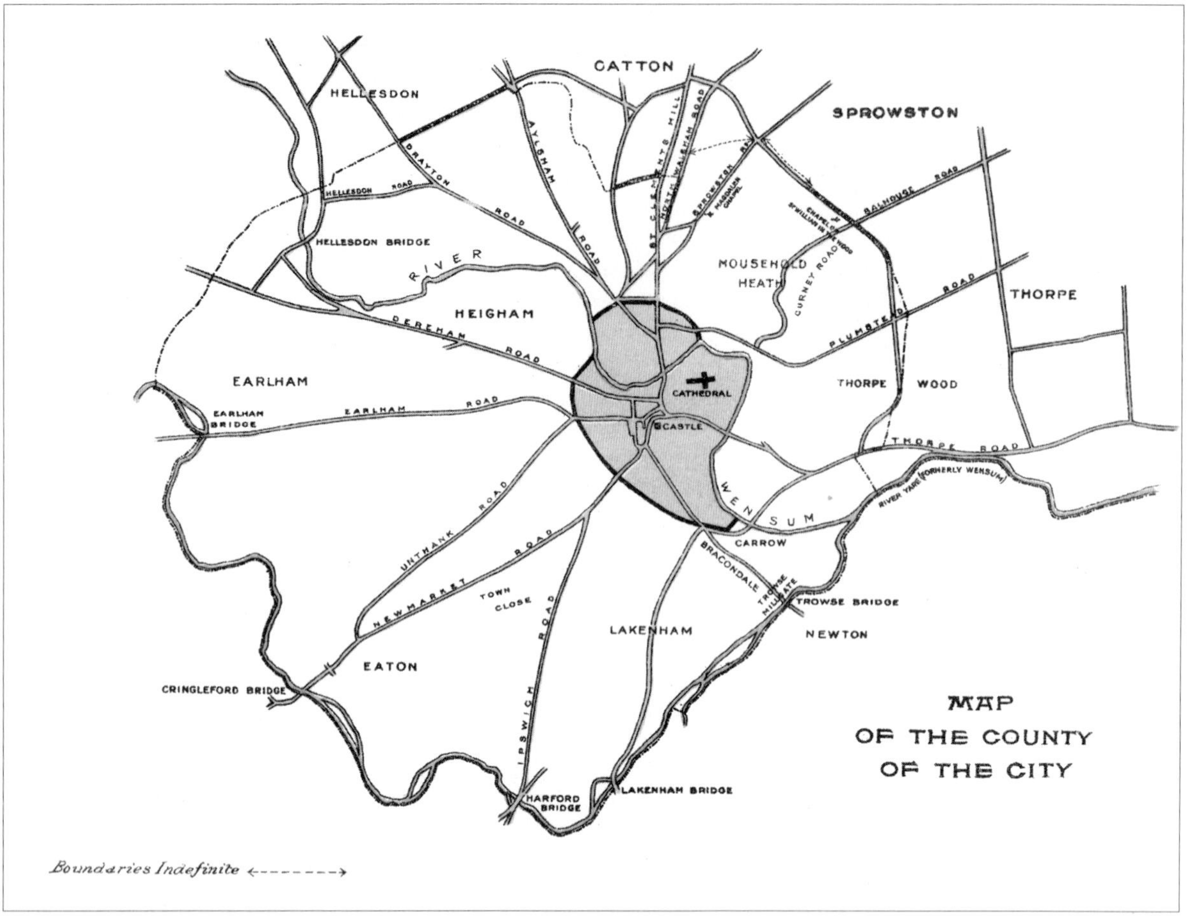

MAP
OF THE COUNTY
OF THE CITY

Boundaries Indefinite ←--------→

Above: 52 *The boundary of Norwich as set out by the charter of Philip and Mary.*

Below left: 53 *Orders in Dutch to the immigrant weavers in the city.*
Below centre: 54 *'Bank Plain'. The word 'Plain' for a square or open space is a characteristic of Norwich.*

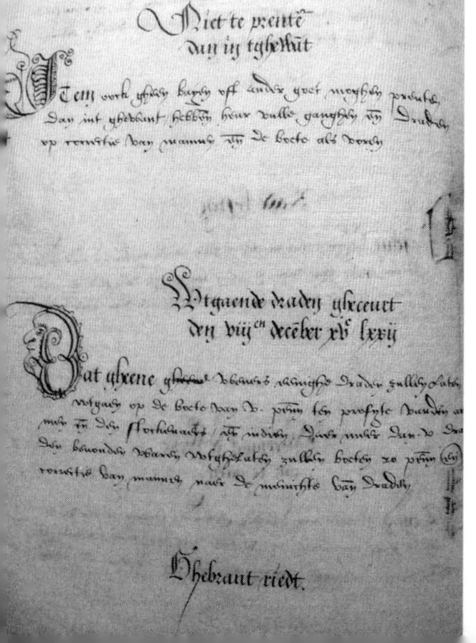

55 *Weavers' windows, a feature of several city buildings.*

Many more followed over the next few years. By 1568, according to a return of 'aliens' in the city archives, there were 1,132 Dutch speakers and 339 French speakers in the city. By 1579, there were 6,000 'Strangers' in the city, out of a population of about 16,000, so that they made up over a third of the city's inhabitants, the largest percentage of any city in England, although the actual number of immigrants settling in London was greater.[9]

Although the first Strangers were invited in, many of the others were refugees fleeing persecution, and suffering the kinds of experiences familiar to refugees throughout the centuries. One of these was Janus Gruter, born at Antwerp in 1560, whose family fled to Norwich when he was a small boy. He went on to Cambridge University, and later became one the greatest literary figures in Europe. His mother wrote a letter back to a friend describing the flight. They arrived first at London:

> then we journeyed 90 miles with four children for two months by land on a waggon and came to a town called Norwich where there were about 1200 Flemings and among them all not one person that I had ever seen before. We did not know what to do to earn our living there. The trade was the spinning of wool and preparing of bays, in which we had no skill, so we had to join together with other people and bought wool and supplied the poor people with wool and took bays in exchange and sent them to London to sell them there. There we chanced upon a merchant who, when the day for payment came and we thought to have our money, was bankrupt, and £450 Flemish was lost; that was our first welcome. The second was that the same man who was in partnership with us left England secretly to cross to Flushing with £300 sterling and on arrival at Flushing he jumped into the water for fear of the Spaniards who came alongside, and sank with all the money and never came up again. And so we lost that too.[10]

A fascinating archive used to exist in the town of Ypres of letters written by the refugee strangers at Norwich back to their families and friends there. In one letter, Clais van Wervekin wrote to his wife: 'You would never believe how friendly the people are together and the English are the same and quite loving to our nation.' Inevitably some customs

Below left: 56 *Dutch-style gables in the Cathedral Close.*
Below right: 57a, b *Mulberry tree at St Mary the Less, planted to honour the immigrants of the 16th century, with the same tree in winter.*

were different, so he asked her to bring with her 'a dough trough, for there are none in England' and also some dishes in which to make butter 'for all Netherlanders and Flemings make their own butter, for here it is all pig fats'. In another letter, a young man, Gilles Navegeer, wrote to his grandmother back in Ypres that he and his family 'are living in great quietness and peace'. The family had been able to find employment of various kinds – his brother was learning the trade of a cutler, one sister worked in a brewery, a younger one spun thread, while a third sister, Synken, presumably just an infant, 'played all day'.[11]

Most of the immigrants, like the original 30, were weavers. They were organised by a committee known as the Governors of the Drapery and by their church leaders. They appointed 'politic men' (eight Dutch speakers and four Walloons) to be their representatives in dealings with the English. They brought with them new techniques, known as the New Draperies, the characteristics of which were summed up by Joan Thirsk:

> The New Draperies represented innumerable different kinds of cloths whose number was constantly being enlarged; their spectacular success as a *group* has totally smothered curiosity in the history of each individual type of cloth, as well as obscuring the fortunes of associated handicraft industries which developed alongside the New Draperies and were also large, but separate, employers of labour. In Norwich, one of the first centres in which the New Draperies started, lace making, ribbon making and stocking knitting all became thriving, expanding occupations, simultaneously stimulated, if not started, by foreign craftsmen.[12]

The two new communities could be rivals; in November 1575 the elders of the Dutch community came to the mayor's court with a new material, bombazine. They asked to have a monopoly of its production, but the Walloons complained that this was unfair on them. The Dutch satisfied the court that they had been the first to produce bombazine and they were allowed their monopoly. In 1577 the Walloons themselves went to the court, asking for new regulations for the making of mockadoes, and that the Dutch be ordered to observe these new rules.

The refugees brought many other skills to the city, including printing. The first printer in Norwich was Anthony de Solempne, who came to England from Brabant in 1567 with his wife and two sons. In the next four years he printed eight books in the city, all in Dutch except one. He became a freeman of Norwich in 1570 and took on the selling of Rhenish wine, apparently giving up printing. Two further Dutch books printed in Norwich were probably by another refugee printer, Albert Christian from Holland. Peter Peterson, a second-generation immigrant, was a goldsmith, making four silver communion cups for the Dutch church in about 1580.

Each community had its own church. Bishop Parkhurst allowed the French speakers to worship in the chapel of the Bishop's Palace. They then used the church of St Mary the Less, where services continued until 1820. The Dutch community worshipped in Blackfriars' Hall. The most well-known of the pastors there was John Elison, whose memorial can be seen on the wall and who, along with his wife Maria, had the distinction of being painted by Rembrandt; the portraits, seen by Silas Neville at the Colbys' house in Yarmouth in 1772, are now in the Museum of Fine Arts in Boston, USA. Baptism registers survive for the Dutch church from 1598 onwards; the first entries are sisters, perhaps twins, Cleya and Rachel, the children of Clayes van Guelen.

However, the numbers worshipping in these churches were comparatively small, as most Strangers soon integrated into the city. Peter Peterson asks in his will to be buried in the church of St Andrew 'in the chapel where I usually sit', so he must have worshipped there for several years. Memorials to Dutch-speaking incomers in the city's Anglican churches include those to van Kurnbeck, who died in 1579, in St Mary Coslany, and the de Hem family (see p.97) in St Michael at Plea. Descendants of the Kurnbecks remained in the city, Sarah Ceunebroeck, the daughter of Abraham and Abigail, being baptised in the Dutch church in 1619; the family lived in the parish of St Michael Coslany.

Inevitably, not everyone welcomed the newcomers. In 1570 John Throgmorton and other country gentry tried to organise a protest against the Strangers, but there seems to have been little support in the city; the Strangers were here to stay. Ironically, the one work in English that Solempne printed was a broadsheet of poetry by Thomas Brooke, an associate of Throgmorton, written while he was in prison awaiting execution for his part in the plot against the Strangers. However, city authorities were happy to inform central government of the many benefits the refugees had brought to the city, such as new ideas that provided jobs for both immigrants and locals, new foods (root crops) that helped all the poor and, above all, setting an example to the people of Norwich, especially the young, in their skill and their hard work. The document concludes, 'We think our city happy to enjoy them.'[13]

Other influences continue to this day. The large windows on the upper floors of houses, introduced by weavers to provide as much light as possible onto their looms, are known in Norfolk as lucams, a word taken directly from the French word *lucarnes*. Open spaces in Norwich are called Plains rather than Squares, from the Dutch word 'plein'. The Dutch also brought with them their pet canaries, and these became an important element of city life. By the early 18th century, many Norwich people were indulging in canary breeding and the Norwich 'plain-head' canary has become a recognised breed. Everyone knows that the nickname of Norwich City Football Club is the 'Canaries', but not everyone remembers this reflects of the contribution to city life by Dutch-speaking refugees 500 years ago.

The Dutch speakers also brought with them a love of gardening. As early as 1575, a gardener from the Low Countries, Joos Brake, had settled in Norwich and was being employed by local gentry to lay out their gardens. In the 17th century, according to Thomas Fuller, a special kind of rose grown in the city had been introduced by them. Florists' Feasts took place at St Andrew's Hall every year from at least the 1630s and probably earlier; these, the Chelsea Flower Shows of their day, are said to have been introduced by these flower-loving newcomers.[14]

The new immigrants largely merged into the local community within two generations. A note in the city archives records that the number of persons in the Dutch congregation was 1,200 in 1613, falling to 999 in 1624 and to 678 in 1634; of these, 575 were second-generation immigrants, that is born in Norwich to immigrant parents. Some of the first generation may have returned to the Continent, but most will have ceased to be part of the Dutch congregation because they had been assimilated into the city's population and attended Anglican churches. The merging of the French-speaking and English communities can be illustrated from the career of Peter de Laune, pastor of the French church in Norwich from 1599: he was installed rector of Harleston and Redenhall in 1629, while retaining his pastorship of the French church.

There was another group of incomers to the city following the Revocation of the Edict of Nantes in 1698, which made the situation for French Protestants very difficult and many chose to find a new life in Britain. Francois Jacolumbine fled to Norwich from France in about 1698 and practised physic in the city. His son, Peter Colombine, born in 1697, married Marie, daughter of Gaston Martineau, from another refugee family, in 1719. Peter and his son, Francis, both served as mayors (in 1755 and 1776), showing how quickly an immigrant family became part of the city establishment. Further romance in the story lies in the fact that they are direct ancestors of Catherine Middleton, wife of Prince William and future queen of England.

After the Strangers

Elizabeth I visited Norwich in August 1578, entering through St Stephen's Gate and staying in the city for almost a week. She knighted the mayor, Robert Wood, and said of her visit, 'I have laid up in my breast such good will, as I shall never forget Norwich.' The city has four traditions about the visit, all probably false. She did not stay, as often claimed, at the *Maid's Head*, but at the Bishop's Palace in the Close. She did not dine with local nobility in the cloister of the cathedral (this idea is based on a misreading of some words in Blomefield). Her entourage probably did not bring the plague with them from London; there was a severe outbreak in 1579, as we shall see, but this was many months after the royal visit. The chancel of St John Maddermarket church was almost certainly not pulled down to make room for her carriage to pass, as there is no evidence that the church was ever longer than it is today.[15]

The holiday we now call Guy Fawkes' Day was introduced in 1606, but was only taken up slowly across the country. Ronald Hutton cites Norwich as being one of the towns most enthusiastic in taking it up, with church services, music and artillery salutes. In 1633 three people – Robert Balleston and John and Luke Brand – were before the mayor's court for taking the celebrations too far: they pulled the doors off two houses, those of Arthur Cordy and Mr Gammoon, and burnt them on the 'bonefyer'.[16]

St George's guild had only survived the Reformation by removing its religious function and using its funds to clean the river. Saints could no longer be represented, so both George and Margaret had to go. In April 1550, the corporation sold all the costumes and the dinner became just a municipal feast. They resolved to restore it in 1555, but it lapsed once more with the accession of Elizabeth. The dragon continued in sole procession, with trumpets and drums, and fellows dressed up as fools, but it was abolished in 1645, along with the idea of saints' days of any kind. It was revived again in 1660 at the Restoration, but the character of the day had altered, and 'Old Snap' survived only as an element in a parade to honour the election of a new mayor. Celia Fiennes noted how the citizens celebrated the election of a new mayor by washing and plastering their houses, hanging flags in the street where the new mayor lived, and with 'plays and all sorts of shows' on the actual day.

58 *The visit of Queen Elizabeth, as portrayed in a pageant by Nugent Monck; compare this image of the city with that of Mottram's book, shown as the frontispiece.*

In 1611 the mayor's procession was the scene of a major tragedy. Blomefield tells the story:

> On the 18th of June (it being the gild-day) a sumptuous pageant was prepared at the new mayor's gate on Tombland, and certain fireworks, as had been usual, were fired off in the evening, some of which breaking, frighted the people (who very numerous) to such a degree, that there were no less than 33 persons trodden down and pressed to death, as the register of the parish of St Simon and Jude declares.

The burial register names six people buried on 19 June 1611 – Edmund Hall of Ludham (had he travelled into town for the show?), Robert Love, Margaret Dybald, Ann Bagla, Rose Firman and Joane Bacon. It adds, 'these 6 and 27 more, weare all slayne at the fyer works in Tumbland, Mr Thomas Anguishe then entering his mayoralty'. Other burials of victims took place elsewhere, including two in the register for St Peter Mancroft: John Duke, a tailor, and a boy named Thomas Lambert, with this note: 'these two with thirty more were pressed to death in ye crowde on ye guile night'. Anguish's house was at the north end of Tombland, where the front entrance of the *Maid's Head* now stands, and the fireworks were set off in front of it. As a result of the tragedy, fireworks were banned from future celebrations; although they are now once again a feature of the Mayor's Day celebrations each June, the conditions in which they are set off are naturally far better controlled.

The Crown enforced a change in the way the city was governed in the early 17th century. The freemen had selected junior aldermen as one or both of their nominations in seven of the 10 mayoral elections prior to 1618. The magistrates invariably elected the most senior of the two. In 1618 the freemen chose Richard Rosse, who ranked 10th in seniority, and Henry Fawcett, who ranked seventh; indeed, Rosse had only been an alderman for one year, although both men had been on the common council for at least 15 years. Rosse was chosen and this led to an order from the king that in future the most senior alderman who had not previously served as mayor must be chosen. This, of course, meant the end of free elections, but no effort was made to make Norwich a closed corporation in which the magistrates chose their own successors, as happened in some other towns.[17]

The corporation had control over two lectureships at St Andrew's church, and always sponsored Puritans. They preached in St Andrew's Plain, which had been established by the Black Friars (see p.33). The space was called the Green Yard, an obvious rival to the open preaching space of the cathedral, also called the Green Yard. In 1622 Bishop Harsnett forbade Sunday morning sermons and lectures in the city, ordering parishioners to attend the sermons at the cathedral instead. In the following year, more than 300 citizens signed a petition lamenting the loss of the sermons; unfortunately the names of the signatories do not survive. Lectures at St Andrew's continued on Mondays and Fridays. A group of Norfolk men established a corporation to buy up the advowsons of city churches, so that they could appoint ministers of their own choosing, and put a leading Puritan, William Bridge, in as rector of St Peter Hungate.

When Matthew Wren became Bishop in 1635, a crackdown on Puritan preaching began. He compelled the magistrates to attend the cathedral service and sermon every Sunday. He suspended eight Norwich ministers, including Bridge, and carried out a visitation to enforce uniformity of worship in parish churches. There were successes on both sides: the corporation managed to restore the Puritan sympathiser John Carter to St Peter Mancroft, but others left the city. Bridge went to Holland; when Laud reported this to the king, Charles scribbled in the margin of the letter, 'Let him go: We are well rid of him.'[18]

Wren's policies of High Church Anglicanism drove perhaps 500 people out of Norwich, some to Holland and more to America. One of these was Thomas Allen, the son of a Norwich dyer and a former pupil at Norwich Grammar School, who became rector of St Edmund's in 1634. Soon in trouble for not putting rails around the altar in his church, he fled to Holland and later went to America, where he was installed as minister of the church at Charlestown in 1638. Among his congregation there were recent immigrants John Harvard and his wife, Anne. Harvard died in 1638, and Allen acted as executor of his will, administering the bequest which led to the foundation of Harvard College; he also married Harvard's widow.[19]

Allen came back to England in 1651, Norwich Corporation appointing him a city preacher. He became rector of St George Tombland in 1656 but conducted services without the Anglican prayer book. Unsurprisingly he was ejected under the return of the old order in the 1660s, but continued to minister to a Congregationalist congregation and survived into a more tolerant era, being licensed under the Declaration of Indulgence in 1672; he died in the following year.

Emigrants included Norwich grocers such as John Baker and Simon Huntingdon. Baker was a man of some standing – he took with him not only his wife, Elizabeth, but also four servants – Samuel Arres, Bridget Bull and Ann and Mary Alexarson. Huntingdon was already 50 when he emigrated and he did not live to see the New World, dying on the voyage. However, his two sons who were with him lived to help found the town of Norwich in Connecticut. A direct descendant, George Sumner Huntingdon, was the first to describe the disease of Huntingdon's chorea; this is especially appropriate as the disease is one characteristic of East Anglia (the rate is twice that of the rest of Britain).

For some, the actual voyage across the Atlantic was only one in a series of journeys. Samuel Lincoln had moved into Norwich from Hingham to train as a weaver before deciding to emigrate to America with his master, Francis Lawes; his descendants included President Abraham Lincoln. William Ludkin, a Norwich locksmith, emigrated to Hingham in Massachusetts and later moved to Boston. Two Norwich weavers who emigrated in the 1630s are known to have 'made good' in America, as shown by their possessions at the time of their deaths. John Pierce left cotton fabric and yarn, and also a treble viol; his goods were valued at £285. Even more successful was Nicholas Busby, who, like Huntingdon, was already 50 when he left for the New World in 1637; he became a prosperous merchant in Boston and when he died in 1657 left possessions valued at over £1,000.

Although the majority on Norwich council was disposed towards Puritanism, Wren did have support in the city, one correspondent informing him, 'our Norwich Puritans, though they be more civil, yet they are as malicious, and more crafty, than those of Ipswich'. When the mayor and a majority of the corporation petitioned the king in favour of nonconforming ministers, 12 members wrote to Wren expressing their dissent; several of these were among the royalist minority expelled from the corporation a few years later.

On 28 July 1642, Captain Moses Treadwell appeared in the city with a commission for levying 100 volunteers for the royalist forces. The mayor's court ordered him not to beat his drum, and, when he refused to obey, he was arrested and sent to London as a prisoner. The magistrates ordered that in future the city gates were to be locked and a double watch set up. They then took steps to defend the city: the walls were repaired and several gates blocked up, with the rest now to be locked at nine o'clock every night. A few royalist supporters left the city to be with the king, including Augustine Briggs, who survived the war to become a Norwich MP in the reign of Charles II.[20]

On the council there was a purge of royalists. Rosse and three others were removed in March 1643, and in May John Freeman was impeached by his ward. He managed to keep his rank as alderman, but 11 months later Alexander Anguish was ejected on a trumped-up charge of fraud and corruption.

Norwich was one of the cities where women formed committees to raise funds for troops of horse for Parliament. Originally the intention was to supply foot soldiers, but Cromwell asked for a troop of horsemen, offering to supply the horses himself. In fact, it was the younger citizens, both male and female, who contributed money, and the city itself paid the shortfall of over £60 to raise the troop. In August 1643, Cromwell took the 'Norwich Maiden Troop', as these soldiers were known, into his own regiment. Inevitably, the women raising the money were mocked in royalist propaganda, one pamphlet suggesting that 'the busy girls' would never find husbands, as men would think ladies who were untrue to their king were likely to be untrue to their husbands as well. The troop remained together in the service of Parliament until the Restoration.[21]

In September 1641 the House of Commons passed an order forbidding people to bow at the name of Jesus, allowing the removal of altar rails, and calling for the removal of images. Cathedral officials took away the communion rails themselves to prevent trouble, but in May 1643 a mob led by two alderman and one of the sheriffs forced their way into the cathedral, smashing stained-glass windows and burning relics, hymn books and surplices. Joseph Hall, who had become Bishop of Norwich in 1642, wrote:

> Lord, what work was here! What clattering of glass! What beating down of walls! What tearing down of monuments! What pulling down of seats! What wresting out of irons and brass from the windows and graves![22]

Hall described the cathedral a year later as 'filled with musketeers drinking and tobacconing as freely as if it had been turned into an alehouse'. He was evicted from the Bishop's Palace, but lived in a house in the Close through the summer of 1644, preaching when he could. He then moved to a house in Heigham, which gave us the street name Old Palace Street. Hall lived here for 10 years, sometimes preaching in the local parish church. He was buried here after his death in 1656; the church with his skeleton monument and the 'Palace', by then the *Dolphin* inn, were destroyed by German bombs almost three centuries later. The inn – unlike the church – has since been rebuilt.

The cathedral was even used for the billeting of troops, as an eyewitness account by an otherwise unknown Mr Wease shows – it is not difficult to work out which side he supported:

> Mr Wease sayeth: he see Capt Garret exercise his troop of horse on horsback upon Christmas Day in Christ Church [i.e., Norwich Cathedral] and he had an unkle was one of the troope whos horse slipt upon a stone in the church there and fell downe and broake his unkle's legg, whose name was Richard Wease: he see the Foote company of Volunteers exercise in the Quire of the Church upon a Sunday. They marched up to the Alter and turned their back upon it in greate derision lifting up their bumbs and holding down their heads against it in a deriding manner, ther Capt was Major Sherewood who hanged himselfe, ther Lieutenant was one Craske that was smitten with sudden death at Mr Ben Baker's, ther ensign was one Heath that formerly lived in great splender but died very poore, one of ther Sergeant's name was Brathwayte who hanged himself next door of St John Maddermarket church, another Sergeant's name was Downing who hanged himselfe in Racky Woode, and had hanged ther about 14 dayes and was full of flyes and vermine. Mr Wease did take 22d out of his pocket as he did hang.[23]

Mr Wease was clear that the Puritans had brought these events upon themselves by their 'sacrilege'. Others thought they had not gone far enough, including the Corporation of Great Yarmouth, who petitioned

Parliament in 1650 that 'you will be pleased to grant us such a part of the lead and other useful materials of that vast and altogether useless cathedral in Norwich, towards the building of a work house to employ our almost starved poor, and repairing our piers'. Fortunately for future residents of Norwich, nothing was done. There is one reminder in the cathedral of those troubled times; a musket ball can still be seen embedded in Bishop Goldwell's tomb![24]

Some of the parish churches also embraced Puritanism. In 1643 the churchwardens at St Lawrence recorded, 'laid out to Goodman Perfitt for putting out the superstitious inscriptions on the church windows and the pulling down of crucifixes 1s.8d.' In March 1644, the mayor's court ordered that religious paintings be taken out of the churches of St Peter Mancroft and St Swithin and publicly burnt in the market place.[25]

The mayor in 1647-8 was John Utting, who had royalist sympathies. In December local apprentices petitioned him that Christmas Day be celebrated. Parliamentarians wanted Christmas Day to be just like any other day, with the shops and markets open and everyone going about their daily business. Under a law of 1644, it was forbidden to decorate one's house, carol singing was outlawed and on Christmas Day mince pies and roast beef and plum pudding (then known as plum porridge) were specifically banned. The Norwich authorities, as good Parliamentarians, took this seriously. In 1645, for example, they met on Christmas Eve and issued an order 'that all the Ministers in this city should have notice given that they forbeare to observe tomorrow being the 25 December as a festival'.[26]

59 *Cleer's map of 1699, showing Committee Street.*

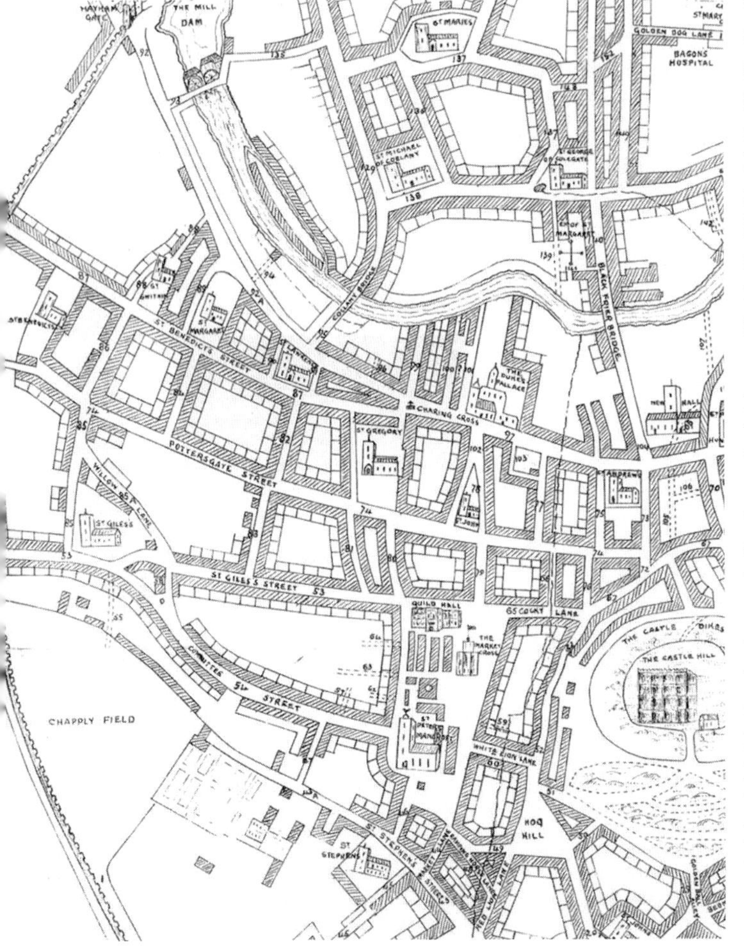

Norwich was one of several towns in East Anglia where attempts to enforce these rules led to riots in December 1647. The apprentices of Norwich gathered in the Castle Yard on 1 December, and put their names to a petition to the mayor urging that Christmas Day be observed in the city, but their petition was in vain and violence was inevitable.

The most significant event in Norwich in the 1640s, also in Utting's mayoralty, is known to history as 'the Great Blowe'. The details can be pieced together from the collection of 278 depositions of witnesses leading up to it, held among the city archives and transcribed by Walter Rye. In April 1648, some Norwich Puritans petitioned Parliament complaining that their ministers were being slighted, and demanding that pictures and images remaining in the city's churches should be destroyed.

Three of their leaders, including Thomas Ashwell, went to London and succeeded in getting an order from Parliament that Utting should be dismissed from office and brought to London. Utting's supporters in Norwich started raising a petition in his favour. On Sunday 23 April, rumours spread that he was about to be arrested. A crowd, estimated at about 2,000, gathered and broke into Ashwell's house, opposite the churchyard of St Michael at Plea. They stole arms that they found there and moved on to the houses of other 'enemies', Thomas Browne (not the well-known doctor discussed on p.113) and Adrian Parmenter, who lived on the market place. They then moved to the Committee House, where the county arms and armour were stored; this was where the Bethel Hospital was later built.[27]

The Committee House was in the charge of Samuel Cawston or Cawthorne; he had the gates and doors locked, but in the tumult a shot from inside the building killed a boy in the crowd. Enraged, the mob broke in and began to pillage; one man was seen to rush out with a hat full of gunpowder, while more powder was observed on the stairs. Not surprisingly, there was a huge explosion. A report in the *House of Commons Journal* says that 40 people were killed, while other sources put the number considerably higher: a sermon by William Bridge before Parliament on 17 May talks of 'nigh two or three hundred' victims, and a contemporary pamphlet puts it at 'above 200'. A few show up in local burial registers: three people 'slain by gunpowder' were buried at St Peter Mancroft on 24 April, and seven others at St Stephen, including a youth named Henry Wilson, perhaps the boy shot outside the Committee House.

Troops of Colonel Fleetwood's command had arrived in the city at about the time of the explosion. It appears that the rioters tried to trap them in the city by closing the Brazen Gates and Ber Street Gate; if so, the troopers were too strong for them and soon rounded them up. On the next day John Utting rode to London and Parliament of his own accord, presumably to prevent further trouble.

Cawthorne had been one of those vandalising the cathedral the previous Christmas, and Wease thought that he was responsible for the disaster, describing him as:

> a great toole to the Committee-men, and an abhorrer of the Church and the day that the Committee howse was blown upp, a very little before the Gunpowder did take fire, he came running from thence and stopt not till he was out at Bishopsgate tho his dwelling howse was upon Tombeland next Mr Wease and all along as he came he cryed out that we should hear presently of 3 or 400 men blowne up, and all did believe that he laid a match and a traine of powder to do it, and ther was to that number then destroyed of persons that sawe what ruine the rebellion had brought upon the King and the Church that made them rise for King Charles and his Govournement, and these that escaped from being blown up. Capt Garret came in with a Troop of horse, and such as they met with they murdered in the streets tho none of the mutineers, others that they met with afterward they apprehended and tried them by a pretend High Court of Justice (as then called) and hangd them up as mutineers and Traytors to the state.[28]

R.W. Ketton-Cremer has transcribed two letters written at the time describing the events in terms similar to the air raids that struck Norwich three centuries later. Joseph Payne, who lived in the house we now call Strangers' Hall, wrote to a relative in London, 'tis reported that at least four score are slain and divers wounded; they are now pulling the mangled bodies out of the rubbish'. He reported that the glass had been blown out of the windows of his own house and that of Mr (John) Hobart. Hobart was in London, but Payne took in his children, who not surprisingly were 'something affrighted'. As with air raids, looting was a possibility; a letter written to Hobart two days later by Justinian Lewyn informed him that two houses of his, one in St Giles and one in St Gregory, had been badly damaged by the blast: 'I took care to board up the windows of your lower rooms.'

On Christmas Day 1648, a large number of local people were charged with involvement in the riot; 26 were fined, seven imprisoned, two whipped and nine acquitted. Eight men – William True, dyer, Charles Emerson (no occupation given), Anthony Wilson, blacksmith, Edward Graye, oatmeal maker, Henry Coward or Goward, saddler, Christopher Hill, brazier, and two brothers, Thomas and John Bidewell, both labourers – were sentenced to death. On 2 January 1649, the eight were publicly hanged in the castle ditches, along with two elderly women, Anne Dant and Margaret Turrell, who had been convicted at the same court of witchcraft. Emerson's body was presumably claimed by supporters as he was buried in St Lawrence church, the burial register describing him as 'one of the pretended mutineers when the then Committee house was blown up with 80 barrels of powder'. Ketton-Cremer describes them as 'ordinary men who had blundered into an ill-conceived demonstration against the dominant power'.[29]

The city assembly officially welcomed the execution of Charles I, sending a letter of congratulation to Cromwell. However, there were still supporters of the royalist cause, and in 1650 there was an attempted royalist rising in Norfolk. Encouraged by a man named 'Smith alias Kitchingham', they met together at Easton Heath, west of the city. It soon emerged that Smith had been a traitor, 'a decoy duck to draw in all the Royalists', and on his evidence many Royalist supporters found themselves in prison. Twenty-four people were tried at St Andrew's Hall in December; six men – William Wilson, Nathaniel Bennett, William Trett, Edmund Brady, David Purslow and Robert Betts – were hanged in the market place, soon followed by two others, Major Francis Roberts (who, according to Mackerell, was hanged outside the door of his own house in the market place), and Lieutenant John Barber or Barbor. Five years later, in March 1655, there was a further royalist rising in the county, and Norwich magistrates put the city on alert and set up night watches.[30]

In 1658 the assembly sent a letter to Oliver Cromwell praising his rule, and after his death they sent a letter of support to Richard, his son and successor. They wrote of Oliver, 'his piety, his wisdome and valor soe eminently appeared in him whilest he lived as the memory will remayne to future ages, the loss of wch head will make the whole body to tremble'. However, in January 1660, when General Monck and his army were approaching London from Scotland, the city sent him an address of support, although the return of the king is not actually mentioned; the address has 794 signatures, including 14 aldermen and 25 common councillors. The return of the Stuarts was celebrated in the city with the ringing of church bells, by order of the assembly. The Corporation Act of 1661 ordered that those improperly ejected from office be restored, at the expense of those who had taken their places, and in Norwich four aldermen, including Adrian Parmenter, were dismissed from office.[31]

Charles II visited Norwich on 28 September 1671. There was some confusion at the time of his arrival as he came along the Yarmouth road, while the Queen was due to arrive later the same day on the London road. Mayor and corporation duly waited for the king at 1 p.m., but he was so late that the whole party could not cross the city in time to greet the Queen, and they had to send Lord Howard's sons and the town clerk to meet her – with the city's apologies. The problem sorted, the king was met with great enthusiasm – and with a gift of 200 guineas. It was the first royal visit since that of Queen Elizabeth a century earlier, and was to be the last until 1909.[32]

Six months later, Charles passed the Declaration of Indulgence, which suspended penal laws against Dissenters and Catholics; however, Catholics could only worship in their own houses and Dissenters in places approved of by the government. There was a small Catholic community in the city, including its most prominent citizen, the Duke of Norfolk, but it was the Dissenters who were to flourish in Norwich over the succeeding centuries.

Trade and Industry

Visitors to Norwich were impressed by its activity. Baskerville wrote in 1681, 'it is a great city and full of people', and Celia Fiennes said in 1698, 'the whole City lookes like what it is, a rich thriveing industrious place'. She commented that 'all the town' span yarn, 'for the Crapes, Callimanco and Damaskes which is the whole business of the place'. There was enormous wealth to be made from the textile business; the merchant Robert Jannys, whose portrait can be seen in Blackfriars' Hall, was reckoned to have more wealth than the entire city of Rochester. Another wealthy family was the Godsalves; Thomas was sufficiently important to be painted by Holbein in 1528, along with his son John, who was painted again by the same master in 1532. One worsted weaver, James Rigg of St Clement's, left an estate worth almost £500 when he died in 1674; most of this was stock, including camlets worth almost £150 and £30 of 'greasy wool', but he also owned books and paintings. In the 1690s, Robert Cooke was described as 'the wealthiest man in the city'; he and his brother Thomas made their fortune in the weaving business, and devoted some of the wealth to founding Cooke's Hospital on Rose Lane, intended for weavers too old to work – provided they had behaved 'soberly and honestly'.

In the 1570s, one in seven new freemen was connected with the textile trade. This rose to one in three in the 1620s and to about half of the new freemen in the 1670s. Norwich was still an agricultural centre and all textile and similar work stopped during harvest time – a Norwich bylaw ordered all worsted weavers to leave off work for about a month. Fishing, too, remained important, and fish was a source of cheap protein; when a special harvest of herring was brought upriver to Norwich in 1666, the town clerk wrote that 'twelve herrings a penny here fills many an empty belly'.

There were tensions among the weavers, illustrated by a bizarre case before the church courts in July 1680, noted by David Peacock. Two witnesses – John King and Nathaniel Maxey – claimed to have peeped through the kitchen window of the house of Anne Batterlie and seen her in the act of adultery with Andrew Faireman. The accused hotly denied the charge, saying that the case had been brought at the instigation of an enemy of Faireman's, one John Metcalf, and that Batterlie's kitchen window was too small for anyone to have seen into the chamber – someone appears to have then enlarged it to strengthen the case, incidentally showing the poor quality of the building. Everyone involved in the case was a worsted weaver – Faireman was a warden of the Weavers' Guild, and Maxey, 'a very loose living man', had had a bolt of his stuff rejected as defective, so there was much bitterness. The outcome of the case is not known.[33]

60 *The probate inventory of Robert Wales, Norwich grocer, 1699; note the enormous value of his stocks of sugar and tobacco.*

Weaving was kick-started in the city by the 'Strangers', as we have seen, and this also applied to other trades. Eighteen citizens of Norwich from a wide range of trades started a new craft in 1543: the making of felt hats. They brought into the city six or seven Frenchmen who were skilled in the work. Later some of these same citizens were part of a group promoting the making of russells (a worsted fabric whose name probably comes from the town of Rysell, now Lille).

Probate inventories enable us to see how people lived; Thelma Morris has looked at those of some dornix weavers. John Hayward, who died in 1626, had three looms, a draft loom, a warping stage, dornix yarn and cloth and over 100 yards of Woolsey cloth. Another weaver, Thomas Barker, who lived in St Michael Coslany, was a much richer man; there were at least eight rooms in his house, five of which were heated, and also attics and outhouses. He appears to have bought and sold cloth as well as manufacturing it. The inventory of a third dornix weaver, Thomas Chambers, illustrates the risk in any business in the days before insurance, as Thelma Morris points out. His debts, including £7 unpaid rent and a £14 dyer's bill, exceeded the value of his possessions; he had been sick for some time before his death, which had no doubt been his financial ruin. He left a widow, Amelia, who had to sort out his affairs.[34]

Norwich led the way in the making of stockings, becoming the foremost centre for knitted jersey stockings (originally developed, as the name implies, in the Channel Islands), which were exported to France, Holland and Germany. In 1615 two thirds of the long wool employed in the New Draperies was used to make cloth, and one third to make stockings. Enormous quantities were involved. Aulnage (taxation) records show that in the last quarter of 1580, tax was paid on 2,640 pairs, which, Joan

Thirsk estimates, would amount to the work of perhaps 100 knitters. By 1600, Thomas Wilson estimated that young child knitters of jersey in the city were earning in total £12,000 a year. In the 1620s, Norwich and Yarmouth houses were exporting 70,000 pairs of stockings a year, mainly to Rotterdam. The decline of the trade came in the early 18th century when Midlands producers began using frames rather than knitting by hand.[35]

The city was also the leading centre outside London for the manufacture of starch, made from bran and used in stiffening the ruffs so important in late Tudor and Stuart England and later for pillowcases and table cloths; Norwich supplied the needs of housewives as far away as Staffordshire and Yorkshire. The waste could be fed to pigs, of which many were kept, often illegally, in the city. Some people thought that the use of wheat for starch was a scandal when others were starving for lack of bread, but the industry continued to expand in the following centuries.

The market place was the heart of the city, and many of the city's activities were focussed upon it. A group of feisty city women caused trouble there on Saturday, 20 July 1532, the matter coming before the aldermen on 3 August. Two of those involved, Elizabeth Baret and Agnes Haddon, gave evidence. A group of women took control of a cartload of wheat which had been unloaded and piled up beside the Market Cross, by whom nobody knew. They discussed how much they should charge, and then sold the wheat at a price they fixed themselves, rather than the price that had been set by the mayor. One of the women was Agnes Oldeman, wife of Henry Oldeman, a common councillor, who seems to have 'shopped' the women to the authorities on the following day. According to Agnes Haddon, there was a threat of further trouble after evensong on Sunday. About a dozen women – one carrying two children – met with her and four other women (one of whom was Agnes Oldeman); the larger group told them that some women had been put into 'the Hall' for selling the wheat and suggested further action be taken: 'Let us go and help them out'. However, or so Agnes said in her evidence, they decided not to meddle any further.

Twelve women were before the court on 3 August: the three already mentioned, Agnes Meredith, Alianora Yong, Alice Pern, Kateryn Tolle, Alice Hawes, Elizabeth Grey, Anna Waryns, Margery Heynes and someone named Estrowe (no first name given). The aldermen took a stern view against what they called the late insurrection of women, and all 13 were sentenced to be tied at the cart's tail and 'whipped severely with whips' round about the market. Alianora Yong was let off because she was infirm, and some others may have paid a fine instead, but at least five of women paid the painful penalty.

Baskerville wrote about Norwich Market:

> They not as in London allowing markets in several places, make it vastly full of provisions, especially on Saturdays, where I saw the greatest shambles for butchers' meat I had ever yet seen … They setting their goods in ranges as near as may be one above another, only allowing room for single persons to pass between.

Like many a visitor to a prosperous town, he was shocked by the prices; at the fish stalls 'they asked me for one pike under two foot 2s. 6d. and for a pot of pickled oysters they would have a shilling'. Celia Fiennes noted that, contrary to Baskerville's statement, there were several markets – a 'broad space called hay market which is on a hill, a very steep descent', a market to sell hogs, stalls for county butchers and the town butchers, and next to it 'a large market for fish which are all at a little distance from the heart of the Citty so is not annoy'd with them'. Like Baskerville, she was impressed by the sheer size: 'a very large Market place and Hall and Cross for fruite and little things every day, and also a place under pillars for the Corn market'.[36]

Towards the end of the period the number and range of shops in the city became much greater. William Browne, who died in 1700, had a coffee-room in his house, and in the same year the corporation let out part of St Andrew's Hall to be used as a coffee-house. Coffee pots and tea-kettles turn up in city probate inventories from the early 18th century. There were booksellers, usually near the Guildhall as Jarrold's is today. William Oliver traded there in the later 17th century, and a sale catalogue printed after his death in 1689 lists religious works, poetry, handbooks on gardening, and also novels and a selection of joke books. There is still a – now barely recognisable – Tudor shopfront at 15 Bedford Street.[37]

The corporation could regulate trade by limiting it to freemen and by exerting control over them. In 1602 a beer brewer named Thomas Norford was punished for unseemly words and bad behaviour by being deprived of his freedom; he submitted in the following year and was made a freeman once more. In 1608 John Cockshead was disenfranchised for 'being known to be a notorious drunkard and of late charged with blasphemy'. Changes of trade are also recorded: in 1554 Robert Collard and Thomas Swanton, who had both been enrolled as cordwainers (shoemakers), asked to be enrolled again, Collard as a fishmonger, Swanton as a haberdasher; both requests were granted. An eye would be kept open for illegal traders; on one day in June 1708, for example, five people were summoned for keeping shops in the city although they were not freemen.

It was not just freemen who had to bow to authority. In 1603 Robert Gibson, a city alderman, got into trouble. In that year, the mayor rode through the city to make sure people removed their hangings, which were thought to harbour plague. Gibson refused to do so, taunting the mayor, 'I would who dare pull them down', but the mayor was a match for him, replying, 'That dare I', and pulling down the hangings himself. Gibson was both removed from his office as alderman and disenfranchised. He had been a benefactor to the city as well as a troublemaker: he had built the conduit from St Lawrence's well for public use – all at his own expense, as the surviving inscription (off Westwick Street) is careful to inform us.

Another troublemaker was John Kettle, a basket-maker by trade. Nominated by the common council for sheriff in 1627, he called himself 'the people's champion' and said that the aldermen were 'worse than devils'. There was a large electorate – about 20 to 30 per cent of adult males could vote in local elections, and, when Kettle lost by just 10 votes, he charged the aldermen with rigging the poll. He held a protest meeting at the *Maid's Head* but the authorities eventually defeated him; he was imprisoned for three months and forced to make a humble submission before mayor and aldermen.[38]

The roads were not paved, of course, and travelling conditions in winter could be very difficult: Kempe described the road to Norwich along which he danced (see p.111) as 'this foule way [in which] I could find no ease, the lane being full of holes, sometimes I skipt up to the waist'. Despite the difficulties, there were regular coaches between Norwich and London. On 20 July 1665, a advertisement proclaimed that all passenger coaches between London and Norwich were to stop because of the plague. In 1681 a coach was running from the *Saracen's Head* in Aldgate to Norwich. There was a regular service by river to Yarmouth, costing six pence in 1667. In 1712 20 passengers on a wherry were drowned when the boat sank.

The Poor and the Sick

The Tudor authorities were very aware of the difficulties of dealing with the poor, and these suddenly became much greater with the dissolution of the monasteries, which brought to an end the charitable giving at Norwich Cathedral priory and Carrow nunnery, and also brought to an end the hospitals run by canons or nuns. They were keen to distinguish between the 'impotent' poor who could not work because of ill health and therefore deserved support, and the idle poor. There was no concept of unemployment in Tudor Britain: if anyone was fit enough to work but was not working, they were to blame and should be punished. In 1547 an Act was passed saying that the impotent poor should be the responsibility of the place where they were born. This was the origin of the system that prevailed for almost three centuries, and meant that paupers were examined as to their place of settlement and then forcibly removed to that place. Norwich soon provided an extreme example. A 'blind cripple' called Mary Ambree was found begging in Magdalen Street. After she was examined, it was decided her true place of settlement was Newcastle-upon-Tyne; after she had spent several weeks in Magdalen Gates lazar house, she was put on a cart to begin the long enforced journey to her 'home'.[39]

The 1547 Act ordered that the sick poor should be provided with suitable houses. In Norwich the city took over the Great Hospital and the leper houses outside the city walls. Henry VIII had intended to dissolve the Great Hospital as a monastic institution and give it to the city. He died before this could be done, but his successor, Edward VI, issued a Letter Patent ordering that:

> The aforesaid late hospital of St Giles shall henceforth be a place and house for the poor there to be maintained and it should be called God's House or the Poor's house in Holmestrete in the City of Norwich, of the foundation of ourself and King Henry the eighth our father for ever.

This meant one major change: for the first time women were now admitted, leading to the establishment of a woman's ward in the chancel of St Helen's church.

The Act also said what was to be done to the idle poor: they were to be punished for their idleness, and might be forced to wear an iron collar around their legs or necks. There are a few references to this punishment being inflicted in Norwich, but, it appears, always after an actual criminal act had been committed and not for mere idleness as such. In 1559 a servant named Thomas Huson, who ate someone else's chicken, was ordered to wear a 'clogg' on his leg. When another servant, William Bannocke, confessed that he had run away from his master three times, the court ordered 'that he shall have a ryng aboute his neck according to the statute'.[40]

Norwich had experimented with a poor rate in the 1540s, the first provincial city to do so, but its real attempt to come to grips with the problem came in 1570. First came the assessment of the problem – the Census of the Poor – then came the attempted solution. The census provides a unique insight into how the poor lived in a Tudor city, although it has one major drawback – it does not include the 'Strangers', who were responsible for caring for their own poor. It names 2,539 people as paupers or potential paupers, perhaps 14 per cent of the total native population and, inevitably, a greater proportion of the elderly: Margaret Pelling estimates that two in five elderly people in the city fell into poverty. Of those whose birthplaces are recorded, about half were not born in Norwich, and so many were ordered to depart.

The census shows that very young children knitted or spun, or were learning these skills; in some cases children as young as six are described as 'idle', implying that they should have been working, and some families are explicitly said in the census to be dependent on the income of a child. The census shows how dependent the city was on textiles: three quarters of the married women mentioned in it were engaged in textile manufacture, some (where the husband was sick or otherwise unemployed) as the chief provider for the family. Most of the other women mentioned in the census are said to 'helpe others', which Wrightson sums up as 'fetching and carrying, washing and scrubbing'.[41]

The solution was the Orders for Control and Relief of the Poor (note the order of the two priorities), issued in 1571. According to their preamble, the ratepayers of the city felt aggrieved that

> The city was so replenished with great numbers [of] poor people, both men, women and children to the number of 2,300 persons who for the most part went daily abroad from door to door counterfeiting a kind of work but indeed did very little or none at all.

These sturdy beggars, it was claimed, were so overfed that their trail could be followed by the excess food and drink that they threw into the street! In 1573 all the unemployed had to go to the Market Cross with their tools to be available for work, but again those in genuine distress were catered for, and a bone-setter was appointed to provide free treatment to those who could not afford to pay. The measures seem to have had some effect, Sir John Harrington calling Norwich 'another Utopia' in which 'the people live so orderly, the streets kept so cleanly, the tradesmen, young and old, so industrious; the better part so provident ... that it is rare to meet a beggar there, as it is common to meet them in Westminster'.

Begging was forbidden and a 'Bridewell' was set up, an institution where the poor could be forced to work. The first one was in the old St Paul's Hospital buildings, which became the city Bridewell in 1571. The Orders for the Poor of that year say that men could be set to work there grinding malt while women could be made to 'spinne and carde'.

In 1583 the corporation bought the larger property known today as the Bridewell, formerly a private house, as the Mayor's Court Book explains:

> Whereas the inhabitants of this city of long time have been at great and excessive charges in maintaining the poor people within the same city which increase more and more by reason that so many young idle persons and bastards do daily increase, and no convenient house hath been provided for a Bridewell to keep and stay the said idle persons to some honest work and labour: the magistrates therefore of the same city have provided and bought the great house of Mr Baron Sotherton situate in St Andrew's nigh the churchyard there, in a place most fit for such a purpose.

61 *St Paul's church; the first Bridewell was next to the churchyard.*

According to Paul Griffiths, a total of 1,085 people were sent to the Bridewell in the first 75 years after 1571. There are only 64 entries before 1600, compared with no less than 640 in the two decades between 1620 and 1640, showing a massive increase in the use of the facility by the magistrates.[42]

Many of the people involved with the Bridewell were clearly quite young, although ages are rarely given. In June 1605, two boys – Robert Mayer and William Jackson – were committed to the Bridewell suspected of cutting purses; both occur in other cases in which Mayer is recorded as being aged 16 and Jackson only twelve. The youngest person sent to the Bridewell was an exceptional case: nine-year-old Jonathan Albry was before the court in 1631, described as 'usually begging' in the city. He was given new clothing at the expense of his parish, St Peter Parmentergate, and ordered to be set to work in the Bridewell, but he was discharged at the request of his mother and set to work for Thomas Carre. In 1632 14-year-old Michael Rix was ordered to be punished in the Bridewell for 'lewd and evill speeches'.

There was a group of masterless young men and women that the mayor's court found difficult to control, and they drifted in and out of the city and its Bridewell. Some, like Jane Sellars in the 1620s, went on to commit burglary, which could lead to branding, prison sentences, and even, in her case at least, to death by hanging. Everything that is known about Jane Sellars is recorded in her appearances before the courts, listed in Table II. Was she a villain or a victim?

Most unusually, the Mayor's Court Book lists the people present in the Bridewell on a particular day, 18 June 1634. There were 10 of them

62 *The entrance to the Bridewell, St Andrew's Hill.*

Table II: *The 'crimes' of Jane Sellars.*

25 June 1623 MC	Found idling at Trowse: whipped and sent to Bridewell
17 Apr 1624 MC	Found 'living idly' – committed to Bridewell and set to work
12 Apr 1626 MC	Before the Mayor's Court: she told the court that at Michaelmas she was apprenticed with Thomas Robinson of Yarmouth for a year; she was to have thirty shillings wages. Therefore she is punished and sent thither with a pass
19 Apr 1626 MC	Committed to Bridewell to be forthcoming at the Sessions
9 Aug 1626 MC	Discharged from Bridewell and given two days to leave Norwich
21 Oct 1626 MC	'Being vagrant and out of service' is committed to Bridewell until she be retained in service
25 Nov 1626 MC	'For living idly' is committed to Bridewell
5 May 1627 MC	JS described as 'servant to Henry Dey'; ordered to go home to her master, in the meantime to remain in the Bridewell
31 Oct 1627 MC	For running away from her master, she is 'punished at the post and put again to Bridewell'
7 Dec 1628 MC	Sent to Bridewell, 'there to be sett in worke till further order'
14 Nov 1629 MC	For michery (petty theft) and ill rule: to be whipped 'at the post'
24 Nov 1629 MC	For michery and ill rule: is 'punished in the Assembly chamber'
Aug 1630 QS	Before Quarter Sessions for first time: charged with theft of six pairs of stockings, worth eight shillings on 21 April. She confessed to the felony, but not apparent what her sentence was. Next two entries suggest she was probably in prison while awaiting her trial
1 May 1630 MC	Child of Jane Sellars is put to wife of Matthew Grove of St Swithins to be kept: she is to have 16 pence a week during the time she shall keep the same
4 Aug 1630 MC	Jane's child taken from Groves' wife and delivered back to Jane
5 Jan 1631 MC	Jane punished at the post for 'lewdness and ill rule'
12 Jan 1631 MC	Jane to be punished at the Bridewell for ill rule
4 Apr 1631 QS	Before Quarter Sessions accused of stealing a linen bodice, two shirts and two smocks worth five shillings in total, from William Colles: acquitted by the jury. Her co-defendant Thomas Clements also acquitted, sent to Bridewell for three days then returned to his master Roger Brooke
8 Aug 1631 QS	Accused of a felony, value under ten shillings. Branded and ordered to be set on work at the Bridewell. She had stolen worsted 'rolestaves', a linen bodice, an apron and a smock (total value 3s. 6d.) from Elizabeth Farmer on 3 May
31 Aug 1631 MC	Committed to Bridewell for begging
29 Oct 1631 MC	Jane ordered to be discharged from Bridewell on the following Monday (31 Oct): she promises to leave Norwich and go to Yarmouth to get her a service
12 Dec 1631 QS	Before Quarter Sessions accused that between eight and ten in the morning of 21 November, she entered the house of Elizabeth Abell. The items she stole are enumerated: a woman's raffe, a linen bodice, two 'pillowbeares', a handkerchief, a neck-cloth, a woman's cloak, a tunic, a smock, an apron, an old petticoat, a diaper napkin, a printed box and two small pieces of linen. The total value of the goods came to under twelve shillings and some, like the handkerchief and the box, were only worth a penny each. Ann Bensly was accused of receiving the property but the fates of the two women were to be very different: Ann was found not guilty and set free, while Jane was convicted – and sentenced to death by hanging. She had no chattels.

MC = mayor's court; QS = Court of Quarter Sessions.

Source: *NRO, NCR 11a, 16a; 20a. Sellars' story was brought to my attention by a work by Paul Griffiths, 'Masterless Young people in Norwich, 1560-1645', in Griffiths, Fox and Hindle (eds),* The experience of authority in early modern England *(1996), pp.146-86.*

and we can look at three cases to paint a picture of the kind of lives that led to a stay there.

1. JOAN WEETING. She had first appeared before the Quarter Sessions and been branded and ordered to return to her master in Hanworth. If she ever went, she soon came back and was committed to the Bridewell, but released in August 1630 on promising to go to Holland. She was punished in October for tearing up her pass and was given a new one. She was back a week later when she was set to work in the Bridewell, where she remained until at least 22 June 1631; she must have been released some time after that as on 28 July 1632 she was ordered to be sent to the Bridewell unless she found a service within a month. She was then out of the court for almost two years, but not inactive as on 28 May 1634 she was once more confined to the Bridewell, this time for having given birth to a bastard child (if her baby was with her there on 18 June, it is not mentioned in the list); she was discharged on 6 August on once more promising to go to Holland, but again she did not go – on 17 September she was up before the mayor's court yet again, this time for ill rule, and was once more committed to the Bridewell.
2. MERABLE BARTRUM. In July 1633, she came before the mayor's court claiming that she was pregnant by her master, Ambrose Crane, whom she had since left by mutual consent; she was now both with child and without a home. In January 1634, she confessed to the court that she was not in fact pregnant. She was committed to the Bridewell, and was still there on 18 June 1634. She must have been released some time after, as she came before the court once more on 11 April 1635, having been taken for 'idling' one night in the company of three men (none of whom were charged with anything). The court considering her 'a woman of lewd conversation', she was again sent to the Bridewell.
3. ARTHUR WHITE. An apprentice to Robert Sinderland, twisterer, he was confined to the Bridewell for an unknown reason. He was there in January 1634, but was released in March at the request of Sinderland's wife. Sinderland and White clearly could not get on; in May, Alderman Gostling tried to get the two together to make peace between them but this must have failed as White was back in the Bridewell on 18 June. In September 1634, he was discharged to go to sea from Yarmouth with a man described as his brother, James Cookson; the court gave him 10 shillings for new clothing to help him on his way.

The mayor's court also exercised powers now associated more with social workers. In August 1583, Stephen Quynce alias Prynne was before the court. He had a wife and five children, but had been going about the country with another woman, Anne Mallerd, posing as man and wife; they were sentenced to a whipping about the market place. Anne's parents, Philip and Johane Mallerd, were part of the deception as they had all been living in Maidstone, and they, too, were whipped. All four were then sent to the stocks, and Prynne was put in prison until he could find sureties for his good behaviour. He put up £20 and was released;

in a Tudor equivalent of an ASBO, he was forbidden to keep company with Anne except in church or the open market place. In 1622 a Norwich mother who was beating her child had it taken away, and was forced to pay for its maintenance by someone else. Eleven years later, John Roote damaged a child's eye; he was ordered to pay compensation of 1s. 8d a week, which went to the child's mother.

Two major charities were founded in the 17th century – the Children's Hospital and Doughty's Hospital. The Children's Hospital was founded under the will of Thomas Anguish, who died in 1618 leaving a house and estate in St Edmund's for the purpose. Other citizens gave or bequeathed money and the house was opened on Fishergate in 1621, when 14 boys were admitted. The number increased to 21 in the 18th century and to 30 in 1798. The hospital benefited again under the will of Thomas Tesmond, who died in 1626, leaving 69 acres in Bixley to the corporation to fund sermons. The residue of the income was to go to the Children's Hospital.[43]

Anguish seems to have intended his hospital to be for both boys and girls but there is no evidence that girls were ever admitted. In 1649 mayor Robert Baron left £250 for the training up of 'women children' and in 1656 Henry Whitingham of London left £200 for the same purpose. The girls seem to have been lodged in St Andrew's Hall until 1664, when they moved into a house on what is now Golden Dog Lane. Accounts survive from 1653 when there were only two girls there; by Blomefield's time there were 21 girls in the hospital. The Mayor's Court Book for 1675-6 records that the girls in the Girls' Hospital were set to work spinning wool on great wheels under the tuition of a 'knowing person'.[44]

63 *Doughty's Hospital, photograph taken in 1911.*

William Doughty wrote to the mayor's court from Dereham in 1677 saying that he intended to live in Norwich and would like to be free from rates and charges. The court agreed; presumably he had already promised to endow a hospital in the city. Doughty died in 1688, leaving £6,000 to trustees to buy a piece of land and build a hospital for poor old men and women. He made some specific orders – it was to have a court in the middle with a gate so narrow that a cart could not come into the court; the hospital was to be run by a bachelor as master (this clause of his will was very soon forgotten) and was to accommodate 24 men and eight women. It should not cost more than £600 to buy the site and put up the building. The rest of the money was to be used to buy land in Norfolk 'not subject to be overflowne with the sea'. He calculated that the land would provide an income of £250 a year to keep up the buildings and give the old people 2s. a week each, and a gown when they first came to the hospital.[45]

Each parish in the city was responsible for its own poor. A fairly typical case is that of Jane Lusher and her children in St John Maddermarket. She was paid three shillings in 1636/7 'in her sickness' but she died soon afterwards, leaving three orphaned children. The parish then paid 'the widow Cooper' 10 pence a week to look after the children. Probably two of them died soon after; in the following year Mrs Cooper was receiving money for just one Lusher child and the end of the story comes in the same year when she was given a further two shillings 'for the burial of it'.

The overseers were always keen to shift responsibility for a poor person elsewhere if they could. An entry in the St Andrew's overseers accounts in 1673/4 says bluntly: 'Paid Mary Hastings at several times and to goodie downes to get her oute of the parish 00. 13. 6.' Occasionally the poor law authorities took even more decisive action to rid themselves of long-term burdens: the overseers of St John Maddermarket paid £1 10s. in 1658-9 'to send away 2 of goody Blunt's sons to new Ingland'.[46]

Treatment of the poor in Norwich was revolutionised by an Act of 1711, under which the whole of Norwich was made into one parish for the poor, apart from the Close and the Strangers' congregations. Guardians of the Poor were set up, comprising the mayor and aldermen and 32 people chosen by the freemen, eight being chosen from each ward. The poor were to be maintained in workhouses in St Andrew's Hall, a wing of the former Duke's Palace and outside St Augustine's Gates.

The Norwich Book of the Poor shows that about 11 per cent of the adults named in the book are sick or disabled. From these figures Pelling estimates that people in Norwich over 60 had a one in four chance of being severely disabled. She comments that 'a minimum of 7 per cent of the urban population at any time might be grossly infectious, repulsive, confined within doors, bedridden, or unable to see'. However, the city already had a reputation as a centre of healing. Simon Bushe, aged 12, was brought to Norwich from Scottow on a cart by someone who told him he would have 'meat enough in Norwich and a surgeon to heal him'. He may well have been right – in 1580 the mayor's court ordered that a lame boy be given a joint of veal or mutton twice a week while he was recovering. The surgeon given responsibility for the boy had the appropriate name of William Fever.[47]

Dutch and Walloons looked after their own sick as they did their own poor. There are two references in the 1570s to the city employing Dutch physicians. Second-generation immigrants born in the city would not suffer any restrictions and the names of some Dutch doctors are known. John Cropp came from Flanders as a surgeon in 1567. His son, also called John Cropp, obtained a licence to practise in Norwich in 1602 and is mentioned in the letters of Katherine Paston.[48]

The lazar houses, situated just outside the city gates, were increasingly supervised by the mayor's court. They consisted of one central building and a number of small cottages. Often a husband and wife acted as joint keepers and the woman might carry on as sole keeper after her husband died. The city used the lazar houses for treatment of conditions that affected the patient's ability to work. The keeper of the lazar house at Magdalen Gate was paid to receive from the Bridewell a 'loathsome boy' who had been sent back to Norwich because he had been born in Ber Street. Most of the lazar houses continued until about 1700. St Augustine's was then used as an infirmary for aged poor people who were unfit for work, and it was being used for the same purpose in 1814. 'By the early 19th century, the Magdalen gates lazar house had changed from leperhouse to "almshouse" to workhouse and finally to alehouse, the last being … not so far from the first as might be imagined.'[49]

The Plague

Norwich kept weekly reports of the number of burials in the city from 1579 to 1646; there is no parallel to this outside London. From these we can trace the waves of plague that hit the city. The first was in the mayoral year of 1579-80, when 4,831 people died in Norwich, 4,193 of plague. More than 2,000 of these were Strangers, which probably represents one quarter of the entire population of the city. The doors and windows of plague victim's houses would be boarded up so that nobody could get in or out. This would happen for as long as there was plague in the house, and for one month after the last plague victim there had recovered or died, so that the period of incarceration might be two months or even more. Arrangements were made to provide food for those inside – and a watch set to make sure no one left the house.[50]

The earliest burial figures do not specify the number of deaths from plague, but show its dramatic effects on the city: there were well over 200 burials a week in the summer of 1579, peaking at 352 in the week ending 15 August, then gradually falling back to a more normal rate of about 30 a week at the end of the year. In both St Peter Mancroft and St Stephen, the average number of burials in the years before 1579 was about 17 a year; in 1579, 248 people were buried in St Stephens, and 243 in St Peter Mancroft, 106 in August alone in the latter.

The next major epidemic was from August 1603 to July 1604. In this time 3,841 were buried, almost 3,000 of plague. This means that, once again, nearly a quarter of the city's inhabitants died in one year. Parishes that suffered especially badly in 1579 may have been less affected two decades later; the peak monthly burial figure in St Peter Mancroft in this epidemic was 37 in September, nothing like the earlier outbreak, though bad enough for those families involved. One memorial of this outbreak is that of the de Hem family in St Michael at Plea church, with its skull and other emblems of mortality. Dutch immigrant Jacques de Hem was buried on 25 September 1603, his wife and a child too young to have a name on 5 October, and Prudence, the family's maid, on 6 December.

64 *Hems family memorial in St Michael at Plea church.*

In the summer of 1626, there was a relatively small outbreak of plague, especially affecting the parish of St Margaret's on St Benedict's Street. By combining the orders of the mayor's court with the burial register we can see how individual families were affected, taking three families, the Andersons, the Hawkyns and the Whalls, as examples. Mary Anderson, daughter of Thomas Anderson, died of plague on 30 July followed by a second daughter, Ann, on 10 August. The house was then boarded up but the plague continued its deadly work, claiming two more children and their mother, Mary, within the next three days. She was the last to die; Thomas himself survived the plague. Mary, the daughter of William Harwyn, was buried on 20 July. William himself died on the morning of the following day and was buried in his local churchyard just one day after his death; this was normal practice at the time. The house was then boarded up and a week later another daughter, Anne, died; there were no subsequent deaths in the family. John Whall buried his daughter Mary on 8 August and his wife, also Mary, two days later. The house was then boarded up and three more children died in quick succession, the last two being buried together on 19 August. There was then a long pause and the family must have hoped that the plague had passed, but another daughter, Ursuley, succumbed almost a month later, being buried on 17 September.

In 1630, the mayor's court took prompt action as soon as plague entered the city. On 26 June, two people were reported as having died of plague in the previous week. John Camp was ordered to destroy dogs, hogs, cats and tame doves found loose in the streets. Watchmen were appointed to attend the pesthouses on Butter Hills night and day, both to keep other people away and to provide provisions and 'reasonable wages' to those inside – and also to restrain them from going out. A Mrs Sandcraft was paid seven pence a day to provide the provisions and to carry water to the pesthouse. Several private houses were shut up after the deaths of a family member. The measures were successful: there were very few more deaths, and those trapped in their houses were gradually liberated, the Tolls after six weeks, William Hafford after ten. On 14 August, widow Coe and goodwife Banister, both of St Margaret, were let out of their houses after seven weeks but the court was still cautious, their local churchwarden being told to make sure that they did not 'thrust themselves into company'. Thanksgiving services were held on 17 August; this outbreak of plague was over.

Above: 65 *Churchyard of St Stephen.*
Below: 66 *Churchyard of St Peter Mancroft. Both parishes saw many burials during outbreaks of plague.*

The outbreak of 1631 appears to have been coped with less successfully, perhaps because it occurred unusually early in the year. On 9 April, Alderman Shipdam told the court that plague had broken out in St Augustine's: on investigation, one person turned out to have died over three weeks earlier, and four more since. Two houses in the parish were involved. The details show a natural human reaction to the outbreak. One house was that of Adrian Latry; his wife and two children had died. Latry had put his surviving child into the care of a neighbour, widow Lavine, and had himself gone to the house of a Joseph Latry, presumably a relative. Of course, this was against the isolationist principles of the court, and Latry was ordered to take his child and go back to his own house to take their chances there. It was decided to put a roof on the Black Tower for use as a pest house and also to build two pest houses on Butter Hills in the same places as they had been the previous year; a carpenter was appointed to build them and construct the tower roof.

Not everyone submitted gracefully to the orders of the mayor's court. In 1631, when there were plague deaths in Robert Howse's house in St Margaret's, a watchman was set at his gate. The court sent one of the city marshals to tell Howse that if he did not consent to the nailing up of his doors, the mayor himself would come down and see it done. Howse remained truculent, repeating that he would not allow his door to be nailed up, and saying he would be glad if the mayor did come, adding, 'What, will Mr Mayor make my house a pesthouse or will he starve me?' There were other hints of trouble at the same time: John Bromely was ordered to be whipped and sent to the Bridewell for resisting a watchman appointed by the mayor, and for abuse to an alderman. It was decided to empty the two towers of the Brazen Gates and turn one into a prison 'for turbulent persons in this time of infection'. Similar measures had been necessary in 1625, and then, as Paul Slack noted, 'the unruly infected' were 'manacled and kept carefully' in the tower; this was the ultimate penalty that the civic authorities inflicted upon the recalcitrant in times of crisis.

The court issued regulations to control the plague in May 1637, repeated in August 1638:

1. Imprimis, that there shall be a meeting of the Justices of peace and Aldermen of this City in the council chamber of this city every Wednesday in the afternoon at two o'clock.
2. Item that every Justice of the Peace and Alderman shall at every such meeting inform themselves by all good means what parishes and houses are at the time of such Assembly infected.
3. Item they shall cause to be appointed in every parish as well infected as not infected certain persons to view the bodies of all such as shall die before they be suffered to be buried and to certify the Minister of the church and churchwardens or other principal officers or their substitute of what probable disease the said persons died.
4. Item the houses out of which there shall die any of the plague being so certified by the viewers or otherwise known or where it shall be understood that any person remained sick of the plague be closed upon all parts during the time of restraint namely six weeks after the sickness in the same house ceased.
5. Item that watchmen be appointed who must be sworn to attend and watch the several infected houses and apprehend any person that shall come out of their house contrary to the order of any Justice of the Peace or Alderman and the same persons be imprisoned in the stock.
6. Item some special mark shall be made and fixed to the doors of every of the infected houses and where such houses shall be inns or alehouses the signs shall be taken down and some cross or mark as aforesaid set upon the door.
7. Item such as are or shall be appointed keepers buriers and searchers or to have anything to do with persons or houses infected shall not go abroad the streets or put themselves into any company without some mark on their upper garment or bearing a red wand in their hands. And always in their going from place to place to go next to the channel.
8. Item that the Officer for Certificates shall weekly enquire diligently of the searchers the clerks of the parishes and others especially such as are sworn to the end he may make a true certificate weekly of the just and certain number of persons dying of the plague.

67 *Black Tower, used as a pest-house in times of plague.*

9. Item that the clothes and bedding of persons dying of the infection be buried burned or very well aired and if the owners of the same be poor then the same to be recompensed out of the taxations.
10. Item if any person shall break or contempt any of the orders aforesaid or any other orders by the mayor, justices and aldermen lawfully devised then every such offender shall be punished by imprisonment or if there shall be cause by binding them over before the Lords of the [Privy] Council.
11. Item that such schools as are near to any place infected shall be suppressed as time shall give occasion.
12. Item that the aldermen of every ward in this city shall take care that there be no unnecessary concourse or assembly of people within this city for any purpose or occasion whatsoever.
13. Item that every alderman do duly examine the disbursements of the overseers to the infected and make the warrants to the treasurers for payment of the same so as there be care had.
14. Item all persons dying of the infection to be buried in the morning before sun rising or in the evening after sun setting and that no chiming of bells or concourse of people be permitted at such burials.
15. Item every aldermen is desired to give such further orders to all inferior officers as they shall upon every occasion think fit for preventing of every inconvenience that may anyway occasion the increase of the infection.

The last great outbreak was in 1665-6, and the number of plague burials, along with the total number of burials and the number of baptisms, for each parish between 3 October 1665 and 3 October 1666 were published in *Norwich Records* (1736). These figures are not completely reliable, if only because the plague continued beyond 3 October 1666 in some parishes, but make a good starting point. Comparing the deaths with the population totals for each parish from the first census of the city, that of 1693, shows the parts of the city worst affected by the 1666 plague. The seven parishes worst hit (those where the number of burials exceeded 10 per cent of the 1693 population) were St Peter Southgate, St Etheldreda, St Julian, St Peter Parmountergate, All Saints, St Margaret and St James. This suggests the plague was worst in the parishes that housed the poorest in the city; five of the seven are recorded by Walter Rye as being among those 14 parishes with no more than one house rated as high as four pence in the first surviving Norwich rate book (1633-4), and this would probably be six if St Etheldreda were not omitted from his analysis of the rate book.

The policy of isolating the infected in their own homes meant that there were cases of whole families being wiped out. The first three plague burials in St Stephen's, for example, were all in one family, of a haberdasher named John Style. His daughter Sarah was buried on 15 May and a son, Samuel, two weeks later; John himself followed on 9 June. The first deaths at St Julian's also came within a single family: Thomas Downing lost all his five children to the plague in 12 days in April 1666, and he himself was buried on 5 May.

One natural response to a plague epidemic, for those who could afford it, was to move out of the city. A government agent visited Norwich in July 1666, commenting: 'the city looks sadly; most of the chief shopkeepers in the market are gone and the shops shut up'. He thought a quarter of the city's population would be gone within 10 days. This could cause problems: if the wealthy left, jobs would dry up, forcing the poor to seek alms, and the poor might also try to squat in houses left empty by those fleeing to the country. Riots were expected, the town clerk admitting, 'Wee are in greater feare of the poore than the plague, all our monie beinge gone.' The city had to borrow £200 to get through the crisis.[51]

Some of the city's leaders fled the city; others stayed to issue orders to control the spread of the disease. A number of aldermen remained even after most common councillors had fled. The city assembly met only once during the epidemic of 1579 and not at all during the height of the 1666 outbreak. However, the mayor's court, composed of aldermen, met almost as regularly as at normal times. In July 1666, the Quarter Sessions ordered what remained of Norwich market to be transferred to a site outside the city walls during the outbreak of plague. This was to stop country people coming into the city and so 'prevent the scatteringe of that Noysome pestilence'.

In 1795 over a hundred skeletons were dug up in Lakenham. With them was a Norwich tradesman's token for 1664, so these were probably victims of this wave of the plague. Steps taken to control the plague were expensive and not always effective. In Norwich, one of those employed as a bearer of the dead stole goods from an infected house and fled to Yarmouth and then to Colchester with a 'lewd woman'.

Plague never came back after 1666, and smallpox was the most feared disease of the later 17th and 18th centuries. There was an outbreak in Norwich in 1669-70 when Thomas Browne wrote, 'upwards of 300 families fell down in less than a fortnight'. In January 1670 the town clerk wrote, 'the smallpox rageth still amongst us, and poverty daily invades us like an armed man'. There was another outbreak in 1681-2.[52]

Schooling

Before the Reformation, such schools as existed were maintained by monks and nuns. When they disappeared, town authorities had to fill the breach, and the statutes of Henry VIII set up a choir school and a grammar school. In 1538 the choir school had eight boys and in 1540 the grammar school had 20 boys. The grammar school moved to Blackfriars in 1541 but was back in the Close by 1546. Norwich also secured a grammar school in connection with the Great Hospital under the will of Henry VIII. In 1551 the school made its final move – the former carnary chapel in the Close was bought and the school moved into the building around which it is still centred.

However, there was more schooling than we might expect. A compulsory rate maintained a few children in the Great Hospital, where they were taught their letters. Several of the 952 children mentioned in the Mayor's Book of the Poor are said to be going to school. In each parish, select women were provided to supervise up to 12 women and children in the cloth industry; the children were taught to read and write as well as to work. When the child was old enough he or she was apprenticed or set to work. In an order of the Assembly of 1592 we read of schools of writing, reading and knitting being closed because of sickness.

Religion

A few people were burnt for heresy at the Lollards' Pit in the first third of the 16th century. The most well-known was Thomas Bilney, who preached against abuses connected with saints' cults. After a preaching tour that began in Norfolk in 1527, he was convicted of heresy before the Bishop of London, but avoided punishment by recanting. Returning to Norwich, he took up preaching again and reputedly gave a copy of Tyndale's New Testament to Katherine Manne, the anchoress at the Dominican friary. He was convicted by the church courts and handed over to the city authorities, who had no choice as to their actions: he was executed by burning on 17 August 1531. A plaque near the spot calls Bilney 'the spiritual father of the Reformation', but G.R. Elton wrote that he was 'never a protestant but certainly not sound on the Mass'.[53]

Mary Tudor became queen in 1553; she tried to undo the Reformation and restore the old religion. She appointed John Hopton as Bishop of Norwich in 1554. Under his rule 48 people in the diocese were burnt for heresy, many at Lollards' Pit. Only two of them were actually from Norwich, both 'ordinary' working women but of extraordinary courage, prepared to die horribly for their faith. Elizabeth Cooper, the wife of a pewterer, stood up to interrupt a service in St Andrew's, and to revoke an earlier recantation she had made of her Protestant beliefs. She was burnt at the Pit alongside a man from Lynn in July 1557. Among the watching crowd was Cicely Ormes, the wife of a worsted weaver from St Lawrence's parish. Inspired by their example, she cried aloud that 'she would pledge on the same cup that they drank on'. She remained true to her faith throughout a year's examination and imprisonment before finally meeting her own death by burning in September 1558. The bravery of these two Norwich women lives on after five centuries as Muriel McClendon makes clear: 'Elizabeth Cooper and Cicely Ormes were arrested only because they stood up, Cooper in church and Ormes at Cooper's execution, and publicly announced their adherence to Protestantism. No one had betrayed them or reported their heresy to the authorities, nor had the civil or ecclesiastical powers discovered them through an investigation.'

The churches were now expected to have the ritual aids that most had just sold. Eighteen city churches were summoned by the church court and asked if they had the necessary ornaments and if they had removed Bible texts painted on the walls. Only five churches were able to say that they had the ornaments.[54]

After Mary's death her Protestant sister Elizabeth became queen and the Reformation in England was assured. Queen Elizabeth relied on her Archbishop of Canterbury, Matthew Parker, to settle the Reformation. He had been born in Norwich and his father was a worsted weaver. The tomb of Parker's parents can still be seen in the churchyard of St Clement. Fuller wrote of Parker, 'he was a parker indeed – careful to keep the fences and shut the gates of discipline against all such night-stealers as would invade the same'; it is said that the way he poked his nose into the affairs of his clergy gave rise to the phrase 'nosy parker'.

68 *Lollards' Pit, where many martyrs died, as seen today.*

69 *St Augustine's church with its distinctive tower of red brick.*

Few Anglican churches were built in this period, the exceptions being St Stephen, where the nave was built in 1545 to 1550 and the tower in 1601, and St Augustine, whose tower was rebuilt in 1687 using red brick, unusual in Norwich; the worshippers became known as 'the red steeplers'.

The Renaissance could be said to have come to the city in the arcade piers of St Stephen, and at St George Colegate, with the terracotta tomb of Robert Jannys, who died in 1533. Other characteristic tombs of the age show figures kneeling at a prayer desk, often with husband and wife facing each other and with sons and daughters kneeling behind the parent of their gender. Three 16th-century mayors kneel facing their wives in Norwich churches – Nicholas Sotherton in St John Maddermarket, Robert Suckling in St Andrew's, Thomas Pettus in Sts Simon and Jude. Other splendid tombs come from the early 17th century – Sir John and Lady Suckling in St Andrew's, Sir John Pettus in Sts Simon and Jude, and Richard Berney in St Peter Parmentergate.

The mayor's court kept its ears open and punished words as well as deeds. A wheelwright called Matthew Hamont was convicted at Norwich Guildhall in 1578 for speaking slanderous words against the queen's majesty. He was condemned to pay £100 to the queen or else have his ears cut off. Obviously he could not or would not pay such a vast sum and his ears were indeed removed on the pillory in the market place on 13 May. Clearly thought to be a threat, he was returned to prison and tried for heresies including having said the New Testament was 'but mere foolishness, a story of men, or rather a mere fable'. For this he was burnt in the castle ditch on 20 May 1578.[55]

Now it was Roman Catholics who were prepared to die for their faith, the most notable being Thomas Tunstall. He had trained as a priest abroad, and on returning to England was imprisoned at Wisbech castle. He managed to escape but was re-arrested and brought to Norwich gaol. Condemned by the next Assizes, he was hanged, drawn and quartered at Magdalen Gate on 13 July 1616. He had a special devotion to St Benedict and, at his own request, his severed head was displayed upon St Benedict's Gate.[56]

The first Independent church in Norwich was that of Robert Browne, who came to Norwich with Robert Harrison in 1580; Browne was chaplain at the Great Hospital. The two were among 175 Norwich men who sent a petition to the queen calling for the establishment of a Presbyterian church order in about 1580, and they formed the first separatist church in the city. Browne was elected pastor and Harrison its teacher; 'Brownists' are mentioned in Shakespeare's *Twelfth Night*. After a year of persecution, the community moved abroad to Middleberg.

William Bridge returned to Norwich in 1640, bringing church members with him; some settled in Norwich and others in Yarmouth. In 1644 the two churches separated, and in 1647 Timothy Armitage succeeded Bridge as pastor of the Norwich community. For half a century, the church had no settled meeting place. In 1693 the building now known as the Old Meeting House was built. As Ian C. Hannah wrote, 'in its imposing austerity the old chapel speaks of the deep but simple faith of those by whose hands it was raised. The atmosphere seems so redolent of New England that even in Norwich one instinctively looks round for the pine trees of the forest.' The building also shows its Dutch origins as the stones in front of the entrances are from Holland.[57]

The fabric of the cathedral suffered less than many others during the Commonwealth. Alderman Christopher Jay spent nearly £200 of his own money carrying out maintenance – after the Restoration he insisted on the return of his money. In October 1662 a Dutch tourist, William Shellink, reported that the cathedral and cloisters had been 'restored as new'. By 1670 the chapter had spent £2,800 on repairs apart from what it had received as donations (at least £870) and also spent £1,542 renovating houses in the Close.[58]

Jay has another claim on the affections of Norwich people: in 1657 he was living at Samson and Hercules House and he may well have been responsible for the two statues, described by Pevsner as 'the two most debonair and sleepy of English strong men'. They were moved into the back yard in 1759 but returned to their rightful positions at the front of the house at the end of the 19th century. Hercules has a lion skin, while, as a shepherd, Samson carries a lamb.

The first Norwich man to be converted to the Society of Friends was Thomas Symonds and the earliest Quaker meetings were held from 1654 in

70 *Tomb of the Suckling family in St Andrew's church.*

his house. Land in Goat Lane was bought for a meeting house in 1676 and in 1678 the Meeting decided 'it shall be 40 foot long and 30 foot wide … and a partition made to run with wheeles to enlarge or lessen the rome as occasion requires'. It opened in 1679 and in 1699 a second meeting house at Gildencroft was opened. In 1700 there were about five hundred Quakers in Norwich. The community had bought land in Gildencroft for their graveyard in 1671. At first grave stones were put up but in 1717 the Yearly Meeting decided they should be removed and no more set up.

The Roman Catholic community in Norwich was not large but the faith was never wiped out. Between 1574 and 1616, 49 students from Norfolk were ordained into the Roman Catholic priesthood after studying at seminaries in Europe. The Compton Census of 1676 lists 62 Roman Catholics living in the city with the greatest concentration – 13 people – living in the Close.[59]

Popular superstitions are reflected in several cases of supposed witchcraft before the courts in the 16th and 17th centuries:

> Jane Blogg indicted at Norwich City Quarter Sessions September 1657 not having God before her eyes but being seduced by the instigation of the Devil on 14 Feb. 1652 did devise devillish arts called inchantments witchcrafts charmes and Sorceries in and upon Elizabeth Noblet widow in her body did wickedly divellishly feloniously of her malice before thought did practice by reason of the said arts whereupon the said Elizabeth Noblet was much tormented and did languish from 14 Feb. 1652 until 10 July 1653 and by reason of the aforesaid practice did die and the jurors said she did feloniously do murther against the public peace …

According to Blomefield, a woman called Mary Oliver was executed for witchcraft in 1659 and her goods were ordered to be sold for the benefit of the citizens. We have already mentioned Anne Dant and Margaret Turrell (p.85), hanged as witches in 1648 alongside the 'Great Blow' rioters in the castle ditches.[60]

Housing

The population of Norwich was about 12,000 in 1520, 15,000 in 1600, and had risen to about 30,000 in 1700. There are few records about their houses but some information can be gleaned from the archives, and some houses of the period survive.

The effects of the 1507 fire were devastating, and may explain why so few medieval buildings survive in the city apart from the stone churches. However, there are some obvious exceptions, like the *Britons' Arms*, the only building in Elm Hill not to have burnt down in 1507. Augustine Steward rebuilt much of the street, including the buildings now called Paston House and Pettus House. Houses built after the fire, like those on Elm Hill, were generally built with rubble walls on the ground floor with timber framing above, and might be of two or three storeys. Houses like these are shown on the two earliest maps of the city, the Sanctuary

71a, b *The Old Meeting, exterior and interior.*

Map of 1541 (which only covers parts of the city; see p.62) and William Cunningham's map of 1558; Brian Ayers has pointed out that almost all of the 70 or so houses shown on the Sanctuary Map have a chimney.[61]

The city was in decay even before the fires, as an Act of 1495 refers to the large number of houses unlet and becoming ruined. Continuing problems are reflected in the fact that many of the sites where property was burned down in 1507 remained empty for decades. An Act of Parliament of 1534 ordered the rebuilding of all 'burnt grounds' or at least their enclosure within stone walls, otherwise the mayor could enter and seize the property. An assembly minute of 1538 refers to an empty piece of land by the *Princes* inn where locals used to throw 'muck and other vile matter'. Properties taken over by the city at this date – 30 years after the fire – included that to the west of the churchyard of St Mary the Less and to the east of that of St George Tombland.[62]

The city took steps to prevent a repetition of the 1507 disaster. On 18 May 1509 the assembly ordered that in future all new buildings should be roofed with 'thaktyle' and not with 'thakke' under penalty of a 20s. fine. This was renewed in 1531 but repealed in 1532; people were now at liberty to roof their buildings with 'slatte, tyle or reeyd'. As this implies, the thatch was usually reed, normal for Norfolk but uncommon elsewhere in the country where straw is used; when there was a rumour in 1640 that Catholics were about to set fire to the city, a boy called Alexander Pritchard thought that the houses by Bracondale 'being reeded houses would burne bravely'. There are about half a dozen thatched houses in Norwich today, the most central being the former *Barking Dickey* on Westlegate.[63]

Detailed orders against fire were issued by the city in 1570. All roofs now had to be covered with tile, slate or lead (the first mention of lead as a roofing material). Buckets and a ladder had to be provided at every church. Each alderman was also to have buckets and a ladder available at his house, along with every citizen chosen into the livery. Every great ward was to supply 'one crome of iron with ringes and ropes fixed to the same' and four long ladders. Every small ward was to have buckets.[64]

The Mayor's Court Books record measures taken against fire. There was one fire engine, and ladders and buckets were kept at St Andrew's Hall and the Guildhall. In 1679 a second engine was ordered from London and Daniel Fromantel was paid £2 a year to keep the two engines in order. Two more engines were ordered in the 1680s.

Celia Fiennes commented on the houses in the city on her visit in 1698, noting that the buildings were old-fashioned by London standards, with much tiling, and the buildings were of timber and plaster on lathes. Sometimes the plaster was struck out into squares

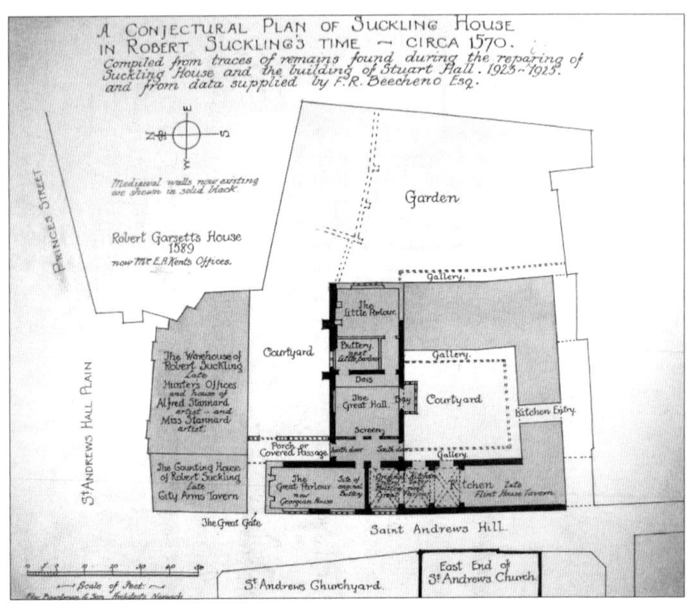

72 *Stuart and Suckling House, now Cinema City; reconstruction drawing of the Tudor house.*

73 *St Gregory's Alley; the present open space in front of the church was formerly its churchyard.*

in imitation of stone, and there is a very good example of this style in Princes Street; 'some they build high and contract the roofs resembling the London houses, but none of brick except some few beyond the river which are built of some of the rich factors like the London buildings'. Mackerell, writing three decades later, noted how brick houses had recently spread on both sides of the river. It was expensive to replace a timber-framed house with a brick one, and one solution was to use mathematical tiles on the walls of such a building, designed to imitate bricks; a classic example in Norwich is the building at the corner of Muspole and Duke Streets.[65]

One characteristic of Norwich buildings is the use of the curved pantile rather than the flat tile more common elsewhere. Pantiles are another debt owed to Holland, from where they began to be imported in the 17th century; they were often glazed black, which can appear blue in bright sunlight. Rounded Dutch-style gables are also common in the city, and there are some fine examples in the Cathedral Close.[66]

Waste products were supposed to be cleared away by scavengers, but houses beside the river made direct use of its flow. In 1689 little Caroline Body, aged two or three, was sitting on the seat in 'a house of office' in her father's house by the river in St Andrew's when she fell through and was washed into the river and drowned. The city's cleanliness was regulated by the courts; in 1648, Joseph Holbacke was before the Quarter Sessions for leasing a house in Mancroft without a latrine.[67]

Keeping the city and river clean was a continual preoccupation of the mayor's court. Details of how the river was 'fyed' (a word for river cleaning, which perhaps gives us the name 'Fye Bridge') are given in an assembly order of 1543: the river was split with boards and posts to create a sluice into which the water was forced, so that gravel could be carried away from the dry portion of the river bed.

In 1590 the authorities looked up previous regulations from 1466 onwards, and issued six pages of new ones. The older rules included the appointment of a channel raker in 1517 and of scavengers in 1569. There was now to be a scavenger in each parish to warn householders to sweep the street or grounds adjoining their property each week; the penalty for non-compliance was 40 shillings, which would be used directly on the river and streets. It was ordered that trades deemed to be 'annoyers of the river' were to pay a higher rate for cleaning it than others. A dozen trades are named including dyers, tanners, parchment-makers and washers of sheep, and also people whose trade was on the river – boatmen, keelmen and fishermen.[68] In 1675 the keeper of the market cross was paid £5 10s. a year to sweep the market once a week and the city bridges and waste grounds once a fortnight. Bylaws were passed by the city in 1686:

> to cleanse the Streets and Channels from Dirt, Coulder and other filth lying there, which by sudden Rain is washed into the said River by means whereof laden Keels and Lighters cannot pass as formerly; and the Citizens themselves are no less annoyed, and the said River will be in a short time destroyed if some speedy remedy be not provided.[69]

74a, b *House in Prince's Street of the kind mentioned by Celia Fiennes.*

In 1700 an Act of Parliament was passed for lighting the city streets and Thomas Lombe was appointed to set up the lamps. The workhouse Act of 1711 included a clause ordering every householder whose property adjoined a public way to set candles or visible lights on the outside walls of their houses from Michaelmas to Lady Day. They were to keep them lit until 11 o'clock at night. Blomefield, writing about 30 years later, was not impressed with the results: 'By virtue of which Act the Streets are enlightened with lamps, which being of the old fashion, and not globular, and standing at a great distance from one another, do not well perform their design'.[70]

Crime

Major crimes such as murder and rape continued to be dealt with by the Court of Assizes, which met twice each year in the county, once in Norwich and once at Thetford. The royal judges came up from London to hold the court, and all its records are at the Public Record Office in London. As always, there were a few sensational cases. One that reached the Privy Council is described by Ralph Houlbrooke. In 1548 Agnes Randolf claimed that when she was 11 years old she was riding across Mousehold Heath when she was abducted by John Atkinson, who forced her to marry him. Atkinson said she had consented and that she was 12 years old, not 11; the exact age is important as 12 was the legal age for a girl to marry. The verdict seems to have been that, although she was indeed of age, the 'marriage' was not valid as it had not been consummated.[71]

Another notorious Norwich crime involved two young men from the county's top families. In July 1684, Thomas Berney (21) and Thomas

Bedingfield (27), who were on the Grand Jury of the Assizes, were drinking together in the *Maid's Head* when they quarrelled; Berney chased Bedingfield through the streets, his rapier drawn, eventually catching him and stabbing several times, some in the back, and Bedingfield died. As the Assize judges were in town, justice was swift: Berney was tried the following day, condemned to death and publicly hanged at Town Close a fortnight later. There may have been more to the case than meets the eye: Goddard Johnson, writing in the 19th century, wrote that 'it is generally believed that one Detravers a Dancing master was the Principal Agent in that Quarrel'. The Town Close, outside the city gate, was a favourite execution place; a century earlier, in 1583, George Shipdham was hanged there for the murder of his wife and children, and remained hanging for a year before his brother, Henry, obtained permission to take his body down.[72]

The most tragic murder case in this period was probably that of Robert 'Gaffer' Watts, a weaver living in the *Old Globe* inn on Botolph Street. He was noted for his jealous behaviour towards his wife. One night in 1701 a man told Mrs Watts that her husband wanted her wedding ring for a moment to settle a bet about its exact weight. She let him borrow it and he took it to Watts, who immediately assumed his wife had cuckolded him. Watts went straight home and murdered his wife; for this he was hanged outside his own door. The inn – not surprisingly – was said to be haunted by the poor woman's ghost. The *Old Globe* was pulled down in 1875 and the site is now a car park next to the Anglia Square shopping centre.[73]

The Tudor period saw the rise of the Court of Quarter Sessions, where local magistrates tried lesser crimes and also dealt with administrative and civil matters, such as disputes about rates, bastardy cases, and maintaining roads and bridges. As a borough, Norwich had its own Court of Quarter Sessions, completely separate from that of the county. However, both courts were actually held in Norwich, the city court at the Guildhall and the county one at the Shire Hall on top of the castle mound – this area was still technically part of the county of Norfolk and not of the city of Norwich. The court of Quarter Sessions began to deal with capital offences by the early years of the 16th century: John Hobbes was hanged in 1511, William Garwood, alias Barker, in 1580 for the theft of two horses, Jonas Goldsmyth, Henry Yaxley and Robert Bloye in December 1611, and William Ellis and Alexander Figg in April 1612. The court was explicitly granted the right to execute criminals under a charter of Charles II, but rarely if ever did so after that date; the report of the Municipal Commissioners in 1834 says that the right was never exercised. Jane Sellars (p.93) may well have been the last person to be hanged by this court.

Lesser crimes were punished with the whip, the cage, the pillory and the ducking stool. Children were not spared the whip: in 1561, seven-year-old Margaret Bryne was brought before the mayor charged with picking the pocket of a servant in the house. At first denying it, she then confessed that she had done it, giving the money to 10-year-old Elizabeth Seman; they were both punished by being whipped with rods.

Leisure and Learning

It has already been noted that the area within the city walls was as large as that of London, which meant there was plenty of land that was not built on. The Gildencroft was still an open space. On 12 April 1671, the inhabitants of the area were told by the mayor's court to stop spoiling the grass by 'immoderate Campings and Dauncings there'; camping here refers to the primitive ancestor of the modern game of football, especially popular in East Anglia.

The city was famous for its gardens. Fuller wrote in 1662:

> Norwich is (as you please) either a city in an orchard, or an orchard in a city, so equally are houses and trees blended in it; so that the pleasure and the populousness of the people meet here together. Yet in this mixture the inhabitants participate nothing of the rusticalness of the one but altogether of the urbanity of the other ... The Dutch brought hither with them not only their profitable crafts but pleasurable curiousities. They were the first that advanced the use and reputation of flowers in this city ... the rose of roses (rosa mundi) had its first being in this city.

Nine years later John Evelyn commented, 'The suburbs are large, the prospect sweete, and other amoenities, not omitting the flower gardens, which all the Inhabitans excell in'.[74]

Theatre companies performed in local inns, as illustrated by an incident in 1583 in the *Red Lion* inn (which gives its name to Red Lion Street). A local man named Wysdon sneaked into the Saturday afternoon performance without paying. Two of the actors – one, Bentley, dressed as a duke, the other, Singer, wearing a false beard – rushed off the stage and chased Wysdon down the street. A member of the audience, Henry Browne (a servant of Sir William Paston), also joined in the chase. As they reached St Stephen's, a bystander hit Bentley with a stone; Browne and Singer attacked the man with their swords and he was taken into a nearby house where he died soon afterwards.[75]

The Norwich waits were founded in 1408. In Elizabeth I's time they usually lived in the 'Suffragans' Tenements' in Bank Street. These were built by John Underwood, suffragan to Bishop Nykke, and had his badge and initials on the spandrels of the door frame. From the 18th century they were associated with the house on King Street once Isaac's, which is why it is commonly known as the Music House; the earliest known use of the name is in the *Norwich Gazette* in 1723. On 25 January 1589 (note the date – this was soon after the Spanish Armada):

> was read in court a letter sent to Mr. mayor and his brethren from Sir Francis Drake whereby he desired that the waytes of this city may be sent to him to go the new intended voyage. Whereunto the waytes being here called do all assent whereupon it is agreed that they shall have 6 cloaks of Stamell cloth made them ready before go and that a wagon shall be provided to carry them and their instruments. And that they shall have £4 to buy them 3 new howboys and one treble recorder ...

Peter Spratt was to be paid 10 shillings for a new sackbut case. Drake's expedition was to Spain and Portugal. Three of the waits died on the voyage; the survivors were each paid 50 shillings for the year and the same amount was given to the widows of those who did not return.[76]

Norwich had its place in the literary renaissance under Elizabeth I. The Earl of Surrey, discussed on p.112, was known as the 'poet-earl'. Robert Greene, born in Norwich in 1560, is most famous for his criticisms of William Shakespeare:

> There is an upstart Crow, beautified with our feathers, that with his Tyger's heart wrapped in a player's hide supposes he is as well able to bumbast out a blank verse as the best of you, and being an absolute Johannes factotum is in his own conceit the only Shake-scene in a country.

Greene went to Norwich Grammar School but spent most of his career in London writing romantic novels, including *Pandosto*, from which Shakespeare took the plot for his play *A Winter's Tale*.[77]

Another writer associated with Norwich was Thomas Deloney, who was probably born in the city, although he made his name in London; Thomas Nashe calls him the 'balleting silk-weaver of Norwich'. His ballads earned him disapproval in the 1580s because of the way one of them referred to Queen Elizabeth. He turned to novels and published three at the end of the 1590s. They were *Jack of Newbury*, *The Gentle Craft* and *Thomas of Reading*. Although the plots are simple, the dialogue and the background details are very real, and they are almost the only books that describe life among Tudor weavers, clothiers and shoemakers. *The Gentle Craft* was the source for Thomas Dekker's great play *The Shoemaker's Holiday* (1599).[78]

William Kempe was a clown with a flair for self-advertisement. He is famous for his dance in 1599 from London to Norwich, ending with a leap into the churchyard of Saint John Maddermarket; an account, *Kempe's Nine Daie Wonder* was published in 1600. It was a form of morris dance, enabling a contemporary, William Rowley, to satirise it as a 'Wild Morridge to Norridge'!

Norwich is often said to have been the first city in England to set up a public library, but Clive Wilkins-Jones defines the claim more precisely: 'Norwich City Library was the first library to be established by a city administration in England outside London in a building that was corporately owned'. It was established by an assembly order of 3 May 1608, with three rooms in the house of the sword bearer adjoining St Andrew's Hall being converted into a library for the use of visiting preachers. It remained a reference library until 1716, when it was decided that books could be borrowed. John Pettus, mayor in 1608, is traditionally regarded as the founder, and he contributed some of the original books.[79]

Printing was re-introduced to Norwich, after a long lapse, by Francis Burges, who set up an office near the Red Well in 1700. In September 1701 he published the *Norwich Post*, the first newspaper to be printed outside London. Burges died in 1706 aged only 30 and is buried in St Andrew's church. Henry Crossgrove printed the *Norwich Gazette* at his house near St Giles' Gate in December 1706. Crossgrove became a freeman in 1710, the first printer to be recorded in the Norwich Freeman's lists since Anthony Solempne 140 years earlier.

The Howard Family

Mount Surrey was the house on St Leonard's Hill built by the Earl of Surrey, the poet and son of the 3rd Duke of Norfolk. It was near the site of the former monastic cell of St Leonard's. Surrey began building his new house in Italian Renaissance design in 1544, richly furnishing it with Turkish tapestries and carpets. He had another palace in Norwich called Surrey Court, in Surrey Street. Surrey's translation of the *Aenid* introduced blank verse to England, and he also developed the form of sonnet later to be used by Shakespeare.

Surrey was charged with using the coat of arms of Edward the Confessor, which only the monarch was entitled to use, and was beheaded on Tower Hill on 19 January 1547, aged only 30. His houses did not long outlast him. Mount Surrey was sacked during Kett's rebellion and later fell into ruin; not a stone remains. Surrey Court was barely finished when he was executed. His father sold the building to the Wodehouse family and the site of the house is now occupied by Aviva's Surrey House.

The Duke of Norfolk had built his own town house in Norwich in 1540 on what is now Duke Street. The 4th Duke greatly enlarged the family palace. It was a quadrangle with a court in the centre and an entrance in the middle of the south side. The north and south ranges were three storeys high and the other two ranges four storeys high. It had a bowling alley and a covered tennis court. The duke is said to have boasted that 'his estate was worth little less than the whole realm of Scotland, in the ill state to which the wars reduced it; and that when he was in his own tennis court at Norwich, he thought himself as great as a king'.[80]

The 6th Duke also spent a lot of money on the palace. It was during this rebuilding that Charles II stayed there in 1671 as the guest of Lord Henry Howard, the duke's brother (the duke himself was insane and lived in retirement in Padua). The tennis court was turned into a kitchen and the bowling alley into five separate dining rooms. There is no known list of the people the king brought with him but the queen's retinue comprised 55 people, from her Lord Chamberlain to the laundrymaid.[81]

The Duke's Palace was the largest private house in the city. In the Hearth tax returns of 1666 it was assessed at £2 10s., which equates to 50 hearths. Thomas Baskerville in 1681 thought it was 'seated in a dunghole place' and that 'though it has cost the Duke already £30,000 in building … hath but little room for garden and is pent on al sides both on this and the other side of the river with tradesmen's and dyers' houses'.[82]

The palace was already in decay when Celia Fiennes visited the city in 1698. She wrote:

> There is in the middle of the town the Duke of Norfolk's house of brick and stone with severall towers and turrets and balls that looks well, with large gardens, but the inside is all demolish'd. Only the walls stand and a few rooms for offices, but nothing of slate or tolerable for use.

The connection of the Dukes of Norfolk with the city came to a dramatic end in 1710, when the mayor Thomas Havers refused to allow the duke to enter the city in procession with his private Company of Comedians

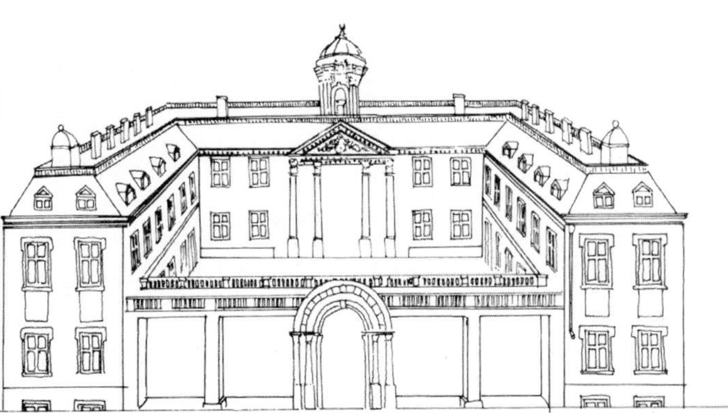

75 *The Duke's Palace, on the south bank of the river.*

sounding trumpets and flying banners. Havers may have feared a Jacobite riot, as the Dukes were Roman Catholics. The duke demolished most of his palace the following year, letting one wing to the Guardians of the Poor, who used it as a workhouse. The Roman Catholic chapel survived until the 1960s, when it was being used as a billiard room – it was pulled down to make way for a multi-storey car park. Some fragments of the palace are said to have been recycled, such as the stone pillars of the doorway of the Harveys' house on Colegate.

These were not the only properties in the city owned by the family. Lord Henry Howard bought the former Augustine friary site in King Street in about 1670, and built on it the property now called Howard House. He turned the rest into a pleasure ground; Edward Browne, son of the Thomas Browne discussed below, wrote that he intended it for a place of 'walking and recreation', had created 40ft-wide walks and was planning a bowling green. The bowling green was indeed laid out and lasted until around 1720, when the then owner, Mr Bosely, let it out as a garden. According to William Hudson, a later gardener grew hops on it, and this led to the name of the public house eventually built on the site – the *Hop Pole*.[83]

Thomas Browne

Thomas Browne was born in 1605. He studied medicine in Montpelier, Padua and Leyden before settling in Norwich in 1637. In 1642 his book *Religio Medici* was published by a London printer without his permission. Browne was a moderate rather than an ardent royalist and included Puritans such as the Hobarts among his friends. He devoted the war years to his enormous work generally known as *Enquiries Into Vulgar Errors*, which contains no reference to the war. He had a great reputation in his own day. The diarist John Evelyn sought his opinion on gardens and trees, and the historian William Dugdale about the Fens and about a fossil fish-bone he had found.

When Charles II visited Norwich in 1671 he was entertained with a banquet in St Andrew's Hall and took advantage of the occasion to knight Thomas Browne. John Evelyn, who was with the king, went on to Browne's house; this was in the Haymarket, and Sir Thomas also rented land in the Close, still known as Browne's Meadow. Evelyn was impressed: 'His whole house and garden being a paradise and cabinet of rarities, and that of the best collection, especially medals, books, plants and natural things.' One thing Evelyn could hardly have missed is the enormous wooden overmantel now in the Castle Museum. This was taken from Browne's house when it was demolished in 1842. It has the arms of King James I on it, so it must have been installed in the house by Browne's predecessor there, Alexander Anguish, who was mayor in 1629.

Browne died in 1682 and was buried in St Peter Mancroft. In one of his books he had written, 'But who knows the fate of his bones or how often he is to be buried? Who hath the oracle of his ashes or whither they are to be scattered?' However, he could hardly have foreseen the fate of his own skull. In 1840 the vicar of St Peter Mancroft was digging a grave in the chancel for his wife when he accidentally opened Browne's coffin. It seems that the antiquarian Robert Fitch 'borrowed' Browne's skull and coffin plate to make copies of them. He probably intended to put them back but the tomb was sealed up again before he could do so. After some time both skull and coffin plate wound up in the museum of the Norfolk and Norwich Hospital and in 1901 a silver and glass casket was provided. The church was not happy about this and in 1922 the skull was again buried in the chancel of St Peter Mancroft.[84]

76 *Sir Thomas Browne.*

Thomas Browne is supposed to be the originator of some words in use today, such as 'electricity', 'hallucination' and 'antediluvian'. Digressive by modern standards, his character was summed up by the Victorian poet John Addington Symonds: 'There is something inconclusive in the habit of his fancy, a delight in intellectual twilight, a moth-like flitting to and fro in regions where no certainty can be attained.'

The Stuart period ended on 1 August 1714 with the death of Queen Anne. She was succeeded by the German prince, George of Hanover. Some people preferred the claims of James II and his descendants (or pretended to, as an excuse to attack the established order), and these people, known as Jacobites, appear frequently in the many riots that characterised city life in the Georgian period.

77 *Browne remembered, the statue on Haymarket shown when it was the centre of a green space.*

FOUR

Georgian Norwich

There was a change in city government in 1729, under an Act for better regulating elections in Norwich. The freemen were now to elect only three councillors for each ward, the remainder being chosen by the three and not directly elected. As the three naturally chose men of their own way of thinking, this helped towards the two-party system. The system continued until 1835 but was not entirely a success. In 1834 the Municipal Commissioners drew attention to the bribery and corruption to which it led, saying bluntly: 'Bribery in Norwich is as common as the sun at noon'.[1]

This period saw the end of the guild of St George – and eventually of Snap. By the 1720s prominent citizens were becoming unhappy with its expense and the guild was finished when one of the aldermen, William Clarke, refused to join. The responsibility for organising Guild Day passed to a city committee. Francis Skipperton was the first dragon-bearer under the new order of things, and he continued every year for the next 15 years. The arms of the city were painted onto standards and onto the caps worn by the standard-bearers so that everyone knew who was now organising the event. The procession was now starting from the house of the mayor-elect and the day was a splendid one: Richard Bradley noted in 1728 how many sweet-smelling flowers that grew in profusion near Norwich were strewn in the streets on feast day. By the 19th century, the mayor might well have lived outside the old city walls, which were in any case regarded as in the way. In 1825 a hole was knocked in the city wall at Pottergate and an arch of boughs made to allow the procession to pass through it in style.[2]

The city's armaments were employed in the celebrations. Parson Woodforde, the diarist rector of Witchingham, sometimes came into Norwich to see the pageant. In June 1781 he summed the day up: 'Bells ringing, Flaggs flying and Cannons roaring'.

A new dragon was constructed in the 1730s, made of basketwork and covered with painted cloth; it could flap its wings and distend its head! It was repaired in 1753, and in 1819 the corporation paid £11 1s. for further repairs. Ten years later, 10 shillings was spent on 'straps for Snap'. However, his time was almost up. The 1835 Municipal Corporation Act swept away much of the pageantry of towns. On 16 June 1835, Guild Day was celebrated for the last time – officially at least. Snap made his last formal appearance in the procession, after appearing for at least 415 years, apart from a brief interlude in the Puritan Norwich of the 1640s. In the evening, 800 people attended the dinner at St Andrew's Hall, followed by a dance at the Assembly Rooms. It was the end of an era.

Rioting continued to be a feature of urban life. One way of showing one's radicalism was to celebrate anniversaries relating to the Stuarts rather than the Hanoverians. Restoration Day or Oak Apple Day, 29 May, was the day to celebrate the restoration of King Charles II. In 1715, according to Hutton, 'the bells at Norwich rang for the whole of Restoration Day, the streets were strewn with flowers, and sprigs of oak were worn by most people in hats or bosoms'. In 1723, as the *Norwich Gazette* noted, the birthday of King George was celebrated 'with all the usual demonstrations of joy and loyalty' but the city really showed its views in the way it celebrated the anniversary of the restoration of Charles II, the day after the royal birthday: 'besides ringing of bells, firing of guns, and bonfires, the streets were strewn with seggs, oaken boughs set up at the doors, and in some streets garlands and pictures hung out, and variety of antick and comick dances'.[3]

In 1740 there were riots in Norwich because of the scarcity of grain. A crowd went to every baker in the city and fixed a sign on the door bearing the words: 'Wheat at sixteen shillings a coomb'. They seized a keel on the river loaded with wheat and rye, and marched out of the city gates demanding money and ale from farmers and treading down the corn of those who refused them. The magistrates called in soldiers who fired on the crowd, killing one of the rioters and seven innocent bystanders. In the same year there was a five-day riot in the city over the price of mackerel.[4]

The worst of the riots in Norwich was in 1766. On Saturday 27 September, a mob assembled in the market place at about two in the afternoon and began destroying provisions there. After an hour they moved on to the New Mills, partly destroying them. They spent the evening breaking into the houses of various bakers and brewers in the city, finally partly demolishing the *White Horse* alehouse in the Haymarket shortly before midnight. The mob gathered again on the next day and marched to Trowse mills but the miller there appears to have placated them; instead they plundered the house of Mr Money in Trowse. On their way back to the city they attacked a granary belonging to Margaret Linsey and boarded a boat on the river, throwing its contents overboard. Back in Norwich they attacked the houses of two bakers in Conesford and Tombland.[5]

City authorities seem to have panicked. John Gay wrote to the Earl of Buckinghamshire at Blickling, telling him that Mr Money's house in

Trowse had been almost demolished, and added a dramatic postscript – 'hear a Malthouse by Conisford Gates just now fired'. Lord Barrington wrote from London to the Earl:

> I am at this moment sending by express orders for two Troops of Dragoons to march from Colchester to Norwich to assist the magistrates there. It may be useful to acquaint you, let the call be ever so urgent, I can send no further military aid into Norfolk; for the troops of the whole Kingdom are imploy'd.

The mayor John Patteson had to go out and read the Riot Act to the mob. Before he did, he handed his chain of office to his sister-in-law, who acted as mayoress, saying 'Take care of this, little mother, God knows if I shall come back alive.'[6]

In the end the city coped without outside help. The mayor called out the citizens, who were armed with staves and succeeded in making 30 arrests. On 2 October, Barrington wrote, 'Norwich has the singular honour of reducing a mob without military aid, an example which I hope other Places will endeavour to imitate.' Two days later he wrote seeking revenge: 'Pray hang as many of your prisoners as possible.' The mayor took a different line. He referred to the prisoners as 'unhappy convicts' and said that troops would be needed in case there were further riots at their execution. The cases were tried before a special commission and eight rioters were sentenced to death but only two, John Hall and David Long, were in fact executed. They were hanged at Norwich Castle on 10 January 1767. Four others were transported for life. Some cases came before other courts: two women were tried at the Norwich Quarter Sessions in connection with the riots, Elizabeth Parr being given three months imprisonment and Susanna Soons bound over to keep the peace.

Many in Norwich welcomed the French Revolution of 1789. Dissenters, merchants and professional men set up a Revolution Society, and Radical Clubs were set up by artisans from 1792; at one time there were more than 40 clubs with 2,000 members. They met in tavern cellars to hear readings from the works of the Thetford-born radical Thomas Paine, and studied *The Cabinet*, a journal strongly in favour of the French Revolution. By 1793 the radical Corresponding Society of London had a link with Norwich. The revolution was warmly greeted at the Baptist chapel of St Paul's. On 29 May 1797 John Thelwall, 'the spokesman for English radicalism', came to speak in the city, but a party of dragoons went to the lecture room and smashed it up, and then attacked and partly destroyed the *Shakespeare* public house next door. Eventually some officers restored order but by then the landlord of the *Shakespeare* had fallen from a garret window and been badly hurt. One man, Luke Rice, was accused at the next Assizes of encouraging the soldiers, but he was acquitted on a technicality. Penny Corfield cites a poster that appeared on the walls of Norwich in 1793: 'Weep, ye who grind the Face of the Poor, oppress the People, and starve the industrious *Mechanic*.'[7]

Many who sympathised with the French Revolution turned against it when the French king was executed. They included Colonel John

Money, who joined the service of France in July 1792, but resigned his commission six months later after the execution, writing to the *Norfolk Chronicle,* 'when I engaged to serve these people they had a King and Constitution; now they have neither – they are all mad and the army think so'. However, some continued to support radicalism. Jonathan Davey was present at the trial of Thomas Hardy, the radical, for treason in London in October 1794; at its end, Davey rode straight back to Norwich, riding through the night and arriving at St Paul's chapel the following morning, where Wilks was leading the service. 'Wilks was in the pulpit when Davey entered, and he broke off to enquire: "What news, brother?" "Not Guilty!" "Then let us sing 'Praise God from whom all blessings flow.'"'[8]

On Valentine's Day 1797 the Norfolk hero Admiral Nelson had a great victory over the Spanish fleet at St Vincent. The Spanish rear-admiral Don Xavier Winthuysen surrendered to Nelson, gave him his sword and died that same night. Nelson presented the sword to the city. On 26 February he wrote, 'I know no place where it would give me or my family more pleasure to have it kept, than in the Capital City of the County in which I had the Honour to be born.' Norwich granted Nelson the freedom of the city. In 1800 the city commissioned Sir William Beechey to paint a portrait showing both Nelson and the sword; city accounts show that £210 was paid to Beechey for Nelson's portrait in 1800-1. The portrait, with its elaborate frame, can be seen today in Blackfriars' Hall; the sword is in the Castle Museum.[9]

William Windham was MP for the city from 1784. A Whig and a friend of Charles James Fox, he was a strong supporter of the war against France, and William Pitt made him his Secretary of War in 1794. On taking office he had to stand for re-election and, although he won easily, the election was a rowdy affair. His opponents' supporters carried aloft a loom wreathed in mourning to symbolise the death of the Norwich weaving trade because of the war. Windham's supporters replied with a model guillotine which chopped the head off a female doll and was labelled, 'This is French liberty'. Pitt and Windham both resigned from the government on the issue of Catholic emancipation in 1801. Windham opposed the peace treaty made with France at Amiens in 1802, and it was probably because of this that he lost his seat at Norwich.[10]

Norwich's 18th-century reputation for radicalism continued into the 19th century. William Smith, MP for the city from 1802 to 1830 (with a short gap in 1806-7), was a dissenter in religion and a radical in politics. Born in Clapham in 1756, he was the son of a wealthy grocer. A friend of William Wilberforce, he played an important role in the campaign to abolish the slave trade in 1807, and subsequently slavery in the Empire. In 1828 he presided over the repeal of the Test Acts, which allowed full rights to the Roman Catholics in England. Smith died in London on 31 May 1835. His son Benjamin Smith, also a radical and free-thinker, was MP for Norwich from 1838 to 1847; he supported the repeal of the corn laws. Benjamin's children included the women's rights activist Barbara Leigh Smith Bodichon. He died in London in 1860.

On 23 June 1815 news of Wellington's victory at Waterloo reached Norwich, five days after the battle had been fought. Four days later, news arrived of Napoleon's abdication and a bonfire was lit in the market place 'with the stalls from the fishmarket and other stolen material'.[11]

There was a demonstration against the passing of the Corn Bill at the Agricultural Show in 1815 and riots in the city. A crowd threw fireballs into the Guildhall, and then marched to the New Mills, breaking windows on the way. They broke into the mill, throwing some of the flour they found into the river and stealing the rest. They went on to smash windows in St Andrew's, Bank Street, Tombland and Magdalen Street before being dispersed by special constables.

Elections were times of disorder in the city, and there was a great deal of corruption, bribery and even physical violence. In August 1727, dirt, oyster shells and stones were thrown and the sheriffs threatened with violence by the mob. At the mayoral election the following May, a stone was hurled at the outgoing mayor, John Harvey, by a mob that had followed him home, fortunately missing him; the culprit was a barber from St Paul's named Cropton. Things were no better a century later. On 10 September 1827, a group of voters, including a man named James Bailey, were taken away by force to prevent them voting in the election for aldermen on the 12th. They were taken to the *Castle* pub in Wroxham, then to the *Swan* in Horning, on to an inn in Smallburgh and finally to the Ridlington *Plough*; in each inn, they were allowed to drink and eat all they liked. They were set free after the voting. Bailey was a sick man, and much disturbed by all the enforced travelling; on 22 September, he burst a blood vessel and died. Some blamed his 'kidnappers', but at his inquest evidence was given that he had been well enough after the adventure to be selling programmes at the Music Festival on 18-20 September – 'his attendance at the Festival took the onus off his captors'.

78 *Looking at the city from Rosary Road.*

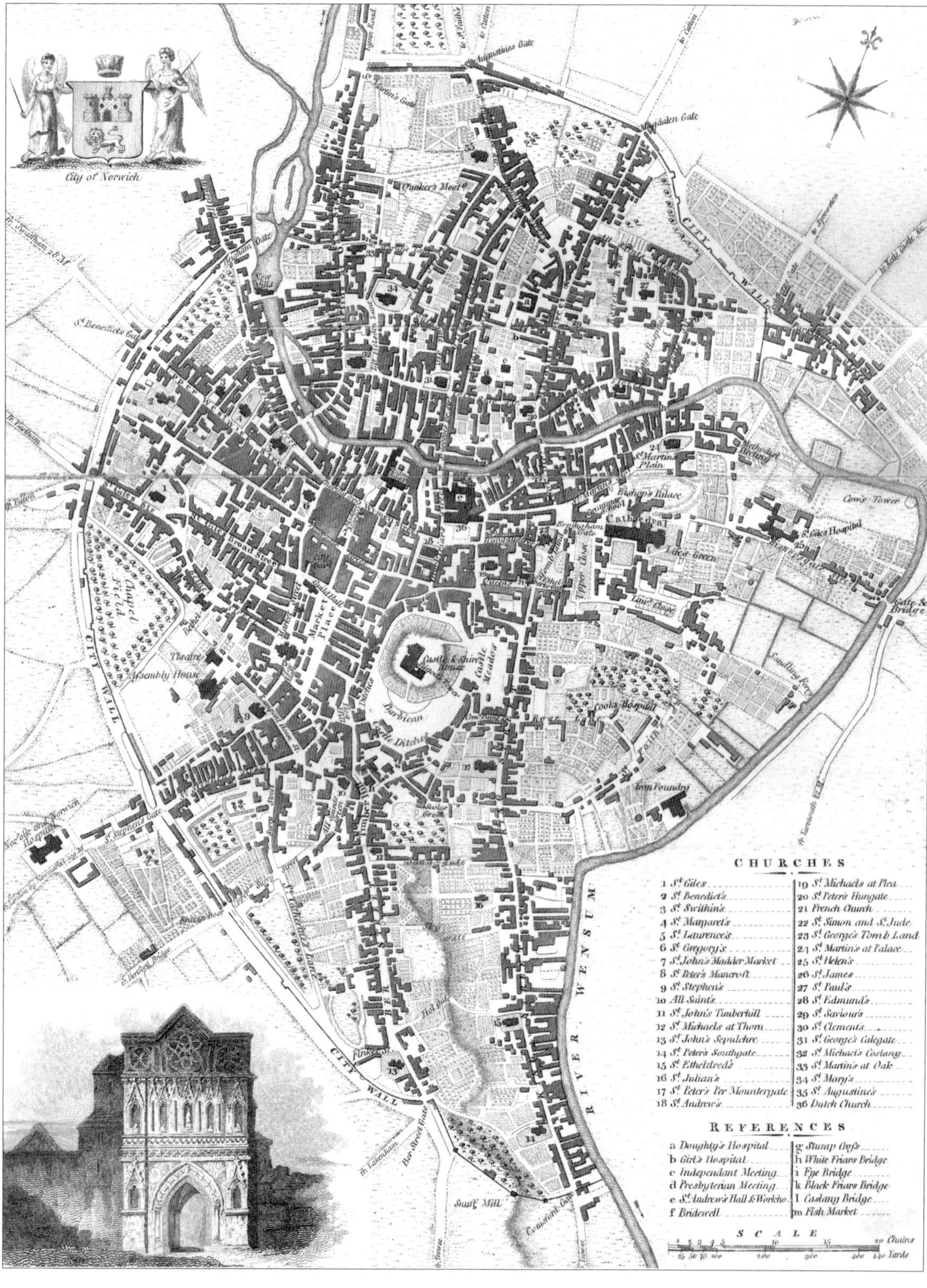
City of Norwich
Magdalen Gate
Augustines Gate
St Benedicts Gate
St Stephen's Gate
Quaker's Meet
Market Place
Castle & Shire House
Barbican
Castle Meadow
Chapel Field
Theatre
Assembly House
Bishop's Palace
Cathedral
St Martin's Plain
Methodist Meeting
St Giles Hospital
Cow's Tower
Cooks Hospital
Iron Foundry
City Wall
River Wensum
Snuff Mill
CHURCHES
1 St Giles
2 St Benedict's
3 St Swithin's
4 St Margaret's
5 St Laurence's
6 St Gregory's
7 St John's Madder Market
8 St Peter's Mancroft
9 St Stephen's
10 All Saints
11 St John's Timberhill
12 St Michaels at Thorn
13 St John's Sepulchre
14 St Peter's Southgate
15 St Etheldred's
16 St Julian's
17 St Peter's Per Mountergate
18 St Andrew's
19 St Michaels at Plea
20 St Peter's Hungate
21 French Church
22 St Simon and St Jude
23 St George's Tomb Land
24 St Martin's at Palace
25 St Helen's
26 St James
27 St Paul's
28 St Edmund's
29 St Saviour's
30 St Clements
31 St George's Colegate
32 St Michael's Costany
33 St Martin's at Oak
34 St Mary's
35 St Augustine's
36 Dutch Church
REFERENCES
a Doughty's Hospital
b Girl's Hospital
c Independant Meeting
d Presbyterian Meeting
e St Andrew's Hall & Workho.
f Bridewell
g Stump Cross
h White Friars Bridge
i Fye Bridge
k Black Friars Bridge
l Costany Bridge
m Fish Market
SCALE
1 2 3 4 5 10 15 20 Chains
25 50 75 100 200 300 400 440 Yards

79 *Plan of Georgian Norwich; note the large amount of open space within the city walls.*

There were more riots in the city in 1830. On 29 November, sawyers assembled on St Catherine's Plain to discuss their wages and then went to a saw-mill at New Catton belonging to a Robert Calver, where they destroyed the machinery and set the building alight. A week later, on 6 December, silk weavers rioted at a silk manufactory in St Martin's belonging to Henry and Edward Willett, breaking windows and cutting the silk in 26 looms. The damage was claimed to come to over £250.[12]

In 1832 it was the soldiers in the barracks who mutinied. When Colonel Keane gave the command 'Attention' on one occasion, not a soldier obeyed. Keane picked a man at random – Philip Pitman – and had him given 200 lashes. At a subsequent court martial, four soldiers were transported, John Martin for life, and Thomas Almond, Henry Bone and John Clayson for lesser terms. A fifth soldier, Charles Edwards, was sentenced to 12 months in prison, five non-commissioned officers were reduced to the ranks and the regimental Sergeant Major was suspended.

Trade and Industry

Georgian Norwich was still the second largest city in England, with a population of about 30,000 in 1714. Its wealth was still based on wool – Macaulay called Norwich 'the chief seat of the chief manufacture of the realm'. The records of the freemen of the city show how the weavers dominated; according to Penelope Corfield, the numbers of freemen admitted involved in the production rose from 23 per cent in 1600-19 to 58 per cent a century later. The register for 1714-52 printed by the Norfolk Record Society runs to 100 pages, of which 40 are filled with the names of worsted weavers. Their status was also rising and they were joining the city elite; no weaver became a mayor between 1600 and 1640, but there were a total of 15 weaver mayors between 1640 and 1700, more than from any other occupational group.[13]

The Norwich worsted trade grew rapidly throughout the early 18th century, outselling Exeter serges because Norwich wages were lower. A range of fabrics were developed, some of pure worsted and some of worsted and silk and, by the end of the century, of worsted and cotton. The first Prime Minister, Robert Walpole, was a Norfolk man and through his influence an Act was passed in 1721 against the wearing of calicoes. Walpole also used his influence to ensure that court mourning dress should consist of Norwich crepes.

Daniel Defoe wrote in 1724:

> If a stranger was only to ride through or view the City of Norwich for a day, he would have much more reason to think there was a town without inhabitants … but on the contrary, if he was to view the city either on a Sabbath Day, or any public occasion, he would wonder where all the people could dwell, the multitude is so great; but the case is this; the inhabitants being all so busy at their manufactures, dwell in their garrets at their looms and in their combing-shops, so they call them, twisting-mills and other work-houses, almost all the works they are employed on being done within doors.[14]

By 1750 Norwich had developed a range of high-quality fabrics. Regulations protected the textile industry: in 1700 the English were forbidden to import printed cotton cloth and between 1720 and 1774 it was illegal to wear it even if it was made in England. After 1713 exports of worsted and Norwich stuffs captured a world market. The Spanish trade, for example, leapt from £31,000 in 1711 to £112,000 in 1721. An anonymous diary in the Cornwall Record Office describes a visit to Norwich in 1757:

> The Town vastly populous, employing an Infinite Number of Hands in the Manufactory of Crapes and Stuffs, for which Norwich is famous ... You see every woman and child almost with their wool fixt to the top of a stick carried in their Left Hand, which they draw out and twist with their right without the use of a spinning wheel or any other Instrument.

Daniel Defoe saw a booth at Stourbridge fair belonging to a dealer in Norwich stuffs, with goods on display said to be worth £20,000.[15]

The Norwich woolcombers showed their muscle in 1752 when they took strike action. The woolcombers objected to the employment of a man named Trye who they said was a colt (that is, a man who had not served an apprenticeship) and a thief. Three hundred men left their work and retired to heathland at Rackheath where they camped out, supported by purse clubs, for several weeks, until they had won their point.[16]

The worsted trade declined at the end of the 18th century. Arthur Young noticed the decline in 1771 and blamed the war with the American colonies; however, he estimated that there were still 12,000 looms in the city. The outbreak of war with France hit the trade hard and by 1791 the trade was dependent on the orders of the East India Company for worsted camlets. A further blow came in 1794, when the Empress of Russia prohibited imports from England.[17]

There were other reasons for the decline of weaving in Norwich. According to the Hammonds, Norwich merchants would not take the risk of introducing machinery to a hostile people, and instead concentrated on making new stuffs, often a mixture of silk and wool. As soon as a fabric became popular it was copied more cheaply in Yorkshire, where new technology and the use of water power in large-scale mills allowed goods to be produced quicker and cheaper than in Norwich. Yorkshire flooded the Eastern markets with cheap imitations after the East India Company lost the monopoly on trade with India in 1813 and with China in 1833. When the company stopped exporting Norwich cloth it was 'a blow as serious as any [the city] had suffered since the Black Death ... Disastrous unemployment, semi-unemployment and rioting followed.'[18]

Some efforts were made to keep up with rivals, such as the jacquard loom. A French development of the draw-loom, it used punched cards on the harness for the automatic selection of the colours; 'by this ingenious contrivance, the most complicated patterns can be introduced upon the different fabrics, with the same ease as the plainest'. It first came to Norwich in about 1830, probably introduced by Willett and Nephew; the

80a, b *Typical apprenticeship indentures: Thomas Taylor, wool comber and William Towler, worsted weaver.*

new technology was perhaps the cause of the riot against their manufactory already mentioned (p.119).

Norwich flourished as long as it did by concentrating on the luxury end of the market, as M.J. Daunton appreciated:

> Norwich was essentially a survival, a persistence of old forms of production. Mass production by steam power and factories did not immediately triumph over high quality production on handicraft lines. Norwich kept its niche as long as this was so. What is also true is that Norwich did not foster the development of these new forms. It survived for some time, but it was being acted upon by a process in which it did not participate. Sooner or later its niche would disappear before the assault of the new forces at work in the economy. Once again, the town was left with the residual function of social and regional capital of an agricultural hinterland.[19]

Large-scale industrial mills intended to match those in the North were finally introduced to Norwich in the 1830s; the idea was for

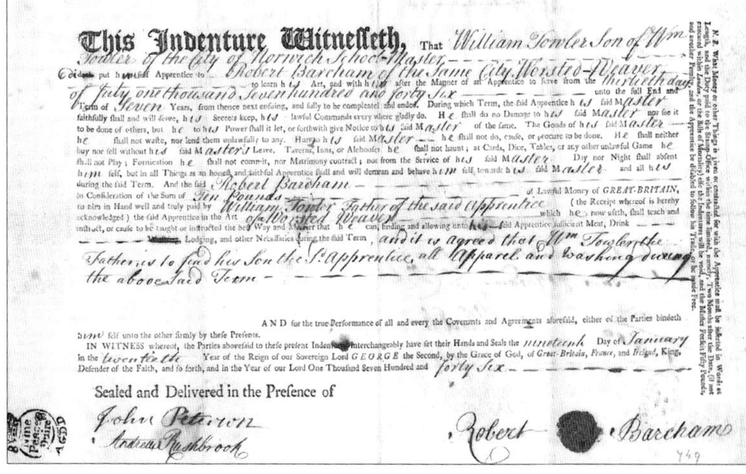

This Indenture Witneſſeth, That William Towler Son of Wm Towler of the City of Norwich School-Master put himſelf Apprentice to Robert Barcham of the Same City Worsted-Weaver to learn his Art, and with him after the Manner of an Apprentice to ſerve from the thirtieth day of July one thousand Seven hundred and forty Six unto the full End and Term of Seven Years, from thence next enſuing, and fully to be compleated and ended. During which Term, the ſaid Apprentice his ſaid Master faithfully ſhall and will ſerve, his Secrets keep, his lawful Commands every where gladly do. He ſhall do no Damage to his ſaid Master nor ſee it to be done of others, but he to his Power ſhall it let, or forthwith give Notice to his ſaid Master of the ſame. The Goods of his ſaid Master he ſhall not waſte, nor lend them unlawfully to any. Hurt to his ſaid Master he ſhall not do, cauſe, or procure to be done. He ſhall neither buy nor ſell without his ſaid Master's Leave. Taverns, Inns, or Alehouſes he ſhall not haunt; at Cards, Dice, Tables, or any other unlawful Game he ſhall not Play; Fornication he ſhall not commit, nor Matrimony contract; nor from the Service of his ſaid Master Day nor Night ſhall abſent himſelf, but in all Things as an honeſt and faithful Apprentice ſhall and will demean and behave himſelf towards his ſaid Master and all his during the ſaid Term. And the ſaid Robert Barcham in Conſideration of the Sum of Ten Pounds of Lawful Money of GREAT-BRITAIN, to him in Hand well and truly paid by William Towler Father of the said Apprentice (the Receipt whereof is hereby acknowledged) the ſaid Apprentice in the Art of a Worsted Weaver which he now uſeth, ſhall teach and inſtruct, or cauſe to be taught or inſtructed the beſt Way and Manner that he can, finding and allowing unto his ſaid Apprentice ſufficient Meat, Drink Lodging, and other Neceſſaries during the ſaid Term, and it is agreed that Wm Towler the Father is to find his Son the Sd Apprentice, all Apparel and washing during the abovesaid Term

AND for the true Performance of all and every the Covenants and Agreements aforeſaid, either of the Parties bindeth himſelf unto the other firmly by theſe Preſents.

IN WITNESS whereof, the Parties aboveſaid to theſe preſent Indentures interchangeably have ſet their Hands and Seals the nineteenth Day of January in the twentieth Year of the Reign of our Sovereign Lord GEORGE the Second, by the Grace of God, of Great-Britain, France, and Ireland, King, Defender of the Faith, and ſo forth, and in the Year of our Lord One Thouſand Seven Hundred and forty Six

Sealed and Delivered in the Preſence of

John Peterson

Andrew Rushbrook

Robert Barcham

749

Norwich people to spin their own yarn rather than taking it from mills in Yorkshire and elsewhere. On 29 August 1833, the Norwich Court of Guardians held a meeting to discuss a proposal by Samuel Bignold to establish a joint stock company. On 5 September, a meeting was held at the Guildhall and the Norwich Yarn Company was formed; by 1 October, £26,000 had been subscribed in shares of £100 each. The first stone of the new factory was laid by Bignold on 27 February 1834, when a procession wound its way from Lakenham to the site in St Edmunds, with people dressed as Bishop Blaize, shepherds and shepherdesses – Blaize was the patron saint of woolcombers and figured in Norwich processions for many centuries. Woodforde witnessed one on 24 March 1783, commenting: 'I never saw so great a Multitude of people in my Life collected together, the Market-Place was as full as it could be, both in the area, at the Windows and on the Tops of the Houses.'

The mill was soon at work, and when Bignold visited in 1836, there were 300 workers there, together with 60 reelers and 200 child labourers. In June 1836, the Norwich Yarn Company held another meeting at the Guildhall, saying that the mill was not large enough – fully occupied, it could supply scarcely a third of the yarn needed for the city. It was decided to increase the capital by issuing another 700 shares of £100 each and to build a new mill one third larger than the first one. A new piece of ground was bought by Mr Youngman, the first stone being again laid by Bignold on 1 December 1836, after another joyful procession; John Sell Cotman sketched the event and sold the subsequent prints, giving all the profits for the benefit of the poor. On the occasion of Queen Victoria's coronation on 28 June 1838, 1,000 employees of the Yarn Factory were dined in 10 parties at 10 public houses. A new chimney for the factory, 165 foot high, was completed beside Whitefriars Bridge on 10 November 1838.

81 *Panorama of Norwich from the east.*

Meanwhile another enterprise, the Lakenham Yarn Company, built the Albion Mills on King Street in 1836, five storeys high with a semicircular tower for the latrines. It had two 70-horsepower engines for the power spinning of worsted.

Other aspects of the industry did flourish. The Norwich shawl was developed as a cheaper alternative to shawls woven in Kashmir. The problem was to make the wool soft enough to be a passable imitation of the Indian shawls made from the wool of cashmere goats. The solution was to use a combination of wool and silk; it was developed by P.J. Knights, who won an award from the Society of Arts and Sciences for having woven a shawl counterpane four yards square without a seam, 'which was never before done in England: it is very beautifully ornamented with flowers, jointly the work of the loom and the needle'. He originally worked for John Harvey in Colegate, but soon struck out on his own and brought the art of shawl-making to perfection.[20]

By 1802, there were 12 shawl manufacturers in the city. At first the design was embroidered by women and children, but by the beginning of the 19th century the design was woven in on a drawloom; this was known as a 'fillover' shawl. The peak period for the shawl was in the decades between 1850 and 1870, the finest of all probably being those produced by Clabburn, Son and Crisp: one of their shawls was given to Princess Alexandra on her marriage to the Prince of Wales in 1863. Jane, the wife of Thomas Coke of Holkham Hall, was apparently the first to see that the material would make tapestries for walls and couches; she filled up parts of the Hall with 'this beautiful article' and started a new fashion.[21]

Joseph Grout introduced crepe making to the city in 1822; this was made from twisted silk yarn and used exclusively for mourning clothes. Grout's crepe factory impressed Mr Marten, a Nonconformist minister from London, in 1825: 'The works are in several floors and the winding, twisting, bobbing etc are by Machinery moved by a beautiful 20 Horsepower Engine.' He was not so impressed with the working conditions, however:

> These operations are watched and conducted by more than seventy females, some so young as 7 to 8 years of age. These are on foot from seven in the Morning till eight in the Evg watching the thread, repairing the broken and seeing that all go on well – occasionally supplying Oil where wanted to prevent evil from frictions – Only that they have half an hour for breakfast and an hour for dinner – And these little Girls earn some 5/- some 5/6 per week.[22]

Marten was also interested in home workers: 'Seeing a loom going in a private house as we passed we asked the woman who was weaving Norwich crape and learned that she could by close application weave eleven yards each day.'

By the end of the century boot and shoe making was increasing in importance. According to Eric Fowler:

> One James Smith, who kept a shop in Norwich market place in 1792, is credited with having been the first man to manufacture boots and shoes in stock sizes, instead of making them up to the requirements of each individual customer. He thus paved the way for the mass production of boots and shoes in factories.

James Southall and Co. was established in 1792 and is said to be the oldest shoemaking concern in England. Bally and Haldinstein was founded in 1799.[23]

Norwich market remained the heart of the city. Money was spent on improving the facilities – the fish market was paved in 1727 and the main market 'new paved' in 1731. In the following year the Market Cross was pulled down, as was the Shearing Cross, 'a neat, ancient stone pillar' outside what is now Strangers' Hall. The Market Cross was a major feature as it was between 60 and 70 feet high with a chapel in the middle, which was converted into a storehouse at the Reformation. The cross contained the approved measure for weighing grain and other goods, chained to a pillar for anyone to use. Meat, eggs and cheese were sold by farmers' wives not from stalls but from 'peds', semi-circular baskets, carried one on each side of a packhorse. In 1783 Parson Woodforde bought three pairs of sole, two crabs and a lobster at the fish market, paying 8s. 4d., which included an earlier purchase.[24]

The market place continued to attract the notice of diarists and writers of journals. The diary of Silas Neville for Saturday 19 October 1777 records: 'After breakfast took a walk thro' the Market, it being Market Day. It is certainly one of the largest and best-furnished in England, the fowls, turkeys etc. so fat and neatly trussed, the men and women who sell them so clean and neat.' In 1782 William Marshall came to Norwich to see the clover-seed market and was told that the biggest dealer had sold six and a half hundredweight of seed that afternoon.[25] Joshua Larwood, a Norfolk rector, noted in 1800:

> the market-place, which is nearly an oblong square, and a very fine one, lies upon a slope with exactly sufficient inclination to show to advantage the successive rows of peds (semi-circular hampers) as you view them from the bottom. The market women are ranged in equidistant rows, with a regularity little short of military precision; between these rectilinear divisions sufficient space is preserved to admit the concourse of buyers.[26]

82 *Norwich Market Cross.*

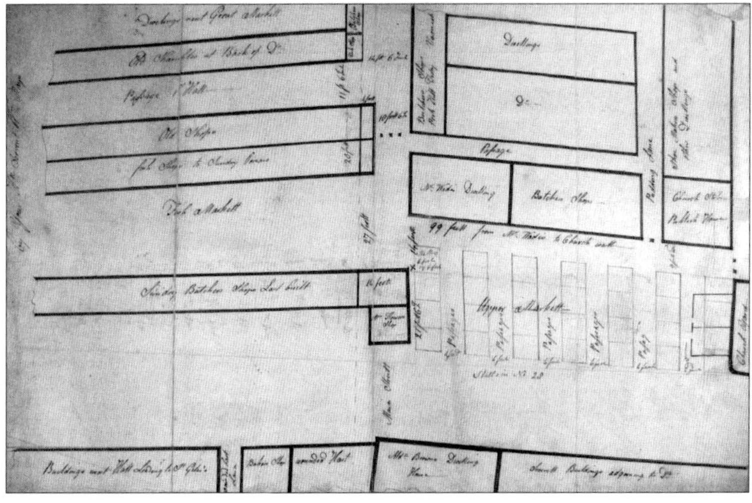

83 *Plan of the market place in the 18th century.*

84 *Gurney's Bank, Bank Plain, at the junction with London Street.*

William Cobbett visited in 1821 and reported:

> The meat and poultry and vegetable market is beautiful. It is kept in a large open square in the middle, or nearly so, of the City. The ground is a pretty sharp slope, so that you see all at once. It resembles one of the French markets, only there the vendors are all standing and gabbling like parrots, and the meat is lean, and bloody, and nasty, and the people snuffy, and grimy, in hands and face, the contrary, precisely the contrary of which is the case, in this beautiful market at Norwich, where the women have a sort of uniform brown great coat, with white aprons and bibs (I think they call them) going from the apron up to the bosom. They equal in neatness (for nothing can surpass) the market women in Philadelphia.

The century saw the beginnings of banking and insurance in the city, serving farmers in the surrounding countryside as well as the city's own residents. The first bank in Norwich was that of Charles Weston, founded in 1756 in the market place. It was one of the first provincial banks in England. Gurney's was founded off Pitt Street in 1775, moving to Redwell Plain in 1779, now Bank Plain in its honour. The bank occupied the house of a wine merchant, Alderman Poole, his wine cellars becoming the bank's vaults. Richard Gurney married into the London banking family Barclays, and Gurney's was a key element in the growth of Barclays Bank into a nationwide concern. Peck's *Directory* of 1802 lists five banking firms in Norwich, and a branch of the Bank of England opened in Norwich in 1827.[27]

The firm that was to become Norwich Union originated in 1783 when Thomas Bignold moved to Norwich from Westerham in Kent. According to the traditional story, he tried to insure his luggage for the journey but was told that kind of insurance just did not exist. He replied, 'There is nothing that is uninsurable, the question is merely would those who would fain be insured pay the price?' The Norwich General Assurance Company was set up in 1792, with Bignold as its secretary. In 1797 he set up the Norwich Union Fire Office, followed by a life insurance office in 1808. The firm soon extended their business into Europe; in the 1820s they had agencies at Bordeaux and Lisbon. The firm operated at first from an office in Gentleman's Walk, but in about 1820 the Bignolds bought the house in Surrey Street (now called Bignold House, beside the present bus station), and later expanded to fill most of the street.[28]

Another firm to become associated with the city was founded in 1823 when John Jarrold and his four sons came to the city in 1823 from Woodbridge. The original business was on the opposite side of London Street to the present firm. He concentrated on printing, book selling and patent medicines, expanding to other goods over the 19th century. Other factories were also being set up to make a wide range of products; Hills and Underwood, vinegar makers, were established in 1762.

Norwich was becoming more than ever a city of shopkeepers. In the 1783 *Directory* there are 40 grocers, 30 butchers, 60 bakers, 30 drapers and mercers, 24 hosiers, hatters and milliners, 12 booksellers and six chemists. Penelope Corfield notes that 13 per cent of those listed in the 1783 *Trade Directory* are women, 208 people in all, including businesswomen and manufacturers: 'the presence of all these women, without fanfare, indicated that economic imperatives were quietly eroding the old cultural and legal barriers to women's business careers'.[29]

Expectations were increasing. In 1793 Edward Leathes wrote home to his mother in Norwich asking for an increase in his clothing allowance:

> I agree with you that Manners make the Man but what are Manners in a ragged coat, dirty waistcoat and threadbare breaches, at the same time I know that a gentleman may appear as well with ten as twenty coats a year, but I by no means wish for either, I shall be content with three.[30]

The Norwich Paving Commissioners were set up in 1806 under an Act for better paving, lighting, cleansing, watching and otherwise improving the city of Norwich. They levied a rate to raise £5,000 a year and paved the main streets, including St Stephen's, St Giles and what is now London Street. The city already had 900 oil lamps, some put up by the corporation and others by individual citizens. The Board increased the number to 1,200 lamps. In the 1820s, gas brought improved lighting to the city. The first gas lamp was the 'Gasolier', a four-branched giant in the centre of the market place; this lasted for about 60 years before being replaced with electricity. Messrs Taylor and Martineau established a small works in what is now Malthouse Road in 1815, using oil – probably whale oil – as fuel. They moved to the site at the bottom of what is now called Gas Hill in 1830, changing their fuel from oil to coal, which was brought by river. Demand led to additional works at World's End, even closer to the river, in 1851. The latter works have since closed, but those at Gas Hill continue to function; the present gas holder, built in 1894, is still a prominent industrial feature of the city.[31]

Communications

In 1745 coaches were advertised in the *Norwich Mercury* as running from Norwich to London over the Christmas period, 'to carry Fowles and presents as usual'; these coaches took three days. According to the *Norfolk Chronicle*, about 6,000 turkeys went to London on the Christmas coaches, and this service continued to run until it were superseded by the railway. In December 1810, 12 carriages were loaded with poultry and game. The first regular coach to the capital was the 'Norwich Machine' from 1762, which took two days. In the summer of 1761 a coach began running from Norwich to London in 20 hours, and the 'Flying Machine' was advertised in 1769 as doing the journey in one day. Mail coaches began to run between Norwich and London in 1785, doing the journey in 15 hours. By 1802 the Norwich Mail Coach Office was running two coaches to London every day, one via Ipswich and one via Newmarket. The new technology frightened some: Parson Woodforde's sister 'shook like an aspin leave' as she took her first ever coach journey from the *Angel* in the market place in 1778.

In 1707 an Act was passed to continue the Acts of 1694-5 for making a turnpike road from Norwich to Thetford, the first turnpike in Norfolk and reputedly the first in England. The road only extended from Hethersett to Attleborough, and did not reach Town Close in Norwich until 1767. Norfolk was slow in turnpiking but a clutch of roads were made in 1770, including those from St Stephen's Gate to Trowse and from Bishop Bridge to Caister, the main road to Yarmouth before the Acle Straight was built. Between 1766 and 1823, 10 of the main roads to the city were taken over by turnpike trustees, who were able to spend much more money on improving them than parish highway surveyors could. Accidents were common; in August 1776 Raven Hardy, aged nine, wrote in his mother's diary, 'Mamma Pappa Billy Polly and I went to Norwich and as we came back overturned the cart and frightened us all out of our wits. Billy hurt his thigh and we thought it had broke.'[32]

In August 1808 a shutter telegraph system between London and Yarmouth via Norwich began to operate. It had 19 stations, including one fixed to a windmill at Thorpe Hill, from which the road name Telegraph Lane is taken. In good visibility a message could travel from London to Yarmouth in 17 minutes. The system was really for military purposes and it closed down in 1815 after the defeat of Napoleon.

A coach service was advertised between Yarmouth and Norwich in 1725; a new boat service was put in operation to rival it, the owners promising that 'no fare was fixed, but it was left wholly to the generosity of the public'. Six people were drowned when the *Royal Charlotte* was overturned by a 'roger' in 1782. Various expedients were tried to speed

up the links, including the introduction of steam power on the river. The first steamship in the UK was in 1812, on the Clyde, with a Norwich-Yarmouth route following in August 1813 when it was advertised that a steam packet owned by Richard Wright would travel between the two towns each day; the journey took a little over three hours and the cost of the trip was 4s. 6d. The steam barge, as it was generally called, was the *Experiment*; it helped keep the river open in the first two weeks of 1814 but the river then froze over and the steam boat service came to an end, starting up again in April. There were other steam boats too, such as the *Nelson*, owned by Thomas Watts, and Wright soon had a second one in service, the *Telegraph*.

On Good Friday 1817, the *Telegraph's* boiler burst just after she had left Foundry Bridge. Eight adults were killed on board, including the steersman William Nickerson, and a two-year-old boy was thrown overboard by the force of the explosion and drowned. Six others were seriously injured and two more of these died later of their injuries. The boiler had only one safety valve and it was apparently overloaded to increase the pressure and hence the power and speed. On 8 May 1817, Charles Harvey, MP for Norwich, raised the question of the safety of steamships in Parliament. A Parliamentary committee recommended that all such boilers should have at least two safety valves, one of which should be inaccessible to the engineman. Harvey drafted a Bill on the subject, but it was lost when Parliament was dissolved in June 1818.[33]

After the disaster, Wright converted the *Experiment* to be run by four horses walking round a platform to create the necessary energy to turn the paddle shaft; the horses were changed halfway. However, Watts continued to operate the *Nelson*, saying Harvey had inspected it and confirmed that it conformed to the committee's recommendations. The Norwich hairdresser John Bilby recorded in his diary that he met a young lady on the *Nelson* on a pleasure trip to Yarmouth in September 1819, who later became his wife.

When Marten visited Norfolk in 1825, he went from London to Yarmouth by paddle steamer, taking 17 hours. From there he took a steam vessel upriver to Norwich and this leg of his journey took five hours; he saw just one other steam vessel, the one travelling downstream, but also 'many large sailing boats (here called wherries) well covered by their hatches and deeply laden'. The speed of this traffic depended on the wind and the tides. The *Excursions* says that an unladen wherry could do the trip between Norwich and Yarmouth in five hours but a laden one took from 12 to 16 hours.[34]

In 1825 it was proposed to build a horse-drawn tramway from Norwich to Ipswich to transport goods from Norfolk to London, but the expense of the scheme put off potential investors. In the same year a road and ship route was established between Norwich and London. This offered fast sailing ships (later a steamship as well) between London and Ipswich to meet goods taken to and from Ipswich by road. However, the service was never reliable because the road between Norwich and Ipswich was so bad. As late as 1846 it was said to be at times almost impassable.[35]

Opposite: 85 *'On the river Wensum' by Henry Ninham; note the women washing clothes in the river.*

The roads and bridges in the city also received attention, probably not before time. Dorothy Wordsworth, the great poet's sister, had been less than impressed with Norwich. She visited the city while staying with her aunt and uncle at Forncett St Peter between 1788 and 1794, writing: 'It is an immensely large place; but the streets in general are very ugly, and they are all so ill-paved and dirty, as almost entirely to take away the pleasure of walking.' Gentleman's Walk was laid out at the end of the century. A manuscript *Guide to Norwich* by William Stephenson says:

> The broad Pavement of Scotch Granite which runs the whole extent of the East Side of the Market Place was erected at the expense of the Owners and occupiers of the respective shops in 179- [*sic*] and will always reflect an honour on their Public Spirit ... This Promenade is on Market Day the rendervaux [*sic*] of the Gentlemen and Farmers and is hence denominated the Gentleman Walk.[36]

Even in 1825, Marten noted that, although the principal streets had flat pavements for the foot passengers, the rest were 'paved with small

86 *The river with several kinds of shipping, Bishop's Bridge in the distance. Note the sheep grazing within the cathedral precincts.*

pebbles and flints uneasy to the foot and on which one cannot walk either steadily or comfortably'. Davey Place, between the market and the castle ditches, was cut through in 1812 at the personal expense of Alderman Davey, who pulled down the *King's Head* hotel to make the space. He is supposed to have caused a sensation by announcing 'Gentlemen I intend to put a hole in the King's Head!' People thought he planned to kill George III and a guard was placed on his house.

Exchange Street was knocked through from the market place to Bedford Street in 1828 and extended down the hill to St Andrew's four years later. In contrast, a chain could be stretched across the north end of St George's Bridge Street to prevent through-traffic. This was a direct ancestor of the permanent posts put up on the bridge at the beginning of the 21st century, once again allowing only pedestrian traffic across the bridge.[37]

87 *Parish boundary signs on the wall of the* Coach and Horses, *Bethel Street.*

Keeping the streets clean and in repair involved the householder much more directly than today. Each ward employed a scavenger whose work including making presentments at court against those who had offended. On 23 August 1734, to take a typical example, the scavenger for the Long Ward (an informal name for East Wymer ward) brought presentments against four men: John Crotch for not taking up his street dirt, John Doyle for making a muck heap at his stable in Pigg Lane, and Thomas Rayner and Samuel Sharp for not sweeping their streets. Occasionally the scavenger himself might be at fault: in 1751 Thomas Pinchion took dirt out of the cockey in St Andrew's but failed to provide carts to remove it, to the annoyance of nearby householders. Failing to sweep one's street was by far the most common cause of complaint, others including placing tubs or laying timber in the street in front of one's house. Street repair was also an issue. In September 1771 the authorities stated that: 'It is the custom of the city of Norwich for the owners or occupiers of houses and grounds to repair and amend the highways as far as their property fronts the same, each occupier repairing as far as the middle of the highway', except where the corporation had been accustomed to make the repairs 'time out of mind'. They were making a case against four men accused of failing to maintain their parts of St Michael at Thorn Lane – Stackhouse Tompson, Jeremiah Russell, John Andrew and a Mr Barrett. Russell was the worst offender: he had 'thrown shitt and rubbish' over the lane as a partial repair, and put down posts to secure the footpath.[38]

Buildings had to be maintained or allowed to fall into ruin. Parts of the deserted Duke's Palace became ruinous; on 24 September 1739 three children were killed when a wall in Duke's Palace Yard fell on them. The tower of St Andrew's Hall fell down in 1712 but the building was still used for corporation banquets and for the Assize Courts. On the advice of the Tonnage Committee the Market Cross was pulled down in 1732; the stone was sold for £125. Mackerell disapproved of this act of destruction, writing: 'Market cross pulled down which in all probability with a little repairing would have stood many ages, for the mortar with which it was built was as hard as the flints themselves and broke several of the workmen's tools in battering it down.' Its octagonal base is now marked out in the paving between the modern market stalls.

The gate on Bishop's Bridge was pulled down in 1791 and the other gates in the city walls soon followed; they had all gone by 1810. They were pulled down because they impeded traffic and also because they were thought to restrict the flow of air and thus encourage the spread of diseases. We know what the gates looked like because drawings survive by John Kirkpatrick (see fig. 29), on which the later paintings by Henry Ninham were based.

The first cast-iron bridge in Norwich was that at Coslany, built by James Frost and opened in 1804, which is still in use but now only for foot traffic. (Sir John Soane's bridge at St George's is earlier – 1783/4 – but only the railings are cast iron; the bridge itself is of stone). Duke's Palace Bridge was opened in 1822. This was also of cast iron, and can still be seen in the city, now part of the entrance to the Castle Mall car park.

Bridges were built as investments, tolls being charged on the Duke's Palace Bridge until 1855, when the corporation took it over. Two rival groups built bridges downstream of Bishop's Bridge, which had been the lowest crossing point for many centuries. Carrow Bridge was built in 1810 as a private toll bridge, mainly used by cows going between Trowse marshes and the cattle market. The bridge, originally a fixed structure, was rebuilt as a swing bridge in 1833 and continued to charge tolls until 1900. The present bridge was built in 1923 on a site 75 yards upstream from the old one.

The first Foundry Bridge was opened in 1811; a 10-year-old boy drowned after falling off the structure when it was being built. It was also a toll bridge, the toll house of which has developed into the *Anglers' Rest* public house. On the opening of the railway a new bridge was built at a cost of £6,000, of which the railway company paid half. The new bridge was toll-free and was replaced by the present bridge in 1888 – it is 50 feet wide and cost £12,000.

'Norwich A Port'

In the 1820s coal was the chief import in Norwich, being unloaded at Yarmouth into barges which could each carry 28 tons up the river. The shipping interests of Norwich and Yarmouth had combined to form the Norwich and Yarmouth Navigation in 1682; the original Act had to be renewed every year. Because Breydon Water is very shallow, boats coming upriver had to draw less than three feet. By the early 19th century some Norwich businessmen were prepared to invest in schemes to deepen the river, the movement becoming known as 'Norwich A Port'; there was once a public house of this name in the city.

William Cubitt, a Norfolk civil engineer, drew up a scheme in 1814. He proposed to dredge the river where needed and to construct a cut along the south side of Breydon Water, which he thought could be done for £35,000. In 1820 he produced an alternative plan to make a new outlet to the sea at Lowestoft instead. The Norwich and Lowestoft Navigation Bill was defeated in Parliament in 1826 but a new Bill was passed in the following year. Cubitt's plan was to widen and deepen the river between Foundry and Carrow bridges, dredge the river to a minimum of 12 feet to Low Street near Reedham, excavate a cut from there to the Waveney, dredge and straighten Oulton Dyke, dig a channel across Oulton Broad, and construct a harbour at Lowestoft, then just a fishing village. There would need to be a lock between Lake Lothing and Oulton Broad. The cost was now estimated to be £100,000. The first spadeful of earth was dug in 1827 by Crisp Brown, a city alderman, maltster and prominent supporter of the 'Norwich A Port' movement.

There were difficulties at the Norwich end, because of problems in getting beneath Bishop's Bridge and a fall in the water levels after alterations to Yarmouth Harbour in 1826-7. The usual way of getting a wherry under the city bridges was by 'bowsing', running a line out to a convenient post and hauling the boat forwards; according to Robert Malster it 'was not unknown' for a wherry to take three days to get the mile and a half from Bishop's Bridge to New Mills in the 1830s.[39]

The 'New Cut' across the marshes at Reedham to Lowestoft opened on 30 September 1833 when the first two ships – the *Squire* and the *City of Norwich* – arrived in the city. Norwich was a port at last but the celebrations were muted as the son of the master of the *City of Norwich* had fallen overboard in Surlingham Reach and drowned. The new waterway was put to good use in April 1834 when the *Sarah* took 54 convicts directly from Norwich to Australia, saving the county the expense of taking them to London overland. Crisp Brown did not live to see his dream come true, dying in 1830 while on an Atlantic voyage.

Health

Georgian Norwich saw the establishment of two hospitals that served the city well into the 20th century – the Bethel and the 'Norfolk and Norwich'. Mary Chapman, the founder of the Bethel, was born in 1647, the daughter of John Mann, an alderman of Norwich. In 1682 she married Samuel Chapman, who became rector of Thorpe in 1670. He died in 1700, leaving £200 each for the Children's and Doughty's Hospitals. On 24 February 1712 his widow, Mary, took a lease from the corporation of the Committee House and adjoining land for 1,000 years at a peppercorn rent. A very detailed agreement was drawn up with Richard Starling, carpenter, and Edward Freeman, mason, to build the hospital; the total cost of the building was to be £314 2s. 6d.

The hospital was intended for curable lunatics who were citizens of Norwich too poor to pay for their own treatment. The first recorded patient fulfilling these terms was Philip Lewis, who was admitted in 1725; he was a former apprentice with a carpenter in Newgate. He had been disordered in his senses for five years and his brother could not afford to look after him any longer. Those whose family could afford to pay might also be admitted on a scale of charges up to a maximum of eight shillings a week. Many citizens of Norwich gave generously to the Bethel and their names were recorded on donation boards. They included Benjamin Wrench, the physician who attended the hospital for 22 years from 1725; he gave back his entire salary which amounted to £352. The largest donation was £2,733 9s. 2d. by George England in 1897. Three gifts of £1,000 each were by Bartholomew Balderston and Thomas Vere in 1766, and by Robert Denn in 1829.[40]

For the wealthy, there were private lunatic asylums. Mary Hardy's diary records that on 30 June 1777 she visited Red House, a private mental home off Queen's Road; 'every patient there cost a 100 guineas a year'.[41]

William Fellowes is regarded as the founder of the Norfolk and Norwich Hospital, but he brought to fruition a scheme which had been long discussed. The Voluntary Hospital System had begun in 1719, and by 1750 11 towns had them. As early as 1744 a letter to the *Norwich Gazette* advocated that Norfolk should follow the example of Devon and set up a county hospital. Thomas Hayter, the Bishop of Norwich between 1749 and 1761, chaired meetings in the city on the subject. In 1758 he asked Benjamin Gooch to examine the hospitals in London with a view to establishing a county hospital, and plans were prepared. There was a loss of momentum when Hayter left Norwich, but in August 1770 William Fellowes called an open meeting and a subscription fund was opened. Three acres of land were acquired, leased from the Great Hospital at a token rent of £6 a year – with a proviso that this should be doubled if the premises ceased to be used for hospital purposes.

William Ivory was appointed architect, and gave his services for four years without charge. Progress then was rapid: the first out-patients were seen in July 1772 and the first in-patients were admitted in November of the same year. The first staff of the hospital consisted of four physicians and four surgeons, all unpaid.[42]

The 'Norfolk and Norwich' was founded as a charity, and it received only patients recommended by subscribers as being too poor to pay. Casualties were admitted but, if they were able to, they had to pay one shilling a day subsistence; as early as 1774 the management decided to charge a patient who was 'above the need of charitable help'. It became famous for its treatment of bladder stones, which was unusually common in Norfolk, suggesting that the diet was poor and over-dependent on cereals.

The hospital soon built up a good reputation. Woodforde visited it on 2 April 1789 and wrote:

> I think I never saw an Hospital kept in a better and more clean, airy manner. All the poor Creatures in it appeared quite cheerful and grateful in their present complaints. I saw there a Stone that was taken out of a man by Mr Donne, and the man now living, of a most extraordinary Nature, called the Mulberry Stone, the Colour and make of the Mulberry, but very large. The poor man was a long time under the Operation.

In 1805 James Neild inspected the Norfolk and Norwich and said, 'It does honour to the county, and is one of the best I have seen.'

Opposite: 88 *The water supply: the New Mills and the proposed reservoir in Chapelfield.*

Benjamin Gooch was the leading surgeon in East Anglia in the 18th century. He published a textbook of surgery in 1758 and was the innovator of 'Gooch's splints', which were in common use until the 1920s when they were replaced by plaster of Paris. Gooch also played a leading part in the founding of the Norfolk and Norwich Hospital. Another well-known doctor in the city was James Alderson, who prescribed without charge for 400-500 people every week at his house in Colegate. In 1768 Norwich was divided into three districts for medical purposes, and the first three district surgeons were William Donne, Joseph Rogers and David Martineau.[43]

One institution that continues to flourish in the 21st century is that for the blind, in Magpie Road/Magdalen Street, founded by Thomas Tawell (who had himself become blind) in 1805. It was meant both as an asylum for the old and a school for the young. Thomas Tawell's monument in the cathedral tells the story:

> In the year 1805 he purchased a spacious dwelling House with extensive garden Grounds in St Paul's in this City and settled them by legal Instruments for a perpetual Hospital and School for Indigent Blind Persons. This magnificent Gift, aided by the Patronage of other benevolent Characters have secured an Asylum for the pitiable Objects of his Bounty whose melancholy Situation he could but too well estimate having himself passed many Years deprived of the Blessing of Sight.

The old were admitted at the age of 55, while pupils were admitted at the age of 12 and stayed until they had learned a skill or trade. The young girls were employed in knitting and netting, the boys in making rope, twine, sacks, baskets, carpeting and rope mats. Tawell died in 1820 and his monument is within the chantry of Bishop Richard Nykke, who was himself 'decrepit and blind' when he died some 400 years earlier.[44]

Inoculation against smallpox by giving the patient a mild attack was practised in England from the 18th century but it was risky – not only might the attack be fatal but the disease might spread to others. Blomefield was an opponent of inoculation and dreaded catching the disease; he stayed away from Norwich several times in the 1740s when smallpox was rampant and this delayed his work on the Norwich section of his *History*, almost allowing his bitter rival Benjamin Mackerell to get his own history of Norwich into print first. Blomefield's father had died of smallpox in 1737 so his fear was understandable, and in 1752, at the age of 47, he did indeed die from smallpox. To prevent the spread of smallpox the inoculation was done in special 'inoculation houses'. In 1784 Parson Woodforde visited one near St Stephen's church in Norwich where the four children of Squire Custance of Weston Longville were inoculated.[45]

In the 19th century vaccination slowly replaced inoculation in the fight against smallpox. In 1805 it was announced that nearly 400 of the poor in the city had been vaccinated. In 1812 Edward Rigby persuaded the Guardians of the Poor to pay 2s. 6d. to any of the poor who produced a

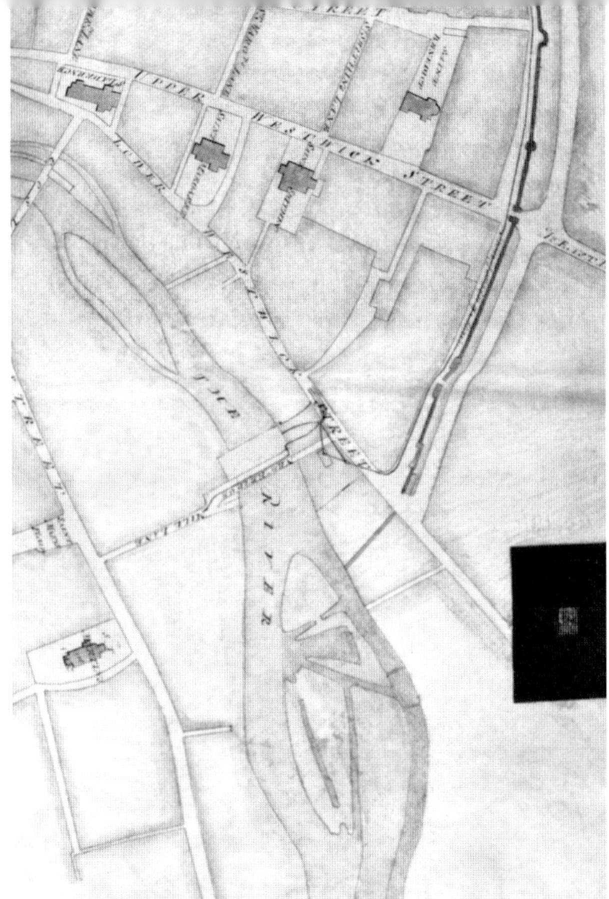

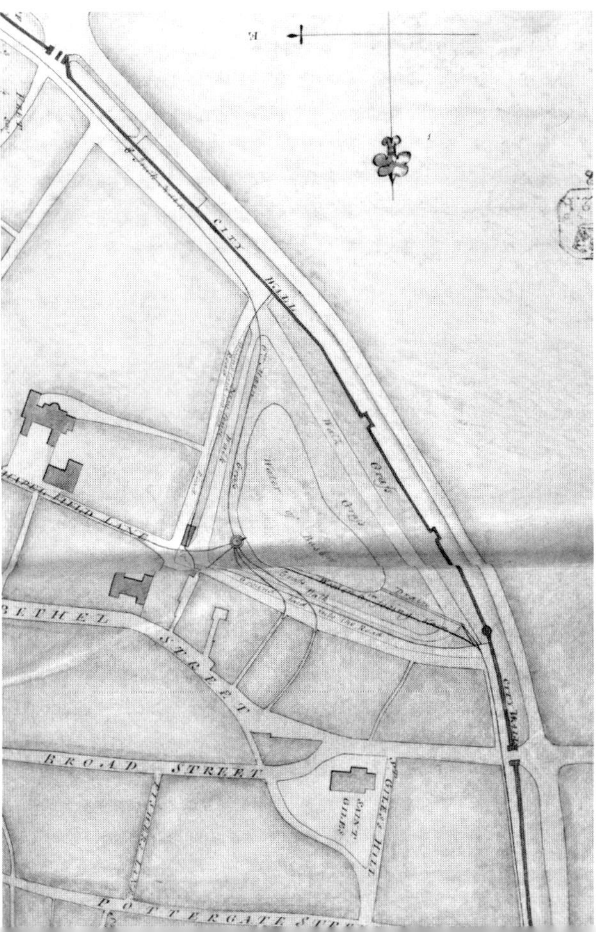

certificate of vaccination and the scheme made Rigby nationally famous. However, smallpox broke out in 1813 with 65 deaths in the city, and in 1819 there were over 500 deaths from smallpox in Norwich between January and September, nearly all of children.

The early 19th century saw many new private charitable bodies set up in the health field. A Dispensary was opened in Pottergate in 1804 to render medical and surgical help to the poor; 'about 2,000 are relieved yearly'. Norwich Society for Relieving the Sick Poor was founded in 1815 and run by a committee of ladies who visited the poor in their homes, giving money, linen and flannel. The society was funded by donations and by annual sales.

The Norfolk and Norwich Infirmary for the cure of eye disease was established in Pottergate in 1822. The Norfolk and Norwich Magdalen was founded on Life's Green in the Close in 1827 'to afford an asylum to females who have deviated from the paths of virtue and may be desirous of being restored to their station in Society. 385 have passed through the house and many are now in respectable situations.' As the Close was increasingly becoming a haven for the 'respectable', some objected to the Magdalen being there. Dean Pellew moved a chestnut tree in the Deanery garden so he would not see the house from his back windows. In the 1840s the Magdalen was moved to Chapelfield.[46]

One of the great risks to health was the water supply. Most of the poor drew their water from wells or from the river. William Arderon was appointed clerk and manager at the New Mills in about 1729, at a salary of £60 a year. He wrote of 'the too frequent practice in Norwich of turning their Old Wells into Boghouses, this undoubtedly mixes with the waters that supply other wells and makes them vastly unwholesome as well as intollerably disagreeable'. Apart from the quality of the water, it was dangerous enough just to fetch it; in 1760 Sarah Batcheler, aged 10, drowned falling off a defective staithe in St Martin at Oak while fetching a pitcher of water. In 1784 an old man fell into the river and drowned while fetching water at St Anne's staithe. Conditions were even more difficult in winter; in December 1784, 11-year-old John Miller slipped on the icy staithe when fetching water, fell in to the river and drowned.

The first attempt to provide water to parts of the city through lead pipes was made by two London plumbers in 1584; water was conveyed to the market place, making use of a cistern in the tower of St Lawrence church. A century later there was a reservoir in Tombland, which was taken down and replaced with an obelisk in 1786. The present obelisk was put up by J.H. Gurney in 1860 when the first was taken down, but, sadly, no longer provides water. In 1788 Robert Mylne was commissioned to report on the waterworks. On the expiry of the current lease on the New Mills in 1793, the corporation advertised for proposals to improve the water supply, and in 1794 they accepted those of William White and Robert Crane. Their plan included building a reservoir on Chapelfield. They appointed Joseph Bramah as their engineer. Mylne was asked to report on the progress of the works and his highly critical report appeared in 1798, followed by Bramah's equally spirited defence. The reservoir was an added city attraction but also an added danger – two 13-year-old boys, Charles Stiles and James Nudds, died after falling through the ice when playing on the reservoir in 1808 and 1813 respectively.

Industrial accidents were common. In 1820 Stephen Sutton, aged 18, was struck on the head by a sail while working at his master's mill in Pockthorpe. He was taken to the Norfolk and Norwich Hospital where he died. In 1824 Edmond Hurne aged 56 and Noah Larter aged 64 were at work with four other men at their master's marl pit in Thorpe. They were barrowing away earth and sand to reach the chalk when the earth collapsed under them – they fell 60 or 70 feet and were buried under 30 or 40 cartloads of earth. It took half an hour to dig them out, by which time both men were dead. Inquests like theirs give a sense of the 18th-century city; those for a typical year, 1737, are listed in Table III.

Table III: *Inquests in Norwich, May to December 1737*

18 May	George Bilby	17	Hanged himself from his loom
31 May	William Fulcher	16	Went to wash himself at Fullers' Hole and drowned
3 July	Esther Maltby	2	Pitched her head into a tub of water in the garden and drowned
25 July	John Middleton	9	Kicked by a colt at Magdalen Fair
6 Aug	Benjamin Sheppard	34	Hanged himself from a loom
11 Aug	John Balls	35	When digging for marl, stifled by earth falling on him
11 Aug	Samuel Green	25	When digging for marl, stifled by earth falling on him
11 Aug	William Newhouse	50	When digging for marl, stifled by earth falling on him
17 Aug	Susan Ward	47	Poisoned herself
1 Sep	Sarah Hott	17	'visited by the hand of God - natural death'
23 Sep	Samuel Lane	30	Hanged himself
7 Oct	Samuel Norton	5	While playing on a staithe between Coslany and Blackfriars Bridge, fell into the river and drowned
12 Oct	Elizabeth Lefevre	79	While asleep by the fire, her clothes caught alight
1 Nov	Robert Trollop	22	Hanged himself from his loom
7 Dec	William Webster	40	Hanged himself

Source: *NRO, NCR 6a, City Inquests.*

The Poor

In the 1770s Norwich workhouse had an average of 1,200 inmates in winter; 600 were able-bodied and the rest were either children or 'impotent' poor. The population of the city was between 20,000 and 30,000 and so perhaps one person in 25 was living in the workhouse. For some the workhouse conditions proved unbearable: William Priest, aged 32, threw himself from a window in Duke's Palace workhouse in 1798. On 8 May 1827 an inquest held at the *Trowel and Hammer* heard that on 2 May Francis Clark, aged 11, and another boy called John Smith, being 'Paupers in the Workhouse in the parish of St Andrew', tried to escape from the workhouse through the privy. Smith climbed on to the privy roof with a muck fork to try to raise the spars of the roof. Unfortunately he dropped the fork, which fell and struck Clark on the head. He was taken to the Norfolk and Norwich Hospital where he lingered until 7 May, when he died.

For the Guardians the problem was always to provide a subsistence allowance for the poor without alienating the ratepayers. Maximilian de Lazowski wrote about his visit to Norwich in 1784: 'The Poor Tax is enormous. It is 8s. 4d. in the pound sterling on the rent of each house. There are surely very few examples of a tax as high as this. It amounts in all to £18,000 sterling (last year, but it is not usually so much).' The Guardians were always looking for economies they could make. They decided it was cheaper to buy bread from the baker than make it themselves because the workhouse inmates did not have the skills – 'a great waste of flour had been made, an extravagant quantity of yeast had been used, and the dough so improperly compounded and so imperfectly fermented as not to admit of the due increase'. In the same way, they decided in 1788 that it was cheaper to buy beer than to make it themselves.[47]

In October 1805 James Neild wrote to the *Gentleman's Magazine* about the conditions in the Duke's Palace workhouse:

> The building is old. The average number in the house about five hundred and fifty. In the first room I visited there were forty two beds, ten of them cribs for single persons, and the others had two in each, there being seventy-four persons in this room. At the entrance, and in the room, is a most offensive and indecent privy, something like a watchman's box, and so much out of repair, and so situated, that the sexes cannot be separated when decency most requires it. The paupers ate, drank and slept on their beds, having no other room to live in … In the boys' room were offensive tubs as urinals; these are emptied daily into a sink in the room, and it did not appear to have been lately washed. One bed in the room was particularly offensive; from an infirmity of the boy who slept in it, his urine passed completely through the bedding, and was suffered to accumulate on the floor to a very putrid degree.

However, Norwich did not allow this savage indictment to go unchallenged. John Gurney wrote a long reply to the *Gentleman's Magazine* in December 1805, claiming that the privy Neild objected to was in fact 'a night-stool, enclosed in a box as described applied to the use of those whose age or infirmity disqualified them from going downstairs'. He said Neild was wrong to say it was used by both sexes – the room was a male ward and the only female there was a wife of one of the paupers who acted as a nurse. Gurney admitted that the inmates had no other room to go to but denied totally the criticism of the boys' ward: 'I am well assured the vessels described were every morning emptied and cleaned, and that the floor under the particular bed described was so frequently washed as to render a putrid accumulation impossible.'[48]

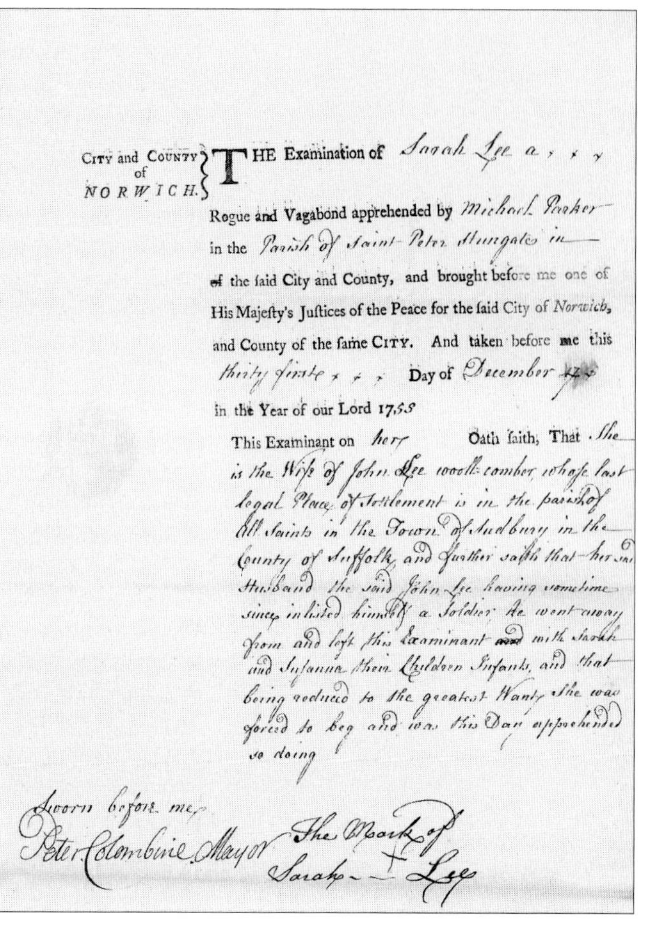

CITY and COUNTY of NORWICH. THE Examination of Sarah Lee a , , ,
Rogue and Vagabond apprehended by Michael Parker
in the Parish of Saint Peter Hungate in
of the faid City and County, and brought before me one of His Majefty's Juftices of the Peace for the faid City of *Norwich*, and County of the fame CITY. And taken before me this thirty first , , , Day of December [illegible]
in the Year of our Lord 1755

This Examinant on her Oath faith, That She is the Wife of John Lee woolcomber whose last legal Place of Settlement is in the parish of All Saints in the Town of Sudbury in the County of Suffolk and further saith that her said Husband the said John Lee having sometime since inlisted himself a Soldier He went away from and left this Examinant with Sarah and Susanna their Children Infants, and that being reduced to the greatest Want She was forced to beg and was this Day apprehended so doing

Sworn before me,
Peter Colombine Mayor
The Mark of Sarah + Lee

89 *Examination of Sarah Lee, left destitute after her husband deserted her and their two children; she was sent back to her home town of Sudbury.*

In 1812 Neild raised the case of one boy in the workhouse who was forced every night to sleep in an iron collar with projecting prongs and with a large log chained to his ankle. The authorities said he was an incorrigible thief and absconder and this was the only way he could be restrained. There was another benefit: 'it acts as an example to deter other paupers from similar misconduct'.[49]

Private citizens continued to leave bequests to the less well-off in their city. Peter Seaman, mayor in 1709, left the thatched house in St Swithin's Alley and land in St Julian's parish, the profits from the properties to be used to pay for apprenticing poor boys. John Norman was mayor in 1714; he died in 1724 and is buried in Catton church. He left his estate for educating and apprenticing sons of his relatives and of his first wife, and 60 years after his death for erecting a hospital for boys. Norman's charity still helps fund the education of the alderman's descendants.[50]

Penny Corfield says that Norwich must have had at least 400 'incomers' every year in the 1670s and 1680s to explain the population growth, and a similar sort of figure must have applied throughout the 18th century. Because the authorities tried to send the destitute back to where they came from, records of their examinations provide details of the lives of a class of people otherwise poorly recorded. Between 1742 and 1762, 433 paupers and vagrants were removed from the city to their place of origin. Of these 40 per cent came from East Anglia but the others came from further afield: 33 per cent from Scotland and 16 per cent from Ireland. Sixty years later, patterns of movement were much the same. Between January and September 1828, Norwich magistrates examined 269 people applying for relief, of whom 79 claimed to have legal settlement in the city, 132 came from elsewhere in Norfolk, 25 from Suffolk and 22 from elsewhere in England. Five came from further afield: three from Ireland, one from Scotland and one from Guernsey. David Souden estimates that urban-born immigrants came to Norwich from an average distance of 93 kilometres away.[51]

There appears to have been a rounding up of vagrants in the winter of 1759-60: 25 people came before the courts, most being sentenced to a deterrent term in the Bridewell followed by a public whipping in the market place on market day and a forced return to their place of legal settlement. Six were men, and three of these, Edward Wright, James and Thomas Leadbeater, were each sentenced to six months. Most of the women received sentences of 14 days to three months, although the variation was very wide, from just one night, up to the full six months for Elizabeth Grimes. There was no clear pattern either to the length of sentence or to the whipping. In only one case is the quantity of the latter specified – Elizabeth Thomas received 20 lashes – and no reason is given for the occasional decision to have a private whipping. In two cases, those of Catherine Tatlock and Mary Tompson, the decision as to a private or public punishment is left to the mayor. In just one of the 25 cases is a concern shown for health, Hannah Frankling being sentenced to three months in the Bridewell, but 'in the meantime the doctor to do what is necessary unto her'; she is also one of the very few not be given a whipping. After serving their time, the vagrant would be given a pass to go back to their home parish, wherever that was (only one is specified, Mary Quintin from Wymondham), and be taken by the officials to just outside the gates at St Stephen's. This may not always have been effective; there is at least one case of a woman left outside the gates who simply went back in, to appear again before the magistrates a little while later.[52]

However, poor people were not always sent back home. There was a whole group of Essex paupers living in Norwich who received a weekly allowance of two shillings each from the overseers of the poor of Braintree parish, sent by bank order to the overseers of Norwich, who then handed it out to them. The Braintree paupers were even visited several times by representatives of their parish vestry to see if their allowances should be continued. Susan Spooner and her bedridden sister were living in Norwich but their place of settlement was Braintree. In 1831 the representatives said of the Spooner sisters, 'both weave Silk but can get very little to do – a complaint general throughout the trade'.[53]

A few came from even further away, adding to the cosmopolitan mix in the city. Marten was accosted in a city street by 'two Italian Image lads', trying to sell paintings and busts of famous figures. He surprised them by speaking in their language, learning that they were originally from Florence, and had walked to Norwich from London carrying their goods on their heads; the journey had taken them five days. There were some black and minority ethnic residents of Georgian Norwich as well, such as James Albert, a black abolitionist who worked as a weaver in the city in the 1760s, and the two men known only as 'Cotton' and 'Charley' painted by John Dempsey in the 1820s, whose portraits are now in the Tasmanian Museum and Art Gallery. One 'vagrant' who died in the

Bridewell was Samuel Turner, a native of Martinique in the West Indies; he was 69 years old when on 29 January 1819 he was confined, 'in a very weak state of health, being troubled with a spitting of blood, and languished until Thursday [11] February when he died'. There were black servants in the city, too, such as William Darby, whose more famous son is mentioned in the next chapter, and Joseph Diana, servant to Robert Herring in Bracondale: he later moved to a new employer in Fakenham, and was sentenced to seven years transportation for theft in 1792.

Marten noted the same characteristic of Norwich that had struck Harrington, another visitor from London, two and half a centuries earlier: during his walks over several days he was not accosted by a single beggar.

The Bridewell

There was a major fire at the Bridewell in 1751, described in the local newspapers such as the *Norwich Mercury*:

> Fire broke out last Tuesday morning [22 October] at about 2 am in a warehouse in Bridewell Alley belonging to Mr Britiff, household broker – the most terrible, before it was extinguished, that has been known in this city for many years. The flames in a very short time extended to the City Bridewell, and entirely consumed the same, with several houses adjoining. Volunteers worked at the fire engines, and carried buckets of water, but the fire was not got under control until six in the morning.

At the next assembly, it was noted that Joseph Chamberlain had presented two new fire engines to the city.

The most well-known inhabitant of the Bridewell was Peter the Wild Man, who was there at the time of the fire. The story appears in the *Norwich Mercury* of 9 November 1751:

> About two months since a man near 40 years of age with a wild countenance and long beard was taken up for strolling in the streets. When the fire broke out, he would not make his escape with the other prisoners and was unwilling to be moved to the workhouse. When any questions were ask'd him, he always answered by a strange noise that could not be understood.

Naturally, Norwich people could not know his name or where he came from, but eventually someone saw the following advertisement in the *London Evening Post*:

> Lost or strayed away, from Broadway in the parish of Northchurch, near Berkhamstead in the county of Hertford, about three months ago, Peter the Wild Youth, a black hairy man, about five feet eight inches high; he cannot speak to be understood, but makes a kind of humming noise, and answers in that manner to the name of Peter. Whoever will bring him to Mr Thomas Fenn's, at the place above said, shall receive all reasonable charges, and a handsome gratuity.

Peter was returned to Broadway. He had first been found in the woods near Hamelin in Germany in 1726 'walking on his hands and feet, climbing trees like a squirrel, and feeding on grass and moss'. He appeared to be about 14 years old. He was brought to London by George I, becoming the sensation of the season in fashionable society, and is mentioned by Swift and Defoe. However, his moment of fame soon passed and he was boarded out at the king's expense. He was of low intelligence and became an alcoholic but lived to a good age, dying in 1785. The name of the *Wild Man* for the adjoining public house comes from this period, being first recorded in October 1751.

The Bridewell was rebuilt and the new building continued as a place of enforced residence for vagabonds, prostitutes and petty criminals. Eleven women were in the Bridewell awaiting trial in November 1779; three (Rebecca Fickling, Elizabeth Turner and Elizabeth Virgo) were accused of fornication in the open air. They were presumably prostitutes, but in no case is any man accused with them. Three others were committed for the 'crime' of rough-sleeping (Anne Tuck in an outhouse in St Stephens; Elizabeth Girte 'found wandering and lodging in the open air', also in St Stephens; Elizabeth Smith 'found wandering and lodging in an alehouse in St John Sepulchre, without giving a good account of herself or having any legal settlement'). Five were committed not for any crime but merely on reputation – Anne Whitred and Anne Chapman as 'lewd, idle, disorderly person of ill fame and bad repute', and Anne Vines, Anne Spillman and Anne Huble as of 'ill fame and bad report'. All had been committed by one of the aldermen, usually the mayor, John Thurlow, and had been in the Bridewell for some time, Anne Tuck for just five days short of six months – on the command of one alderman, and without having faced any kind of trial.

Other examples of people in the Bridewell included two Blofield girls who, according to C.B. Jewson, went on a shop-lifting spree in the city in 1791, taking two women's hats from Oxley's shop on the Walk, linen from John Browne's ironmongery and books and cards from William Stephenson's shop, where they had gone pretending they wanted to buy a children's book. They were tried by the Assize court and sentenced to six months' hard labour and solitary confinement in the Bridewell. Elizabeth Larter was sentenced to three months in the Bridewell for theft in April 1801, but with no mention of further punishment; in contrast, Alice Jones, found guilty at the same court of stealing a calf's head worth a shilling, was sentenced to 12 months in the Bridewell – with the extra punishments of solitary confinement and hard labour.[54]

Three babies died in the Bridewell in this period, short-term residents staying with their mothers, classed as vagrants. Thomas Sweeten aged just 14 weeks was in a consumptive state when he died in 1784, and one-year-old Thomas Rants died of smallpox in 1827; both were with their mothers. The most tragic case was in November 1809, when a heavily pregnant Elizabeth Sparrow was picked up as a vagrant. Suffering from typhus fever, she gave birth to a son, Anthony, in the Bridewell and died, probably on the same day; just four days later, baby Anthony, 'suffering stoppages and convulsions', followed his mother to the grave.

Several people killed themselves in the Bridewell. In June 1801 Benjamin Pygall, aged 24, slit his throat with a pruning knife while he was being held there; he was awaiting trial for stealing horses and turning them into dog meat. The inquest verdict was suicide and the return is endorsed 'Paid for burial of Benjamin Pygall in the public Highway £1. 1s. 0d.'; he must have been one of the last people in England to suffer this fate. His clothes and possessions passed to the authorities, and were listed. He had eight shillings and a halfpenny in cash – and also an 'old silver watch' which was sold for 18s. The clothes he was wearing were one twill slop, one fustian jacket, one linen waistcoat, one pair fustian breeches, one shirt, one pair worsted stockings, one silk handkerchief. He had no other possessions.[55]

Other people were sent to the Bridewell as a punishment for misbehaviour in the workhouse, such as John Fox in 1763. He had cut a piece of crape upon a loom in the workhouse as an act of defiance; he was removed to the Bridewell for a short time and then taken back to the workhouse to receive 20 lashes of the whip. All the poor people and children in the institution were ordered to watch – once again, the punishment was used as a deterrent. In 1769 the Guardians ordered that disorderly persons committed 'to that part of the workhouse called Bridewell' should have no provisions sent to them except bread, unless they were ill; the Bridewell was part of the workhouse system as well as the prison system in Norwich.

In 1826 Gabriel Bell 'hanged himself, with a blanket and a handkerchief tied together, from an iron grating fastened into the window frame in his cell'. By this time, central government was making increasing demands on prisons, emphasising the need for work, and for classification and separation of different groups of prisoners. The Bridewell introduced a treadmill in the 1820s, but its small yard did not allow for segregation of prisoners. When the new city gaol was opened, it replaced both the old gaol and the Bridewell; the latter was sold and became a tobacco factory and later a shoe factory.

The campaign against slavery

Norwich was one of the leading cities in the campaign against the slave trade, one of the great issues of the late 18th century. Norwich Quakers were very active in the campaign, both collectively and as individuals. Anthony Benezet, an American Quaker opposed to slavery, corresponded with John and Henry Gurney of Norwich in 1772. In 1783 the Yearly Meeting petitioned Parliament against the slave trade; signatories included members of the Gurney family and also David Barclay and Samuel Hoare from London, both related to the Gurneys. They set up a committee, which distributed pamphlets such as 'The Case of Our Fellow-Creature, the Oppressed Africans' issued by the National Committee.

Such petitions were an important weapon in the campaign, and several were organised by individuals and others by the city assembly. A 'numerous and respectable' meeting on 8 February 1792 unanimously agreed to send a petition to the Commons against the African slave traffic, and when the Quarterly Assembly of the corporation met later in the month they drew up a parallel petition for the abolition of a trade 'so disgraceful to a Christian country and incompatible with the sentiments or feelings of humanity.'

Other people took direct action by boycotting products made by slave labour, especially sugar. This was something in which women could take the lead as they usually made the purchases for the household. Some households stopped using sugar altogether, but more commonly people only bought sugar produced by free labour. The *Norfolk Chronicle*, whose editor, William Stephenson, was a leading campaigner against the slave trade, supported the cause:

> The consumption of sugar in this country is so immense that the quantity used by individuals will have an important effect. A family that uses five pounds of sugar per week, with the proportion of rum, will, by abstaining from the consumption twenty-one months, prevent the slavery or murder of **ONE FELLOW CREATURE**; eight such families in 19 years and a half, prevent the slavery of 100; and 38,000 would totally prevent the slave trade to supply our islands. Nay, so necessarily connected are our consumption of the commodity, and the misery resulting from it, that in every pound of sugar used (the produce of slaves imported from Africa) we may be considered as consuming two ounces of human flesh, besides an alarming number of seamen destroyed by the slave trade, and the inconceivable anguish and misery that must result from parents being torn from their families, villages burnt, and continual suspicion, terror and dismay spread through an extensive country. A Frenchman observes that he cannot look on a piece of sugar without conceiving it ***stained with spots of human blood***. It is therefore incumbent on us **TO ABSTAIN FROM THE USE OF SUGAR AND RUM, until our West Indian planters themselves have prohibited the importation of additional slaves, and commenced as speedy and effectual a subversion of slavery in their islands, as the circumstances and situation of the slaves will admit; or till we can obtain the produce of the sugar cane in some other mode, unconnected with slavery and unpolluted with blood.**

Norwich became one of the leading towns in this boycott, a Birmingham newspaper writing in 1791 that in Norwich 'sugar is now positively banished from the most polite and fashionable tea-tables'.

One leading anti-slavery campaigner was Ouladah Equiano, one of the few former slaves to have left a written record of their experiences. In 1789 he published his autobiography, *The Interesting Narrative of the Life of Olaudah Equiano, or Gustavus Vassa, the African*. It went through many editions and has been described as 'the most important single literary contribution to the campaign for the abolition of slavery'. Norfolk people paid for a new edition of the book to be published in

Norwich in 1794. The names of the subscribers are listed in the front; they include many well-known names such as the surgeons James Alderson, Joseph Clover and Edward Rigby, and members of the Gurney and Martineau families.

After the slave trade had been abolished by Britain in 1807, British navy ships patrolled the ocean, taking control of ships full of slaves in order to give them their freedom. The freed slaves usually went to Sierra Leone to start a new life, but three African boys taken out of a Portuguese slave ship by Captain Irby of the frigate *Amelia* were sent by him to Norwich for education; they were baptised at St Peter Mancroft on 30 May 1813. The fact that these three were brought back must mean they were too young to look after themselves, and that they had no one on board the ship to care for them. They were given the names of Paulo Loando, Edward Mackenzie, and Charles Fortunatus Freeman. We do not know what their African names had been nor what happened to them in later life. They emerge from anonymity just for one moment in this Norwich church two centuries ago.

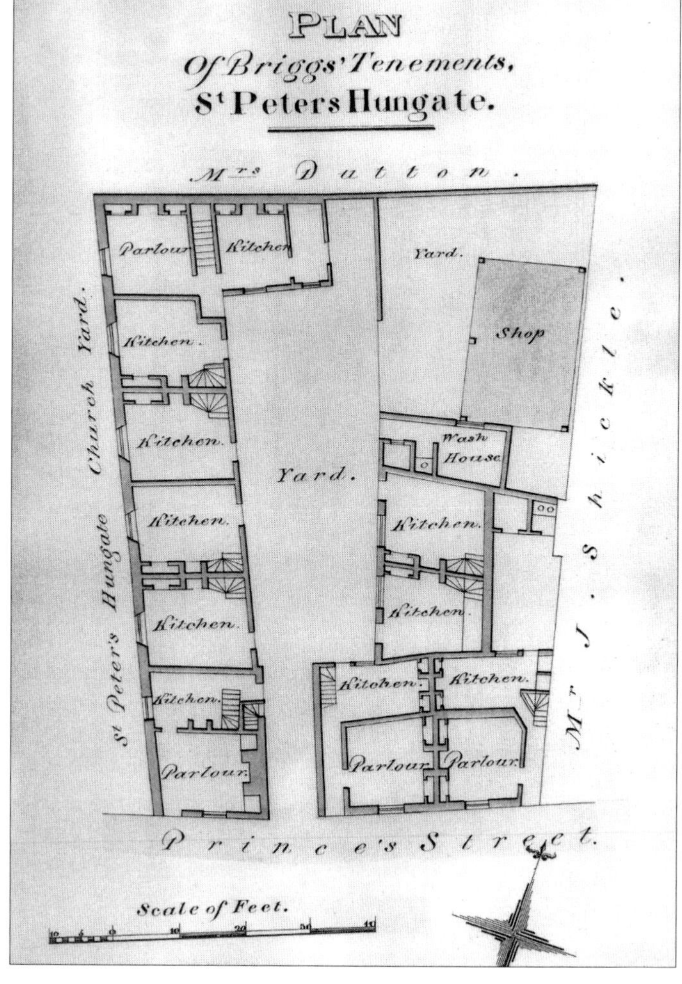

90 *Murrell's yard, St Peter Hungate; note the communal wash house and privy.*

There was a second campaign in the 1820s to abolish not just the slave trade but the institution of slavery itself. The boycott and the petition were again important weapons, and Norwich was once again in the forefront: Elizabeth Fry and Thomas Fowell Buxton have had their work in this field commemorated in plaques on the wall of the Quaker Meeting House in Upper Goat Lane. William Smith also campaigned for the cause, presenting Parliament with an anti-slavery petition organised after a meeting at St Andrew's Hall in 1828; it had 10,125 signatures and was 150 feet long.

Housing

Norwich had many fine houses, some of which are shown around Corbridge's map of 1724; 13 families in St Peter Mancroft had five or more servants in 1694. In contrast were the slum areas, especially along the river where the poor people crowded together in alleys and yards. One of the poorest parishes was St Peter Parmountergate, where W. Hudson analysed the people who voted in 1768: 114 people cast their votes and their names are recorded. Hudson compared the names with those who paid church rates – only 27 of them did so. All the others were presumably in holdings of rentals of less than 40 shillings value.[56]

There were still no sewers in the modern sense, and toilets were in outside sheds from which the night soil had to be removed. In 1749 Daniel Steward, 'whilst in the privy house belonging to the house of John Thaxter, the boards at the back being old and decayed, fell into the receptacle and suffocated'. The inquest jury, on hearing this, tried to fine the owner of the house 40 shillings for his negligence but the coroner appears to have been unsure if they had the power to do this. Many people naturally used the river as a public convenience and there are several inquests for people who drowned when they fell from staithes while relieving themselves.

The low-lying part of the city was, as always, liable to floods. In October 1762, eight churches and between two and three thousand houses were underwater, while on 27 February 1784 Neville recorded that the lower parts of the town were flooded, with boats plying in the streets.[57]

Fire remained a constant danger. There was a Christmas Day tragedy in 1766 when George Ward's house on Ber Street burnt down; Ward and two sons escaped, but his wife, two children, his mother, an infant grandchild (Lucy Nixon) and a maidservant (17-year-old Elizabeth Garrod) all died. The strength of the fire can be deduced from the entry in the St John Sepulchre burial register: 'These six where all burn and the remains buried in one coffin'. The inquest jury decided that the cause was 'a linen sheet hanging near a fire in the parlour catching fire'. Fatal accidents where children or elderly people allowed their clothes to catch alight were common. On 30 September 1746 the Shire House on Castle Hill was completely destroyed by fire and in February 1773 two felons died in a blaze at the county gaol.

Lazowski was not impressed when he visited the city in 1784: 'Norwich, like all ancient cities, is badly planned and built. It is not that there are no good or beautiful houses, but a well built house on a bad site or in a narrow street can never appear more than mediocre.' However, there are many fine Georgian houses in the city. They include Churchman House, built of red brick in about 1730, and several good houses in Magdalen Street and Colegate, including 20 Colegate, which has a fireplace with two cherubs on the pediment said to have come from the Duke's Palace. Some of the most ornate Georgian houses in Norwich are in King Street and in the Surrey Street and All Saints' Green areas.[58]

Some of the Norwich architects of this time are nationally famous. Matthew Brettingham worked at Holkham Hall and built the Shire Hall to replace the one that burnt down in 1746 – his has now gone, too. The leading Norwich architect was Thomas Ivory, who became carpenter for the Great Hospital in 1751 and held this job until his death in 1779. His best surviving buildings are St Helen's House in Bishopgate, the Assembly Rooms, the Octagon Chapel (see p.152) and the block of large terraced houses on Surrey Street. Pevsner and Wilson say: 'Norwich can be proud of its Assembly House. No other town of its size in England has anything like it except of course for a spa like Bath.' However, an anonymous diarist called it 'a very large, tall, grand affair, by far the tallest in the city. I have not mentioned these things to our honour but rather to our shame, and must also add to our madness too, seeing trade is so very sickly and nobody knows when it will recover'. Another Norwich architect was William Wilkins, who adapted the castle for the county gaol – which had been rebuilt only three years earlier by John Soane – in 1792-3. His son, William Wilkins junior, went on to build the National Gallery in London.[59]

Arderon wrote about Norwich buildings:

> The Houses and other Buildings in Norwich have formerly been constructed for the most part of flintstone and lime. Some of the flints being cut exactly square, and so curiously perform'd as not to admit of a Knife's Blade between them ... A remarkable example of this is to be seen at Bridewell, St Andrews ... A great many of the Cellars are arched and very strong and capable of preserving goods from fire [the undercrofts referred to on p.53] ... The modern manner of building is now with Bricke, tho' of very bad soft sort, composed of a little Clay and a great deal of sand.[60]

Daily life in the city is recorded in the journal of John Bilby; born in 1801, attending what he describes as 'a play school', he became an apprentice hairdresser at the age of 13, becoming a hairdresser himself and then, from 1832, landlord of the *Dog* in St Paul's. He met his future wife, as we have seen (p.130), in September 1819, but the process of getting married was a slow one. They bought a 'very handsome' chest of drawers together in February 1822 and he joined a Furniture Club in April. The banns were called in November 1822; Bilby's prospective father-in-law, Mr Payne, provided the couple with a bedstead, mattress and the linen, and the marriage took place at St Saviour's church on 25 November, Bilby recording that he 'spent the day comfortably and had a large supper party in the evening at Mr Payne's house'. The Bilbys had several children, including a daughter, Rebecca, born, as her father proudly records, at a quarter to ten on the night of 7 February 1828. Her life was a short one: she died of smallpox in 1831. Bilby himself was only 36 when he died in 1837.[61]

Schools

The 18th century was the age of the charity school and the Norwich schools were described proudly by Mackerell:

> The first charity schools in this city were begun on the 24th June 1700 *viz.* one in the parish of St Ethelred [*sic*], a second in St Benedict's, a third in St Mary's, the fourth in St James's, in each of which twenty five poor children are taught to read, write and cypher, and some of them at proper ages are bound out apprentices. These are under the tuition of four masters, when any of them have finished their learning they have a new Bible given to them gratis.[62]

In 1707 Bishop Trimnell and other Anglican clergymen raised money to set up more charity schools

> for poor children of both sexes to be taught reading, writing and arithmatick, the boys cloathed with coats, capps and bands, the girls with gowns ... the girls are also taught use of their needles so far as is necessary for them in order to their being serviceable in the necessary affairs of a family.

The schools were funded by sermons and by private contributions.

The first Sunday School in Norwich was set up in 1785 in St Stephen's and many other parishes followed suit. The first Nonconformist Sunday School was opened by the Methodists in 1808; by 1835, 5,861 children attended Sunday School, 3,327 of whom were at Nonconformist schools. By 1877 there were over 7,000 enrolled in Nonconformist schools alone. The chief aim of Anglican schools was to provide religious instruction to poorer children, often to supplement that taught at day schools. Nonconformists, in contrast, saw their schools as the spearheads of conversion. The first and main objective was to teach reading and also writing (which often was not taught in Anglican Sunday Schools, as many thought it would give children ideas beyond their station in life).[63]

The general development of day schools in the early 19th century also came from the churches. The British and Foreign School Society was founded on the basis of work by Joseph Lancaster, who visited Norwich in 1810 to give lectures on his system of education. In 1811 a free school for boys on his plan was established by public subscription and with the support of leading Nonconformists like Joseph Gurney and Jeremiah Colman. No less than 537 pupils enrolled during the first year, but a large number of them stayed for only a week or so. The school was intended to be nondenominational, but Anglicans preferred to start their own schools with specifically Church of England teaching. They combined with the charity schools to buy land in Aldred's Court in St Peter Hungate and established a large school to replace all their small scattered ones. However, many small schools continued to be founded and by 1839 there were 28 day schools in the city with 2,632 children on their books.

The Boys' and Girls' Hospitals were really institutions where orphans or the children of the poor were trained for useful work. The Boys' Hospital was on Fishergate, where 34 boys were taught to read and write before being bound out as apprentices, while the Girls' Hospital, on Golden Dog Lane, took 24 girls and 'taught everything to fit them for servants or apprentices'. When going out, the girls wore blue gowns and the boys blue coats and red caps.

Alongside the charity schools were small fee-paying schools, such the Ladies Seminary School founded by Mrs Ruth Carver on West Pottergate in 1823. She took in 15 girls at a time and ran the school for 41 years; in 1895 the school moved to larger premises at Lonsdale House, and many Norwich ladies recall their schooldays at Lonsdale School. Mrs Carver's school was for day pupils but similar schools might take in boarders, as did the nearby and almost contemporary 'Classical and Commercial Academy for Young Gentlemen' run by Mr Turner at Pottergate Street House.

There was a growth in the education of adults as well – in 1815 Norwich was one of 14 towns in England that had a school for adults. With increasing literacy came a growing demand for cheap educational literature, such as the *Penny Encyclopaedia*. The Corresponding Society contributed by lending out books and pamphlets.

Religion

Apart from charity schools, the 18th century was not a time of great achievement in the Church of England. Many of the 18th-century bishops hardly ever came to Norwich and one, Robert Butts, was known mainly for his fondness of the bowling green. Silas Neville was unimpressed with Bishop Yonge's preaching, writing in his diary on 21 August 1772: 'Heard an inanimate sermon at the cathedral by Dr Philip Yonge, Bishop of this Diocese for the benefit of the Norfolk Hospital. This fat blown-up fellow is said to be one of the best preachers in the Establishment. But it is low in preachers if that is the case.' John Wesley was in Norwich on Sunday 17 October 1790 and noted that only two sermons were preached that day in the city's 36 churches; they were at the cathedral and at St Peter Mancroft.[64]

George Horne became bishop in 1790, moving from Canterbury with his wife and three daughters. On their first morning his daughter remembered him saying 'this is banishment indeed', but he soon came to enjoy the garden of the Bishop's Palace. A later bishop, Bathurst, although he was the only bishop to vote for the Great Reform Act, was not an active pastor: in his time the diocese of Norwich was known as 'The Dead See'. Bathurst's third son, Benjamin, was involved in an unsolved mystery on 25 November 1809, when he was aged 26. Returning from a secret

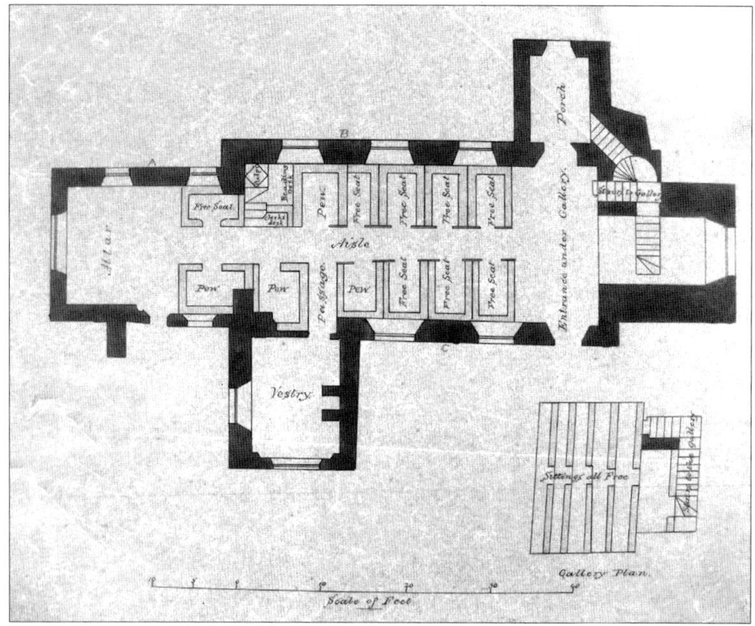

91 *Inside a Georgian church: the plan of St Peter Southgate.*

diplomatic mission near Vienna, he had a meal at a post-house near the Prussian border. Witnesses saw him standing by his carriage, then he was never seen again. Bishop Bathurst died in 1837, leaving 2,000 books and 2,650 bottles of wine. His statue, by Sir Francis Chantrey, can be seen in the cathedral.

The cathedral was becoming a tourist attraction, though many people found it a disappointment. Marchioness Gray wrote in 1760, 'the cathedral itself is large but not I think fine' and her husband thought the Bishop's Palace 'a rambling unpleasant house'. Seventy years later, William Cobbett wrote of the 'offensive and corroding matter, which is so disgusting to the sight round the magnificent pile at Norwich'. Woodforde noted that there was a fire in the cathedral in June 1801, 'a Thousand Pounds of Damage supposed done'.[65]

No new Anglican churches were built in the city in the Georgian period. St George Colegate has fine Georgian fittings – a west gallery on Tuscan columns, a reredos of dark wood with columns and pilasters, and a pulpit with back panel and tester. The spire of St Gregory, prominent on many engravings of the city, was blown down in a gale on 15 January 1806. John Wesley wrote of St Peter Mancroft:

> I scarcely remember ever to have seen a more beautiful parish church; the more so because its beauty results not from foreign ornaments, but from the very form and structure of it. It is very large, and of uncommon height, and the sides are almost all window; so that it has an awful and venerable look, and at the same time surprisingly cheerful.

From the middle of the century the Methodists were influential in Norwich. The first preacher John Wesley sent to Norwich was Samuel Larwood, but he only stayed two weeks. John and Charles Wesley themselves came in July 1754 and Charles stayed on. James Wheatley had arrived in Norwich in 1751 but he was not sent by Wesley; he had been expelled from Methodism two months earlier.

After about six weeks riots began occurring at his meetings. Details are given in a contemporary diary for 3 February 1752:

> This morning poor Mr. Wheatly preached at the Tabernacle, but was invested by the mob upon the Castle Ditches: fifty or more of Mr. Wheatly's friends undertook to surround and protect him. The mob (some think) was from nine to ten thousand strong; neither side had stayes, but drums, clapboards, and all instruments of noise; there was dreadful fighting on both sides, for the mob obliged the others to dispute every inch of ground – some who saw it said they had fought like furies on both sides. Mr. W. could not get away, he was shamefully handled, his hat and wig lost, his head broken in several places, his clothes rent, and himself all over mire and dirt; at length he was driven through the Griffin yard and took sanctuary in a house hard by, till the mayor sent his officers to release and guard him.

However, he persisted and the diary records similar riots on 11 and 14 March and again in August. Wheatley obtained a preaching licence in December 1752. His triumph was short-lived. He was accused before

92 *The Octagon Chapel.*

the Norwich Consistory Court in 1756 of misappropriating funds and of adultery with several young ladies. He lost the case and also lost appeals in 1757 and 1759. He then gave up preaching but still came to Norwich practising 'physick'.[66]

The most well-known Dissenter church was the Octagon Chapel, attended by William Taylor, the Aldersons, the Martineaus and James Smith. The Octagon Chapel was built in 1754-6; the architect was Thomas Ivory, but Vic Nierop-Reading, who with great insight describes the style as a return to 'temple architecture', suggests that the minister, John Taylor, and his son were responsible for the design. Almost £4,000 was subscribed, at least ten people contributing more than £100 each, illustrating the wealth within the Norwich Dissenting community. John Wesley wrote, 'I was shown Dr Taylor's new Meeting House, perhaps the most elegant one in Norfolk … the Communion Table is fine mahogany, the very latches of the pew doors are polished brass. How can it be thought that the old coarse gospel should find admission here?' However, he recommended the design as one Methodist churches could follow. Some Anglicans took against it, calling it 'the Devil's cucumber frame'.[67]

The Baptist movement flourished in Norwich, two of their best-known leaders being Joseph Kinghorn, minister of St Mary's Baptist church from 1789 until his death in 1832, and the radical Mark Wilks. Marten was at Kinghorn's service on 11 September 1825, describing him as 'a thin tall old gentleman, very plain in his attire, simple in appearance' – and noting that there were 300 people at the meeting. Wilks arrived in Norwich in 1776 as minister of Whitefriars' Tabernacle. He took a large part of the congregation with him to St Paul's chapel two years later and served there until 1814, when he opened a new chapel at Friars' Quay. He died in 1819.

The Independent Chapel on Princes Street was founded in 1819 by a breakaway group from the tabernacle on Bishopgate Street. The first pastor, John Alexander, remained in post for 47 years. The church was rebuilt in 1868 by Edward Boardman, whose father had been one of the first members of the church, and he added the Sunday School in 1881; it is now called Boardman House.

The Rosary cemetery was the first nondenominational cemetery in England. It was established in 1819 by Thomas Drummond, a Presbyterian minister, and his wife was the first burial in 1821, being reinterred here from the Octagon Chapel. In the next 80 years some 18,000 burials took place. It was naturally favoured by Nonconformists but many Anglican families used it too and, with its hillside site and its trees, it is the most atmospheric burial place in the city. The cemetery passed into the care of the city council in 1954, and is cared for by an enthusiastic group of volunteer 'Friends of the Rosary'.

93 *Maddermarket Chapel, the first Roman Catholic church in the city after the Catholic Relief Acts, and later the Maddermarket Theatre.*

Roman Catholics were forbidden public worship until 1778, but after the Catholic Relief Act of 1791 allowed the building of Roman Catholic places of worship, they bought a plot of land in St John's Alley formerly part of the garden of Strangers' Hall. The chapel opened in 1794 and in 1797 they bought Strangers' Hall itself for use as their Presbytery, a purpose it served until 1880. By 1801 the Jesuits had a chapel in St Swithin's Lane; this became a school after the Willow Lane chapel was built in 1827 following the Catholic Emancipation Act. The architect was J.T. Patience, who also designed the Friends' Meeting House in Upper Goat Lane; this replaced the one in which Elizabeth Fry was married.[68]

Popular superstitions are reflected in an advertisement of 11 February 1725 in the *Norwich Gazette*:

> Whereas I, Hester Brown Percy, of St Augustine's, have falsely and indifferently charged one Mary Parker, of St Martin at Oak, with being a witch and in great measure the author of the pains and afflictions I have for some years laboured under, which charge I now believe to be absolutely groundless and may be prejudicial to the said Mary Parker: therefore I do here publicly declare that I am fully satisfied that the said Mary Parker is perfectly innocent of the charge I have made against her …

Norwich was the site of at least one case of the sale of wives: a man who purchased a wife turned out to be already married and to have turned his own wife out of doors. A crowd hustled him in anger in 'one of those disgusting scenes which are a disgrace to civilised society'.[69]

Crime

Hanging was still the most common punishment for most types of crime but it no longer took place at the scene of the crime, the market cross or the 'hanging tree' at Town Close. All hangings were now conducted outside the castle, where they attracted large and boisterous crowds. In 1805 Martha Alden murdered her husband Samuel while he was asleep, striking him repeatedly with a billhook. For this she was executed on Castle Hill on 31 July 1807. Her ghost was supposed to walk on the Hill; in December of that year a party of drunken men attempted to invoke the ghost and they were kept in prison for two days to sober up. Perhaps her ghost was still haunting the castle 15 years later: an official report for the castle gaol in 1820 said that three men waiting in the cells to be transported were driven out of their minds by the sight of a ghost.[70]

Some executions were especially gruesome. John Pycroft was executed on Castle Hill on 16 August 1819 for poisoning his infant child. 'The culprit had a diminutive form and decrepit figure; when the platform fell his chest expanded at intervals during the space of 7 or 8 minutes although every precaution was taken to shorten his sufferings by the addition of some heavy appendages.' After he finally died his body was displayed to public view at the Shirehouse and then dissected by surgeons. In the case of Richard Nockolds it was his own family who displayed the body. Nockolds was found guilty of setting fire to straw stacks at Wood Dalling and was executed at Castle Hill on 9 April 1831. The body was handed over to his widow. Apparently because of her poverty she displayed his body at their cottage outside the Barrack gates in Pockthorpe, charging a penny for a view; 'a considerable sum was in this way raised for the

94 *A public hanging outside Norwich Castle.*

95 *Proposed new city prison on Gaol Hill.*

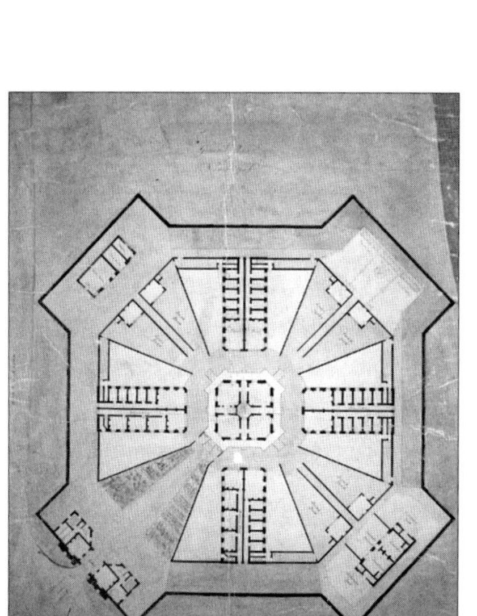

96 *The new city prison outside St Giles' Gate.*

widow'. Nockolds was eventually buried at St James Pockthorpe church on 13 April. To some of those filing past his corpse, Nockolds may have been a local hero: he was a weaver, and apparently the leader of a group involved in both urban and rural protest, among whom he was known as 'the Governor'. According to the prison chaplain, James Brown, he was one of 'a large gang in Norwich connected with the horrible crimes lately committed – men ripe for any atrocity'.[71]

There was a shortage of bodies for dissection in medical schools, which was only partly satisfied by the release of the bodies of a very small number of murderers. An Act of 1752 ordered many more murderers' bodies to be given up for dissection after hanging. The first in Norwich to suffer this fate was John Rye, hanged for murder on 19 March 1777 and then taken to the new hospital for dissection.

This was still not enough, and Norwich had its share of body snatching. In 1815 the stables of the *Duke's Palace* inn were used by resurrection men pretending to be apple merchants, but one night the ostler found three sacks containing corpses which turned out to have recently been buried at Hainford. The body-snatchers were never caught. In February 1823, suspicion was aroused by the frequency with which trunks were sent to London by the 'Telegraph' coach; on investigation they turned out to be bodies. An inquest among the Norwich city archives on an unknown man records: 'his body was found in a box in a coach offices occupied by the proprietors of the Telegraph Coach ... with a direction To Be Conveyed To London'. There were no marks of violence on the body – these were body snatchers, not murderers. The body was later identified as that of George Brundall, recently buried in Lakenham churchyard. Two men, Joseph Collins and Thomas Crowe, were eventually tried, sentenced to three months' imprisonment and fined £50. The 1832 Anatomy Act authorised the use of the corpses of the poor, and with this much increased legal supply, the body snatchers died out.[72]

Criminals were occasionally transported to the American colonies in the 18th century. This came to an end with the American War of Independence and from 1788 many convicted prisoners were transported to Australia instead. In 1783, at the age of 20, Henry Cabell was condemned to death with his father and brother for breaking into a house at Alburgh. All three were sentenced to hanging but Cabell's sentence was commuted to 14 years' transportation to the American colonies. However, America had declared independence and could no longer be used as a dumping ground for convicts, so Cabell stayed in Norwich Castle awaiting his fate. While there he fell in love with a girl also waiting to be transported, Susannah Holmes. They were both transported, landing at Port Jackson on 26 January 1788; Cabell is supposed to have carried the new governor ashore on his shoulders and thus to have been the first person on the fleet actually to set foot on the land. [73]

The city prison was on Gaol Hill, on the site later occupied by the Subscription Library. A return survives listing the prisoners in the gaol on 1 January 1736, and how long they had been in the prison. There were 85 inmates, six of whom were already in the gaol when this particular gaoler took over in September 1729, over six years earlier. Only three of the prisoners were women – Sarah Roper, who was one of those already a prisoner in 1729, and Catherine Coppin and Hannah Lancaster, both of whom had been committed in 1732.[74]

By the 1820s, this prison was too small; it was originally proposed to build a new one on the same site but in the end a large space was acquired just outside the city wall at St Giles' Gate. It was a design in accordance with the latest ideas; Marten visited it when it was being built and noted: 'The Governor's House is in the centre and from the several windows he can at all times inspect every part of the prison.' Like all prisons of its time, it housed both criminals and debtors; those among the latter who had the cash could hire a private room for four shillings a week.

Trials were held at the Quarter Session every three months, and twice a year by the Assize courts; the length of one's wait would depend on how the crime fitted into the pattern, as some cases in 1791 illustrate. It could be uncomfortably swift: Mary Hindes, caught stealing a petticoat and some stockings from a washing line in the castle ditches on 16 August 1791, was tried next day by the Assizes, which happened to be in session, and immediately started her sentence of six months in the Bridewell. However, Margaret Hamilton, who committed three thefts from city shops in November 1791, remained in prison over Christmas before eventually being sentenced to six months in prison; as these example suggest, there was no clear distinction between a sentence in the Bridewell and one in the gaol. Some people might be incarcerated for weeks and then acquitted at their trial, such as Mary Loveday, accused of stealing two beaver hats from Oxley's in the market place, but found not guilty by the Assize jury.[75]

Petty criminals, like the vagrants discussed on p.143, were physically punished and often publicly humiliated, as illustrated by the cases of two women before the magistrates on 28 October 1771. Margaret Pullien stole a shirt and a handkerchief worth 10 pence, and her punishment was to be sent to the Bridewell 'to be privately whipped till her back be bloody'. Elizabeth Gillings, also known as Elizabeth Sword, stole two handkerchiefs and an apron worth nine pence in total; she was sentenced 'to be stripped and publicly whipped' the following Saturday.

The 1830 riot (p.119) showed the inadequacy of Norwich's law enforcement: the city called out 200 Chelsea pensioners to try to preserve the peace. Central government was not happy. On 15 January 1830, a letter from Whitehall on behalf of Robert Peel was sent to the city authorities:

> I am directed by Mr Secretary Peel to inform you that he has heard with deep regret of the commission of another outrage of a most aggravated character in the City of Norwich. Mr Peel considers that the state of the City of Norwich with respect to its Police is very discreditable, and that some energetic measures ought to be forthwith adopted for the purpose of preventing the disorder and outrage which have recently taken place, apparently with perfect impunity.
>
> Mr Peel is prepared to send down two or three, or even a greater number, of active and intelligent Police Officers, provided the Local Authorities will undertake to pay the expenses of their Employment.[76]

The first police force was set up in the city in March 1836, on the model of that founded in London seven years earlier. The force consisted of 18 men and one superintendent; they wore a dark blue uniform with a waterproof cape. In 1840 the night watch became night constables and they were soon incorporated into the police force proper, which by 1851 numbered 80 men. In November 1846, the corporation delegated the Watch Committee to:

> appoint a fire brigade of six men, whose business it will be to attend all fires in Norwich ... The men in the daytime are to act as common policemen, and to sleep near the station house, where the engine is kept, each night, that they may be ready in case of alarm.

97 *Elizabeth Fry, born Elizabeth Gurney.*

Elizabeth Fry

The state of English prisons was to be transformed by one of the most famous women associated with Norwich, Elizabeth Fry. She was born Elizabeth Gurney at Gurney's Court off Magdalen Street in 1780, the fourth of 12 children of the banker John Gurney and his wife Catherine Bell. They were wealthy, and, when Elizabeth was six, they moved out of the city and rented Earlham Hall, now part of the University of East Anglia. She married Joseph Fry in the Goat Lane chapel in Norwich in 1810 and moved with him to London. Soon after this she became an active Quaker and she was formerly acknowledged a minister in 1811.

The work for which she is justly famous is prison reform. She visited Newgate Prison in London for the first time in January 1813 and was appalled by the conditions in which the female prisoners lived. She wrote to her small children, 'I have lately been twice to Newgate to see the poor prisoners who had poor little infants without clothing, or with very little and I think if you saw how small a piece of bread they are allowed you would be very sorry.' Conditions for poor women in gaol were awful: prisoners whose relatives had money could buy food, drink, clothes and privacy but those with nothing were herded together in large rooms, with no clothing apart from what they arrived in, no access to basins or towels and a bare survival ration of meat and bread. It was Elizabeth Fry who spent 30 years making people aware of these conditions and led the way in suggesting changes.

Elizabeth Livingstone summed up her work: 'She campaigned for the separation of the sexes, classification of criminals, female supervision of women, and the provision of secular and religious instruction'. She was well in advance of her time in her view that the government should provide work for prisoners and pay them for it. Even in her own lifetime, she was a role model for many. An American minister visiting England wrote:

> Two days ago I saw the greatest curiosity in London, aye and in England too, compared to which Westminster Abbey, the Tower, Somerset House, the British Museum, nay Parliament itself, sink into insignificance. I have seen Elizabeth Fry in Newgate, and I have witnessed there the most miraculous effect of true Christianity upon the most depraved of human beings.

Later she visited other countries and her ideas improved the conditions of female prisoners all the way across Europe and as far away as Russia.

Elizabeth Fry took up other causes too. She regularly inspected the ships of female prisoners being transported to Australia and made suggestions to improve their lot on board and when they arrived in Australia. Finding the body of a dead boy on a frozen winter night in London led her to set up a group of ladies to run a night shelter, providing soup and bread as well as a bed for the night.

The author Dennis Bardens thought that Elizabeth Fry had a special relevance to the 21st century, a time when an increasing number of women are being sent to prison, two thirds of them with dependent children. 'Elizabeth approached the women prisoners in Newgate as a mother, appealing to them to consider the welfare of their children.' She died in 1845 and is buried in the Quaker burial ground in Barking.[77]

Leisure and Art

The 18th century saw a flowering of culture in the city, including its first purpose-built theatre, and its Assembly House next door. In the Georgian period the city boasted the most famous botanist in the country, its own school of art and some of the leading thinkers, writers and musicians in England. It also saw the Norfolk and Norwich Museum, opened in a room in Haymarket in 1825, moving to a purpose-built site on Post Office Street (now Exchange Street) in 1833. It moved again to Museum Court in 1838, where it remained until 1894.

The Theatre Royal was designed by the Norwich architect Thomas Ivory. Built in 1758, it was only the second purpose-built theatre in England. It was very small and 40 years later another Norwich architect, William Wilkins, was complaining that 'a lady must be separated from

Opposite: 98 *Theatre Royal, as built in the 18th century.*

the Arm of her protector both on entering, and on leaving the lobby … it really is otherwise impossible that ladies can reach their carriages without danger of spoiling their Dresses and being squeezed perhaps between Doorkeepers, Porters and prostitutes'.[78]

In 1791 a subscription was raised to buy up an inn in Lady Lane seen as a 'nursery of vice and debauchery' and a cause of offence to those going to the nearby theatre. On 26 October 1799, the magistrates issued an order to stop up a lane known as Chapelfield Lane running through Bell Yard:

> the said footpath has in the Day time as well as by night been frequented by Idle disorderly indecent and wicked persons as well Men as Women by reason whereof the Morals of the youth of this city (passing through the said footway or passage) are liable to become corrupt and depraved.

The theatre itself could be a scene of trouble. Five men – Henry MacNeil, Joseph Travers, Richard Dewguard, Anthony Harris and Robert Evans – came before the courts after a riot there on 29 March 1800. All five were in the 85th Regiment of Foot, Travers a lieutenant, the others ensigns. They all pleaded guilty, and each was fined £5. In 1821 it was reported that:

> on Wednesday night last, some person most wantonly threw a glass bottle from the gallery upon the stage. Mr Smith, the manager, attended by the mayor's officers, immediately went up and with a laudable perseverance discovered the offender, who proved to be a young man of the name of Wheeler (son of the late Mr Wheeler formerly of this theatre). He was lodged in Bridewell, and on Thursday committed by the mayor to the same prison for the space of on month, for the offence.[79]

Norwich people made their contribution to the dramatic arts. Hannah Brand, born in the city in 1754, the daughter of a tailor, both wrote and starred in the play *Huniades* at Drury Lane in 1792. It was a flop, but in 1798 she included it in her volume *Plays and Poems*, published in Norwich. Louisa Brunton and her niece Elizabeth were both Norwich-born actresses who achieved fame in London. Louisa's father, John Brunton, was actor-manager at the Norwich Theatre Royal, and she cemented her fame by her marriage in 1807 to William, Earl of Craven. One place to celebrate the romance of the stage is in St Peter Mancroft churchyard, where the tomb of Sophia Ann Goddard can still be seen. One of the best-known London actresses of her day, she moved to Norwich in December 1798, but died of consumption aged only 26 in March 1801. She was engaged to John Yallop, responsible for the tomb; he later became a mayor of Norwich.

Before the theatre the *White Swan* inn (on the Millennium Library site) had been the centre of acting in Norwich. The inn was associated with the Norwich Company of Comedians from at least 1727, when it advertised in the *Norwich Mercury* a 'Tragedy call'd the Fall of Saguntum, With Entertainments of Singing and Dancing'. The Comedians made it their permanent home in 1731. Charles Macklin played Macbeth here in 1747. The *White Swan* declined as a centre of drama when the new theatre opened in 1758 but still held variety shows and also more popular entertainments: it was one of the centres of cock-fighting in the city.

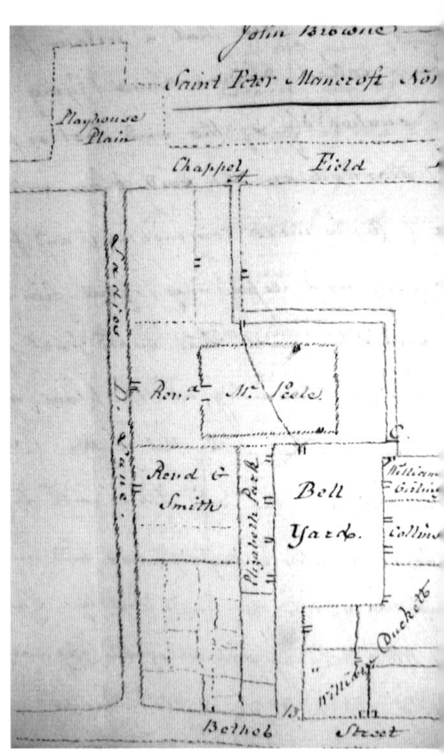

99 *Magistrates' order closing the path across Bell Yard; this whole area is now under the Millenium Library.*

The largest entertainments were held at St Andrew's Hall. When Parson Woodforde went to see Madame Mara sing there ('I never heard so fine a voice'), there were 911 in the audience and it took him an hour to get back to his coach afterwards. The ground floor of the Assembly Rooms had partitions so that it could be used for three functions, or opened up for a large dance. The pubs and inns provided a huge variety of entertainment. The quack doctor Graham advertised his show at the *Maid's Head* – 'he will deliver his very celebrated Lecture to Gentleman, on the Propagation of the Human Species, and on the Arts of exalting and rendering permanent the Joys of the Marriage Bed'. On 19 December 1785, Parson Woodforde came to Norwich with a friend, eating boiled beef and a saddle of mutton at the *King's Head*. In the afternoon they went to the *Rampant Horse* inn to see a 'learned pigg': 'he would spell any word or Number from the Letters and Figures that were placed before him'. He paid one shilling for this entertainment. In the evening they went to an astronomy lecture at the Assembly Rooms, for which Woodford paid 2s. 6d. and he 'was highly pleased with it'. They had a late supper at the *King's Head*, where they spent the night. Before Madame Tussaud and her wax figures became a London attraction, she toured the country, exhibiting at Norwich on two occasions: in 1819 at the *Angel* Inn, and in 1825 at the much larger Assembly Rooms. One of the most famous musicians to perform in the city was the Italian violinist Nicolo Paganini, who gave concerts at the Corn Hall and the Theatre Royal in 1831.[80]

A well-known name in the city is that of Noverre, a French Protestant family who left their home country for London after the Edict of Nantes and came to Norwich in about 1794. Augustin Noverre died at the Chantry in 1805. His son and grandson, both named Frank, were dancing masters at the Assembly House for a century, the first building his own room there in about 1856. Frank jr sold it to the Girls' School (which had taken over the rest of the building) in 1901; it later became the Noverre Cinema, and is now the Noverre Room.

There was a taste for exotic animals, and in 1788 a large tiger was exhibited at the *Bear* inn; it broke loose and devoured a monkey. In December 1816, George Wombwell was in Norwich exhibiting his 'Royal Menagerie' at the castle ditches over Christmas. The star attraction was a rhinoceros which was claimed to be the only one in Europe. It was actually auctioned at Norwich cattle market and fetched £300.[81]

Many 'sports' involved animals, and would now be regarded as barbaric. There were cock-fighting pits at the *Maid's Head*, while bull-baiting could be watched on Ber Street. Thomas Coke of Holkham had part-ownership of a bull here, said never to have been 'pinned' by the dogs; one day a farmer, seeing the bull throw a number of dogs in succession, called out, 'Lawk! It's like batting at cricket!'[82]

An attempt to revive the sport of camping took place at Norwich Cricket Ground in 1831 when a match was held between Norwich and Blofield, accompanied by wrestling. According to the *Norwich Mercury*,

100 *The Assembly House, on the site of the medieval College of St Mary in the Fields.*

it 'was attended by an immense number of persons both from the city and the country, who appeared to be highly amused with the games'. However, it is the last known camping match held in the city.[83]

Mackerell was proud of the city's inns.

> For good-fellow-ship perhaps not one city in England can match us. The gentlemen and better sort of tradesmen keep their clubs constantly every night in the week some at one tavern some at another, neither are the alehouses empty, for there are many persons of good fashion and credit that meet every night at one or other of these houses besides great numbers that are filled with poor labouring working men who go to these houses to refresh themselves after they have left work.

However, Arderon was not so impressed. He describes what he calls a:

> particular custom in Norwich – Both rich and poor when they meet in Taverns or Alehouses, pis into a large pewter Chamber pot (when they have occasion) wch stands in the Corner of every Publick Room, and there it stands stinking till it is full and often it runs about the Room, in a very nasty manner.[84]

In fact, there was probably an element of recycling involved, the urine being collected and used by dyers in their industrial processes. Neville was also not impressed, confiding to his diary in 1772, 'I do not like the *White Swan*, where I set up at Norwich. But none of the principal inns are agreable and all of them dear.' Some of the inns of Norwich survive from this period, such as the *Ribs of Beef*, first recorded under that name in 1743.

A sign of increasing leisure – for some classes at least – was the Pleasure Gardens in the city. The New Spring Gardens between St Faiths Lane and the river was founded in 1739; the Wilderness began in 1748 and was illuminated by 1768; Ranelagh Gardens outside St Stephen's Gates had fireworks and an illuminated Grand Walk by 1768. All the gardens had fireworks displays; in 1782 a man was killed at Bunn's Gardens by the fireworks while they were being prepared. There were public baths at Chapelfield; charges in 1789 were 5s. for a hot bath, 2s. 6d. for tepid and 1s. for cold. The radical Mark Wilks showed an entrepreneurial side to his character when he set up a bath house on the river in Heigham in 1789.[85]

A 1781 *History of Norwich* says of Chapelfield, 'this delightful sport is much resorted to, and may be justly called the city mall', but other sources say that Chapelfield was not much used by the genteel because of the number of disorderly boys congregating there, especially on Sundays. They preferred the area around the castle where, according to the *Norfolk Tour*:

> Beauty holds its daily court
> And all the Norwich belles resort.

The Gardens were the centre of the late 18th-century craze of ballooning. James Deeker, who sold experimental balloons in London, announced that on 1 June 1785 he would make a balloon ascent from Quantrell's Gardens in Norwich. A violent storm damaged the balloon but Deeker tried to ascend anyway; unfortunately the fabric had torn and he fell rapidly, landing unharmed at Sisland. On 23 June he tried again and in a flight of 45 minutes reached Topcroft.

On 23 July John Money had a try, also starting from Quantrell's Gardens. His was a charity event and the money raised from the 700 fee-paying spectators went to the Norfolk and Norwich Hospital. The balloon rose and was in sight for 45 minutes as it drifted slowly to the south-east. Money tried to let out gas but the valve would not open and he eventually came down in the sea about 20 miles off Southwold. A Dutch boat which passed did not stop, apparently mistaking the balloon for a sea monster! After clinging to the balloon for five hours, Money was spotted by the Harwich revenue cutter, which pulled him aboard. He was put ashore at Lowestoft next morning and arrived at his home in Crown Point in a post-chaise.[86]

Norwich Public Library was founded in 1784, a private venture funded by subscriptions. Norwich Literary Institution followed in 1822; they combined to form the Norfolk and Norwich Library in 1886. The library was built on the site of the old city gaol on Guildhall Hill in 1837. The architect was Patience; the façade was rebuilt at the end of the 19th century after a fire. The library closed in 1977 and many of its books passed to the Norwich School.

In 1820 the famous 'pugilist' Ned Painter moved to Norwich, taking over the *Sun and Anchor* in Lobster Lane. Born near Manchester, he had lost to Tom Oliver ('the Chelsea gardener') in 1814 and fought Thomas Winter ('Tom Spring') twice in 1818. Painter was defeated in the first fight but gained his revenge in the second. He planned to retire from the ring when he moved to Norwich but he was persuaded to fight Oliver once more. The contest took place at North Walsham before a crowd of about 20,000, and is described by George Borrow in *Lavengro*. Painter won after 12 rounds and announced his final retirement at a dinner held in his honour after the fight. In 1843 he was found guilty of thrashing a corn merchant called Jeremiah Cross at the *Rising Sun* in Norwich. After this he passed into obscurity; his death in Lakenham in 1852 was not even noted in Mackie's *Annals*.

These fights were, of course, savage affairs compared with modern contests. In 1820 a prize fight at St Faith's lasted 65 rounds. Three years later a man named Purdy died after a fight near Bishop Bridge. The courts were in sympathy with the pugilists: Painter was fined a mere shilling even though Cross was hospitalised after the assault. Purdy's opponent, Grint, received only three months' imprisonment.[87]

Norwich was the centre of its own social scene, as is shown in letters and journals of the time. Humphrey Repton, the landscape gardener, spent some time at Norwich Grammar School, and was then educated for four years in Holland. He returned to Norwich in 1768 and worked in a textile house for five years. He went to dances and was something of a dandy, as he recalled: 'In those days of my puppy-age every article of my dress was assiduously studied … I recall to mind the white coat lined with blue satin, and trimmed with silver fringe, in which I was supposed to captivate all hearts on one occasion.' He did indeed marry one of the young ladies in the social circle, Mary Clarke.[88]

A Norwich doctor, John Greene Crosse, was more critical of Norwich society, writing about a 'Grand Sessions Ball' held in 1815: 'it struck me as being a sort of market for stale as well as fresh goods. I took up this notion of it from seeing so many mothers leading their bare-necked daughters about with them … the market was certainly overstocked.' He spent much of his spare time playing chess with another city doctor, John Polidori, later to become famous as the author of *The Vampyre*, arguably the first ever vampire novel. Harriet Martineau recalled the impact he made in the city:

> About this time there came to Norwich a foreigner who excited an unaccountable interest in our house … it was poor Polidori, well known afterwards as Lord Byron's physician, as the author of The *Vampyre*, and as having committed suicide under gambling difficulties. When we knew him he was a harum-scarum young man – taken up by William Taylor as William Taylor did take up harum-scarum young men.

It is tempting to think that some of the themes in *The Vampyre* that appeared in the thousands of vampire novels and films that followed, such as deserted ruins in the moonlight, were inspired by Polidori's time in Norwich.[89]

Norwich was also the place where several Gothic novels were written. Rachel Hunter, who lived in the city from 1795 to her death in 1813, was the author of many works including *Letitia, or the Castle without a Spectre*, and *Lady Maclairn, the Victim of Villany*; her books were derided by Jane Austen.

Sir James Edward Smith

Sir James Edward Smith was born in Norwich in 1759, the son of a wealthy wool merchant. He studied medicine and botany in Edinburgh and London. When in London in 1784 he bought the whole collection of books, manuscripts and natural history specimens of the great Swedish botanist Linnaeus for a bargain 1,000 guineas. They consisted of 19,000 pages of pressed flowers and descriptive volumes. When the King of Sweden heard of the sale he sent a ship to intercept the one carrying the collection, but it was too late and the precious cargo arrived safely in England. Smith moved back to Norwich in 1796, bringing the collection with him to his house at 29 Surrey Street, where it was kept for 20 years. When he returned to this city, the Bishop of Carlisle wrote to him, 'at the distance of Norwich you will be quite buried alive' but it was here that he wrote his most famous works including the text of *Sowerby's Botany* and *The English Flora*. Smith also founded the Linnaean Society, which bought the collection (for 3,000 guineas) on Smith's death in 1828. They are now at Burlington House in London.[90]

One of James Smith's students was William Hooker, born in Norwich in 1785. Hooker founded the Royal Botanical Gardens at Kew in 1841 and was its director until his death in 1865. He was followed in the post by his son, Joseph Hooker.

Literary and Artistic Life

A Lecture on Art and Letters in Georgian Norwich describes literary life in the city: 'Norwich like one of its neighbouring broads forms a sort of literary backwater wherein were hatched many of the young fry of letters, several of whom escaping later into the mainstream of English literature became comparatively big fish.'[91]

William Taylor was born in 1765 of Norwich parents and became one of the leaders of political, philosophical and debating societies in Norwich. He travelled widely and met Goethe at Weimar in 1782, and was known as a translator of German poetry. Mrs Barbauld wrote to Taylor: 'Do you know that you made Walter Scott a poet? So he told me the other day. It was, he says, your ballad of Lenore that inspired him.' Harriet Martineau notes that in Taylor's time Norwich was known as 'the Athens of England', and he tried to enrich the literary life of the city by inviting the poet Robert Southey to live here. Southey replied that the letter excited a half-desire to diet for life upon Norfolk puddings, turnips and turkeys. However, he moved to Italy instead.[92]

Amelia Opie was born in Calvert Street in 1769. She lost her mother early and lived as companion to her father, Dr Alderson, becoming hostess to her father's friends. She married the artist John Opie in 1798 and the couple lived in London. In 1801 she published her novel *Father and Daughter*, of which Walter Scott wrote that 'he had cried over more than he ever cried over such things'. John Opie died in 1807. After his death, Amelia came back to Norwich and became increasingly involved with the Society of Friends. Harriet Martineau thought she did this in an attempt to gain a second husband in the person of the philanthropist Joseph John Gurney. She published her last novel in 1822 and was formally received into the Society in 1825. She died in 1853 and is buried in the Society of Friends' graveyard in Gildencroft.

Harriet Martineau was the sixth child of Thomas and Harriet Martineau and was born in 1802 in Gurney's Court off Magdalen Street, in the same room as Elizabeth Gurney, later famous as Elizabeth Fry. She was a sickly, introverted child who was almost deaf in adolescence. She wrote essays and stories in the 1820s and later, and travelled widely, including America and the Middle East. She cured herself of illness through Mesmerism, a popular form of hypnosis. Her first novel, which she always considered her best, was *Deerbrook*, published in 1839, its fans including Charlotte Brontë, described by Martineau as 'exceedingly small with melting, burning eyes and with much serenity of soul'. Martineau's best-read work today is her *Autobiography*, with its barbed comments on her contemporaries. Harriet died in 1872. Harriet's brother James Martineau became the most eminent Unitarian writer of his generation. He was principal of Manchester New College from 1869 to 1885, and wrote several religious books when he was in his 80s. He died, aged 95, in 1900.[93]

Another Norwich woman to achieve a certain literary fame was Elizabeth Bentley. She was born in All Saints Norwich in 1767, the only child of a shoemaker, who taught her to read and spell. In 1791 one of the city's debating societies, the United Friars, decided to publish her verse, and secured over 1,500 subscribers for the book. A second volume was published in 1821. The poet William Cowper referred to 'the Norwich maiden's strong natural genius'; her themes included animal welfare and the abolition of slavery. She spent the last years of her life in Doughty's Hospital and died, aged 72, in 1839.

One of the most famous names to come out of Georgian Norwich is that of Hansard, although few who use *Hansard's Parliamentary Debates* probably recognise the connection with the city. Luke Hansard was born in Norwich in 1752 and became an apprentice to a Norwich printer, Stephen White. He moved to London and his speed and accuracy in printing Parliamentary papers has resulted in his name being attached to the official record of the British Parliament, and to that of some Commonwealth countries too. He died in London in 1828.

Few people reach the height of their fame when they are three years old, but this was the fate of William Crotch, born in Green's Lane in St George Colegate on 5 July 1775. His father was a carpenter and built an organ for his own use. William was able to play 'God Save The King' on this when he was two years and three weeks old; before he was three, he 'learned several tunes which he could play with great exactness'. He was an instant sensation and became 'a child prodigy without parallel in the history of music'. He played before a large crowd at Norwich in February 1778 and his mother then took him on tour; he played before the King and Queen at Buckingham Palace on 1 January 1779, appeared in London again in October 1779 and then 'toured' throughout the country. He went on to write three oratorios and a good deal of church music. The *Pocket County Companion* calls his oratorio *Palestine* 'the finest work of the kind ever produced by an Englishman up to that time'. He was the first principal of the Royal Academy of Music in London from 1822 to 1832 and wrote books on the theory of musical composition. His last public performance was at the Handel festival in Westminster Abbey in 1834. He died in 1847 on a visit to his son, who was master of Taunton Grammar School, and is buried at Bishop's Hull in Somerset.[94]

Perhaps the fame of William Crotch contributed to the success of the first Norwich Music Festival, which was held in 1824. It was organised by Richard Mackenzie Bacon, the editor of the *Norwich Mercury*, to raise funds for the Norfolk and Norwich Hospital. The first festival raised £2,400 and it became a triennial event. It is the second oldest music festival in England (the oldest being the Three Choirs Festival in Hereford, Worcester and Gloucester).

Another Norwich resident who has contributed to the musical life of England is Sarah Ann Glover. Born in 1786, the daughter of Edward

Glover, the curate at St Lawrence, she developed the Norwich Sol-fa ('do-re-mi') system of learning musical notes. Her system was developed by the Revd John Curwen into the Tonic Sol-fa system still in use. Sarah also developed the Glass Harmonica, examples of which can be seen in the Strangers' Hall and Bridewell museums. She left Norwich in 1851, moving first to Cromer and then to Hereford, and she died at Great Malvern in 1867.[95]

The turn of the century saw a flourishing of painting in the city, leading to the group of artists known as the Norwich School of Artists – Norwich is the only city in Britain to have a school named after it. The name is given to three generations of Norwich-based landscape painters who were linked together by master-pupil relationships and family ties. The Norwich Society of Artists was founded in 1803 and held yearly exhibitions from 1805 to 1833. The most important artists were John Crome, John Sell Cotman and Joseph Stannard.

John Crome was born in a public house in 1768, which R.H. Mottram has convincingly identified it as the *Griffin* on King Street, within the old bailey of the castle. At the age of 12 he was errand boy to Dr Edward Rigby and in 1783 he became apprentice to a coach painter. Thomas Harvey introduced him to the famous artist William Beechey, who wrote later: 'Crome when I first knew him must have been about 20 years old and was a very awkward misinformed country lad but extremely shrewd in all his remarks upon art although he wanted words and terms to express his meaning.'[96]

Crome painted signs for several Norwich inns, including the *Three Cranes* in the Lower Close. This sign is now in the Castle Museum, as are many of the urban and rural landscapes for which the School is famous. Crome became a full-time artist and drawing master with the support of local gentry like Harvey, the Gurneys of Earlham and Dawson Turner of Yarmouth. Although most of his landscapes are of Norfolk scenes, he did paint in the Lake District and elsewhere and once visited the Continent. Crome died in April 1821 and is buried in St George Colegate, where there is a plaque to his memory. He had married Phoebe Berney in 1792 and they had 11 children, some of whom also became artists. They lived all their married life in Gildengate, but the house no longer survives. George Borrow wrote expressively of Crome in *Lavengro*:

> he has painted not pictures of the world but English pictures such as Gainsborough might have done; beautiful rural pieces … with trees which might well tempt the wild birds to perch upon them. The little dark man with the brown coat and the top-boots, whose name will one day be considered the chief ornament of the old town, and whose works will at no distant period rank among the proudest pictures of England.

Borrow was right. After Crome's death his reputation grew and eventually he came to rank with Turner and Constable as one of the three major English landscape painters of the century.

John Sell Cotman was born in St Mary Coslany Norwich in 1782 and was a pupil at Norwich Grammar School. He trained in London, moving back to Norwich in 1806. He published etchings of antiquarian scenes and worked in Yarmouth for 12 years under the patronage of Dawson Turner. He made three visits to Europe and after a further 10-year spell in Norwich he went back to London in 1834 to be Teacher of Drawing in the newly founded King's College school. He was not fully recognised in his own time because of his forward-looking style. Cotman died in 1842. From 1823 to 1834 he lived in St Martin at Palace Plain and had a drawing school there. Two of his sons later lived in the same fine Georgian house, now called Cotman House.

Joseph Stannard was born in 1797. He was never a formal member of the Norwich School but his paintings of the coast and rivers of Norfolk were immediately popular and have had a high reputation ever since. In 1824 he painted the 'Thorpe Water Frolic', commissioned by Colonel John Harvey of Thorpe. Harvey refused to buy the painting at first, changing his mind a couple of years later. Stannard's later years were severely restricted by tuberculosis and he died in 1830. The 'Water Frolic' became one of the first Norwich School paintings to be acquired by Norwich Castle Museum after it was bought by J.J. Colman in 1894 for 110 guineas. He presented it to the museum when it moved to the castle later in the same year.

Sculpture in the city was represented by an incomer, Pellegrino Mazzotti, from Lucca, Italy. A figure maker and modeller, he had works exhibited at the Norwich School of Art between 1821 and 1829. In 1822 he married Mary Leeds in St John Maddermarket, and they had four daughters between 1822 and 1827. His first studio was in Strangers' Hall, his second in Goat Lane. He deserted his family in about 1840, moving to Cambridge. Mary died in Norwich in 1861, and Mazzotti himself died in poverty in the Union workhouse in Wisbech in 1879.

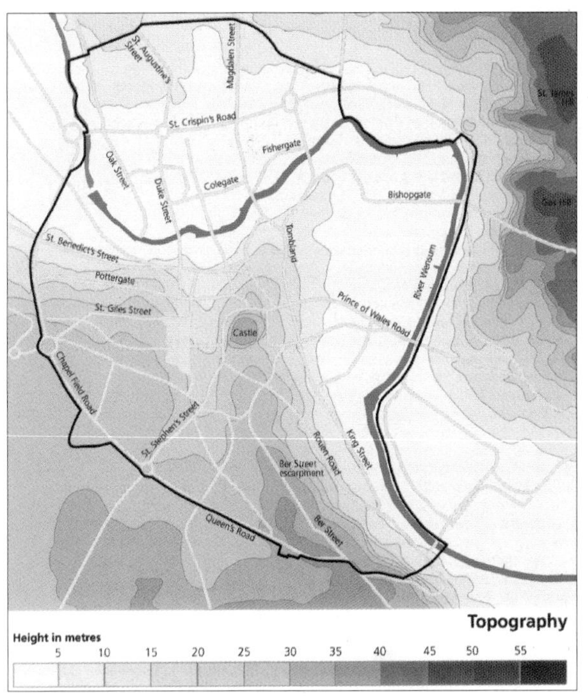

I *Topography of Norwich.*

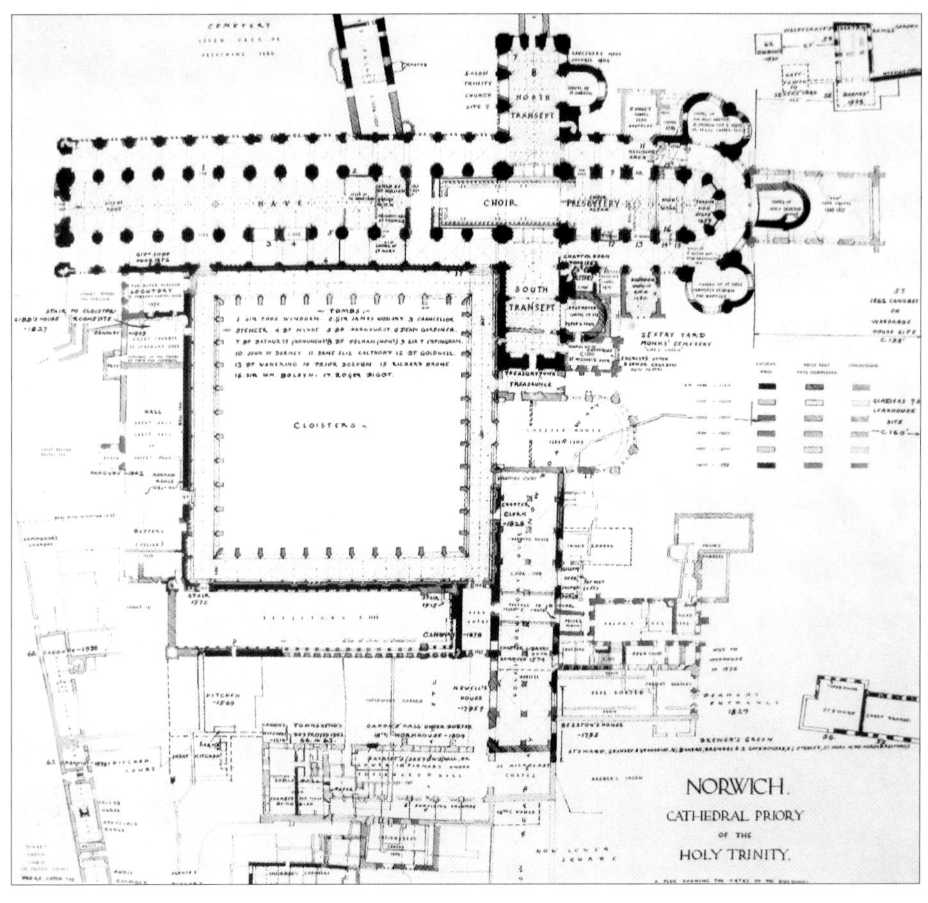

II *Plan of Norwich cathedral and cloister, by A.B. Whittingham.*

III *The south transept of the cathedral. The prior's house, later the Deanery, is on the right.*

IV *Prior Robert Catton and his Benedictine monks, on an agreement between the Cathedral and the city, 1524.*

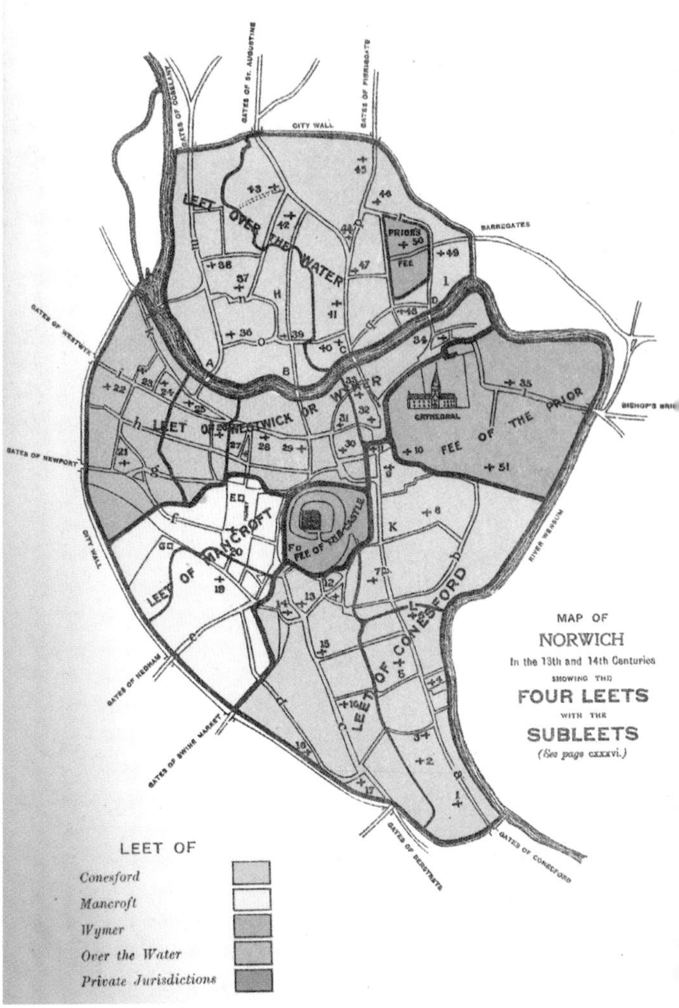

MAP OF
NORWICH
In the 13th and 14th Centuries
SHOWING THE
FOUR LEETS
WITH THE
SUBLEETS
(See page cxxxvi.)

LEET OF OVER THE WATER
LEET OF WESTWICK OR WYMER
LEET OF MANCROFT
LEET OF CONESFORD
FEE OF THE PRIOR
FEE OF THE CASTLE
PRIORS FEE
CATHEDRAL
CITY WALL
BARREGATES
BISHOP'S BRIDGE
RIVER WENSUM

LEET OF
Conesford
Mancroft
Wymer
Over the Water
Private Jurisdictions

V *The leets of early medieval Norwich.*

VI *Seventeenth-century map of Norwich, based on Cunningham's plan of 1558.*

VII *Snap the Dragon, as portrayed in glass at St Andrew's Hall.*

VIII *Snap: the last of many generations of dragons featuring in civic ceremony in Norwich.*

IX *(Above left) Charley, painted by John Dempsey; courtesy Tasmanian Museum and Art Gallery.*

X *(Above) Cotton, painted by John Dempsey, courtesy Tasmanian Museum and Art Gallery.*

XI *Guild Day in Norwich.*

XII, XIII *The interior of Norwich cathedral as painted by David Hodgson.*

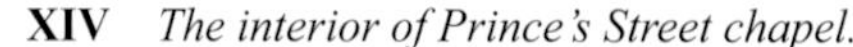

XIV *The interior of Prince's Street chapel.*

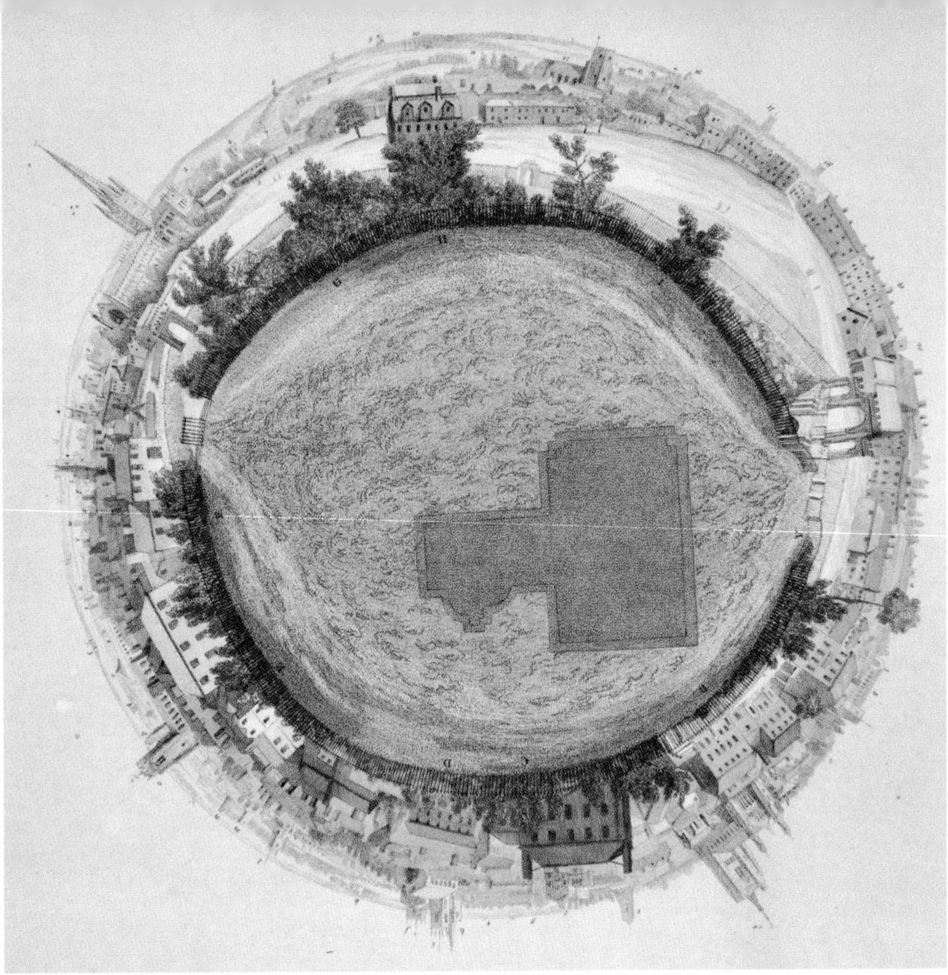

XV *Norwich from the Castle: St Peter Mancroft and the Cathedral are prominent landmarks.*

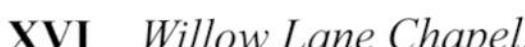

XVI *Willow Lane Chapel.*

XVII *Norwich in 1848*

XVIII *Robert Dixon, 'City Wall, Junction of Barrack Street and Silver Road Norwich'.*

XIX *David Hodgson, 'St Lawrence Church, Norwich'.*

XX *John Thirtle, 'Bishopgate Bridge, Norwich - Evening'.*

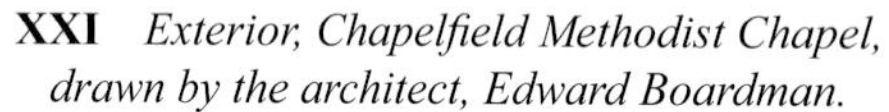

XXI *Exterior, Chapelfield Methodist Chapel, drawn by the architect, Edward Boardman.*

XXII, XXIII *St John's Roman Catholic church: the painting is by Charlotte Nicholls.*

XXIV *Edith Cavell statue, now moved to beside the Erpingham Gate.*

XXV *'Norwich Barracks and their Garrisons'.*

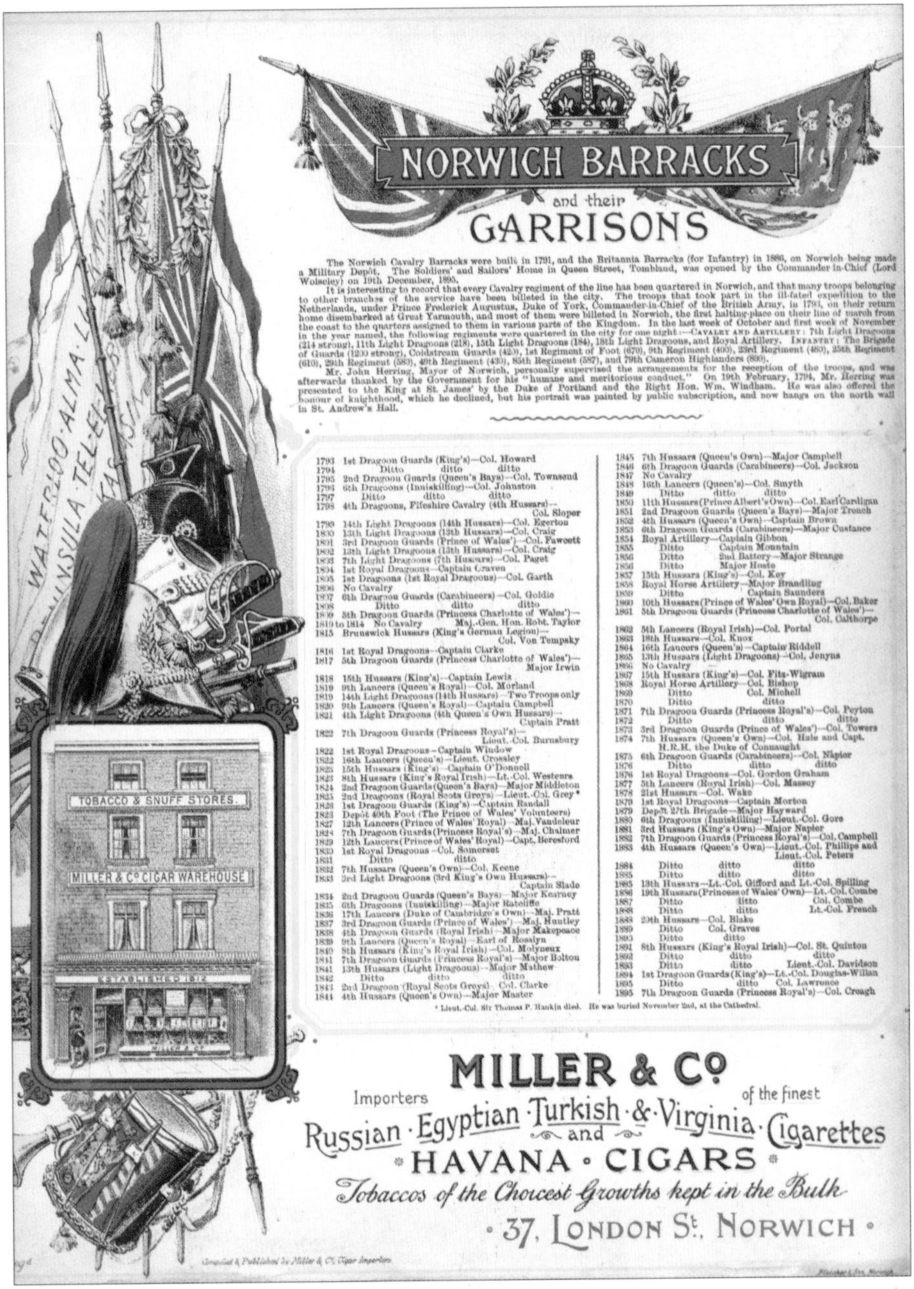

NORWICH BARRACKS and their GARRISONS

The Norwich Cavalry Barracks were built in 1791, and the Britannia Barracks (for Infantry) in 1886, on Norwich being made a Military Depôt. The Soldiers' and Sailors' Home in Queen Street, Tombland, was opened by the Commander-in-Chief (Lord Wolseley) on 19th December, 1895.

It is interesting to record that every Cavalry regiment of the line has been quartered in Norwich, and that many troops belonging to other branches of the service have been billeted in the city. The troops that took part in the ill-fated expedition to the Netherlands, under Prince Frederick Augustus, Duke of York, Commander-in-Chief of the British Army, in 1793, on their return home disembarked at Great Yarmouth, and most of them were billeted in Norwich, the first halting-place on their line of march from the coast to the quarters assigned to them in various parts of the Kingdom. In the last week of October and first week of November in the year named, the following regiments were quartered in the city for one night:—Cavalry and Artillery: 7th Light Dragoons (214 strong), 11th Light Dragoons (218), 15th Light Dragoons (184), 18th Light Dragoons, and Royal Artillery. Infantry: The Brigade of Guards (1200 strong), Coldstream Guards (420), 1st Regiment of Foot (670), 9th Regiment (400), 23rd Regiment (480), 25th Regiment (610), 29th Regiment (580), 49th Regiment (430), 85th Regiment (587), and 79th Cameron Highlanders (800).

Mr. John Herring, Mayor of Norwich, personally supervised the arrangements for the reception of the troops, and was afterwards thanked by the Government for his "humane and meritorious conduct." On 19th February, 1794, Mr. Herring was presented to the King at St. James' by the Duke of Portland and the Right Hon. Wm. Windham. He was also offered the honour of knighthood, which he declined, but his portrait was painted by public subscription, and now hangs on the north wall in St. Andrew's Hall.

1793 1st Dragoon Guards (King's)—Col. Howard
1794 Ditto ditto ditto
1795 2nd Dragoon Guards (Queen's Bays)—Col. Townsend
1796 6th Dragoons (Inniskilling)—Col. Johnston
1797 Ditto ditto ditto
1798 4th Dragoons, Fifeshire Cavalry (4th Hussars)—Col. Sloper
1799 14th Light Dragoons (14th Hussars)—Col. Egerton
1800 13th Light Dragoons (13th Hussars)—Col. Craig
1801 3rd Dragoon Guards (Prince of Wales')—Col. Fawcett
1802 13th Light Dragoons (13th Hussars)—Col. Craig
1803 7th Light Dragoons (7th Hussars)—Col. Paget
1804 1st Royal Dragoons—Captain Craven
1805 1st Dragoons (1st Royal Dragoons)—Col. Garth
1806 No Cavalry
1807 6th Dragoon Guards (Carabineers)—Col. Goldie
1808 Ditto ditto ditto
1809 5th Dragoon Guards (Princess Charlotte of Wales')—Maj.-Gen. Hon. Robt. Taylor
1810 to 1814 No Cavalry
1815 Brunswick Hussars (King's German Legion)—Col. Von Tempsky
1816 1st Royal Dragoons—Captain Clarke
1817 5th Dragoon Guards (Princess Charlotte of Wales')—Major Irwin
1818 15th Hussars (King's)—Captain Lewis
1819 9th Lancers (Queen's Royal)—Col. Morland
1819 14th Light Dragoons (14th Hussars)—Two Troops only
1820 9th Lancers (Queen's Royal)—Captain Campbell
1821 4th Light Dragoons (4th Queen's Own Hussars)—Captain Pratt
1822 7th Dragoon Guards (Princess Royal's)—Lieut.-Col. Burnsbury
1822 1st Royal Dragoons—Captain Window
1822 16th Lancers (Queen's)—Lieut. Crossley
1825 15th Hussars (King's)—Captain O'Donnell
1823 8th Hussars (King's Royal Irish)—Lt.-Col. Westenra
1824 2nd Dragoon Guards (Queen's Bays)—Major Middleton
1825 2nd Dragoons (Royal Scots Greys)—Lieut.-Col. Grey *
1826 1st Dragoon Guards (King's)—Captain Randall
1823 Depôt 40th Foot (The Prince of Wales' Volunteers)
1827 12th Lancers (Prince of Wales' Royal)—Maj. Vandeleur
1828 7th Dragoon Guards (Princess Royal's)—Maj. Chalmer
1829 12th Lancers (Prince of Wales' Royal)—Capt. Beresford
1830 1st Royal Dragoons—Col. Somerset
1831 Ditto ditto
1832 7th Hussars (Queen's Own)—Col. Keene
1833 3rd Light Dragoons (3rd King's Own Hussars)—Captain Slade
1834 2nd Dragoon Guards (Queen's Bays)—Major Kearney
1835 6th Dragoons (Inniskilling)—Major Ratcliffe
1836 17th Lancers (Duke of Cambridge's Own)—Maj. Pratt
1837 3rd Dragoon Guards (Prince of Wales')—Maj. Huntley
1838 4th Dragoon Guards (Royal Irish)—Major Makepeace
1839 9th Lancers (Queen's Royal)—Earl of Rosslyn
1840 8th Hussars (King's Royal Irish)—Col. Molyneux
1841 7th Dragoon Guards (Princess Royal's)—Major Bolton
1841 13th Hussars (Light Dragoons)—Major Mathew
1842 Ditto ditto ditto
1843 2nd Dragoon (Royal Scots Greys)—Col. Clarke
1844 4th Hussars (Queen's Own)—Major Master

1845 7th Hussars (Queen's Own)—Major Campbell
1846 6th Dragoon Guards (Carabineers)—Col. Jackson
1847 No Cavalry
1848 16th Lancers (Queen's)—Col. Smyth
1849 Ditto ditto ditto
1850 11th Hussars (Prince Albert's Own)—Col. Earl Cardigan
1851 2nd Dragoon Guards (Queen's Bays)—Major Trench
1852 4th Hussars (Queen's Own)—Captain Brown
1853 6th Dragoon Guards (Carabineers)—Major Custance
1854 Royal Artillery—Captain Gibbon
1855 Ditto Captain Mountain
1856 Ditto 2nd Battery—Major Strange
1856 Ditto Major Hoste
1857 15th Hussars (King's)—Col. Key
1858 Royal Horse Artillery—Major Brandling
1859 Ditto Captain Saunders
1860 10th Hussars (Prince of Wales' Own Royal)—Col. Baker
1861 5th Dragoon Guards (Princess Charlotte of Wales')—Col. Calthorpe
1862 5th Lancers (Royal Irish)—Col. Portal
1863 18th Hussars—Col. Knox
1864 16th Lancers (Queen's)—Captain Riddell
1865 13th Hussars (Light Dragoons)—Col. Jenyns
1866 No Cavalry
1867 15th Hussars (King's)—Col. Fitz-Wigram
1868 Royal Horse Artillery—Col. Bishop
1869 Ditto Col. Michell
1870 Ditto ditto
1871 7th Dragoon Guards (Princess Royal's)—Col. Peyton
1872 Ditto ditto ditto
1873 3rd Dragoon Guards (Prince of Wales')—Col. Towers
1874 7th Hussars (Queen's Own)—Col. Hale and Capt. H.R.H. the Duke of Connaught
1875 6th Dragoon Guards (Carabineers)—Col. Napier
1876 Ditto ditto ditto
1876 1st Royal Dragoons—Col. Gordon Graham
1877 5th Lancers (Royal Irish)—Col. Massey
1878 21st Hussars—Col. Wake
1879 1st Royal Dragoons—Captain Morton
1879 Depôt 27th Brigade—Major Hayward
1880 6th Dragoons (Inniskilling)—Lieut.-Col. Gore
1881 3rd Hussars (King's Own)—Major Napier
1882 7th Dragoon Guards (Princess Royal's)—Col. Campbell
1883 4th Hussars (Queen's Own)—Lieut.-Col. Phillips and Lieut.-Col. Peters
1884 Ditto ditto ditto
1885 Ditto ditto ditto
1885 13th Hussars—Lt.-Col. Gifford and Lt.-Col. Spilling
1886 19th Hussars (Princess of Wales' Own)—Lt.-Col. Combe
1887 Ditto ditto Col. Combe
1888 Ditto ditto Lt.-Col. French
1888 20th Hussars—Col. Blake
1889 Ditto Col. Graves
1890 Ditto ditto
1891 8th Hussars (King's Royal Irish)—Col. St. Quinton
1892 Ditto ditto ditto
1893 Ditto ditto Lieut.-Col. Davidson
1894 1st Dragoon Guards (King's)—Lt.-Col. Douglas-Willan
1895 Ditto ditto Col. Lawrence
1895 7th Dragoon Guards (Princess Royal's)—Col. Creagh

* Lieut.-Col. Sir Thomas P. Hankin died. He was buried November 2nd, at the Cathedral.

TOBACCO & SNUFF STORES.

MILLER & Cº CIGAR WAREHOUSE

ESTABLISHED 1812

Compiled & Published by Miller & Co. Cigar Importers

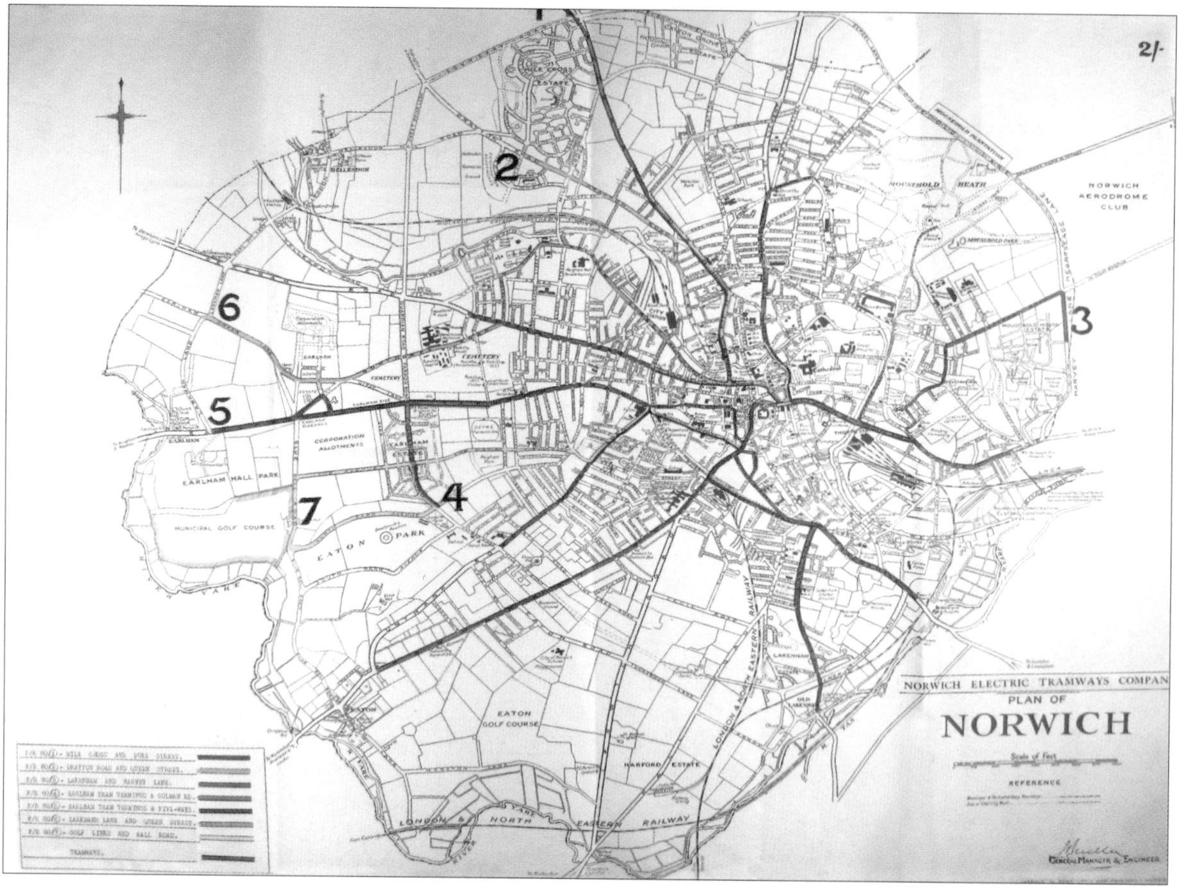

2/-
NORWICH AERODROME CLUB
HOUSEHOLD HEATH
CORPORATION ALLOTMENTS
EARLHAM HALL PARK
MUNICIPAL GOLF COURSE
EATON PARK
EATON GOLF COURSE
HARFORD ESTATE
LONDON & NORTH EASTERN RAILWAY
NORWICH ELECTRIC TRAMWAYS COMPANY
PLAN OF
NORWICH
Scale of Feet
REFERENCE
TRAMWAYS.
GENERAL MANAGER & ENGINEER

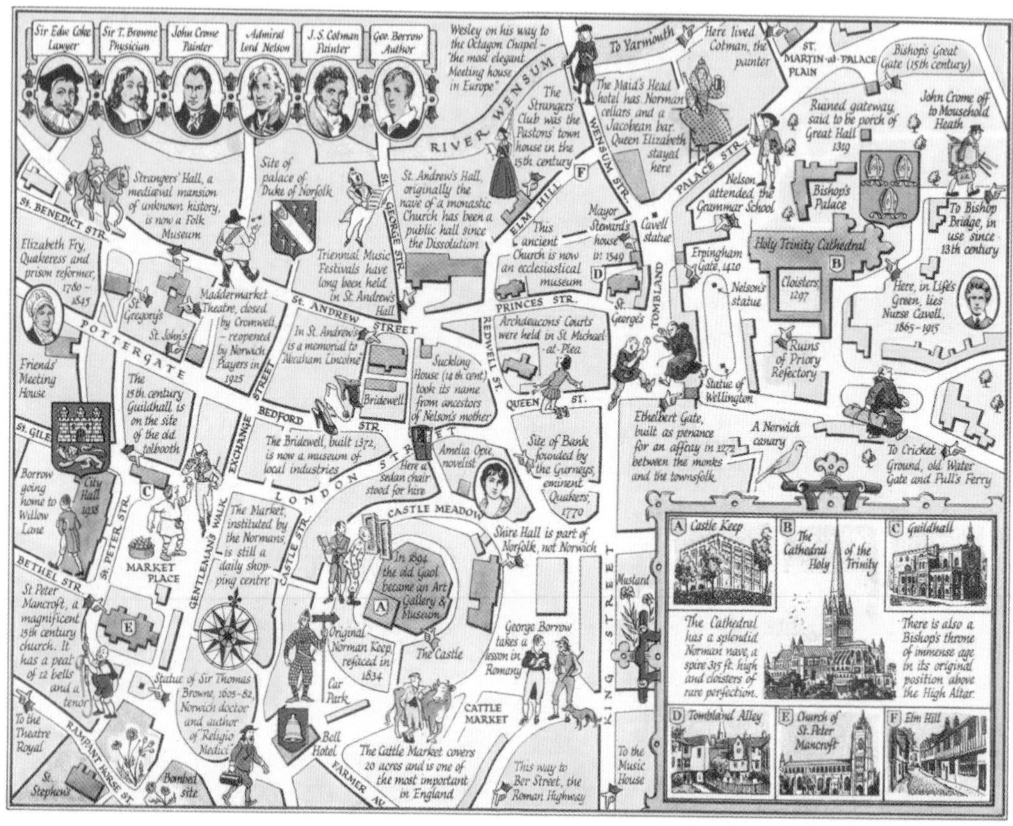
Sir Edw. Coke Lawyer
Sir T. Browne Physician
John Crome Painter
Admiral Lord Nelson
J. S. Cotman Painter
Geo. Borrow Author
Wesley on his way to the Octagon Chapel – "the most elegant Meeting house in Europe"
To Yarmouth
Here lived Cotman, the painter
ST. MARTIN-at-PALACE PLAIN
Bishop's Great Gate (15th century)
RIVER WENSUM
The Strangers' Club was the Pastons' town house in the 15th century
The Maid's Head hotel has Norman cellars and a Jacobean bar. Queen Elizabeth stayed here
Ruined gateway, said to be porch of Great Hall 1319
John Crome off to Mousehold Heath
Strangers' Hall, a mediaeval mansion of unknown history, is now a Folk Museum
Site of palace of Duke of Norfolk
St. Andrew's Hall, originally the nave of a monastic Church has been a public hall since the Dissolution
ELM HILL
WENSUM STR.
PALACE STR.
Nelson attended the Grammar School
Bishop's Palace
To Bishop Bridge, in use since 13th century
ST. BENEDICT STR.
ST. GEORGE STR.
Mayor Steward's house 1549
Cavell statue
This ancient Church is now an ecclesiastical museum
Holy Trinity Cathedral
Elizabeth Fry, Quakeress and prison reformer, 1780–1845
Triennial Music Festivals have long been held in St. Andrew's Hall
Erpingham Gate, 1420
Cloisters 1297
Here, in Life's Green, lies Nurse Cavell, 1865–1915
St. Gregory's
Maddermarket Theatre, closed by Cromwell, – reopened by Norwich Players in 1925
ST. ANDREW STREET
PRINCES STR.
TOMBLAND
Nelson's statue
St. John's
In St. Andrew's is a memorial to 'Abraham Lincoln'
REDWELL ST.
Archdeacons' Courts were held in St. Michael-at-Plea
St. George's
POTTERGATE
Friends' Meeting House
The 15th century Guildhall is on the site of the old tolbooth
EXCHANGE STREET
Suckling House (14th cent.) took its name from ancestors of Nelson's mother
Ruins of Priory Refectory
Statue of Wellington
Bridewell
QUEEN ST.
BEDFORD STR.
Ethelbert Gate, built as penance for an affray in 1272 between the monks and the townsfolk
A Norwich canary
ST. GILES
The Bridewell, built 1372, is now a museum of local industries
LONDON STREET
Here a sedan chair stood for hire
Amelia Opie, novelist
Site of Bank founded by the Gurneys, eminent Quakers, 1770
To Cricket Ground, old Water Gate and Pull's Ferry
Borrow going home to Willow Lane
City Hall 1938
ST. PETER STR.
GENTLEMANS WALK
The Market, instituted by the Normans, is still a daily shopping centre
CASTLE STR.
CASTLE MEADOW
Shire Hall is part of Norfolk, not Norwich
MARKET PLACE
In 1894 the old Gaol became an Art Gallery & Museum
KING STREET
Mustard
BETHEL STR.
St. Peter Mancroft, a magnificent 15th century church. It has a peal of 12 bells and a tenor
Original Norman Keep refaced in 1834
The Castle
George Borrow takes a lesson in Romany
Statue of Sir Thomas Browne, 1605–82, Norwich doctor and author of "Religio Medici"
Car Park
CATTLE MARKET
To the Theatre Royal
RAMPANT HORSE ST.
St. Stephen's
Bombed site
Bell Hotel
The Cattle Market covers 20 acres and is one of the most important in England
This way to Ber Street, the Roman Highway
FARMER AV.
To the Music House
A Castle Keep
B The Cathedral of the Holy Trinity
C Guildhall
The Cathedral has a splendid Norman nave, a spire 315 ft. high and cloisters of rare perfection.
There is also a Bishop's throne of immense age in its original position above the High Altar.
D Tombland Alley
E Church of St. Peter Mancroft
F Elm Hill

Opposite: XXVI *Integrated transport in the 1930s: the red lines are the tramways, the others are bus routes leading from them.*

Below left: XXXVII *Tourist map of Norwich.*

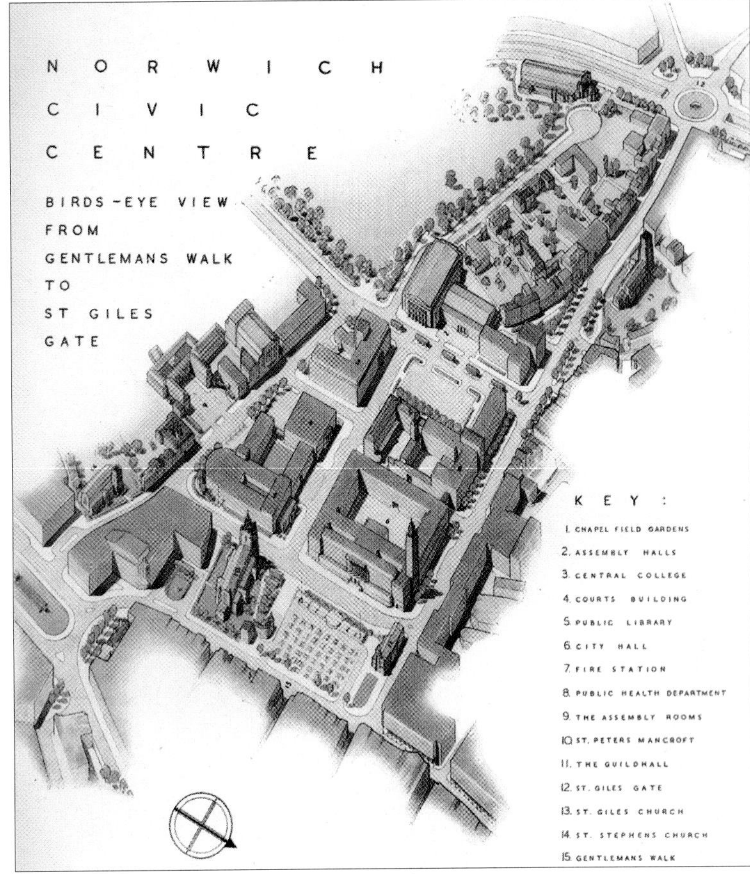

XXVIII *Plans for the post-war city: the City Centre.*

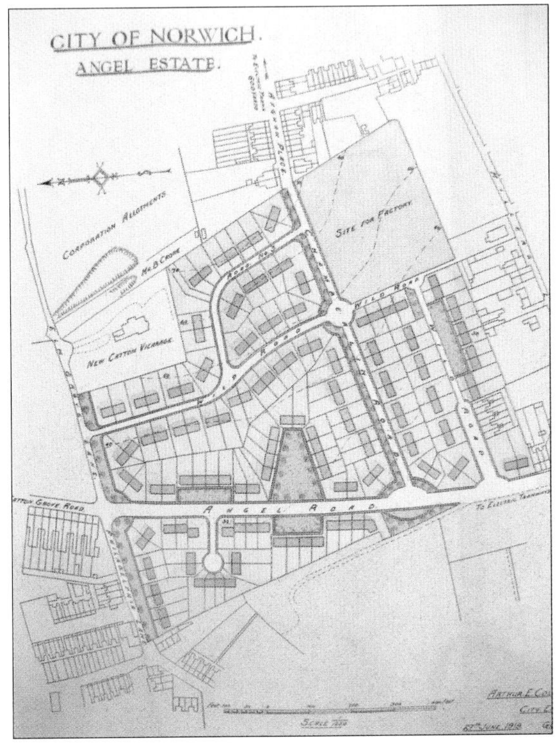

Below: XXIX *Council estates: the planned Angel Road estate, 1919.*

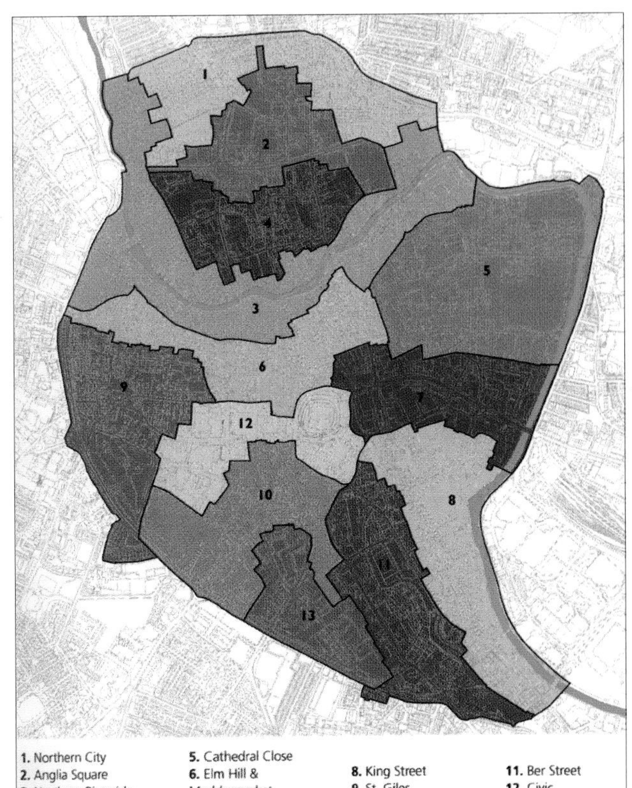

Right: XXX *Conservation Districts of Norwich.*

Clockwise from above:

XXXI *How Norwich merchants saw themselves, overmantel painting at Strangers' Hall.*

XXXII *The* Bell Hotel *(painting by T/Sergeant Ludwig Lund of USAAF).*

XXXIII *The* Castle Hotel *and restaurant (painting by T/Sergeant Ludwig Lund of USAAF).*

L HOTEL
RAC
BELL HOTEL.

GRILL ROOM
CASTLE HOTEL

XXXIV *The Three Mustardeers: Colman's advertising*

XXXV *Norwich shoe designs, 1920s.*

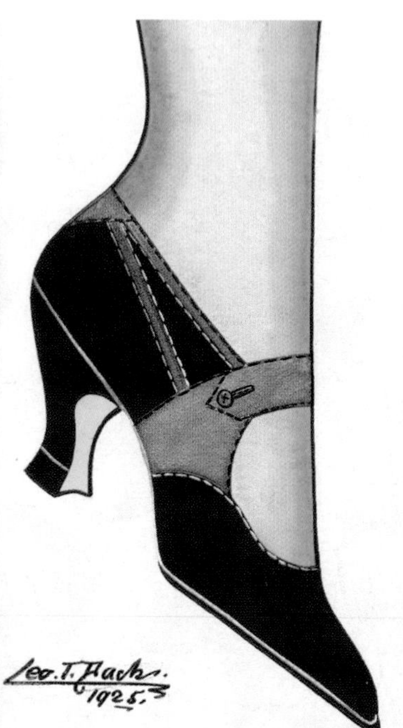

FIVE

Victorian Norwich

In the age of Queen Victoria both local and national authorities began to exercise powers to change the city's infrastructure drastically, transforming people's lives. These included changes in the supply of water, the provision of sewers, the beginnings of slum clearance, the introduction of minimum standards of housing and the start of a system of free education for all.

The population of Norwich rose throughout the 19th century but not at the speed of the cities of the North. The census figures for the city are 36,909 in 1801, 68,195 in 1851, 80,386 in 1871, and 100,964 in 1891.

In the 1830s the Parliamentary Reform Act and the Municipal Reform Act changed the face of government in England. The Parliamentary Reform Act extended the number of people entitled to vote. It made little difference in Norwich: the franchise was very wide already as all freemen were entitled to vote. Two members were still elected for the city and all voters still had two votes. The number of people voting in the first election under the new rules went up by about seven hundred.

The Municipal Reform Act had a much more drastic effect. It extended the franchise in the elections for the city council from all freemen to all male ratepayers, quadrupling the franchise. In 1869 women ratepayers were given the same right to vote in city council elections as male ratepayers and in 1885 Norwich had 2,600 female voters to 14,000 male voters. These women were all single women or widows; married women were held not to have property of their own and therefore were not entitled to vote.

The Act altered the four great wards of the 1404 charter into eight wards. The ratepayers elected councillors who in turn chose aldermen and also the sheriff and the mayor. The title 'corporation' was changed to 'council'. The council was given the power of raising money by imposing a general rate; before this all rates had been raised by *ad hoc* bodies for particular purposes. In 1892 16 wards were established, each with as near the same population as possible. As W. Hudson pointed out at the time, each of these new wards had roughly the same population as the whole city 700 years earlier.

Norwich continued to embrace radical causes. Daniel O'Connell, 'the famous Irish agitator', was in Norwich in November 1837 and addressed a large meeting at St Andrew's Hall. The city also played a part in Chartist activities in the 1830s and 1840s, a movement in which the working classes demanded universal adult suffrage and changes in the Poor Law of 1834. The movement in Norwich began in 1838 when J.R. Stephens from Ashton spoke to rallies in the market place. He told the crowds: 'England stands on a mine; a volcano is beneath her ... Hitherto the people have been held in leash; they can be held back no longer.'[1]

The first Chartist leader in Norwich was John Love, treasurer to the Norwich Weavers' Society and a Primitive Methodist lay preacher. He attacked the new workhouses for separating married couples inside them. Love was committed to non-violent protest and condemned the abortive rising in 1839, the year in which Chartism reached its peak. Violence was expected in the city. On 5 March 1839 Charles Loftus reported to Lord Wodehouse, the Lord Lieutenant of the county, that a man named Land, who lived in Graham's Court in St Peter Mancroft parish, was making pikes for chartists. Radical clubs with supplies of pikes were being held at the *Cottage* behind Patteson's Brew Office in Pockthorpe, the *Angell* in St Martin at Oak, the *Roebuck* in Peafield, Lakenham, and the *Shuttle* in St Augustine's. These were public houses in some of the poorest areas of the city.[2]

In the event there was no violence in Norwich in 1839. After a great meeting on Mousehold Heath, led by Love, the Chartists turned on the churches. They would attend a church in large numbers and sometimes disrupt the proceedings. About five thousand turned up at St Stephen's one Sunday and heckled the vicar when he preached on man's duty to be content with his lot in life, shouting, 'You get £200 a year! Come and weave bombazines!'[3]

Love was rivalled and soon eclipsed in popularity by the orator John Dover. John Ward says that the Norwich chartists 'drove out their early bourgeois leaders, preferring the heady oratory of the promiscuous and rascally publican John Dover – at least until 1841'. Dover was not against violence, and when he was arrested in 1839 pikes, guns and bullets were found in his house. Like any mob orator he ran the risk of angering them too – once he was suspected by the crowd of taking a bribe and they dragged him to the river intending to throw him in. He had to be rescued by the newly formed police force. However, his career came to a sudden end in 1845 when he was sentenced to transportation on a charge of receiving stolen goods. Dover's family were reduced to poverty after his transportation; his wife Martha is described in the 1851 census as a 'pauper, formerly a silk weaver'.[4]

Love also left Norwich in 1845, going to work for the Chartist cause in the north of England. He came back to Norwich in 1848 and spoke to large crowds as the final petition to Parliament was being organised. After the petition failed Chartism died out and Love became destitute;

he was forced into the workhouse against which he had preached so strongly.

Elections to Parliament in the Victorian age were the source of endless disputes, petitions and counter-petitions. In the 1868 election Sir Henry Stracey and Sir William Russell were elected, but after an inquiry it was found that Stracey had offered bribes and was therefore not legally elected. In May 1870 Jacob Henry Tillett was elected to the vacant seat. After a petition this election was also declared invalid and Tillett was unseated. At the subsequent by-election in 1871 Jeremiah James Colman was elected in his place. Both Tillett and Colman were Liberals but in the next election of 1874 the voting was so close that one Liberal and one Conservative were elected. Despite being so close the election was not disputed, but after Tillett was elected in a by-election in the following year there was another petition against him, and once again Tillett was thrown out. This time no by-election was held and the second Norwich seat remained vacant until the 1880 general election. At this election two Liberals – Colman and Tillett – were elected and actually held their seats undisputed for the full five-year term. There was a further dispute after the 1885 election and this time it was the Conservative Harry Bullard who was unseated. J.J. Colman finally retired as MP in 1895 and in that year the city elected two Conservatives for the first time for 60 years.

The last years of the century also saw the beginnings of the Labour party in the city. The Norwich branch of the Independent Labour Party was founded in 1894; its first meeting was at the Victoria Hall, during the 1894 Trades Union Congress, held in Norwich. This meant that figures of national importance were present in the city, including Keir Hardie and another future Labour leader, J.R. Clynes, who remembered the Norwich Congress as the time the union movement committed itself to full-scale nationalisation. A delegate proposed the nationalisation of land and mines; Keir Hardie was on his feet instantly. 'I wish to suggest an amendment,' he began in his arresting manner. 'There can be no argument in favour of nationalising lands and mines which does not apply equally to every form of production. If the mines from which we dig minerals are to be nationalised, why not the railways which carry those minerals? Why not the depots where they are deposited, and the works in which they are manufactured? Why shall the landlord be attacked and the capitalist go free?' After much debate, his amendment that all means of production, distribution and exchange should be nationalised was carried by 219 to 61 votes.

As was customary the TUC held an open-air rally; in 1894 this was on Mousehold Heath. Keir Hardie and John Burns, the chairman of the Congress, were among the speakers. 'Unfortunately at the beginning of the procession heavy rain fell, but this did not deter an enormous concourse of people from the city and the neighbouring towns from coming together.' After the Congress was finished, Hardie and some friends went for a walk in the Cathedral Close. They stood under 'an old Norman arch' to watch the sun set. In the silence, as the lights in the city were being lit, Hardie began to sing the 23rd psalm and all those present joined in. However, the new dawn was not to arrive immediately. Frederick Hoult, a boilermaker at Thorpe Station, stood for the Heigham ward in the city elections of 1894. He was defeated, but the 262 people who voted for him were the first Norwich citizens to vote for a Socialist candidate in any election.[5]

One Norwich radical in the later part of the 19th century was Robert Aspland Cooper, the son of a Unitarian minister. He made his fortune in America, supplying bread to the Unionist armies in the American Civil War. After the war he moved to Norwich and set up a confectionery and biscuit-making business. At its height this was running from three premises – Albion Mills on King Street (better known as Read's Mill from a later owner), and retail outlets on Queen Street and Bank Plain.

Cooper was a freethinker and friend of the atheist MP Charles Bradlaugh, whom he invited to Norwich to give talks on several occasions. In 1891 he published a pamphlet entitled *Free Railway Travel.* This advocated that the state should take over all the railway companies and that travel on trains should be without charge: 'free passenger travel is a primary condition of the comfort and well-being of the whole of the population, and it is especially necessary for the abolition of overcrowding in populous districts, and for the improvements of workmen's dwellings'. His idea was that, instead of living in overcrowded yards close to their work, people would be able to live in more pleasant houses in places like Brundall and Poringland, and travel into work by train free of charge. His pamphlet was reprinted in full in the Norwich radical newspaper *Daylight*, and attracted considerable interest – one supporter was Keir Hardie.

Cooper built for himself a large house on Thorpe Road, appropriately enough opposite the railway station; he called it Aspland House. His son Edward followed him in the confectionery business but died of typhoid in 1894, some six months before his 30th birthday; Cooper was heartbroken and lost interest in his business after the tragedy. Edward Cooper is buried in the Rosary Cemetery; as befits the family's beliefs, the grave has no Christian symbol, but a stone in the shape of a scroll. Cooper died in 1907. His house, too large for later tastes, was split up and later became a nursing home. It was bombed in the war and part of the site became a public library, but it is now part of a private housing development.

Trade and Industry

The weaving industry collapsed in the 19th century and Norwich faced a crisis; by 1845 it could be said: 'It was formerly a great manufacturing city; but it has declined much of late.'[6] The final mill built by the Norwich Yarn Company was St James' Mill, for weaving. It was built by Richard Parkinson (some books say John Brown) and had two steam engines. It opened in 1839, as is recorded on a plaque on the building. The rooms in the factory were let out to different manufacturers who ran 65 spinning frames and 500 power looms, employing 1,000 people at an average wage of seven shillings a week. However, Norwich just could not compete

101 *St James' Mill, with the flag of Jarrold and Sons.*

with Yorkshire, and the Yarn Company had to be wound up. The yarn factory was bought for £14,000 by Messrs E. and R.W. Blake in 1850, a valuation of the stock bringing the total price up to £21,219. By 1869 the number of looms had been cut to 300 'and they are not always at work', and the number of employees at the mill had fallen to below five hundred. St James's Mill survives, one of the most spectacular industrial monuments in the city.

According to the Hand-loom Weavers' Commission report of 1840, weaving was still done at home in the great majority of cases – out of 4,054 looms at work in Norwich, 3,398 were in the weavers' own homes. In 1850 Yorkshire had 746,000 spindles, 40 times the number in Norfolk. The great days of the industry were over. Even in 1869, in spite of the mills, the hand-loom worked in the weaver's own home still played a role in the city. The loom was a large piece of furniture, which explains a feature typical of many older Norwich houses – the unusually tall attics with dormer windows the full height of the roof. By 1900, only about two thousand people were engaged in the textile industry and in the 1901 census there were no worsted weavers at all in the city.

Other parts of the industry did continue to flourish. Printed shawls were made in the city from the 1840s and widely exported. One won a first-class medal at the International Exhibition in Paris in 1855. In 1849 Charles Dickens wrote to his wife Kate: 'I bought you a shawl in Norwich – I don't think much of it. It's Norwich manufacture. That's all I can say. But it's bright and cheery besides – I forgot that.' Whereas the number of worsted weavers fell from 800 in the 1851 census to about 80 in 1891, the decline in silk workers was not so drastic, falling from 4,000 in 1851 to just over 1,000 in 1891.

102 *Monument to Thomas Clabburn in St Augustine's church; note the weavers' shuttles on the coat of arms.*

It was the great growth in boot and shoe making that compensated for the collapse of the weaving industry. The trade employed 1,913 people in 1841 and this had increased to 6,278 in 1861 and to over 7,500 by the end of the century. Successful firms included Howlett and White, founded in 1846, Sexton, Son and Everard in about 1886 and Edwards and Holmes in 1891. The making of clothes also flourished, led by Rivett and Harmer, founded in 1826 and becoming F.W. Harmer and Co. in 1851, who set up a new factory using sewing machines. Their factory, built in St Andrew's in 1891, was praised for its 'light and airy' conditions.

In the later 19th century, Norwich also became a major centre for engineering. Charles Barnard established an ironmonger's business in Norwich market place in 1826 and built the first patented wire-netting machine in 1844; the firm of Barnard, Bishop and Barnard sold this all over the world. The machines were similar to those used in the city for weaving cloth. The foundry was in Pottergate. They also made wrought-iron gates. A pair sent to an exhibition in Vienna in 1873 is now in a Vienna museum and the well-known Norwich Gates made for the entrance to Sandringham are still to be seen there. The firm also made the Slow Combustion or Norwich Stove, known as the Country Parson's Fire Grate.[7]

William Boulton introduced wire-netting machines at his Rose Lane factory in 1868. The firm became Boulton and Paul in 1869, and built their new office in Rose Lane in 1899, incorporating timber from a merchant's hall discovered when slum properties in King Street were being pulled down. They moved to a larger site across the river in the 1920s; the blue and red brick boundary wall on Mountergate and Tudor Hall in Rose Lane survive from their earlier site.

103 *Haldinstein's shoe factory, Queen Street.*

William Scott began to make dynamos in 1883 and was joined in 1888 by Reginald Laurence. The firm was a great success: new works were built in 1896 and a second factory in 1900. Its Gothic frontage near Norwich railway station is a familiar sight to all train passengers.

The timber merchants Jewson's were founded at Earith in Huntingdonshire in 1836 and John Jewson moved to Colegate in 1868. The firm imported timber into the city by boat, offloading at Yarmouth. The first cargo steamer to come to Norwich was the *Saxon Prince*, carrying timber from Viburg for Jewson's.

J. & J. Colman were established as a milling firm at Stoke Holy Cross in 1814, when Jeremiah Colman took over a mill there. Originally used for paper making, it had been converted by a Mr Ames for making mustard. Jeremiah improved the quality of production and the machinery, and began the move in 1856, to a site in Carrow convenient both for river and rail communication. By 1900, the firm had over 2,000 employees. The factory also made the well-known tins in which the mustard was sold, and expanded into the making of starch and later other products such as Almata complete food, oats, semolina and Robinson's barley water. Colman's won medals for their mustard and starch at Dublin in 1865 and Paris in 1868; they also led the way in good treatment of the workforce.

104 *Industrial Norwich, with gasometer, and factory chimneys belching smoke.*

A.J. Caley and Son was established as a chemist in London Street in 1860. In 1863 they started making mineral water in the back of their shop. The firm moved to Chapel Field Road in 1883 and started making cocoa, followed by chocolate in 1886. In 1898 they began making crackers and continued to make mineral water, using water drawn from two artesian wells on the site 400 and 500 feet deep. Coleman's began making tonic wine in the 1880s and was later famous for its tonic wine Wincarnis.

Norwich continued to be a major brewing centre in the 19th century. Because of the predominance of large brewers, Norwich had a lower proportion of pubs brewing their own beer than anywhere else in England. The 1830 Excise Returns show that in the country as a whole one public house in three was brewing its own beer, but in Norwich there were only 37 brewing victuallers and 1,070 victuallers.

The Anchor Brewery was founded beside Coslany Bridge by Richard Bullard and James Watts in 1837. Ten years later the partnership was dissolved and Bullard carried on alone. His son Harry joined the family business and by the end of the century the site covered seven acres. The brewery used water drawn from an artesian well dug into the chalk beneath the brewery site.

The other big breweries were Steward and Patteson in Barrack Street, Youngs, Crawshay and Youngs in King Street and Morgan's also in King Street, many of whose buildings survive in the complex known as Wensum Lodge. The last developed from tragic beginnings: in May 1845 Walter Morgan, who with his brother had just bought Thompson's Brewery in King Street, was found drowned in the fermenting vat there – he was only 23 years old. All the breweries had access to the river for easier transportation of raw materials.[8]

105 *Workers at Steward and Patteson's brewery.*

There was a wide range of other trades of the kind to be found in any large county town. For example, in 1845 Norwich soap makers made over one and a half million tons of soap. Newspaper printing continued and expanded – the *Norfolk Chronicle* and the *Norwich Mercury* were both published once a week. They included international, national and county news; sensational local murder cases took up many pages, including special supplements. They featured local advertising too; in December 1843 Mr Beard of the Royal Bazaar was the first person in Norwich to advertise photographic portraits. Each paper had its own political viewpoint; the *Norfolk News* was founded in 1845 by a group of Liberal Nonconformists dissatisfied with the views of the *Norwich Mercury*. The first daily paper in Norwich, the *Eastern Daily Press*, began publication on 10 October 1870; it is still the city's leading paper, now part of the publishing group Archant.

The provision and cattle markets continued to be the heart of Norwich. Orders for the markets issued in 1872 show that the provision market was normally open every day including Sunday from dawn until very late. In 1882 it was ordered to close at 10 p.m. instead of 11.30 p.m. on Saturdays. Market tolls were 3d. 'for every Stall Ped or other Standing', which was not to exceed three feet in width without special permission from the collector.[9]

Ber Street was known as 'Blood and Guts Street' in the 19th century because of all the butchers – hence the former pub name the *Jolly Butchers*. Cows were driven along the street from Trowse to the cattle market. Once the railway was opened the main traffic came by train – Trowse station had a huge area of animal-holding pens. The livestock market was enlarged and repaved in 1861; even then some people thought it should be moved out of the city, but this was not to happen for another century. Tombland Fair continued, but had become an entertainment rather than a commercial fair, not always of the highest quality. John Hastings and Arthur Crompton came before the Assizes in 1887, charged with keeping a booth

106 *The Victorian Haymarket.*

107 *Early photograph of the southern end of the market place, with St Peter Mancroft behind.*

108 *Horses wait patiently as the market is set up.*

109 *Cabs on a quiet Sunday in the market place in 1898.*

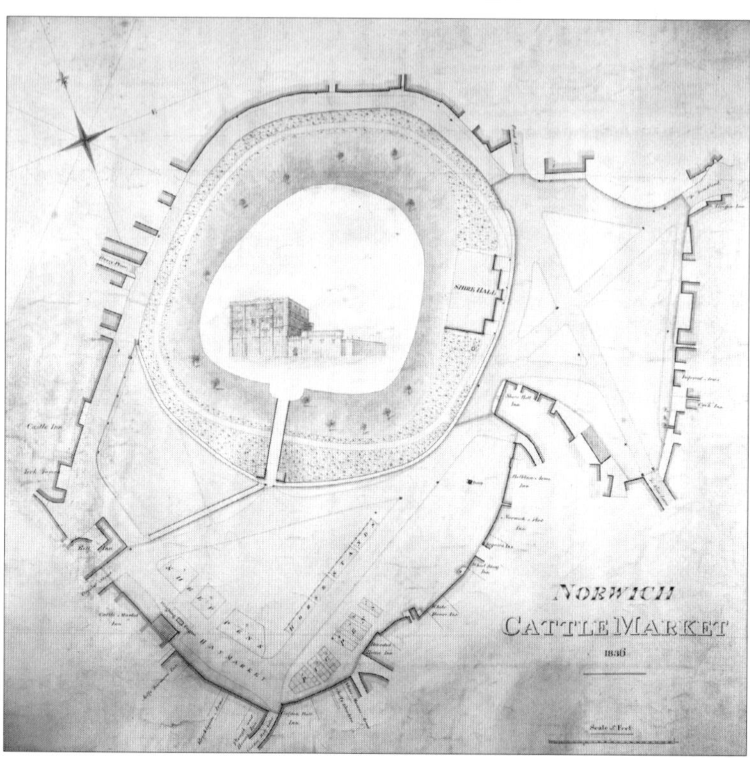

110 *Plan of the cattle market in 1836; note the number of public houses surrounding it.*

Opposite: 111a, b *A crowd watch Barnum's circus elephants and camels go by, 6 September 1898.*

at the Easter Fair of that year 'for the purpose of exhibiting an indecent, disgusting and loathsome performance'; they pleaded guilty to displaying indecent pictures. By 1897, the Easter fair was held on the cattle market. John Barker was killed there when he was trapped between two wagons while setting up his Steam Roundabout on 12 April.

Fire was an ever-present danger in the city. In October 1822 the chandling office of Staff and Chamberlin in St Martin at Palace burnt down. The tallow ran into the river and more than ten cartloads of it were skimmed off the surface of the water by people in boats. On 26 June 1839, the factory of a cabinet maker, Mr Bush of Roach's Court, Fisher's Lane, was destroyed by fire together with the adjoining house of a silk weaver, who lost his machinery and his stock of silk. 'The fire engines were not in a state for such an emergency and many of the leather pipes had to be tied together with handkerchiefs.'[10]

On 20 December 1806 the Norwich Fire Office announced that its travelling fire engine was to be kept at St Peter Mancroft church, from where it could be obtained by sending a man and two horses. Insurance was an expanding business: the total funds of the Norwich Union life insurance office were £1 million in 1830 and £2 million by 1890. Thomas Bignold's son, Samuel, was secretary of both the Fire and Life Insurance Societies for nearly 60 years. In 1864 the Norwich Union took over the Amicable Society, which was the world's first life insurance society, founded in 1706 by Samuel Talbot, Bishop of Oxford; his statue now graces one wing of Skipper's Norwich Union building. An office to cover insurance of accidents was set up in Norwich in 1856 and merged with the Fire Office in 1908.

The banking sector had more than its share of problems. The East of England Bank was established in 1836, with its head office in Norwich and a dozen local branches. It collapsed on 20 July 1864, its directors having been speculating in railway shares; customers found the doors closed. The goodwill was sold to the Provincial Banking corporation and its creditors did eventually receive 20 shillings in the pound, but it took two years.

The bank later known as Overend and Gurney was founded in 1800 by Thomas Richardson and John Overend; Samuel Gurney joined in 1807. Their core business was buying and selling bills of exchange. Samuel Gurney died in 1856. After his death the bank took investments in railways and other long-term investments, and eventually had four million pounds of bad debts. The bank attempted to raise more money by a flotation on the stock exchange and tried to get assistance from the Bank of England – without success. The bank failed on 10 May 1866, leading to a run on the stock exchange on the following day, now known as Black Friday. Panic ensued in London and other cities including

Norwich – more than 200 companies were brought down by the collapse of the bank. On the same day, however, the citizens of Norwich held a meeting in the Guildhall and declared their confidence in the Gurneys, but the Norwich Gurneys had to sell their estates to cover the losses. Barclays came to the rescue, injecting £635,000 into the Norwich bank and putting in new men, still from the Quaker banking world, including Henry Paul Barclay and Samuel Gurney Buxton. In 1868 six directors of Overend and Gurney, including John Henry Gurney and Henry Edmund Gurney, came before the courts, charged with having cheated Dr Alan Thom and other shareholders out of £3,000,000. On 22 December, all the directors were found not guilty. The news was received with acclaim in Norwich, the auctioneer at Norwich Corn Hall announcing it and saying: 'The name of Gurney is an honoured name in Norwich. The Gurneys had ever been friends of the poor and kind and good to all classes.'

112 *Harvey's Crown Bank building, later the post office, then Anglia TV, and now used for apartments.*

Harvey and Hudson's Bank had been founded in 1792 by James Hudson and Robert Harvey; its offices were in King Street. Hudson had previously been in the banking partnership of Hudson and Hatfield, who had run a bank in Haymarket from at least 1783. The bank descended through several generations of the Harvey family to Robert Harvey, who built the Crown Bank premises at the top of Prince of Wales Road in 1866. Lord Wodehouse did not like him, describing him in his diary as 'a mean sod who is afraid to risk his money bags by taking part in politics, tho' he wants to be made a bar[one]t to gratify his petty vanity'. However, the new bank was praised by the 1868 *Directory*: 'The building altogether is very handsome, stands in a fine position, and is a great ornament to the city.' Safety considerations were not forgotten; 'the whole building is also as fire-proof as it is possible to make it'. Two years later the bank came to a dramatic end when Harvey shot himself in the grounds of his house at Crown Point on 15 July 1870, dying three days later. The bank never reopened its doors and it emerged that Harvey had been using bank money for years to speculate on the stock exchange. The fall in prices following the outbreak of the Franco-Prussian War had ruined him. Gurneys bought up the goodwill, but many nerves in the city were shaken. Dean Goulburn knew of a woman who kept her savings in her own house after the bank's collapse – only to lose her nest-egg of £100 to housebreakers in 1874.[11]

Barclays, Gurneys and others amalgamated in 1896 to form Barclay and Co., which immediately became one of the six largest banks in England, a fact reflected in the size and grandeur of the later (1920s) Barclay's Bank building on Bank Plain, on the site of Gurneys bank.

Although there was no great incoming of migrants equivalent to the Strangers of Tudor times, there were plenty of new people arriving in Victorian Norwich. George Rossi, born in Italy, who had been conscripted to fight in Napoleon's army in Spain, came to Norwich in 1815. He set up a goldsmith's business on Exchange Street, which soon moved to Guildhall Hill; George Borrow was a close friend. Rossi died in 1865, and his son, Theodore, took over the business, which lasted four generations until it finally closed in 1936.

The house on St Andrew's Hill now occupied by 'Trudi's' had a very different feel a century ago as it was occupied by Polish Jews, refugees from the Russian progroms of the second half of the 19th century. At the time of the 1901 census it was occupied by Barrett and Sarah Lazarus and their eight children. Barrett and Sarah were both born in Warsaw in the late 1850s. Like many of the Polish Jews, they had first settled in London; six of their children, aged between five and 18 in 1901, were born there. Two more children, aged one year and three months, were born in Norwich, so the family probably moved to the city between 1896 and 1898. Lazarus ran a tailor's business from the house. His eldest son was also a tailor and two other young men in the house at the time of the 1901 census, both born in Lodz, were described as a tailor and a machinist.

Other members of the Russian/Polish diaspora came to Norwich before the Lazarus family; some are recorded in the 1891 census. Most of them were also tailors, such as Joseph Finsburg and his wife Harriet, living at 52 Peacock Street, both born in Poland. Like Lazarus, they spent some time in London before coming to Norwich; their son Reuben was born in Whitechapel in 1887. Living with them in 1891 were seven men and one woman, all born in Poland and all described as tailors: Swev Rosenzweig, Mark Silverman, Hyman Smith, Jacob Remer, Woolf Rudsky, Harris Golstein and Jane Rose. Jane Rose is described as Finsburg's sister; she was single, so had presumably changed her name into a more English form. Another family from Russia/Poland was that of Samuel Harrison and his wife Elizabeth. Living at 21/3 Colegate Street in 1891, they were another much travelled family: they had two children born in Manchester, one in Canada and two in Norwich. With them in 1891 was a visitor, Elias Shapps, also born in Poland. Although the Harrisons and the Finsburgs may have fled Poland with almost nothing, they had made good in their profession of tailoring in England over the years, and each family had a live-in servant.

Another incomer was Dr Harrington Darrell, born in the West Indies of white parents, who practised in Norwich. His surgery was at 12 All Saints' Green, a house under threat in the 1950s but saved thanks to the Norwich Society. A man of wide interests, he also owned a stable of trotting horses. Darrell died in 1920; a memorial was erected to him in the cattle market and more recently moved to a much more prominent site, near the bus stops on Castle Meadow.

Housing and Health

The Victorian period saw a massive increase in the city's housing stock, mainly in terraced housing in the suburbs. In 1821 there were 10,833 houses in Norwich, an increase of 2,300 in the previous 10 years. The 1881 census records 19,777 inhabited houses with 1,011 uninhabited and 246 being built.

Squalor and overcrowding were common in all major cities in England, and Norwich was no exception, especially as the weaving trade declined. The Health of Towns Commissioners reported:

> Norwich, it is feared, has seen its best days as a place of commerce, and would appear to be in that painful state of transition from once flourishing manufacturing prosperity to its entire decline, and must, ere long, revert to its original condition as a capital of an extensive agricultural district. A large portion of its inhabitants are therefore poor, their labour becoming daily lowered in amount and recompense … Neglect and decay are now conspicuous in the streets and quarters occupied by the working classes, so as to render them places of the most dismal aspect.[12]

113 *The growth of a suburb: Lakenham in the 1840s, with housing at Peafield. The city has now spread to cover all of Lakenham. The Tuckswood estate is named after the farm shown on this map.*

Working-class people lived mainly in courts or yards housing anything up to 40 families and with a single doorway leading into the street. These yards often had a single pump for water and unbelievably primitive toilet arrangements. In 1900 there were over 700 yards; their houses often backed onto those of the next yard, so that the only windows were in the front wall of the house. Some yards which were below the main street level were known as 'holes' and, where they were near the river, were always wet. Such houses would be let out for £3 to £5 a year, with some single-room properties at £2 or £3 a year. Terraced housing was developing outside the city walls from the early 19th century, starting with the very low-quality speculative housing at Peafield in Lakenham. Small houses could be rented for £5 to £7 a year; these houses usually had four rooms but often they were shared by more than one family to save expense. By the 1820s larger estates were built at Crook's Place and Union Place. Railway cottages in Thorpe built in the 1840s, with their triangular communal court, still survive.

Of course, not all housing was poor quality. The city had no control over houses already built but it owned much of the land within the city walls and could control the quality of new houses built on its land by stipulating the minimum annual rents and sanitary requirements. Some of the high-quality housing put up from the 1820s onwards survives at the Crescent, the Town Close estate and Victoria Street. By the beginning of the 19th century the richest families like the Harveys, the Gurneys and the Custances had moved out of the city and their places were taken by managers and clerks. By the middle of the century the better paid artisans were moving out too – into newly built houses in the suburbs. The population of Heigham rose from 842 in 1811 to 5,932 in 1841. One resident of Heigham who has left his mark was Henry Trevor, who owned a furniture shop which in 1851 employed 30 men. In 1855 he bought the site next to the city gaol and built the house now called the Beeches. He lavished much care on its garden, which in recent years has been lovingly restored by the Plantation Garden Trust, established in 1980 with the aim of maintaining the garden as it was at the time of Trevor's death in 1890; art historian Roy Strong called it 'one of Norwich's great surprises'.[13]

114 *The 1878 flood: this is Orchard Street off the Dereham Road.*

The 1851 census is the first to give exact ages and places of birth. It shows that, although there was a considerable movement of people into Norwich, it was not nearly so great as into the cities of the North. It also shows that the great part of the city's population still lived in crowded streets and yards. In tiny Flower Pot Yard, off Oak Street, there were seven households. Five of the householders were weavers. There were 22 children living in the yard and out of all its inhabitants, young and old,

only one had not been born in Norfolk. The wealthy lived in streets like Bank Plain, where the eight households employed between them 15 live-in servants (there were none in Flower Pot Yard). The people of Bank Plain were small businessmen. Their origins were different too – half the Bank Plain householders were born outside the county.

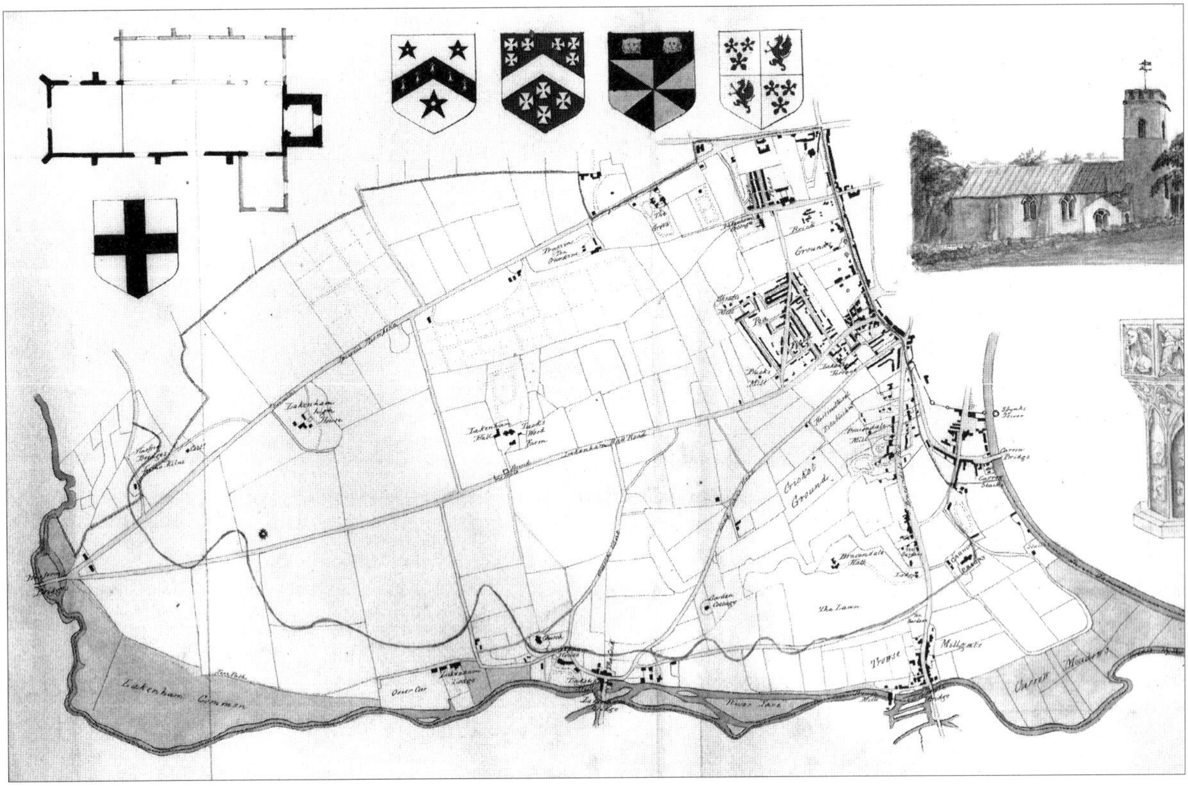

The movements of a more migratory population can be picked up from the census as well. In three inns on Ber Street – the *Fox and Hounds*, the *Jolly Butchers* and the *Bull's Head* – there were 34 lodgers born in all parts of Britain, including one each from Scotland and Ireland. The impact of the railway on jobs is shown in that five of these lodgers (all under 30) were railway workers. Older ways were represented by the Scotsman James Briggs, a 50-year-old drover.

Norwich's first housing by-laws followed the Local Government Act of 1858. New regulations came in from 1889: the minimum room height was to be eight feet, and there had to be 150 feet of open space at the rear. Plans for new houses had to be submitted to the city council, and from 1877 these plans survive as a complete record of new building in the city.

The years after 1877 saw the development of the terraced house in the suburbs, especially off the Earlham, Dereham and Unthank Roads. The process took several stages. The owners of farmland outside the city sold it to developers, who undertook the layout of streets and sewers. They might build the houses themselves or, more commonly, divide them into plots for small firms to do the actual building work.

The houses were then bought in blocks by landlords who rented them out. Standards were enforced by the original ground landlords who put covenants into the title deeds which the builders and later inhabitants had to obey. This might dictate the minimum rent to ensure that only the desired class of person could afford the house, or it might stipulate that any building be used as a house and nothing else – this is why shops and public houses are usually found on corners. Because the development was later than in the industrial cities, the corporation was able to enforce building regulations and the horrors of back-to-back houses were avoided; the only ones surviving in the city are at 27-33 City Road. Characteristic Norwich terraced houses have a small front garden (only a few streets do not have this) and a yard at the back with a toilet, rear access and often another small garden. Few have basements or third storeys.[14]

115 *The Victorian city: (above) the Greenland Fisheries, Oak Street; (below) Hayward's Yard, Ber Street.*

Co-operation between private enterprise and the city is illustrated by Isaac Coaks, who laid out the streets of terraced houses on the Hill in Thorpe Hamlet and also gave land to the council for a school. The names of his six daughters are recorded in the names of the roads – Ethel, Ella, Florence, Marion, Beatrice and Primrose. The first slum clearance programme began in 1877, and in 1899 the city council acquired the power to compel the owners of courts and yards to clear them.

Norwich is not always thought of as a centre for Victorian architecture, but it has some excellent buildings of the period – and some of the best architects in the country worked in the city. Edward Boardman, born in London in 1833, was the founder of the firm Boardman and Son, and he practised in the city from 1860 to 1900. He was the architect of some of the most important buildings in Victorian Norwich, including the rebuilding of the Norfolk and Norwich Hospital, the conversion of the castle from a prison to a museum, the *Royal Hotel*, the London Street Improvement Scheme of 1876-80, and a large number of 'villas' on the Unthank, Newmarket and Ipswich Roads. He also designed the Alexandra Mansions on the Prince of Wales Road, perhaps the first residential flats in Norwich and now part-occupied by a night club. He was a Nonconformist and designed several chapels, including the large block in Princes Street now named Boardman House in his honour.

The other famous Norwich architect was George Skipper (1856-1948), born in Dereham. He made his name with his work at Cromer, and moved his practice to London Street in 1896. The spectacular front of terracotta (made by Gunton's of Costessey and known as Cosseyware) is now part of the frontage of Jarrold's department store; it is described by David Summers as 'a firework in the street scenes of Norwich'. It was followed by the Royal Arcade, in art nouveau style, with glazed Doulton tiles decorated with peacocks; 'a shopping arcade was a novel experience for the city and Skipper's design ensured a unique shopping experience for its inhabitants'. When it opened in May 1899, a local newspaper said, 'It is as if a fragment of the Arabian nights had been dropped into the heart of the old City.' One of the present-day shops, Langley's, has been in the Royal Arcade from the beginning.[15]

Skipper's other works in the city centre include the Norfolk Daily Standard Offices, St Giles, 1899-1901, in white and brown terracotta. The least known is Haymarket Chambers, 1901-2, in terracotta with two towers, each with a trading galley on a plaque near the top. The Norfolk and Norwich Savings Bank (now Commercial Chambers), Red Lion Street, 1901-3, made much use of faience and has a square staircase tower. He was also responsible for the frontage of Jarrold's, the London and Provincial Bank, 1906, Telephone House (Norwich and London Accidental Assurance Association), 1904-6, and the Norwich Union Building. John Betjeman said of Skipper in 1975, 'He is to Norwich what Gaudi is to Barcelona.'

Works of the two architects can be seen side by side in Red Lion Street, where the whole street needed to be widened for trams, allowing state-of-the art architecture to come into the city. The Savings Bank of Skipper already mentioned stands beside Boardman's Veterinary Surgery of 1901-2, in red brick banded with artificial stone and topped by a huge Dutch-style gable. Pevsner calls the ensemble 'tall Dutch-inspired shops and houses punctuated with bits of baroque'.

A third local architect was A.F. Scott (1854-1936), who began his practice in 1886. His buildings include many factories now demolished, as well as Buntings (now Marks & Spencer) in 1912, actually of reinforced concrete; the solid-looking stone frontage is just a facing. Other buildings include Bewick House in Thorpe Road, built in 1894 for Richard Dawson, a bookmaker, with plenty of Cosseyware, and the Jonathan Scott Memorial Hall further up Thorpe Road, built in memory of his father.

116 *Plans of typical Victorian Norwich terrace houses.*

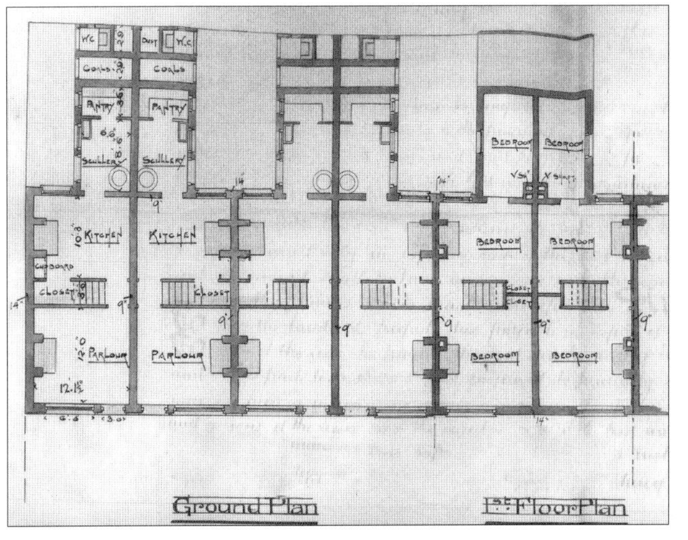

The city also committed itself to improvements in its infrastructure. The building of Thorpe Station led to a new main route developing along London Street, Castle Ditches and Rose Lane, but this route soon became choked with wagons. The London Street Improvement Committee was set up in 1876 and the street and nearby roads were widened over the next few years. The architect was Edward Boardman; the Venetian-style buildings at the market place end of London Street are a legacy of this scheme.

Prince of Wales Road was built in the 1860s to provide a wide direct route to the station and it was taken over by the council in 1865. They pulled down part of the old city wall at Chapelfield and used it as rubble for the new road; obviously they had not yet begun to think about preserving the city's historic heritage. A new and much wider Foundry Bridge was built, the old one being taken down and re-erected at

Heigham. The Foundry Bridge built then is the present bridge – Pevsner and Wilson are wrong to say it has been removed.[16]

Some of the finest large buildings of Victorian Norwich are on Agricultural Hall Plain. The Crown Bank (see p.178) has a fine crown on its pediment by Barnabas Barrett, responsible for several other works in late Victorian Norwich including the pepper-pots on the corners of St Peter Mancroft church tower and the 12 apostles on the flying buttresses on Norwich Cathedral. After the bank collapsed, the building became a post office. Next door is the red brick Agricultural Hall designed by J.B. Pearse and built in 1882. The building was still new when Oscar Wilde visited Norwich in 1884 and lectured here; his subject was 'The House Beautiful'. Opposite is the *Royal Hotel* designed by Edward Boardman in 1897, in a very different style from his heavy Nonconformist chapels. There was plenty of money to be put into Norwich's most prestigious hotel, with its easy access to the railway; it cost almost £24,000!

Above: 117 *The* Royal Hotel, *drawn by its architect Edward Boardman.*

Another Victorian building illustrating the close interdependence between city and country was the Corn Exchange, opened in 1861. There had been a corn market in St Andrew's Hall in 1796, which moved to what is now Exchange Street in 1828. It continued in use until the cattle market moved out of the centre of Norwich. The Exchange closed in 1963; it was demolished and replaced by an extension of Jarrold's. An unusual example of Victorian building that survives today is Crystal House on Cattle Market Street, built in 1863 for Holmes the engineers, with its façade of cast iron and glass – some of the pillars are actually of wood. It is one of the earliest designs of its kind in Britain, and is described by Pevsner as 'one of the most remarkable of Norwich's commercial buildings.'

In the 1870s wood paving was introduced to London Street, Eric Lubbock recalling: 'As I think of Norwich I remember first how the carriage-horses seemed to fill the narrow channel of London Street, how their horses pounded and echoed on the wooden pavement ... The shops of London Street were very brilliant.' By 1883 most of the city centre streets had been paved with wood – over 17,000 square yards in all. Main roads like Newmarket Road, St Stephen's and Ipswich Road had macadamised all-weather surfaces as early as 1835. In 1881 the city council decided to extend its scheme of electric lights from the two it had put up in the market place to the principal streets; however, this was discontinued in 1883, as the city was spending money on building sewers and could not afford to spend on lighting the city as well. In 1891 the prospectus of the Norwich Electricity Company was published and capital of £50,000 was raised in 5,000 shares of £10 each, but it was another two decades before electric street lighting was introduced.[17]

It was in the second half of the century that the twin problems of fresh water supply and disposal of sewage were solved, and conquering these problems revolutionised the way in which people lived. As we saw in the last chapter, the Norwich Water Company took water from the river at New Mills to its reservoir at Chapelfield. However, it supplied only the houses of those willing and able to pay, and even these could only have water for a few hours each day. The water was unfiltered. As late

Below: 118a, b *Rosary cemetery: some examples of the monuments.*

as 1849, only 3,000 of the 15,000 or so houses in the city had access to this supply.

Most people were still using wells or the river. There were 10 public pumps in the city but five of them adjoined churchyards, like the pump at the bottom of St John Maddermarket churchyard which survives to this day. The 2,000 people in Peafield had eight pumps and two wells between them. Supply from the river was also extremely unhealthy. Two of the worst cases are quoted in the *Norwich Mercury* report of 1850. In Water Lane people were taking their water from directly below the dye works and the water was coloured according to the dye being used. People found brown coloured water the best – 'the black spoiled the tea and so did the scarlet'. The worst situation of all was Crown Court Yard in St Benedict's, where 200 people had no water at all except what they fetched from the staithe. There was only one privy in the yard and that emptied into the river just three feet upstream from the staithe; 'parties fetching water first tried the [privy] door to see if anyone was inside. If so, they waited.' Women used to run across Fye Bridge with wraps over their noses to avoid the stench from the river.[18]

In May 1850 William Lee, a government health inspector, visited the city. He noted that the city graveyards were full and were scattered with fragments of bones. He said the city water supply was 'bad in quality and bad in everything that should constitute a water supply'. He reported that 'there were bubbles to be seen rising in the [Chapelfield] reservoir, and the water became dark in colour when the supply was let in by the pipes, and also in Hindes yard slugs were drawn in the water'.[19]

The City of Norwich Waterworks Company was formed in 1850-1, and built Heigham waterworks, the intake for which was upstream of city pollution. The company also built the Lakenham storage reservoir, from which the filtered river water was distributed across the city by gravity. The water quality was described as 'very good indeed' by the Norwich Sanitary Inspector in 1869. The city's water supply was taken over by the city council in 1892 and by Anglian Water Authority in 1974, and is still based on the works at Heigham and Lakenham, together with later works at Thorpe: the 300,000-gallon water tower on Thorpe Heights, built in 1932, is a prominent monument today, and has a historic resonance typical of Norwich, being on almost the exact site of Kett's Oak of Reformation.

In 1850 Lee suggested a sewer from Tombland to Trowse via King Street to intercept all the drains that ran into the river, and a second sewer to drain the higher parts of the city. The sewers were not built. In 1865 the engineer Sir Joseph Bazalgette was called in to advise; he proposed a low-level sewer starting at New Mills, crossing under the river at Bishop Bridge and running to a pumping station near Whitlingham Lane, with a high-level sewer running from Ipswich Road and joining the other near Thorpe Station. This, too, came to nothing.

In 1866 the residents of Thorpe took the city to court and won an injunction to stop the city polluting the river with sewage. The city finally had to act, and drew up a plan similar to Lee's with the low-level sewer running down King Street. The sewage was to be pumped up to Crown Point at Whitlingham.

Work on the sewers finally began in 1868, and sewage began to be delivered to Crown Point in 1871. Far more liquid material was being delivered than expected as water seeped through the brickwork of the sewers; this led to a great deal of work providing iron plating, struts or tubing. The low-level sewer was liable to silt up as it was almost level, giving off foul smells and forcing the removal of the sludge in the sewer by barge, with more offensive odours. New, higher sewers were eventually built with ejector stations to raise sewage from the low-lying parts of the city into the system. The old foul sewers were restored to be used for the removal of storm water. In 1899 a compressor station was opened at New Mills. In the 1960s, because of the massive increase in the quantity of use, the old sewers were reopened and strengthened; many of the drains built by these Victorian engineers are still in use today. One physical sign of this new world under the feet of Norwich citizens is the drain cover in Tombland Alley, which still bears the legend: 'T Crapper Sanitary Engineers'.[20]

As the century passed there were rising expectations in hygiene among the middle classes. When the Social Science Association held an exhibition of 'sanitary appliances' in Norwich in 1873 it was so popular it had to be extended by public demand. Lambert comments: 'That so many should flock to examine water-closets, stink-pipes and the like indicates … the widespread interest in sanitary affairs'. However, the process of connecting all the poorer houses in the city to the sewers was a fairly gradual one – as late as 1893 there were 20,000 houses still without water closets. They were still using privies or a midden – these were emptied at the city's expense but never cleaned.[21]

The diseases most characteristic of the 19th century were smallpox, cholera and typhus. In 1845 two prisoners – Dennis King and John King – died in a smallpox epidemic in the castle gaol, as a result of which 85 prisoners were vaccinated. There were several other outbreaks later in the century, with an epidemic in the spring of 1872; at its height 30 people a week were dying of smallpox in the city. The Roman Catholic priest Edmund Costello died at the Willow Lane presbytery on 2 July 1872, his death hastened by his work among the poor during the epidemic.[22]

Cholera reached England in 1831 and the corporation prepared for it by issuing orders for cleaning the city in the same year. They were not successful; cholera reached Norwich the following year. There were 320 cases of the disease in the city between August and October 1832, and 128 people died. Ideas as to its cause were sometimes inaccurate. Benjamin Armstrong, the vicar of Dereham, wrote on 12 September 1854: 'I am told that the following was done at Norwich, where the pestilence [cholera] is also very bad: a piece of fresh meat being attached to a kite was flown into the air for a couple of hours. When the kite descended, the meat was black and putrid.' He drew a false conclusion: 'this would make it seem that the cause of cholera is in the air rather than arising from the noxious vapours from the earth.'[23]

119 *Jenny Lind, singer who raised money for the city's hospital for children.*

The real problem was impure water, and outbreaks of cholera led to a concern for health in cities. In 1845 John Green Crosse described the city's churchyards as 'depositories of the crumbling remains of our predecessors, accumulated to a height of many feet, and disturbed by every recent interment'. From the 1850s it was forbidden to bury people in the overcrowded city churchyards, and municipal cemeteries were set up. At one time the corporation intended to put a cemetery on Mousehold Heath but in the end land in Earlham was purchased from John Cater in 1855. The Earlham Road cemetery is still in use, but no longer on the edge of the city due to massive later expansion of the urban area. As late as March 1893 an outbreak of cholera was feared in the city and preventive measures were announced.

The Norfolk and Norwich Hospital was almost completely rebuilt by Boardman and Wyatt in 1879-83. At one stage it was proposed to pull down all of the old building but in the end one wing was kept, saving about £2,000. Sir Thomas Wyatt was a famous London architect who had designed Knightsbridge Barracks and the Adelphi Theatre; Boardman later complained that Wyatt took the credit while he (Boardman) did the work. Wyatt was already very ill even before he undertook the commission. He died on 5 August 1880, and Boardman continued alone; the first stage of the work was opened on 30 June 1881. His achievement was acknowledged in an anonymous booklet: 'Mr Boardman's name must ever be associated with a structure which is hardly less admirable for the soundness and just proportions of the fabric, than sacred and venerable for the ends which in time to come it is intended to subserve.'[24]

A new children's hospital in Norwich was built after Jenny Lind, the singer known as the 'Swedish Nightingale', gave two charity concerts at St Andrew's Hall in 1849, and made later visits to the city. Armstrong wrote in 10 April 1862:

> took my elder daughter to a concert to hear Jenny Lind sing. She is a great favourite in Norwich … certainly her powers of song are marvellous. The sustained note on the highest key, the shakes, and above all the 'echo' in the Swedish song, are astonishing, and partake of the nature of ventriloquism.

Jenny Lind's first two concerts raised just over £1,250, and with the proceeds land was bought in Pottergate and a hospital for sick children was built, with 12 beds and an out-patients department. Jenny Lind had high standards – no nurse was to be engaged who could not read and write. In 1897 a new hospital was begun on Colman Road, using money from the Queen Victoria diamond jubilee fund. This hospital opened in 1900 but the out-patients department in Pottergate continued until 1929.

Medicine had to be paid for, of course, and a manslaughter case in 1850 illustrates both the purchase of medicines from local chemists and the city's addiction to opium. Lucy Dix of Magdalen Street sent a young girl, Hannah Barker, who lived next door, down to Messrs Smith, druggists, for a piece of rhubarb. Hannah brought the root back to Lucy in a pill box. She made it up into pills and gave to her husband, William; he died at nine o'clock that evening. The root turned out to be opium, and the shopman Augustine Worts was charged with manslaughter. The verdict of the jury was that Hannah had certainly intended to buy rhubarb; Worts probably misheard her, and assumed she had been sent for opium, 'which is a drug very much used in this city'. Unlike today, it was opium that was commonly seen, and rhubarb that was a rarity; Lucy Dix said she had often seen opium, as her brother and father both used to take it, whereas 'she never saw rhubarb except such as the Jews take about', an interesting insight into cosmopolitan Norwich in Victorian times.[25]

Slow steps were taken to improve care of the mentally ill. The county led the way: the Norfolk County Lunatic Asylum was built at Thorpe in 1814. In 1828 the city built 'a new Bethel at the Infirmary without St Augustine's Gates' on the site of the pest house there, which had become an asylum for aged and infirm paupers capable of holding only 19 lunatics. This was not big enough for its purpose and from the 1840s the Commissioners in Lunacy criticised Norwich's provision for the insane. Under an Act of 1863 the city was ordered to make proper provision for its 'lunatics'. [26]

After 40 years of pressure the city opened a new asylum at Hellesdon in 1880. It was designed to house 311 patients and was jointly funded by the councils of Norwich, Yarmouth, Thetford, Lynn and Bury St Edmunds. The hospital passed to the state in 1948. There were also private madhouses in the city for those whose relatives could afford them; that at Heigham Hall opened in 1833 and did not close until 1960.

In one way Norwich (together with Sheffield) led the way in its treatment of the sick poor, as the Guardians of the Poor in these two towns provided medicines. A separate apothecary was employed to dispense the drugs; this meant the doctor could order what he thought the patient needed, without having to consider the cost to himself. The dispensary was at the workhouse and the doctors gave the sick prescription notes to take there – or the doctor would visit if the patient was too ill to get up. The doctors were under strict instructions to give treatment only to the destitute. During the cholera outbreak of 1832, the Workhouse Committee was instructed 'that strong neat soup, and boiled down rice, and well spiced, be prepared and kept in the workhouse, ready for the paupers attacked with Diarrhoea or Cholera'. This was not just for inmates; poor people living in their own homes could also partake, providing they produced a doctor's certificate.[27]

During the 19th century many bodies were set up with responsibility for health matters such as local health boards, highway boards, school boards, sanitary boards and poor law unions. The Public Health Act of 1872 pulled them together under the control of the Urban Sanitary Authority. The first Medical Officer for Health for the city was appointed in 1873. In his first report he noted that more than a quarter of the deaths in the city were of children under five. He blamed bad diet, bad housing and the use of opiates. He found that many parents did not want their children vaccinated against smallpox and some did not register their children's births in order to avoid this.

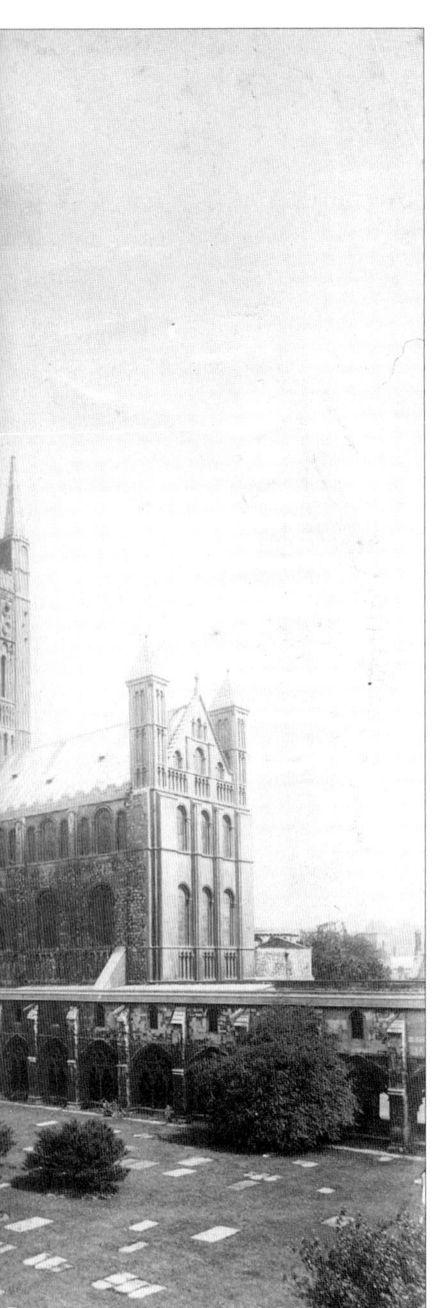

120 *Cathedral cloister as a burial ground for the parish of St Mary in the Marsh.*

The *Lancet* reported that in the period 1870 to 1878 Norwich had the highest mortality rate of 20 large towns that it surveyed. The birth rate was also very high at 32 per thousand – about ten per cent were illegitimate. The Norwich Improvement Act of 1879 gave the city power to enforce the notification of infectious diseases and this led to the detection of many sources of impure water. In 1878 Colman's appointed the first known industrial nurse in the world, Philippa Flowerday.[28]

Giving birth continued to be a home event with the aid of a city midwife. These included Phoebe Crew, who died in 1817; according to her tombstone in St Helen's church she had brought into the world 9,730 children in 40 years' practice. A stone in St Etheldreda churchyard commemorated Elizabeth Elvin, who died in 1849 and 'during 30 years practice as a midwife in this city brought into the world 8529 children'.

Although the first year of life and childbirth were dangerous, people who survived them might live longer than is often thought. The 1854 *Directory* cites seven Norwich people who had lived to be over 100 in the 19th century; only one was male.

Crime and Punishment

There was a gradual liberalisation of the treatment of criminals through the century. Hangings continued to be a popular public spectacle outside the castle until 1867 and transportation to the colonies was abolished the following year. Charles Dickens, who was fascinated by public hangings, wrote to a friend in 1849, 'Norwich, a disappointment, all save its place of execution, which is fit for a gigantic scoundrel's exit'.[29]

Samuel Yarham, who murdered Harriet Candler at Yarmouth, was executed outside the castle on 11 April 1846. This was the same day as Tombland Fair and a total of 30,000 spectators watched the hanging. There were similar huge crowds three years later when the double murderer James Bloomfield Rush was hanged. Many people were disgusted at the revelry and when Hubbard Lingley was hanged in August 1867 it was done at eight o'clock on a Monday morning to discourage crowds. This turned out to be the last public execution in Norwich; later hangings were held in in private within either the city or castle gaols.

The first private hanging involved a sensational case. In June 1851 the hand of a woman was found in Miss Martineau's Plantation in Martineau Lane by a boy called Charles Johnson. Other pieces of the woman turned up, scattered throughout the suburbs of the city. They were kept in spirits of wine in the Guildhall, but the victim could not be identified.

Nearly 20 years later, on 1 January 1869, a man called William Sheward walked in to the Carter Street police station in London and said, 'I have killed my wife. I have kept the secret for years, but I can keep it no longer.' Sheward was living in Tabernacle Street in Norwich when his wife suddenly disappeared in June 1851; at the time he said she had gone away in search of a former lover. In fact he had cut her throat during an argument. He kept her body until it started to smell and then dismembered it, boiling her arms and feet on his stove in the hope they would dissolve. Sheward was hanged in the city gaol on 20 April 1869.

A macabre event occurred at the hanging of Robert Goodale at Norwich Castle in 1885. The *Norfolk Chronicle* reported:

> The lever was pulled, the trap-door fell, and the prisoner who weighed 15 stone and was 5ft. 11ins. in height, and was allowed a drop just short of 6 feet, disappeared from view. To the horror of the bystanders the rope rebounded, and it was thought that by some means it had become unfastened. On looking into the pit below the scaffold the spectators observed the body lying on the ground, with the head still enveloped in the white cap, completely severed from the trunk.[30]

Prisoners in both the castle and the city gaol were made to work on the treadmill. In May 1848 a boy named Benjamin Elsey caught his foot in the castle treadmill; he was taken to the Norfolk and Norwich Hospital where part of his foot had to be amputated. A report by the prison surgeon two years later commented on the high level of malingering among the prisoners, 'chiefly caused by a desire to avoid the tread wheel'. In 1898 questions were asked in Parliament about a boy, Robert Cooper, who was put to work on the treadmill in the castle even though he said he was ill. He was kept at work for several days and his bed was taken from him as a punishment; one morning he was found dead in his cell.

Just over 500 people are listed in the Norwich Quarter Sessions records as being sentenced to transportation between 1788 and 1856. After 1856 there were no more transportation sentences from this court although the system was not abolished until 1868. Table IV lists the last people to be transported from this court, all to Australia. The peak decades were the 1820s to the 1840s, with an average of about fifteen people a year being transported. Their crimes were almost always stealing or receiving stolen goods. As might be expected, it was a mainly young and male population being excluded from society. The youngest was William Tuck, who was only eight years old when he was sentenced to transportation in 1839 for stealing two bottles from doorsteps. On investigation it turned out that he was forced into crime by his father, who would beat him if he came home without having stolen something. Tuck was sent temporarily to a new institution for young offenders at Parkhurst on the Isle of Wight; in 1842, he became one of the 123 'Parkhurst Boys' transported not to Australia but, most unusually, to New Zealand.[31]

The Industrial Schools Act, 1857, empowered magistrates to send children who had committed an offence to an industrial school. Norwich boys were sometimes sent to Red House Industrial School at nearby Buxton, but many children were sent outside the county to schools as far away as Manchester and Stockport. Boys from Norfolk were also sent to training ships, including the *Formidable*, based at Portishead, Bristol. Three sons of John Randell, a labourer of Chapel Street, Lakenham, were before the courts in successive years in their teens and all were sent to the *Formidable*; George, tried in 1884, died there suddenly of

Table IV: *Transportations from the Norwich court of Quarter Sessions.*

Date	Convict	Age	Crime	Length of term
1 Jan 1850	Robert Sadd	24	Stealing wheatmeal (fc)	7
1 Jan 1850	Samuel Pearson	21	Stealing money	7
1 Mar 1850	Hudson Neale	14	Stealing alcohol (fc)	7
1 Mar 1850	John Aldridge	16	Stealing alcohol (fc)	7
28 Jun 1850	George Webb	33	Stealing from a house (fc)	7
15 Oct 1850	Eleanor Allen	19	Stealing clothing (fc)	7
2 Jul 1851	James Base	21	Stealing a bag of money (fc)	10
14 Oct 1851	Thomas Hall	18	Stealing cutlery (fc)	10
29 Jun 1852	Edward Ong	20	Stealing shoes	10
30 Jun 1852	Isaac Lovell	19	Stealing a coat (fc)	10
30 Jun 1852	Edward Aldridge	21	Stealing money (fc)	10
30 Jun 1852	Thomas Bell	25	Breaking and entering	10
5 Jan 1853	William Cork	24	Stealing 12 rabbits (fc)	10
28 Jun 1853	William Platford	26	Stealing a sheep	7
2 Jan 1855	Matilda Leggett	26	Stealing money	14
2 Jan 1855	Mary Ann Howard	21	Stealing money (fc)	14
30 Dec 1856	Maria Chambers	20	Stealing a purse	15

fc = former conviction

Source: *NCR 20a, Quarter Sessions books. Taken from a list of transportations from Norfolk courts compiled by Finn Laplain.*

heart failure on 22 August 1897, while Isaac, tried in 1895, later joined the Royal Navy, serving on the *Lion*.[32]

Two cases in September 1883 show late Victorian attitudes to child crime. In September 1883, two boys, 11-year-old George Hilton and James Cullum aged 12, were caught trying to scale the wall of a garden in St Augustine's with 11 apples they had stolen; Hilton told the constable that 'he did not know how the apples came into his pocket'. Although the younger, Hilton was thought by the magistrates to be the ringleader; he was sent to an industrial school until he reached the age of sixteen. Cullum was merely fined five shillings.

In 1883 an unnamed 12-year-old boy (the fact that he is not named in the *Norwich Mercury*'s account of the trial is itself a significant step forward) was in court charged with theft. He delivered milk for his employee, Watts Dickerson, a dairyman of Alexandra Road, and had supposedly pocketed some of the money the customers paid and kept it for himself. The magistrates fined him for this, but the chairman of the magistrates commented that it was most unwise to put temptation in a lad's way by letting him collect cash.

Life in Norwich Castle prison is described by 'the King of the Norfolk Poachers', sent there for a month at the age of 12 for stealing a rabbit.

> You were called up at six in the morning, got dressed, made your bed up, and with a pail of water had to scrub the floor and table and make everything bright and clean for the day. Breakfast at seven thirty to eight o'clock, then half an hour in Chappel – and was surprisen to hear how the Prisners sang the himns. Nine o'clock we were marched off to the Weel room. There were numbers posted up from one to twelve. The Warder

> in charge would shout out what numbers he wanted to work on the Weel, and those men would stamp it round for fifteen minutes and then come off for five minutes. It was like walking up steps and never getting any higher, but verry hard work and we was kept at it from nine to twelve.
>
> Then came diner, wich was one pint and a half of stir about, composed of one pint of oatmeal, and half a pint of maze meal put in the oven and baked. We were put on the Weel again from one o'clock till four of the afternoon, then we were set to pick okum [which, he tells us elsewhere, was 'old tarry rope'] till eight, wen we went to bed.[33]

121 *Transforming the castle from a prison to a museum.*

The end of transportation meant that more gaol cells was needed, while the efforts of Elizabeth Fry, John Howard and other prison reformers resulted in higher standards of prison accommodation. Norwich's new prison at Mousehold was completed in 1887. Prisoners were moved there from the castle, which had served as a county prison since 1345, and from the city gaol on Earlham Road, which had lasted just 60 years.

The castle was bought by the city council. One proposal was to let it slowly crumble into a 'romantic ruin', but an alternative plan to convert it into a museum was led by John Gurney, who had become blind in 1881, when he was 36 years old. The architect Edward Boardman created a model of the plans, so that Gurney could appreciate what was proposed, and this survives at the Castle Museum. The castle opened as a museum in 1894; admission was free except on two days a week when a charge was imposed. In 1900 a 'Time Ball' was erected, dropping at exactly 10 a.m. every morning so that citizens could set their watches and clocks to the exact time. At first made of iron, its drop was found to be damaging the structure and it was replaced by a ball of wood and canvas; it fell out of use in 1938.

Religion

The 1851 religious census asked people what church they had attended the previous Sunday. The people of Norwich divided into three almost equal groups. One third had been to an Anglican church, one third to a Nonconformist place of worship and one third had not been to any place of worship. The Nonconformists were divided into many groups, of course. Even the Methodists (by far the largest group) were split into four movements, each with their own chapels: the Wesleyan Methodists, the Primitive Methodists, Wesleyan Reform and the Countess of Huntingdon's Connexion.[34]

Several Nonconformist chapels were put up in the 19th century, such as the massive block making up the Prince's Street Congregational church and associated buildings. This was built by Edward Boardman between 1869 and 1879. He worshipped there himself and it is now called Boardman House. Boardman built the Methodist Chapel at Chapelfield, too, and worked at St Mary's Baptist chapel; this was destroyed in the Second World War but has since been rebuilt. The fine 1810 Calvert Street chapel belonging to the Methodists was pulled down by the city council and the Congregational chapel of 1858 at Chapelfield has also gone. Other faiths

122 *Interior of St Peter's Chapel.*

were also building: the Jewish synagogue in St Faith's Lane was opened in 1849. This, too, was destroyed by bombs in the Second World War; the street name Synagogue Lane still exists, apparently the only street in Britain named after a synagogue.

The Salvation Army came to the city in 1882. The Norwich Skating Rink between Bethel Street and St Giles had opened for roller skating in 1876 but folded due to lack of support in less than four years. The Salvation Army bought the building in 1882, converting it at a cost of £290, and it was open shortly before General Booth made his first visit to Norwich, on 9 September 1882. Booth urged his followers to 'Get a drum and arouse Norwich from end to end.' The first leader in Norwich was a woman, Captain Jane Hockey. The present St Giles citadel opened in 1892 and the skating rink later became a builders' store; it is now a shop.

In 1870 the Roman Catholic community in Norwich amounted to about 1,200 people, with 215 children at Catholic schools. In 1869 six sisters of the teaching order of Notre Dame arrived at the Catholic school in Ten Bell Lane and in 1870 they opened a boarding and day school for girls. The end of the century saw the building of St John's Catholic church, built by the Duke of Norfolk, thus renewing the connection between the Dukes and the city that had been severed in 1708.[35]

Five different sites were considered by the Duke of Norfolk and Canon Richard Duckett from the late 1870s. Possibilities included the grounds of the Notre Dame convent in Surrey Street, the existing chapels at Willow Lane and Maddermarket, and the old prison site which had come on the market. Then in February 1879, a fifth possible site came up when Duckett bought a house in St George's Plain with an adjoining dye house, and began to pull down the buildings there. However, when the prison site came on the market once more in September 1879 the Duke bought it at a cost of £7,505. He appointed George Gilbert Scott as his architect, and decided that the church should be in Early English style as this was not well represented in Norwich. Building began in 1884 and the nave and aisles were completed by 1894. Scott's poor health forced him to give up the work and he was succeeded by his brother, John Oldrid Scott; the whole church was finally completed and blessed on 8 December 1910. It had taken about half the length of time of the medieval cathedral. Dr Duckett, who had also established the Convent of the Little Sisters of the Assumption in Chapelfield Road in 1904, died in July 1910 just a few months before the final completion of the church.

Pevsner calls the building 'an amazing church, proof of Victorian generosity and optimism'. Eric Lubbock described it as 'a large and splendid church, scrupulously Gothic, with curious rungs or handles attached to it – as though for the grasp of a giant bending over the pile to lift it bodily in the air, "flying buttresses" they were, I was told.' The church has some fine stained glass by John and Dunstan Powell. After it was opened, the former Willow Lane church became a school.[36]

The Church of England had a revival too, with some clergymen doing vital work among the poor of the slum parishes. One of them was Samuel Stone of St John de Sepulchre, who died in 1848 and is commemorated in the east window there. In the 19th century, Anglican churches were built for the expanding population of the suburbs, including Christ Church, New Catton (1841-2); St Mark, Hall Road (1844); St Matthew, Thorpe Hamlet (1851); Holy Trinity, Essex Street (1860-1); Christ Church, Eaton (1873); St Philip, Heigham Road (1868); St Thomas, Earlham Road (1886).

Several of the city centre churches were neglected for much of the century. A late 19th-century newspaper article says:

> It is fourteen years ago and more now since matins and evensong were said or sung in St Mary's Coslany. St Mary's indeed has long been an eye-sorrow and is now rapidly becoming a nuisance and a source of positive danger to those who live near it … if among those who live in that neighbourhood of yards and slums there is one who has a dead cat or dog for which he can find no place of burial, in the carcase goes, through the fine old traceried windows, every pane of which has long been smashed out.[37]

There was a growing interest in the buildings, however, and by the end of the century every Anglican church had been restored except St Helen and Sts Simon and Jude.

Norwich led the way in a revival of Anglican monasticism. Joseph Leycester Lyne was an Anglican who had become convinced it was his calling to restore to England the monastic life lost when Henry VIII dissolved the monasteries. He gathered together a few followers in Claydon, Suffolk, and in January 1846 they moved to Norwich, taking over a rag merchant's house in Elm Hill. The vicar of St Lawrence, Mr Hillyard, offered to give them daily communion, so the 'monks' would walk there in their robes each morning. They were shouted at and sometimes assaulted; Lyne had to ask for police protection. He now started calling himself Father Ignatius. Armstrong wrote of him (30 January 1864), 'his personal beauty, youth, zeal and eloquence are described as something extraordinary, rising, they say, to the level of a Whitfield or a Wesley'. Lyne built himself a church behind Elm Hill which still exists; he left the city in 1866, later founding a monastery at Llanthony in Wales.

Popular superstitions had not changed much through the centuries. The *Norfolk Chronicle* reported a case in 1843 when a Mrs Kedge complained to the magistrates that a Mrs Clarke had bewitched her 'by sending her and her children a vast number of vermin'. Two months later the city magistrates had another witchcraft case to deal with. Mr and Mrs Curtis claimed to have been bewitched by a Mrs Bell:

> Mrs. Curtis saw Mrs. Bell light a candle and fill it with pins. She then put some red dragon's blood, with some water, into an oyster-shell, and having repeated a form of words over it, her husband's arms and legs were set fast, and when he lay down he could not get up again without somebody helping him.

Norwich and south-eastern Norfolk had its own Valentine's Day custom. This was:

> the leaving of small anonymous gifts for children in parallel to the greetings and presents being made to adults. All through the early 20th century the custom continued to thrive among working-class families in this area, youngsters expecting the visit of an invisible character called 'the Valentine man' or 'Father Valentine' after nightfall on St Valentine's Day. Apparently inspired by Santa Claus, he left sweets, fruit, pencils, or a book for each child on a window-sill or inside a hallway; in reality he could be either a parent or a family friend.

Adults might well receive gifts too, Dean Goulburn noting in his diary his Valentine presents in 1873: a bottle of wine, a box of photographs and a pen-wiper with a dog upon it. Many Norwich people still fondly recall this tradition.[38]

Transport

Pull's Ferry was known for most of its life as Sandling's. Sandling, who had been a chorister at the cathedral in the reign of Queen Elizabeth, kept the ferry in the early 17th century; according to Sir Thomas Browne he lived to be 89 years old. The ferry was named after him until the time of John Pull, who kept the ferry and the adjoining inn from 1796 to 1841, when the licence for the inn lapsed. The ferry continued until 1943. There was another ferry lower down on King Street, giving its name to the *Ferryboat Inn*.

Lowestoft Harbour was rebuilt in 1846, but by this time the railway was replacing the navigation. There were plans for a large new harbour in Norwich, to be named after the Duke of Clarence, but the arrival of the railway killed the idea; the scheme now only survives in the street names Clarence and Lower Clarence Roads and nearby Harbour Road.

Steam packets continued to operate in the 1840s, including the *Dahlia,* built of iron, but, as the railway took more of the trade, the ships focused increasingly on the tripper market. The best-known of them was the steamer *Jenny Lind*, launched at Reedham in 1879, which ran between Norwich and Bramerton Woods End. However, trade on the Norfolk rivers was mainly by wherry. The 1854 *Trade Directory* says:

> The general navigation from Norwich to Yarmouth is by keels and wherries. The latter are peculiar to the rivers of Norfolk and Suffolk; and those used in the Wensum carry from 15 to 40 tons, and draw from three to four feet of water; the mast is at the head, and so balanced by means of lead, that the strength of one man is sufficient to raise or lower it in the event of passing bridges.

Wherries can be seen picking up cargo from warehouses by the river in Norwich in Henry Ninham's painting, 'On the River Wensum, Norwich' (fig. 85). The Norwich builders' merchants Lacey and Lincoln had a number of wherries. Timber was brought by wherry to Jewson's in Colegate and other timber merchants, and sawn planks were unloaded from Scandinavian sailing ships at Yarmouth. They were famously loaded so that they extended right over the cabin and well beyond the hull, producing a stack 20 feet across, which gave just nine inches to spare when passing under Bishop's Bridge. Ice for Norwich tradesmen was also brought up from the Broads by wherry; there was an Ice House off Bracondale above King Street, last used in 1894 but still surviving as a street name. Wherries were built in Norwich at yards in Carrow and Thorpe, and most famously at Petch's Yard opposite Cow Tower. William Petch built wherries here, such as the *Jessie* in 1860 – and was also landlord of the *Horse Barracks* public house in Barrack Street.[39]

The Coach and the Railway

In 1816 there were four coaches a day from Norwich to London. Two Royal Mail coaches left the *Angel* inn at 3.45 p.m., one going via Newmarket and the other via Ipswich. The London Day Coach left the *Rampant Horse* inn at 6 a.m. and took 14 hours. The Telegraph London coach left the *Norfolk Hotel* at 7 a.m., taking 13 hours. These coaches were in competition and the owners of the Day coach announced that they would 'not risk the lives of their passengers by racing against time'. In 1844 there were seven coaches a day from Norwich to London but they were doomed. The first through-train to London ran on 30 July 1845 and by January 1846 the coaching trade was dead.[40]

On 7 February 1835 a 'moveable panorama' of the Liverpool and Manchester Railway was exhibited in the Theatre Royal in Norwich. Two companies put schemes before Parliament in 1836 to connect Norwich to London by railway, but both ran into money problems. In 1841 George and Robert Stephenson decided upon Yarmouth as the starting point of a great east-to-west trunk route across England. The first stage was to be the 20-mile route between Norwich and Yarmouth via Reedham. Work started in 1843; no tunnels were needed, but the river was diverted into a new channel between Trowse Hythe and Wensum Reach as this was cheaper than building swing bridges. The contractor was Samuel Morton Peto, now commemorated by a bust at Norwich railway station.[41]

The Norwich and Yarmouth Railway was formally opened on 30 April 1844. The first public traffic was on 1 May when 1,015 passengers

123 *Exploiting the river: Stewart and Patteson brewery barge.*

were carried, in some discomfort in the case of the third-class passengers: 'The third class are six-wheeled carriages, open, and at present without seats. We trust they will not continue so; the inconvenience of standing, especially to females, during a journey in a cold weather, will be very great'. A considerate husband might bring a carpet stool for his wife, as the Yarmouth murderer Samuel Yarham did in 1846. The fare for third class was 1s. 3d. for one way, compared to 2s. 6d. for second class and 3s. 6d. for first class. By means of the railway, passengers and freight could be carried between Norwich and Yarmouth in 50 minutes.[42]

The Norfolk Railway's line to Cambridge opened in 1845 and the first through train to London ran on 30 July, starting at Trowse as the swing bridge over the river was not finished. The bridge was finished in December 1845; the engineer was George Parker Bidder. On Christmas Eve in the same year, the engine of a train to Norwich left the line at Thetford and the driver and stoker were killed; 'the accident was supposed to be due to the excessive speed at which the train was travelling – fifty-five miles an hour'.[43]

The effects of the railway were dramatic. The *Norfolk Chronicle* said on 25 April 1845: 'During the droving season last year 9,300 beasts were housed at the *Bird in Hand* public house Tasburgh … but so great is the diminution of traffic occasioned by the Norfolk Railway, that during the present season only twelve beasts have been taken in.' On 17 January 1846 the same paper said starkly: 'All the coaches between Norwich and London have ceased to run.' In fact, because Norwich was the last major city to be connected to the main railway system, its mail coaches had survived longer than any others; the last run was on 8 January 1846. The news was not all bad for horse transport; the same newspaper acknowledged that there had been a great increase in horse carriages connecting towns without stations to the railway. In 1875 there were 101 carriers in Norwich, serving 363 towns and villages. It was not until after the First World War that they came to be replaced by motor vehicles.[44]

124 *The first railway station in Norwich, 1845.*

The line to London via Ipswich was opened in 1849 by the Eastern Union Railway, which built its own station out of an old circus building in a pleasure ground off Queen's Road. This was Norwich Victoria and it became something of a white elephant as early as 1851, when the line was linked to Thorpe Station; however, the city forced the railway company to keep it open, with an Act of 1862 forbidding its closure.

The Norwich and Yarmouth line was one of the first to introduce the 'block' system whereby only one train was allowed at a time on each section of line. Even so there was a disaster in 1874 when a train from Yarmouth crashed into the mail train from Norwich on the single-line track in Thorpe. Both drivers and firemen were killed and 23 passengers also died. The fault was with the staff at Brundall who had let the train from Yarmouth through. It was unclear whether the night inspector Alfred Cooper or the telegraph clerk John Robson was responsible; in the end Cooper was jailed for eight months. There is a plaque marking the spot, and several of the crash victims are buried in the Rosary cemetery, some with engravings of the train on their tombstones.[45]

One major piece of early railway engineering to survive is the Lakenham viaduct. Made of red brick and with five arches, this was financed by Samuel Bignold and built in 1849. The present Thorpe Station, of red brick with stone dressings and a zinc-covered dome, was opened on 3 May 1886. The swing bridge leading to it was single track and by 1905 was carrying 170 services a day. In August of that year it was replaced with the present double-track structure; the drum of Bidder's original swing bridge survives, beneath the more recent superstructure.[46]

The third station in Norwich was City Station, off what is now Barker Street. This opened in 1882 and was the terminus of a line from Melton Constable. In 1881 it was planned to extend the railway from City Station along the river edge of the Close to a point opposite Thorpe Station. This would, of course, have meant destroying the medieval Water Gate. The plan was strongly opposed by Dean Goulburn, whose efforts earned him the nickname 'the fighting dean', an allusion to the 'fighting bishop' of 500 years earlier (p.18). It was originally planned to run the railway from City Station right through the centre of Norwich to join the Thorpe line and end in a new station in front of the cattle market. The failure of the scheme meant that all the stations were on the edge of Norwich and there was never a line through the city. The result is, as Arthur Ransome says, that 'Thorpe Station at Norwich is a terminus. Trains from the middle of England and the south run in there, and if they are going on east and north by way of Wroxham, they run out of the station by the way they came in.'[47] Later City Station became part of the Midland and Great Northern Railway Company, offering services to the North Norfolk coast and through-trains to Birmingham. Badly damaged in air raids, City Station was rebuilt after the war but closed to passengers in 1959 and to freight in 1969.

The most profitable route was always that to London. In 1846 trains ran from Shoreditch to Norwich in 260 minutes, making four stops. Just as there had been two coach routes to London, so there were two train routes – one via Colchester, the other via Cambridge. Both routes had about the same number of trains until after the Second World War, when the Colchester route became the only main line between Norwich and

THE

YARMOUTH & NORWICH RAILWAY

Notice is hereby given, that on and after MONDAY NEXT, the

FIRST TRAIN

FROM YARMOUTH

WILL

Leave at a QUARTER BEFORE 8 o'clock,

AND THAT THE TRAINS WILL ONLY STOP

At such Intermediate Stations as are shewn in the Time Table below.

THE SURLINGHAM FERRY STATION

WILL NOT BE USED FOR THE PRESENT.

TIME-TABLE.									FARES. Children in arms, **Free.** Under Ten Years of Age, **Half-price.**		
Down Trains.		DAILY.				SUNDAYS.					
		MORNING.		AFTERN.		MORNING.		AFT.	First Class.	Second Class.	Third Class.
Departure.	Miles.	H. M.	H. M.	H. M.	H. M.	H. M.	H. M.	H. M.	s. d.	s. d.	s. d.
NORWICH . . .		**9**	**11**	**4**	**7**	**7 45**	**9**	**7**	—	—	—
BRUNDALL . . .	6	—	11 10	—	7 10	7 55	9 10	7 10	1 0	0 9	0 6
BUCKENHAM . .	8	9 15	—	4 15	—	8 0	9 15	7 15	1 6	1 0	0 8
CANTLEY .	10	—	11 20	—	7 20	8 5	—	—	2 0	1 6	0 10
REEDHAM . . .	12	9 25	11 25	4 25	7 25	8 10	9 25	7 25	2 6	1 8	1 0
YARMOUTH . . .	20½	—	—	—	—	—	—	—	3 6	2 6	1 3

125 *Norwich-Yarmouth railway timetable, 1844.*

the capital. In the 1960s many of the branch lines disappeared and even more drastic proposals would have left only the line to London open. These came to nothing, but evening and winter trains on the Cromer and Yarmouth lines have had to be subsidised by the county council.

Communications

The electric telegraph service came in with the railways; telegraph companies rented the wires used for railway signals and for the first time communication became almost instantaneous. In November 1846 the London stock market prices were conveyed to Norwich by telegraph. When Isaac Jermy, the recorder of Norwich, and his son were murdered at the isolated Stanfield Hall in 1848, a servant swam the moat, borrowed a horse and rode the three miles to the police station at Wymondham. The police telegraphed Norwich and reinforcements were sent in carriages; they surrounded the house of the suspect James Rush and arrested him there. By 1854 Norwich was provided with services along the lines to Ely, Yarmouth and Fakenham.

The first attempt to promote the telephone in the city was in December 1877, when two telephones of Alexander Graham Bell were brought to Norwich. One was taken to Cromer but an attempt to speak from the Norwich telephone to the Cromer one only produced a mumbling sound. However, in 1881 a cornet solo played into an Edison telephone by a member of the Carrow Works' band was clearly heard down the line in London, and after this progress was rapid. In the same year, the United Telephone Company ran a line from Morgan's Brewery in King Street to Mousehold House, where one of the directors lived. This is the first record of a telephone in Norwich. The first telephone exchange was set up in Exchange Street in 1883 (the street name refers to the earlier Corn Exchange and not to the telephone exchange). A larger one opened in Haymarket in 1894 with 200 subscribers. At first they could only telephone each other and people in Yarmouth and Lowestoft, but the system was extended over the next few years. These humble beginnings led to today's telephone technology.[48]

Poverty

The treatment of the poor in most of England was run under the New Poor Law Act of 1834, which grouped country parishes into unions with a workhouse. However, the parishes of Norwich were already in a union with a workhouse so they did not come under the Act, and the poor law administration established in the city in 1712 lasted until 1863. The Norwich Poor Act of that year made the electoral districts for the Guardians the same as the city wards; it also brought the parish of St Mary in the Marsh into the city system for the first time.

There was no drastic change in policy in 1863, however; as always it was a question of looking after the poor while spending as little of the ratepayers' money as possible. Poverty was probably at its peak in the middle of the century. In 1845 the *Norfolk Chronicle* said that 2,000 to 2,500 were unemployed in the city and 75 per cent of these were weavers. They were costing Norwich ratepayers over £300 each week. By 1848, one in five of the city's population were paupers – in 1847, 35,596 were excused payment of poor rates because of poverty. The capacity of the workhouse at St Andrew's was only 380 but the conditions were good. A poor law commissioner wrote: 'I have never seen bread of such fine quality in any other workhouse, it is equal to any provided for my family.'[49]

It was intended to make workhouses undesirable places and one factor was the threat that the bodies of paupers might be used for dissection (see p.153). In 1848 the Poor Law Commissioners enforced the regulation of separating married men from their wives in workhouses. This led to trouble. In May 1848, 11 paupers were imprisoned for disorderly conduct at the workhouse; they had refused to be separated from their families. They were released on 16 June and spent the day parading around the city with about 200 or 300 supporters. They went back to the workhouse where they were given supper and allowed to talk with their wives. At 9 p.m. the master of the workhouse ordered them to leave their wives and go to the male ward. They refused to do so, and the police were called to take them back to prison. The protest was pre-planned and a large crowd had gathered on St Andrew's Plain and the nearby streets, perhaps 2,000 strong; they followed the police as they escorted the men back to gaol, throwing stones, brickbats, glass bottles and other objects at them, several of the prisoners also being struck. The police walked in two ranks, before and behind the prisoners, up Exchange Street, through the market place and along St Giles.

It was here, just outside the *Black Horse*, that disaster occurred. Constable Thomas Osborne, who was walking next to Constable William Callow in the rear rank, heard him cry out 'Oh I have got it', and he fell; he died of his wounds on 29 June, leaving a widow and five young children. On reaching the gaol, the police deposited their prisoners and again faced the mob, several policemen being hurt in the volleys of stones that were thrown. This time they cleared the street by force; many of the crowd received wounds to their heads from the police truncheons and others were trampled by those making their escape. It was after midnight before the market place was cleared. Two men, William Woods and Isaac Williams, were imprisoned or fined for their part in the riot, but the person who threw the fatal stone was never identified. As for the prisoners, they spent the night at the prison; some then agreed to obey the workhouse rules and went back there, others served a further term of imprisonment.

A new workhouse opened in 1859 on Bowthorpe Road with room for 900 paupers. On an average day there were about 300 people in the workhouse, rising to almost 600 in the 1860s. The number of poor being relieved in their own homes rose from about 1,600 to 4,600 in the same period, as unemployment rose with the collapse of the weaving industry.

Norwich Guardians paid professionals to train poor boys in a craft, usually shoe-making. They also continued to bind out boys as apprentices.

In 1847 a Boys' Home was opened and selected boys went there from the workhouse school, staying on for two or three years after they had found a job. Of the 67 boys sent out from the home between 1847 and 1854 only eight failed to make a living for themselves. A Girls' Home was set up in 1850 where poor girls were trained as domestic servants. In 1880 the Guardians proposed to save money by closing the Boys' Home and sending the boys back to the workhouse. This was opposed by Canon Copeman and his amendment was carried. In the event both homes continued into the 20th century. The Boys' Home was at St Faith's Lane until 1932, when it moved to 58 Earlham Road.

Poverty inevitably forced some women into prostitution, a side of the city that shows up mainly in criminal court records. One such case was in 1891, when the landlord of the *Cattle Market* inn, George Anderson, was charged with allowing the pub to be used as a brothel. The prosecution was based on a police watch on the inn during a Saturday evening, and a round-up of the women involved. Jane Nichols of Union Place admitted going to the inn with a man she did not know and having sex there; another of the women, Ann Fountain of Cartwright's Yard off Rosemary Lane, agreed in court that 'it was her misfortune to walk the streets'. Her husband was a chimney sweep, and her own profession is given as shoe binder. Other women involved included Laura Day of Coburg Street, described as an 'unfortunate', Emma Brown of St Paul's Opening, and Ann Dawson of Harford Street, but not all were necessarily prostitutes: Ann Dawson in particular strongly insisted in court that she was simply having a drink in the pub with a friend. Anderson was fined £20 with costs and forfeited his licence.

Schools

The education reformer James Kay-Shuttleworth wrote his *Report on the Training of Pauper Children* in Norwich in 1838. He said that classrooms should be full of maps, drawings and blackboards and fitted up on the plan used in Dutch schools with all the pupils facing the teacher. The monitorial system should be replaced with the Continental system of teaching children in classes of reasonable size. The curriculum should embrace the three 'Rs', geography, religious instruction and also vocal music as taught in Dutch and German schools.

The sons of richer parents would attend academies such as that of Charles Turner on Pottergate. Boarders paid fees of 20 guineas if under 10 years old, and 25 guineas for older pupils. For this they were taught English, arithmetic, history and book-keeping. Everything else was extra. If they paid they could have lessons in classics, astronomy, drawing, dancing, music, mathematics and natural philosophy.

In 1838 new district schools were opened at St Augustine's Gates by the Bishop of Norwich. They were supported by voluntary contributions and intended to accommodate 450 children, but demand was growing and by 1854 about 700 were attending the school. There were similar but smaller district schools in Surrey Street and Upper Westwick Street.

The Norwich charity schools were smaller institutions. In 1854 there were nine schools with a total of 750 boys and 500 girls. The Central or Model Schools were in Prince's Street for boys and in Broad Street for girls. Although largely funded by subscription, each pupil did have to pay one or two pence a week.

In 1854 there were National schools at Pockthorpe, Lakenham and Heigham, and British schools in the city mission room in Julian Place and in Lakenham. The Dissenters ran their own school in St James' Road with about 200 pupils and also supported the Lancastrian school in College Court. Dissenters' Sunday schools were attended by about 4,000 children in 1854.

Following the formation of the Ragged School Union in 1844, a Ragged School was set up in Norwich in 1848. This functioned on Sundays and two evenings in the week and was supported by Nonconformists and radicals. However, following rioting and disorder in 1857, the school closed down.

The new Norman school, 'a neat Gothic building with a residence for the master', was opened in Cowgate in 1839. Thirty boys were instructed as free scholars and their parents were given £10 a year for their maintenance. When a boy reached 14 he was apprenticed with a premium of £15 and a further £10 if he reached 21 with no complaints about his apprenticeship. Norman's School also took in fee-paying pupils.[50]

The 1851 census shows many small schools in the city. On Bracondale, William Paul with three live-in teachers (all young men between 18 and 21) looked after 37 boys aged between nine and seventeen. Most came from Norfolk or Suffolk but two had been born in India, where their parents were no doubt on colonial service. In Pottergate, Anna Barnsdale looked after nine girls between four and 12, all described as orphans; this was the Girls' Orphan Home and School, supported by voluntary subscriptions. A 17-year-old female lodger, described as a shoe binder, was probably a former pupil.

In 1856 Jeremiah James Colman and his wife started a school for the children of their employees. Parents paid a penny a week for one child and a halfpenny for any others; the money went entirely to school prizes. The school began with 22 pupils and had 324 by 1870.

Under the Education Act of 1870 School Boards were set up. These were intended to supplement the church schools and not to replace them. The Norwich Board estimated that the existing schools provided 8,674 places but that over 5,000 more places were needed, and they began building schools to fill this gap. For the first time, every child in Norwich was to have an education. At first they had to pay a few pennies, but schooling became free in Norwich elementary schools from 1 September 1891.

The School Boards were elected bodies and had an extraordinary method of voting. In Norwich there were 15 people on the Board; every elector had 15 votes and could vote for 15 different candidates, or could put as many votes as they liked onto one candidate – they could vote 15 times for the same person if they wished. This was to allow minority interests onto the Board. For example, there were not enough Roman

Catholics in the city to ensure they would get onto the Board in a normal election, but if each Roman Catholic voted 15 times for the same person, they would get one representative; in practice, this was Canon Duckett, who made a great contribution to the city's educational life, and is now honoured with a street named after him. The system also helped other small groups like the early Socialists; George Roberts, a printer born in Chedgrave, was elected to the School Board in 1899, before going on to later fame as an MP for the city.

Women ratepayers could vote in these elections and also be candidates. The first two women to obtain seats on the Norwich School Board – and thus the first to obtain any official positions of authority in the city – were Charlotte Bignold, the daughter of Sir Samuel, and Mary Anne Birkbeck, both elected in 1881; Bignold School is actually named after Charlotte, and not after her famous father as most people assume. In 1893 Margaret Pillow ran for the Board as the first woman representative of the National Union of Teachers. She was elected and fought hard for teachers' salaries, but was defeated at the next election three years later.

Discipline in these schools was harsh by later standards, as a case in 1883 illustrates. Susannah Reeve was assistant teacher at St Augustine's Board School for infants. One of her pupils was five-year-old Samuel Howard, who one morning was 'disobedient and naughty'. Susannah tied his hands 'very loosely behind his back with a piece of velvet', telling him to stay behind after the class was dismissed for lunch so that she could untie him. Unfortunately she was called away to see the headmistress, and when she came back the bell had gone and all the children had left, including Samuel. He had walked back to his house at Barrack Steps not far away; a few minutes later, Samuel's mother, Amelia Howard, came storming into the school with Samuel – whose hands were still tied behind his back – and, in a fury, struck his teacher in the face. The headmistress, Miss Evans, turned out to have exceptionally liberal views on punishment, by Victorian standards; she said not only that she (Miss Evans) was the only teacher in the school permitted to carry out corporal punishment, but that there was not even a cane in the school at all – 'the tying of hands was so mild a form of punishment that teachers were permitted occasionally to resort to it'. Amelia was fined for the assault, but the magistrates were divided as to whether the tying of hands was a very cruel or a very mild punishment.[51]

Many dioceses established teacher training colleges. In Norwich the first college to train elementary school teachers was set up in a house in the Close in 1839, and in 1853 a building on St George's Plain was bought and adapted for 40 trainee teachers. A purpose-built college was built at a cost of £15,000 and opened in 1892; the name College Road preserves its memory. Most of the students at the college were pupils from elementary schools who had been awarded Queen's scholarships.

The Norwich School of Design opened in 1846, among the earliest in the country; one of the first students was Frederick Sandys, discussed on p.210. The Technical Institute was built in 1899 on St George's Street, with its long face rising directly from the river and with a dome at the corner.

Leisure

In the Victorian period Norwich saw the establishment of two of its best-known open spaces as public parks– Chapelfield and Mousehold Heath. The College of St Mary in the Fields passed to Miles Spencer at the Dissolution; the adjacent Chapelfield Croft was granted to the city by John Worseley in 1569 and has been city property ever since. In Elizabethan times it was used for archery practice and Braun and Hogenberg's map of about 1581 shows archers there. Chapelfield was leased out on condition that the people of Norwich were free to use the grounds for walking or recreation, and that the city chamberlain could dig and take away sand and clay for the repair of the city walls between St Giles' and St Stephen's Gates. In 1656 Lady Hobart tried to stop the citizens having free passage in the field, but this was successfully resisted – so the area has a centuries-long tradition as a public space. A fence was put around it at the beginning of the 18th century, and part of these railings were removed for use in the war effort in the 1940s. Avenues of trees were planted in the field in the mid-18th century by its lessee, Thomas Churchman, who resided at nearby Churchman House.

In 1792 it was taken over by the Norwich Waterworks Company and a reservoir and water tower were built; the reservoir was used in winter for skating. It ceased to be part of the water supply in 1852, but remained as a lake; in that year the council planned to put the Nelson statue, which is now in the Cathedral Close, onto an island in the lake. The plan came to nothing, and the lake and water tower were removed soon after.

Soon after his conversion to the Japanese vogue, Wymondham-born architect Thomas Jeckyll was employed by Barnard, Bishop and Barnard to design for them a great cast-iron pavilion to be shown at the Philadelphia Centennial exhibition of 1876. Two years later it appeared at the Paris exhibition, where it was admired as a technical *tour de force* and a perfect example of the application of Japanese design to contemporary use. The pavilion was bought by the city for about £500 – its original cost had been £2,000. It was set up in Chapelfield but was taken down in 1949; the sunflower frieze from it can still be seen in Heigham Park.

Most of the vast area of Mousehold Heath (known to locals as 'Mussel') lay outside the city; over 1,000 acres of it were enclosed under Parliamentary Acts for Sprowston and Thorpe in 1801. Only the part within the city boundary (about 184 acres) survived as common land. It was owned by the cathedral, who gave it to the city in 1880 on condition that the corporation tried 'all lawful measures to prevent the continuance of trespasses nuisances and unlawful acts and to hold the heath for the advantage of lawful recreation'. John Gurney gave money to make it accessible, and in his year as mayor provided work for the unemployed in laying out a new road across the heath, now named Gurney Road in his honour. Due to lack of grazing, oak and birch trees have reclaimed much of Mousehold Heath in the 20th century, and the open heath loved by Crome and Borrow has been largely lost.[52]

Despite the growth in the number of houses, Norwich was still a city of gardens. In 1845 Thomas Dugdale wrote, 'the houses being generally

126a, b *Jeckyll's Pavilion, and its sunflower remnants in Heigham Park.*

furnished with gardens, [the city] occupies more ground in proportion to its population than any other city in England'.[53]

The Theatre Royal may have undergone something of a decline in popularity in the middle of the century. Bayne wrote sardonically, 'the interior is quite commodious enough for the limited number of patrons which Norwich furnishes to the drama'. However, some great names were attracted to the city: in September 1840, the Hungarian pianist and composer Franz Liszt gave one concert in the Assembly Room and one at the Theatre Royal.

There were other theatres in Norwich in the 19th century, specialising in all forms of variety and popular entertainment. Full-blooded dramas were staged at the Adelphi Theatre in the Ranelagh Gardens, which in 1848 put on a local drama called 'The Spirit of the Loom' showing 'Norwich as it is' with 'Effects of Vice, Drink and Misery, Burning of the Cotton Mill and dreadful conflagration'. The Adephi closed when Victoria Station was built on the site in 1849. Another short-lived theatre was the Vaudeville in St Giles Street, offering a roller-skating rink, cycling, performing dogs and music hall. It closed in 1882 after six years. In March 1898, the freehold of the *Norfolk Hotel* was bought by a syndicate for £9,500 to build 'The Norwich Opera House and Theatre of Vanities' on the site. It later became the Hippodrome Theatre.[54]

Popular entertainment was represented by two nationally important figures, Jem Mace and Pablo Fanque. 'Jem' (James) Mace, born at Beeston near Dereham in 1831, was a bare-knuckle fighter. He won the world title in 1862 against Tom King – the fight lasted 43 rounds. In 1870 he fought Tom Allen in Kenner, a suburb of New Orleans – fighting was not allowed in the city itself. The prize was $10,000 and Mace won in the 10th round; there are now statues to both men on the site. Mace became landlord of the *Swan* in Swan Lane in 1858. He fought to the end of his life, dying at the age of 79 on a boxing tour of Durham. He is sometimes called 'the father of modern boxing'.[55]

'Pablo Fanque', whose real name was William Darby, was born in Norwich of a black father and white mother; it is commonly said that he was the son of John Darby and Mary (*née* Mary Stamp) born in 1796, but this child appears to have died as an infant. However, more recent research has found that they had a second child called William, born in Norwich Workhouse in 1810, which is almost certainly him; his death certificate says that when he died in 1871 he was 75, but this appears to have been an error. Darby was a circus performer, and became the first black circus proprietor in Britain when he established his own show in 1845. He married twice: his first wife died in an accident at Leeds when a gallery collapsed during a performance in 1848. Darby died in Stockport in 1871, and is buried in Leeds. He is mentioned in the Beatles' song 'For the benefit of Mr Kite', perhaps the only Norwich person to have this distinction; John Lennon had seen his name on an old circus poster in an antique shop.

Tradition says that his father was a butler in a Norwich house but this is not certain; this fascinating man awaits a biographer.[56]

One form of civic pride was the erection of statues. The Nelson statue by Thomas Milnes, made of granite, was erected in St Andrew's Hill. The Duke of Wellington statue, in bronze by C.C. Adams was unveiled in the market place by Samuel Bignold in 1854 in front of a crowd of 20,000 people. Nelson was a local hero, of course. Wellington had no direct connection with the city but his son had an estate in Norfolk and had been MP for Norwich. Both statues have, at different times, been moved to the Close. At the top of Agricultural Hall Plain is this author's favourite statue in the city, the bronze angel on the Boer War memorial by George and Fairfax Wade, with delicate drapery across the legs and gorgeous outspread wings.

Norwich was the home of many other Victorian institutions. It was one of the first cities to levy a rate for the purchase of books under the Free Libraries and Museum Act. The Free Library opened in 1857 in St Andrew's at a cost to the corporation of £10,000; in 1883, it comprised a lending library of 7,000 volumes, the City Library of 1,800 volumes and a reference library of 1,100 volumes. In April 1880, the librarian used £10 received from fines for overdue books to buy some local reference books; this was the beginning of what eventually became the Local Studies Library. The privately funded Subscription Library in Guildhall Hill was much larger, with 50,000 books and a specialist law library of 4,000 books.[57]

In May 1850, public baths were opened at Heigham by Mr Sultzer; there was a penny bath, a three-penny bath, and also private baths for those who could afford it. The baths were open from six in the morning to six in the evening, a *Norwich Mercury* reporter noting that 'we had the pleasure of testing the healthful influence of these baths and the accommodation here offered to those who regard bathing even as a luxury is highly satisfactory'. In June 1875 a group of Norwich residents met at the Literary Institute and resolved 'that the establishment of a public swimming bath in Norwich is most desirable'. The estimated capital needed was £1,500 and a site was chosen near the river at Heigham; such facilities were still provided by private enterprise rather than by the city council.

Literary life in Norwich, although not at the peak of the Georgian era, could still furnish some famous names. George Borrow, born at Dereham in 1803, went to Norwich Grammar School and the family lived in Willow Lane until Borrow's marriage to May Clarke in 1839. Abbe Thomas D'Eterville, a refugee from the French revolution who came to Norwich in 1792, taught Borrow French and Italian; William Taylor, the author, taught him German. In 1833 Borrow became an agent and translator for the Bible Society in Spain and Russia. Needing to be in London, he simply walked the 112 miles; it took 27½ hours and he survived on a roll, two apples, a pint of ale and a glass of milk – total cost 5½ pence! His account of his subsequent travels, *The Bible in Spain*, was one of the best-selling books of its time. Harriet Martineau recalled that Borrow becoming an agent of the Bible Society caused 'one burst of laughter from all who remembered the old Norwich days', but Amelia Opie was entranced by the book: 'Long live Don Jorge! He is my delight both night and morning, and my happiest hours are spent in his society.'[58]

Borrow's two books of autobiography, *Lavengro* (1851) and *The Romany Rye* (1857), were not successful at the time but are now valued partly for the picture they give of Norwich and Norfolk life. One interesting detail in the latter is that in discussing the mutiny on the *Bounty* in 1787, Borrow thought men followed the mate, Fletcher Christian, rather than the captain, William Bligh, because Christian was more genteel and came from a better class of family than Bligh. He had this idea from a man whom he does not name, but was obviously Robert Tinkler, who was just 14 when he took part in Bligh's epic voyage and who was in Norwich when Borrow was growing up; Tinkler died in the city in 1820. In this way a book published in 1857 provides direct evidence about an event 70 years earlier.

Mary Wright was born at Sutton, Suffolk, and went to a dame school in Norwich; her drawing master may have been John Crome. Mary's father and brother were ruined when their steam packet blew up in 1817 (see p.129). Mary married Isaac Sewell, son of a prominent Yarmouth grocer; their first child, Anna, was born in Yarmouth in 1820. Mary became famous for writing children's books and books for the poor. Her *Mother's Last Words*, published in 1860, was a long ballad about two young brothers who preferred poverty to thieving. One died of cold and went to heaven, the other lived to be an honest man. It was published by Jarrold's and sold well over a million copies. From 1867 Mary lived at the White House, Catton, now 125 Spixworth Road, and devoted herself to the care of her sick daughter Anna. Anna herself, at the age of 57, wrote her one book, *Black Beauty*, in 1877. Also published by Jarrold's, it was an immediate success and remains one of the most popular children's classics of all time. Anna did not live to see its full success; she died just three months after its publication and is buried, with Mary, at the Friends' Burial Ground at Lammas in Norfolk. They are commemorated – appropriately – by a horses' drinking trough at the bottom of Constitution Hill, not far from their Catton home. This was put up by Anna Sewell's niece.

One Victorian author, not as well known as she should be, was Emma Marshall. Born Emma Martin, she spent the first 10 years of her life in the Old Bank House where her father, Simon Martin, was manager. Later the family moved to the Thorpe Road and as an adult Emma lived in Clifton, where she wrote her books in the 1880s and 1890s, novels based on the lives of famous people including *In the East Country* (Thomas Browne), *Winifrede's Journal* (Bishop Hall) and *Castle Meadow* (John Crome).

Painting did not reach the heights of the early years of the century, but was not moribund. Sir Frederick Sandys, born in a house on Grapes Hill in 1829, became a leading London artist closely associated with the Pre-Raphaelites; he frequently returned to Norwich and city scenes feature as the background of many of his paintings. Lucy Brightwell, born in Thorpe in 1811, studied under John Sell Cotman and exhibited her highly praised etchings in 1839. In 1869 recently-widowed George

Borrow proposed to her, but she turned him down. She died in her house in Surrey Street in 1875.

Margaret Fountaine, diarist, traveller and butterfly collector, moved with her family from Stoke Ferry to Eaton Grange in 1878. Two years later, when she was 18, she noted that 'life now is nothing but a succession of garden parties, dances etc, a constant introduction to the fashionable society around Norwich', but her adventures soon took her very far from the city. She died in the West Indies in 1940, leaving to the Castle Museum her collection of 22,000 butterflies – and the rather frank diaries of an exotic and much travelled life.

Norwich had many other international connections, including Joseph Jackson Fuller. Born in Spanish Town, Jamaica, in 1825, almost certainly a slave, he, along with his father and brother, became a Baptist missionary; all three were in West Africa from 1844. Fuller married Elizabeth Johnson, a Jamaican school teacher, there and they had three children; she died in 1859. In 1861 he married Charlotte Diboll, daughter of Joseph Diboll, an English missionary. In 1869 he visited England for the first time. The Dibolls came from Norfolk and Fuller placed his son Joseph (by his first wife) as an apprentice in a Norwich engineering company. Fuller returned to missionary activity in Africa, and in later life lived in London, dying in Stoke Newington in 1908. Another former slave, Samuel Crowther, preached in the church of St Giles on Sunday, 2 July 1882. Crowther, whose African name was Adjai, had been captured by slavers in 1821, when he was 11 years old. Brought up in Sierra Leone, he became the first black bishop in the Church of England.

We have discussed Jenny Lind's role in the city (p.188), but Norwich had its own musical talents, including Maria Brennan. Born in 1849, her father was a dentist who died before her first birthday; her mother then ran a haberdashery shop in London Street. She was a pupil of Zechariah Buck, the long-serving cathedral organist, and under the name Marie Rosetti achieved worldwide fame, singing in many opera houses including Milan, New York, Moscow and St Petersburg, where she was presented to the Tsar. She married Alfred Barnard, of the Norwich iron merchant family, in 1878 and died in London, aged only 45, in 1895.[59]

SIX

Norwich in the 20th and 21st Centuries

The new century was observed in the city on 1 January 1900 with great celebration. The 20th century saw more changes in Norwich – and in life in England in general – than the previous 900 years.

The first change in the way the city was governed was in 1907. Under the terms of the Local Government Act of 1888, the city boundaries were extended to include parts of the parishes of Sprowston and Catton. On 25 October 1909, Edward VII visited the city and so became the first reigning monarch to come to Norwich since Charles II, 238 years earlier; the fact that he embraced the latest technology by travelling in a motor car – then, a rare sight – added to the numbers who turned out to watch him. There was a much shorter wait for the next royal visit, as George V came to the city on 28 June 1911, just six days after his coronation.

The mayor in 1909 was Walter Rye, discussed on p.244, and he met the king not in formal morning dress but in his usual bowler hat and tweeds – some people thought this cost Rye the knighthood he might otherwise have expected. The following year the chief magistrate of the city became lord mayor rather than mayor. In 1911 it was Eustace Gurney who was host to the royal visitor as lord mayor – and he was duly knighted.

One of the earliest lord mayors sprang from the city's Jewish community: Arthur Samuel, whose father had been a pawnbroker on Timberhill. His mother, Rosetta, was the daughter of Philip Haldinstein, the shoemaker. Samuel went to Norwich Grammar School, but then moved away from the city; indeed, when he was elected mayor of Norwich in 1912, some members of the city council objected that his links with Norwich were not close enough.[1]

The early 20th century saw the beginning of the break-up of the old two-party system of Liberals and Conservatives, and Norwich played its part in this. The first 'Socialist' member of the city council was James 'Fred' Henderson, elected in 1902. Henderson was born in Norwich in

1867, and had spent four months in Norwich Castle prison following food riots in the city in 1885; he claimed that he was one of the last people in England to be forced to work on the treadmill. He was a poet, whom Gladstone had supposedly considered as poet laureate, and also an important political writer; his *The Case for Socialism*, published in 1911, was based on Saturday evening meetings that he held in Norwich, and was translated into many languages. The Norwich Parliamentary by-election of 1904 was the first one in which the Labour party put up a candidate, George Roberts. The Liberals won by 1,820 votes over the Conservatives, with Roberts a poor third, but in 1906 he was elected, becoming one of the first 30 Labour Members of Parliament. He soon became chief whip of the group.[2]

127 *King George V, in Norwich, visiting CNS school in 1911.*

The early years of the century also saw some advances for women in politics. Although they could not vote in Parliamentary elections until after the First World War, they could both vote and stand in other political areas. Some women had become Poor Law Guardians after an Act of 1894 removed property qualifications; among them was Annie Reeves, a member of the Salvation Army, who lived in a slum yard off St Stephens. From 1907, women could stand for the city council; the first was again Annie Reeves, who stood unsuccessfully in 1907 and 1908. However, the first woman to be actually elected to the council was Mabel Clarkson in 1913, having served on the Board of Guardians since 1904; she was elected as a Liberal, but in later life moved to the Labour party. In her 1912 election address, she wrote:

> I know many, in fact most, of the Courts and Yards in our poorer districts, and I do not hesitate to say that some of the dwellings in which some families are living today are a disgrace to the city. Those of us who care for the purity of her homes, for the right of little children to opportunities of health and development, for the prevention of infantile mortality, and of all the unnecessary sickness and suffering caused by overcrowding and bad housing, are bound to make every effort to get rid of the slums.

Norwich had more female council members after the war. One was Lucy Henderson, Fred's wife, and they were the first married couple to serve together on any local authority. The number of females on the

council rose to eight in 1950, and to 18 in 1986, over one third of the council. Norwich was the first city in England to have a female lord mayor, Ethel Colman, daughter of Jeremiah James Colman, elected in 1923; her sister Helen Colman acted as lady mayoress. Another sister, Laura Stuart, was the first female Justice of the Peace in the city, as recorded in a plaque in Stuart Gardens, which she gave to the city in memory of her husband, James Stuart, an important figure in the development of education for adults. Norwich also elected one of the very earliest female Members of Parliament, Dorothy Jewson, of the well-known Jewson timber family. A pre-war suffragette who had worked for women's union rights during the war, she won her seat in December 1923 but was defeated in the next general election, less than a year later. Few have followed her lead. Lady Noel Buxton was a city MP between 1945 and 1950, and a third female MP was elected in 2009, Chloe Smith, who was also one of the youngest people to become a Member of Parliament. Norwich has had a tradition of young politicians: when Arthur South was elected to the city council in 1935 for Catton ward, he was just 22, the youngest councillor in the British Isles. Radical politics saw the rise of the Labour Party, first taking power in City Hall in 1933, and later that of the Green Party, who held 15 seats after the election of May 2011, one of the largest Green groups on any English local council.[3]

Norwich women played their part in the suffragette movement, mainly outside the city. Dorothy Jewson was a member of the WSPU and taught in Richmond, Middlesex, between 1908 and 1911. She was back in Norwich in December 1912, when Emmeline Pankhurst paid a visit to the city, speaking over male jeers and catcalls at St Andrew's Hall; one of the chants the Norwich men employed to drown her out was 'On the Ball, City', a very early use of the song that became Norwich City's anthem. Miriam Pratt, a teacher at St Paul's school in Norwich, set fire to empty buildings in Cambridge in 1911; on being imprisoned in Holloway she went on hunger strike. Violet Aitken shocked her father, Canon William Hay Aitken of Norwich Cathedral, with her window-smashing activities in London in March 1912.

Norwich hit national headlines in 1912 when the city was devastated by flooding. On 26 and 27 August, torrential rain fell continuously for 29 hours; 7.34 inches of rain were recorded. The *Daily Mail* of 28 August caught the drama of those days, exploiting the latest communications technology in a series of timed telephone reports. At 11.15 p.m. on the 27th their reporter in Norwich phoned his London office:

> Norwich was plunged into total darkness at 8.30pm tonight. This was due to water flooding the electric power station to a depth of 6 ft, putting the dynamos out of action. All the streets which are lighted with electricity are in darkness. The fire brigade have sent an engine to try to keep the power station clear of water.
>
> All day long the police have been patrolling the district in boats. Carts were stationed in the flooded streets to carry people from point to point, and ladders were reared up against the houses where women and children took refuge in the top stories for many hours.

At 1 a.m., he telephoned with further news:

> Thousands of people were in the streets, driven from their homes by the advancing waters. It is estimated that 7,000 were rendered homeless in the poorer quarters. The police organised a rescue service by boats to remove the people from their inundated homes. The women and children were taken to schools on higher ground, where mattresses, hurriedly brought from all quarters, were provided for them … I have been told that in the dire necessity of rescuing human beings, animals have had to be left to their fate. Horses and dogs have been seen floating dead in the streets. The work of rescue is rendered the more difficult by the total absence of lights in the streets. Torches are being used. Several men who live in the flooded districts have had to swim to places of safety.
>
> As I am sending this message the work of rescue is still being pressed forward with desperate haste.

A final telephone call at 3 a.m. was in time for the paper's later edition:

> The water is still rising. The whole of the local police force is engaged in rescuing people from houses in the flooded area. The schools in the district are now overcrowded with homeless people … the situation is hourly becoming more serious.

About 3,650 houses were affected by the floodwater, especially in the low- lying areas of the city, north of the river and off the Dereham Road and in an area the *Daily Mail* reporter called 'Ham Street', misunderstanding a Norwich pronunciation of Heigham Street. Three people were killed in the night, and 2,200 people were put up in schools and in other shelters. The next day, food was supplied by boat to those trapped in their homes; Caley's provided milk and hot chocolate in soda-water bottles with a loop at the neck, passed to upper windows with boat-hooks. Carriers, unable to practise their usual trade, made some money by hiring their carts out for rides through the flooded areas. The water subsided on 30 August, but many houses needed repair; 43 were so badly damaged that closing orders were issued on them as being unfit for human habitation, while a further 102 Dangerous Building Notices were given out.

One of the consequences of the flood was a widening of the river near Fishergate to make it less of a bottleneck. Another was that national attention was brought to the poor quality of some of the houses in the city by the news reporters from London, the *Daily Citizen* commenting that Norwich 'has literally hundreds of little, narrow, sunless courts, resembling nothing more than a series of rabbit runs, and the dampness which the waters had left as legacy has never disappeared'. It was estimated that one house in three was below the standard laid down by the Local Government Board, and that one house in five was positively unfit for human habitation.[4]

128a, b *The 1912 floods and repair work afterwards: no health and safety here!*

The *Daily Mail* report mentions electric light, a new development in the city; after a gap of almost thirty years, the city had begun installing electric light in the streets in 1910, and by 1913 there were over 1,750 lamps. The project was the brainchild of the city's electrical engineer, F.M. Long.

Norwich in the First World War

The First World War broke out on 4 August 1914. The city was affected both in the loss of many of its young men and in the lives of those who remained behind. The names of those killed recorded on the Roll of Honour comes to a total of 3,544 men. Many joined the Norfolk Regiment and many fought on the Western Front, in most cases leaving England for the first time in their lives. Two won the highest military honour, the Victoria Cross. Harry Daniels, the son of a Norwich baker, won his for courage during the attack at Neuve Chapelle on 15 March 1915: he carried on cutting the German wire in front of his position despite being badly wounded. Daniels remained in the army until 1942 and later lived in Leeds. Sidney Day won his Victoria Cross on 26 August 1917 for his bravery in clearing trenches of the enemy, and in particular for picking

129 *Local men enlisting at Britannia Barracks in 1914.*

up and throwing back a stick bomb which had landed in his trench occupied by five men, one severely wounded. He was one of the VC holders who accompanied the coffin of the Unknown Soldier into Westminster Abbey on 11 November 1920. Day was born in 1891; his family lived in Ber Street, and he went to St Mark's school, Lakenham, before becoming an apprentice to a butcher in St Catherine's Plain. He later worked as a butcher in Saxmundham and enlisted into the Suffolks when war broke out. Day also survived the war, and in later life he lived in Portsmouth, dying there in 1959. There is a plaque in his honour in St Mark's church, Lakenham.[5]

130 *First World War soldiers on the cattle market.*

However, for Private John Abigail of Thorpe Hamlet the horrors of the war were too much to face. The son of a Norwich carter, he deserted from the 8th Battalion of the Norfolk Regiment at Ypres in 1917 and became one of the 307 British soldiers shot for desertion, the only one from the Norfolk Regiment. His name was omitted from the city Roll of Honour after the war, although it is among the names honoured in St Augustine's church; it was added to the city Roll in the 1990s when a more understanding attitude to these – often very young – 'deserters' emerged.[6]

Norwich men fought in the Middle East campaign as well. The 4th and 5th Battalions of the Norfolk Regiment suffered many losses in the failed attempt to capture Gaza in April 1917, with almost every officer of the 5th Battalion killed or wounded. They included Major W.H. 'Harry' Jewson, the brother of Dorothy. Others served in the navy or in the Royal Flying Corps. Older men played their part as well, and in December 1914 a Volunteer Corps, with a minimum age of 38, was formed for men too old to join the forces. These men patrolled railway lines, guarded bridges against saboteurs, and helped build the airship base at Pulham Market.[7]

St Andrew's Hospital was converted into a war hospital, the mental patients being moved to Hellesdon Hospital to empty the wards. Nearly 45,000 wounded troops were treated at the hospital during the war. Dr David Thomson was Medical Superintendent at Thorpe from 1886 until his death in 1923. He was a close friend of Sir Arthur Conan Doyle, and the author often played cricket with the team from the Thorpe Hospital. Thomson's greatest claim to fame is as the original of one of literature's most famous doctors: Dr Watson, of Sherlock Holmes fame. Apparently Doyle once asked Thomson: 'What do you think of Watson?' Thomson replied: 'I think he's a bit of an ass.' Doyle then said: 'I'm sorry you think that. I rather modelled him on you.'[8]

The Norfolk and Norwich Hospital also played its part, and on 17 October the first casualties arrived – 97 men from the British Expeditionary Force came to the city by train, arriving at Thorpe Station. Fortunately most were only lightly wounded and could make their own way to the hospital, as there was only one city ambulance, drawn by one horse! The *Eastern Daily Press* began an appeal for a new ward at the hospital for wounded soldiers, and this opened in 1915 with space for 60 men. The beds were sponsored by individuals and local businesses; Boulton and Paul, for example, sponsored 10 beds. Many large buildings in the city were used as convalescent homes, such as Sunny Hill House in Thorpe, Catton Hall and the convent of the Little Sisters of the Assumption.[9]

After the first ever air raid in Britain took place, resulting in a small loss of life in Lynn and Yarmouth, black-out restrictions were ordered in the city in January 1915. About 700 men became special constables, both to replace those policemen who had joined the army and to enforce the black-out. In the event there were no raids on the city, although the hospital took in four people badly hurt in an air raid on East Dereham on 8 September 1915. There were many other restrictions on normal life:

131a, b *Healing the sick at the Convent of the Little Sisters of the Assumption.*

public houses were ordered to close at 9.30 each evening and voluntary food rationing was promoted, becoming compulsory for some foods early in 1918. Attitudes sharpened toward foreigners living in the city; all 'aliens' had to register with the police and stay within five miles of their homes. There were about 2,000 registered aliens in the city, mainly Italians.

There was an anti-war movement in the city. By chance, the Independent Labour Party held its annual conference in Norwich in 1915; the two main speakers were Keir Hardie and Ramsay MacDonald. Because of the party's anti-war stance, most Norwich meeting-places refused to stage the conference. In the end a Primitive Methodist minister, the Rev. Storr, allowed them to use the schoolroom attached to his chapel in Queen's Road. The chairman of the Norwich Reception Committee was Herbert Witard and the treasurer was Annie Reeves; the Committee included Ernest Cornwell, later to serve a prison sentence for refusing to join up after conscription was introduced in 1916. ILP delegate Fenner Brockway recalled the Norwich Conference in his autobiography:

> At night Norwich was pitch black; since it was a town near the East Coast not a light showed through the house windows or in the streets. As I approached the ILP Club I saw some ghostly white figures grouped together. Suddenly the strains of 'O God, our Help in Ages Past' rose from them. The vicar had brought his choir to sing outside the hall in protest against the holding of an anti-war meeting.
>
> Hardie made this incident the theme of his opening speech. The little hall was crowded to suffocation and the lights were dimmed. Hardie's bushy white hair and his white beard shone out in the darkness with almost phosphorescent radiance. His head was held high, defiantly; his voice was strong and deep. His speech was the most uncompromising denunciation of war I had heard from him. Mass murder he called it, and the statesmen and parsons and Labour leaders who appealed for recruits were guilty of incitement to murder. His voice nearly broke when he spoke of the tragedy of Socialists murdering each other, but then he spoke confidently of the rebuilding of the International Socialist movement and of the final triumph of Socialism and the ending of war for all time.[10]

The local leader of the movement was Witard, who at the age of 13 had run away to sea but returned to become a city councillor. His political views led to the accusation that he had refused to help with recruiting men into the forces. In the long term, his career was not harmed: he later became leader of the Labour group on the council and its first lord mayor in 1927.

Not all Labour men opposed the war; George Roberts was a strong supporter, and served in several positions in all-party coalition governments after 1915, becoming Minister of Labour under Lloyd George in August 1917. He resigned his seat to fight a by-election, but the anti-war campaigners did not feel they had sufficient support to put up a candidate and Roberts was returned unopposed.

Inevitably, some Norwich manufacturing firms benefited from the war. Boulton and Paul made military aircraft on their Rose Lane site, building a large number of Sopwith Camels. They also produced their own plane, the Bobolink, as a replacement, but it was not a success. They made a total of 2,530 military aeroplanes, and also supplied over 5,000 miles of the wire that defended the trenches. Munitions were made at Laurence Scott and elsewhere, while Mann Egerton began to supply seaplanes to the Admiralty in 1915. Howlett and White made Cossack boots for the Russian army, as well as boots for the Royal Air Force. Many of the engineering positions in these firms were taken by women replacing men at the Front, which allowed women into many new skilled jobs but created problems when the men returned from the war and expected to have their jobs back.

The war also produced one of the most famous of the many strong women that we have recorded, Edith Cavell. She was born in Swardeston in 1865, trained in London as a hospital nurse, and worked in Brussels from 1907. In August 1914 she was on leave in Norwich, staying with her mother in College Road, when she heard that the war had broken out; she at once returned to Brussels, which was later occupied by the German army. Edith looked after wounded soldiers of all nationalities – including German – but also helped over one hundred Allied soldiers escape to neutral territory in Holland, from where they were able to return to Britain and continue the war effort. She was arrested in August 1915 and kept in solitary confinement until her trial. She agreed that she had helped soldiers to leave Belgian soil, and was executed by firing squad on 12 October 1915. Her death shocked many throughout Britain, and was used as propaganda in recruitment campaigns. This was a wilful misunderstanding of her message, which is one for all time: her last words, as she received the sacrament, were: 'Standing as I do, in view of God and eternity, I realise that patriotism is not enough: I must have no hatred or bitterness towards anyone.'

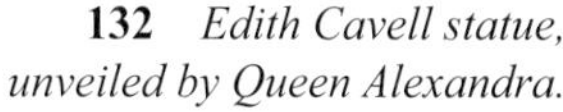

132 *Edith Cavell statue, unveiled by Queen Alexandra.*

Edith was buried where she fell, but in 1919 her body was brought back to England and reburied outside Norwich Cathedral, where her tomb can still be seen; her family preferred this to a burial in Westminster Abbey. A memorial statue to her, in the centre of the road in Tombland, was unveiled by Queen Alexandra; it has since been moved to a more peaceful setting by the Erpingham Gate. It was designed a by local doctor, J. Gordon Munn, and is not admired by all: Pevsner and Wilson see in it a resemblance to a man playing hoopla.[11]

The city war memorial was designed by Edwin Lutyens, who also designed the Cenotaph in Whitehall. It was originally attached to the Guildhall, being formally dedicated in 1927. It was moved to its present site in a small memorial garden in front of City Hall in 1938. This was not found entirely satisfactory: the garden was too small for formal parades and tended to be used by people whom the 16th century would have called 'idlers'. The situation was resolved in 2010 when the memorial was turned around to face St Peter's Street, where the parades can take place. Another memorial is the War Memorial Chapel at the east end of Norwich Cathedral, designed by Sir Charles Nicholson. Unexceptional today, it aroused controversy at the time, reflecting the usual difficulty

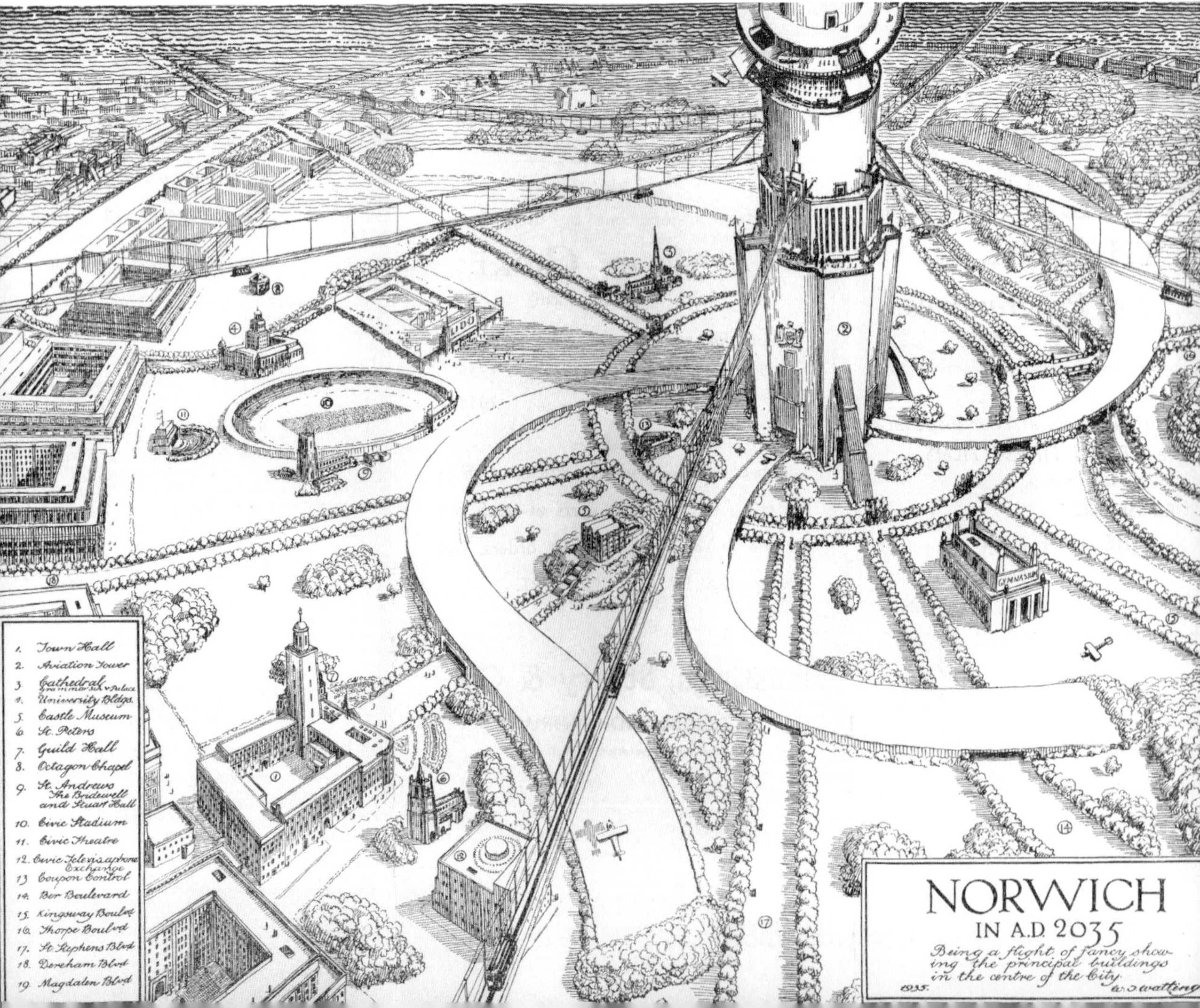

133 *'Norwich in 2035': a satirical look at the city's future, drawn in 1935.*

in adding a 'modern' building to an ancient one; Ethel Colman wrote to the Dean saying that she would not have contributed to the building if she had known how controversial it was going to be.[12]

Perhaps the best memorial is in the form of a book, *The Spanish Farm* by R.H. Mottram. This and its two follow-up novels convey the atmosphere of life on the Western Front as it must have been for so many Norwich men. Mottram, who was lord mayor in 1953-4, wrote other novels as well as books on the city's history, and also played an important role in preserving the building heritage of the city. He died in 1971 and is buried in the Rosary cemetery; there is a memorial to him at St James' lookout, overlooking the city he loved.[13]

George Roberts remained in Lloyd George's government after the war and moved increasingly to the right. In the general election of 1922 he stood as an Independent and won the seat. In October 1923, he completed his political journey by becoming a Conservative. This was a step too far for his Norwich voters and he was defeated in the general election that followed; he died in 1928.

The population of the city was 126,236 in the 1931 census. The census shows the large institutional population of the city, with 875 people in the Bowthorpe Road workhouse alone. There were 537 in the Norfolk and Norwich Hospital, 168 in the Great Hospital and 128 in the Bethel. A large military presence is shown, with 389 people in Britannia Barracks and 380 in the Cavalry Barracks on Barrack Street, while criminality is indicated by the presence of 117 people in Norwich prison on Mousehold Heath.

The most impressive city building of the 1930s is the City Hall; plans for this had been discussed since the early years of the century. The final choice was by competition; well over 100 designs were submitted, which were reduced to a short-list of four. The winning design was by C.H. James and S.R. Pierce; built with bricks from Buckinghamshire, it has attracted differing judgements. James Wentworth Day did not like it, commenting: 'A pity that [the market] is overshadowed by that modernistic monstrosity, the City Hall, which has the proportions of a brick and the complexion of brown Windsor soup', and 'It looks like a precocious modern railway station, only the hoot of engines and the stink of diesel are absent.' However, George Nobbs disagreed: 'The dramatic flight of steps, the noble civic lions, the imposing balcony, and the magnificent tower convey more, to me at least, of the spirit of Norwich than any other building can ever do.' The large bronze doors are works of art in themselves, with portrayals of trades of the city past and present: they are by James Woodford. The elongated lions, also in bronze, are by Alfred Hardiman. City Hall was formally opened on 29 October 1938 by George VI, a vast crowd filling the market place; afterwards the king went to Carrow Road and saw half of the match between Norwich City and Milwall.

As Europe travelled on the road to war, Norwich opened its heart to many refugees. On May Day 1938, 36 children paraded in the market place, refugees from fascist Spain. Preceded by a Spanish Republican flag and with some wearing dresses in their national colours, they sang the Internationale and songs of their own country. One of their number,

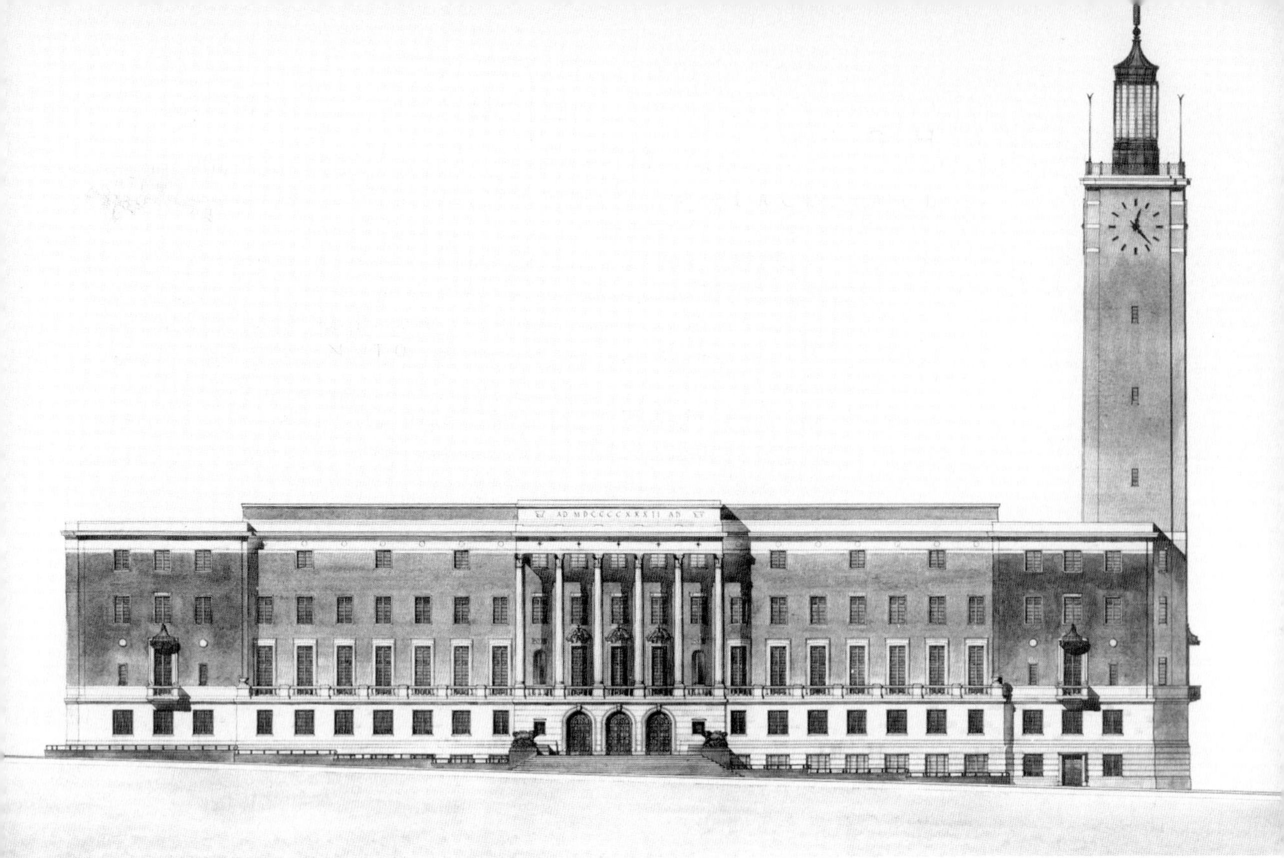

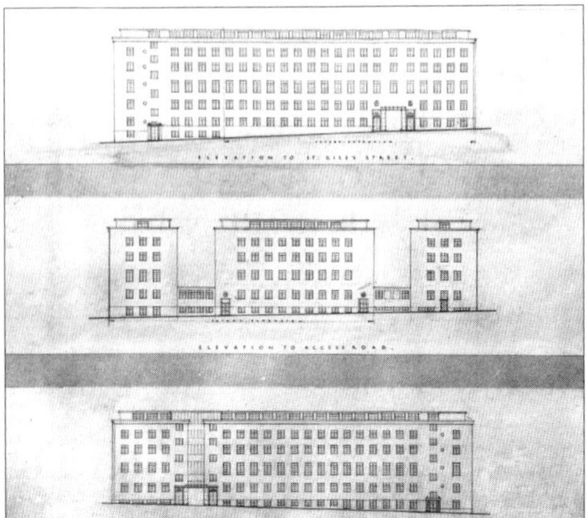

AD MDCCCCXXXII AD

ELEVATION TO ACCESS ROAD.

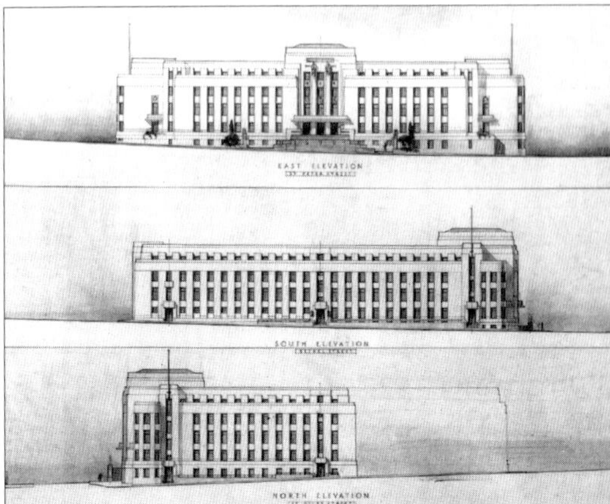

EAST ELEVATION

SOUTH ELEVATION

NORTH ELEVATION

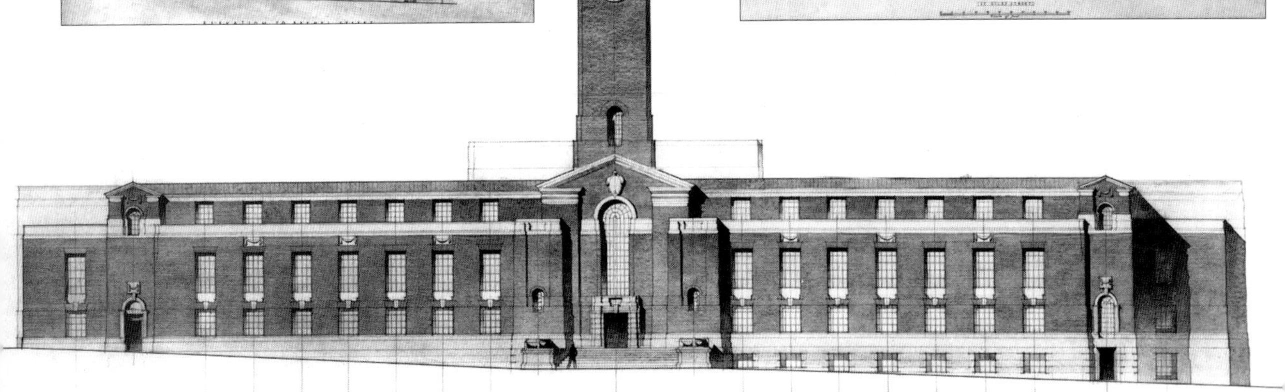

Top left: 134 *Norwich City Hall: the winning design.*

Below left: 135a-c *The other three final designs for City Hall; which would you have chosen?*

a girl of 14, made a speech in Spanish which was afterwards translated for the crowd. A collection was made and the money handed over to the carers of the children.

A larger group of refugee children to arrive in Norwich in the same year were the German and Austrian Jews of the *Kindertransporte*. In December 1938, no less than 520 Jewish children from Vienna arrived at Pakefield Holiday Camp, where they stayed until homes in Britain could be found for them. They had travelled by train all the way, crossing over at the Hook of Holland and landing at Harwich. The *Eastern Daily Press* commented,

> their presence here is in itself a vivid appeal to all who can do so to help the work which is being done in Norwich and the district to raise funds for the maintenance of the refugees and to find adoptive homes for as many as possible of the children – it would be foreign to all the kindly and merciful traditions of British men and women if means were not found also to give some help to these little fugitives of terror.[14]

Mariam Cohen recalled attending a meeting in Norwich at which it was asked, 'Any offers to take children?' Mariam and her husband Percy 'felt you wanted to do something'. They took Kurt Fuchel, born in Vienna in 1931; he soon settled in, but his fears surfaced at the end of each day: 'every night when it was dark, he'd come down the stairs and he'd see the door was locked'. One girl from Austria who went to the Blyth School at this time was Hertha Fischer, who contrasted the two school systems in an article in the school magazine:

> On Saturday, every school in Vienna works as usual until 12 noon, and then they think themselves very, very lucky to have the afternoon free. It surprised me very much that schools in England should have the whole of Saturday off, for it seemed to me most unusual.
>
> The time when English schools begin their lessons, also seemed to me peculiar, because in Vienna at a quarter to eight, all the children have to be at school ready to begin work; while here some people are lucky enough to be still in bed at that time.[15]

Most of the children never saw their parents again as they were victims of the gas chambers. Fuchel was fortunate: his parents had managed to escape to France, but the long separation brought its own problems, as he recalled: 'my parents let go of a seven-year-old and got back a 16-year-old. And my mother, especially, wanted to carry on where she'd left off. And a 16-year-old doesn't like to be treated like a seven-year-old.' Fuchel acknowledged how fortunate he was compared to many: not only had he found his parents but the Cohens of Norwich had become like another set of parents to him. Hertha was one of several of the group who chose to stay in Norwich after the war was over.

The outbreak of the First World War had taken most people by surprise, but the Second World War was widely predicted as Germany became increasingly aggressive. One new development that saved many lives during the war was the blood transfusion service, which was first set up in Norwich in 1939. There were large numbers of volunteers giving blood throughout the war, much of the blood being sent to military hospitals overseas.

In the 1930s, many people were preparing for massive air raids that could devastate cities like Norwich. The contingency plans allowed for many hundreds of deaths, if not thousands, and were so drastic that they were the basis of plans in case of nuclear war in the 1960s. By the outbreak of war, Norwich had built air-raid shelters for 17,000 people and by the start of 1942 there were enough shelters for everyone in the city, just in time as it turned out. The old chalk tunnels under Gas Hill and the Earlham Road were filled with bunks, supposedly still there, and large public shelters were built in many places such as Chapelfield Park and the cattle market, the latter causing some problems when the Castle Mall shopping centre came to be built on the site half a century later. Individual shelters were provided in back gardens, known as Anderson shelters and made up of two curved walls of corrugated, galvanised steel bolted together and covered with earth. Some can still be seen in city gardens, pressed into service as garden sheds. Although they could not stand a direct hit, they undoubtedly saved many lives: in an air raid up to 75 per cent of fatalities come from flying debris, especially glass, and the shelters protected from this danger. Later in the war, people without gardens were provided with Morrison shelters, an immensely strong structure of steel, inside the house.

136 *An Anderson shelter, built by Barnards.*

The first air-raid warning came on the day war broke out, 3 September 1939, but the first raid on Norwich was on 9 July 1940; this time there was no alert. Two planes bombed Barnards on Salhouse Road, and one backed away towards the city, dropping a bomb on Carrow Hill. The hill was crowded with people leaving work at Colman's, many pushing their bicycles up the hill, and five women were killed. More bombs fell on Boulton and Paul's factory on Riverside, and on the nearby locomotive sheds. In all, 27 people were killed in the raid, but it is the five 'Carrow girls' killed on the Hill who are best remembered: the youngest, 18-year-old Gladys Sampson and 19-year-old Bertha Playford, had worked at the factory since leaving school at 13 years old.[16]

The Baedeker Raids

The most serious raids on the city were the 'Baedeker Raids' on the nights of 27 and 29 April 1942. E.C. Le Grice sets the scene:

> A lovely night. The old City bathed in moonlight ... the historic old city, nestling in the quiet valley seemed almost dreamlike. Suddenly the silence was broken by the wail of sirens, the distant throb of engines, the menacing roar of aircraft growing louder and louder, and the night sky was illuminated with the red glare from floating chandeliers of coloured lights like giant fireworks hovering over the sky.[17]

The raids were in retaliation for RAF raids on German civilian populations at Rostock and Lubeck; a German foreign office spokesman announced that the Luftwaffe would destroy every building in England marked with three

137 *Caley's chocolate factory after the first Baedecker air raid.*

stars in the Baedeker guide book. The cities bombed were Norwich, Bath, Canterbury, York and Exeter. On the Monday night, some 185 high-explosive bombs and a large number of incendiaries (fire bombs) were dropped; 162 people were killed and 600 wounded. After a break the following night, the raids resumed on a massive scale on the Wednesday, when 112 high-explosive bombs were dropped and even more incendiaries than on the Monday. This time 69 people were killed and 89 admitted to hospital with serious wounds; the hospital also had to cope with damage to its own buildings. About two thirds of all the people in the city killed in air raids in the war died on those two dreadful nights, the greatest single tragedy occurring when 11 elderly people were killed in a hit on Bowthorpe Lodge on 28 April.

Many local people recorded the events in diaries or letters. Violet Campling of Valpy Avenue wrote to her friend Alice French in Northampton on 1 May:

> Poor Norwich has caught it this time. The swines have struck us very hard and Norwich is ruined. The main streets are out. Our bedrooms are broken about but the windows are in. But we go away every night to the country. People are very good to us & we go to Drayton to sleep in a schoolroom & they give us tea and feed us, & one thing, to get a good night sleep will be a treat. Wed night: my God I thought we were gone. The school next to our 3 houses was struck so you can guess what we felt of it. I prayed as I never prayed before & God heard me … My poor mother is burned out & has just what she stands up in.

138 *Complete destruction of the* Duke of Connaught.

Violet was fortunate: Constance Ward and her three children died that night at nearby 4 Valpy Avenue.[18]

Agnes Podd, an elderly lady of Doris Road, records in her diary 'terrible raids' on both nights of the Baedeker raids, and also notes that there was an attack on the night between them: 'another raid but not a bad one'. Her entry for 30 April records: 'Went to Tharston, everyone leaving the city that could get away, hundreds sleeping in the open. We were fortunate to get in a farmhouse at Tharston at Mr Palmer's. We stayed there till 26 of May.' This sleeping out in the countryside, known as 'trekking', was a natural response to the nightly air raids but disapproved of by the authorities. Olive Anthony recalled that her family's little

139 *The* Dolphin *after an incendiary attack (note the undamaged Anderson shelter).*

bungalow in Costessey was 'just like a bed and breakfast', with families walking there from the city centre.[19]

Le Grice and his family hid under their stairs on the night of 29 April. The house suffered a direct hit, but the stairs still stood:

> bomb after bomb fell shaking the house to its foundations, for we counted 29 H E bombs within a few hundred yards of us. Windows were shattered, ceilings crashed down, the crockery on the cupboard shelves was shaken off, a sugar basin emptied itself on my daughter's head, to be followed by the milk jug, and finally when one bomb fell just opposite, the voice of a warden was heard to say, 'Don't you think you had better come out of there?' We thought we had better come out, and happily that proved to be the last one in the district that night.[20]

Buildings destroyed in the Baedeker raids included the Hippodrome Theatre; Anders Pederson, the Danish trainer of a troupe of sea-lions performing at the theatre, was killed, together with his wife, Dagmar. The photographer George Swain recalled running from his studio next door to see if he could help. The inside of the building was pitch black; suddenly he heard 'a terrible sound – a wailing worse than the whistle of a bomb. It was from one of the sea-lions which the bomb had released. I shall never forget the noise it made, flapping its ungainly way through the dark, empty theatre, crying for its master.' They were not the only animal victims of the war: George, the well-known dray horse at Pockthorpe Brewery and winner of prizes at the Norfolk Show, was killed in his stables on Barrack Street on 1-2 August 1942.[21]

140 *George, dray horse at Steward and Patteson, an air-raid victim.*

Many people displayed great courage in the city, such as the air-raid warden, mentioned by Le Grice and Herbert Witard, who drove from his Bracondale home through the worst of the raid to make sure all was well at Hellesdon Hospital. Women played their part, and many Norwich women became members of the Mutual Aid Good Neighbours' Association (MAGNA), a scheme to help air-raid victims. The Norwich organiser was Ruth Hardy, who had noted that many deaths resulting from shock had occurred in blitzed areas and the only way to combat the effects of shock was to apply immediate warmth. 'We want every housewife in Norwich to offer her home temporarily for such a cause', she said, and 30,000 women in the city took her up, displaying in their windows the MAGNA poster with the words, 'a good neighbour lives here.' Inevitably, not everyone behaved so well, and cases of looting from ruined or empty houses turned up in local courts over the next few months.[22]

There was another severe raid on 27 June 1942, when the bombs dropped were mainly incendiaries, and very many fires were started. Bond's on All Saints' Green, which incorporated the former Thatched Theatre, was reduced to a burnt-out shell. St Mark's school in Lakenham was also destroyed in this raid, the head teacher recording in the school log book: 'I ran through the churchyard just before the 'All-Clear' to see whether the school was safe, and found it a blazing inferno, nothing to be done.' The school re-opened just two days later, occupying the nearby Church Hall.[23]

City Hall was only a year old when war broke out and was the subject of conflicting stories in the city at the time. One story was that William Joyce, Lord Haw-Haw, had said on one of his propaganda broadcasts from Germany, 'The people of Norwich have a new City Hall. It isn't paid for yet, but, never mind, the Luftwaffe will soon put paid to it.' The opposite story was that Hitler asked his pilots to avoid destroying the building; as an architect he is supposed to have admired the design and, in his imagination, seen himself standing in triumph on its balcony once he had conquered Britain. In fact the German pilots came pretty close; the modern building just across Guildhall Hill from the tower stands where a bomb destroyed what was the Clover Leaf Café before the war.

The last conventional air raid was on 6 November 1943, when high-explosive bombs fell on the municipal golf course in Bluebell Road, and incendiaries caused fires in houses off the Unthank Road. No one was killed in the raid. The last person to die as an immediate result of an air raid in Norwich was a nine-year-old boy, Cyril Cranmer, killed on 19 May 1943 after picking up an incendiary bomb that had failed to go off, although Charles Coates died at Bowthorpe Lodge on 10 June 1945 of wounds inflicted during a raid several years earlier. There had been about 45 raids on the city between 1940 and 1943, resulting in 340 deaths – two thirds of them in the two nights of the Baedeker raids – and just over 1,000 serious injuries. About 30,000 houses in the city were damaged.

Hitler's secret weapons, the V-1 flying bomb and the V-2 bombardment rocket, did not kill anyone in the Norwich area. V-1s were seen above the city on 26 June 1944, but none fell there. Just one V-2 fell in the area,

141 *Norwich children during the Second World War, awaiting a military parade.*

landing on Hellesdon golf course on 3 October. The threat was ended as the Allied armies advancing across Europe captured the sites from which they were fired.

Inevitably, there were plane crashes in the city, some with fatal results. On 29 November 1944, an American B-24 Liberator returning to its base at Horsham St Faith struck the tower of St Philip's church in Heigham. The pilot made every effort to avoid coming down in a built-up area, and the plane crashed in the Corporation Yard off Heigham Street; all nine members of crew were killed. Today a plaque on a nearby wall marks their sacrifice. On 4 January 1945, two children, 11-year-old Bryan Jones and five-year-old Mary Kemp, were killed when an American plane crash-landed in the garden where they were playing in Spynke Road.[24]

Another aspect of the war was the removal of many hundreds of children, with their school teachers, out of the danger areas in large cities in September 1939. Norwich was neither a danger area nor a safe area, so evacuees were not allocated to houses in the city, although many arrived at Thorpe Station on their way to billets in Norfolk towns and villages. The situation changed as the Blitz hit London from the summer of 1940, and once more when the V-1s and V-2s devastated London in the summer and autumn of 1944. Many mothers and children, sometimes with grandparents as well, fled to Norwich from the capital. In the summer of 1944, there were over 20,000 such refugees in the Norwich area. On one day in July alone, over 800 arrived at the railway station, the youngest just two weeks old. All were found accommodation of some kind, the lucky ones with families or in empty houses, the less fortunate in Nissen huts.

Norfolk was one of the areas used for bases by the United States Army Air Force, and many people have memories of the Americans dancing at the *Lido* and the *Samson and Hercules* and drinking in the *Bell*. Some

Norwich women, the so-called 'G.I. Brides', found husbands among the airmen and travelled to a new life in America with them after the war. The Americans were better paid than the English, and many Norwich people who were children during the war still recall their generosity. In 1943 they used Carrow Road football stadium to host a rodeo! Almost 7,000 young Americans were killed in action. Even before the end of the war, it was decided to erect a Memorial Library in their honour, and it was formally opened on 13 June 1963 in the presence of nearly 100 Second Air Division veterans.

At least one woman connected with Norwich suffered the horrors of a concentration camp, Elsie Marechal. Born Elsie Bell, she was brought up in Great Yarmouth and undertook her training as a teacher in Norwich. She met Georges Marechal during the First World War and moved to his native Belgium. During the German invasion of the country in 1940, the couple helped Allied servicemen evade capture and make it back to England. For this, Georges was shot and Elsie, together with her young daughter, spent the rest of the war in camps at Ravensbruck and Matthausen. She survived the war and published a short book of poems, as well as relating her experiences to the Teachers' Training College.[25]

Many local people have left records of their experiences during the war. One recalled: 'I was five years old when the war started. I went to Hillside Avenue School, Thorpe St Andrew. I remember being fitted for a gas mask which I had to take everywhere I went.' Others remembered their fears. Josephine Mann recalled that her family 'had a shelter in the garden which I remember sitting in the night when we had the very bad raid with the bombs absolutely raining down. Of course we didn't

142 *Men of the Norfolk Regiment, after serving as prisoners of war, return to Norwich.*

really understand what that was all about – but I remember feeling quite frightened.' The experience of Paul Brett was similar: 'I was dreadfully afraid in the bomb shelter; I don't know how afraid I was … I think my brother told jokes about it and I don't think my mother showed it because she couldn't because of us.' Gladys Courtnell's memory was of food shortages:

> we used to have to queue up in the city for rations – we were allowed one quarter or half a pound of margarine a week, one egg, one loaf of bread, and sixpence worth of mince or corned beef. They were selling broken biscuits at Woolworth's so I queued up for some as they were a luxury. You couldn't get any fruit.[26]

As in the First World War, many city men joined their local regiment, the Norfolks. Three battalions were in Singapore when that city was captured by the Japanese in February 1942, and the survivors spent the rest of the war in prison camps in the most appalling conditions. The 2nd Battalion fought in the Far East, taking part in the decisive Battle of Kohima in May 1944. The 1st Battalion took part in the D-Day landings and the liberation of Europe.[27]

Post-war Norwich

The bombing, added to the slum clearances of the 1930s, created an opportunity for a comprehensive new vision of how the city might be reconstructed after the war. Leonard Hannaford was the city architect and his vision of Norwich in 1943 envisaged the demolition of all property between City Hall and Chapelfield Gardens and the creation of a new city centre. In 1945 *The Norwich Plan* was published; its introduction quotes Aristotle: 'Men come together in cities to live; they remain together in order to live the good life.' However, many of the council's grand plans came to nothing as the money ran out.

Since the war the population of the Norwich area has spread well beyond the city limits, and some boundary adjustments have been made. Under the 1950 Norwich Extension Act the city was extended to include a portion of Caistor St Edmund, the river Yare, and a portion of Thorpe St Andrew. In 1967 following a Boundary Commission report, the city boundary was extended to bring in most of Norwich airport. To the west, the area of Bowthorpe, of 600 acres, was taken in at the same time, the Bowthorpe estate site being bought by the city for £9.5 million; the plan was to accommodate 13,500 people in three 'villages'. The population of Norwich remained constant in the later years of the century: it was 122,083 in the 1971 census, 122,611 in 1991, and 121,550 in 2001. However, the number of people in the conurbation continued to expand rapidly, the growth taking place in areas such as Thorpe St Andrew, Drayton and Taverham, which are in the county of Norfolk rather than the city of Norwich. Many city administrators have thought that the whole built-up area should be brought within its control, but this has always been resisted by those outside its present boundaries. The population of the Norwich

Urban Area has a population of 194,000 – the 31st largest in population of all urban areas in England.

October 1962 saw the Cuban missile crisis. In the words of U Thant, quoted in the *Eastern Daily Press* on 25 October 1962, the 'very existence of mankind was in the balance'. Every house in Norwich, as elsewhere, had received a booklet called *Protect and Survive*, telling the householder how to prepare a room in their house – usually the cupboard under the stairs – as a stronghold in case of nuclear attack. It was expected that the major attack would be on the great cities, which did not include Norwich, but East Anglia was at risk because of the presence of the 'Little Americas' – the air bases at Sculthorpe, Lakenheath and Mildenhall – and the RAF station at Coltishall. The *Eastern Daily Press* for 27 October showed Hugh Fraser, the Secretary of State for Air, at Coltishall watching a firestreak guided missile being attached to a Lightning jet fighter. Second World War evacuation plans were dusted down and made ready but the crisis passed, and the city has never again been so close to war.

143 *Plans for the post-war city: the viaduct over King Street.*

An important change to the running of the city was brought about by the Local Government Reform Act of 1972, carried out in 1974. Norwich lost its county borough status, and some of its powers, such as control over education and libraries, passed to the county council. The city has tried to redress this since, but after much debate the status quo has been confirmed.

On 4 June 1977 over 100,000 people watched parades to celebrate the silver jubilee of Queen Elizabeth, with over 70 streets closed to traffic for parties the following Tuesday; unfortunately it was a day of heavy rain.

The years 1994 and 1995 will long be remembered in the city for disastrous fires. The new Norwich Central Library was formally opened by the Queen Mother on 19 June 1963; on 1 August 1994, it was burnt down following an electrical fault. Many books were lost, as were items held by the Local Studies Library including rare prints and photographs. The Norfolk Record Office shared the building and thus lost its home; fortunately no archives were lost, although some were damaged by water pumped into the building. On 12 April 1995, the historic Assembly House was burnt out. It was very quickly restored to its former glory, while the Library was eventually replaced by the much larger Millennium Library building, which has become the most used library in England. The American Memorial Library has also been rebuilt. The Norfolk Record Office had already outgrown the old library, and the county council eventually decided to place it on the County Hall site; the state-of-the-art building was opened by the Queen in 2003. The Record Office has had a remarkable continuity of service: the first county archivist, Jean Kennedy, MBE, was still in office at the time of the fire; due to retire, she stayed on to see the crisis through. Her successor, Dr John Alban, has brought an increasingly proactive attitude, with many talks and group visits making the Record Office and its treasures better known to the inhabitants of the city.

The new millennium was celebrated in Norwich with the Festival of Light on the night of 31 December/1 January 2000 – a laser show watched by over 90,000 projecting lights between Castle and City Hall. It was

144 *The Norfolk Record Office in the new Archive Centre.*

145 *The Central Library fire, 1 August 1994: firemen carry out armfuls of ancient documents.*

performed twice but disappointed many as it only lasted 15 minutes. Norwich also celebrated the true start of the new millennium in the following year: up to 45,000 people watched images of the past and future projected onto City Hall, followed by £40,000 worth of fireworks let off from the castle and visible all over the city.

The radical traditions of Norwich were upheld in the two national referenda held in Britain. The strength of its links with Europe were reflected in the vote in favour of being part of the European community in 1975, 70.1 per cent of those in Norfolk being in favour, compared with 67.2 per cent in the country as a whole. In the 2011 referendum on the alternative vote, over 18,000 people in Norwich were in favour of change, 45 per cent of

146 *The Queen opens the new Archive Centre in 2003; the County Archivist, Dr J.R. Alban, is with her.*

147 *The Millennium Library, the most visited library in Britain.*

those who voted – the national vote saw only 29 per cent in favour. In an early example of the 'Big Society', Norwich also saw two local referenda, on transport and on Sunday opening, discussed on p.252.

The Making of Livings

The textile trade was in its final decline in the early 20th century. C.B. Hawkins wrote a superb analysis of the city's economy in 1909; in his time, there were still two important silk factories, 'all that is left of the old textile industry of Norwich, which in process of time, is likely to disappear completely'. Even in the first decade of the 20th century there were still a few hand-looms, their workers engaged in hair weaving. Hawkins wrote that 'in the older quarters of the city an observer can still hear the peculiar click-clack of the hand-looms, and if he happens to be in Calvert Street or Peacock Street, where the houses date back to the eighteenth century, he has a perfect example of what industrial Norwich was 150 years ago [that is, in the mid-18th century].'

The first half of the century saw the rise of the shoe making and engineering trades in the city. These sectors declined during the post-war years and have been replaced by an extremely wide range of manufacturing and service industries. Boot and shoe making replaced weaving as the main industry in Norwich well before 1900; in the 1901 census there were over 7,500 people employed in the boot and shoe trade and the number rose to 10,800 by 1931. Hawkins wrote:

> In light shoes and in women's and children's boots – men's are scarcely made at all – Norwich can now compete on equal terms with any other centre. The best ladies' evening shoes, which were till recently made in Paris and Vienna, are now, for example, being made in Norwich.[28]

In 1961 10,000 people were employed in clothing in the city and 9,000 in shoe making. Norwich was making eight million pairs of shoes and ranked fourth as a footwear manufacturer. It specialised in ladies' fashion shoes and children's shoes. A 1961 report noted that teenagers were now buying five pairs of shoes a year:

> Fresh from the restrictions of school life, the teenager looks for style rather than durability. She has had enough of gym tunics and good strong sensible Oxfords. Now she looks for the prettiest shoes she can find, for the most delicate pastel colours, the highest heels, the most pointed toes. But though appearance is all to her at this stage, and though her desire for style must be fulfilled, she must not be disillusioned about quality. She may not look for durability but, if her pretty shoes fall apart at the first summer shower, she is not likely to spend her money on that particular make again.[29]

The trade has since declined and almost all the factories are closed. In the 1984 Census of Employment, only 3,000 were employed in footwear and clothing in the city, about three per cent of the working population. There was only one textile firm in the city, Francis Hinde and Sons,

148a, b *The processes of shoe making.*

employing about 275 people. The last bespoke shoemaker in the city is Bowhill and Elliott in London Street.

The production of food and drink continued to grow in the 20th century. Colman's led the way again in care for its workers. In July 1905 they introduced a graduated pension scheme which reached a maximum of 8s. a week for those who worked until they were 65 years old. In addition everyone contributed 2d. a week to produce an extra 2s. a week, making a total pension of 10s. a week or, if preferred, the extra could be taken as a lump sum. Foremen received extra money. The *Eastern Evening News* commented: 'The pension scheme has been often enough described, but as far as we are aware, it has never yet been paralleled. It has been again and again commended in disinterested quarters as the most liberal thing of its kind known to British industry.' In 1910 there were 97 elderly former workers of Colman's receiving pensions. Wages were generous too; Hawkins wrote,

> the best wages are earned at Carrow where the minimum for labourers is 21s. a week. On the mustard and starch floors the earnings are rather higher and not less than 22s. 6d. a week. There is only one other employer in Norwich where labourers are paid so much, namely the city itself. Street sweepers and other unskilled workers are given a minimum of one guinea a week.[30]

Colman's was one of the firms that supported Captain Scott's expedition to the South Pole in 1911-12; cases of their flour and their ubiquitous mustard tins can still be seen in his hut in the Antarctic, now preserved as a museum. The firm made good use of its riverside site, owning a steam tug, the *Mustard Pot*, which hauled lighters to and from Yarmouth; an image of it adorns the sign of the *Mustard Pot* pub on Thorpe Road. Some

149 *Norwich at work in the 1950s: making chocolate at Caley's.*

12 per cent of the inward traffic of grain was coming by river even in the 1960s. In 1988 the firm employed 1,500 people. It has since become part of the international group Vandenberg Foods.

Caley's was another major employer in the food and drink business. One of their advertisements ran:

> Believe It Or Not! In one year the manufacture of Caley Chocolate uses more than enough milk to float a 10,000 ton Ocean Liner. This amazing fact is particularly interesting to Norfolk people for a large proportion of this milk is produced on Norfolk farms.

Their factory near Chapelfield was destroyed in the Second World War and later rebuilt on the same site. The firm was taken over by Mackintosh and in 1961 was employing 2,100 people. In 1987 they were trading as Rowntree Mackintosh and 2,000 people were employed on the Norwich site making Yorkies, Rolos and Munchies. The company was then bought out by Nestlé, but the factory closed in 1994 with the loss of 900 jobs. Its site is now a shopping centre.[31]

Another firm to close in the 1990s was the grain-milling firm of R.J. Read in King Street. It was one of the last firms to make extensive use of Norwich as a port; foreign grain came up the river and was used for flour and animal feed. Like many factory sites along the river, it has been converted into apartments.

Brewing in Norwich was at its height in the late 18th and 19th centuries. There were four major breweries until 1957, when Bullard's bought up Youngs, Crawshay and Youngs in King Street, reducing the number to three; in 1961, they were employing 900 people. In that year two of the breweries combined against the third: Bullard's and Steward and Patteson together bought up Morgan's for the 400 public houses it owned and sold the brewery to Watney's. This was the beginning of the end. Watney's took over both Bullard's and Steward and Patteson in 1963. Brewing stopped at the Anchor site in 1963 and eventually no beer was brewed in the city at all. In 1974 'real' or unpressurised beer could only be bought in two pubs in the city. However, the demand spread and some small breweries were eventually established again in the city, beginning with those at the *Reindeer* on Dereham Road and then the *Coach and Horses* on Thorpe Road.

Engineering also flourished in the city in the 20th century only to decline towards its end. As we have seen, Boulton and Paul prospered in the First World War and laid out an airfield on Mousehold Heath to test planes. In 1920 they moved to larger premises on the Riverside, at which time they were employing nearly 3,000 people. Afterwards they made

150 *Barnards children's party.*

the framework for the airship R101 and when the great airship was completed it flew over the city, watched by an enormous crowd that cheered as she passed overhead. Unfortunately she crashed at Beauvais in France while on her way to India in October 1930, but it was agreed that the Boulton and Paul frame was in no way to blame for the disaster. In 1961 Boulton and Paul still employed 1,300 people and together with Barnard's they made about half of the total British production of chain-link fencing and wire netting. Barnard's came to an end as an independent company in 1955 when they were taken over by the Sheffield company Tinsley Wire Industries Ltd. They finally ceased trading in 1991. Laurence Scott provided motors and winches for many of the most important ships of the century, including the *Titanic* and the cruise liners *Queen Elizabeth* and *Queen Mary*, as well as equipment for nuclear submarines including the Tridents. In 1995 they made the replacement railings for Westminster Bridge.

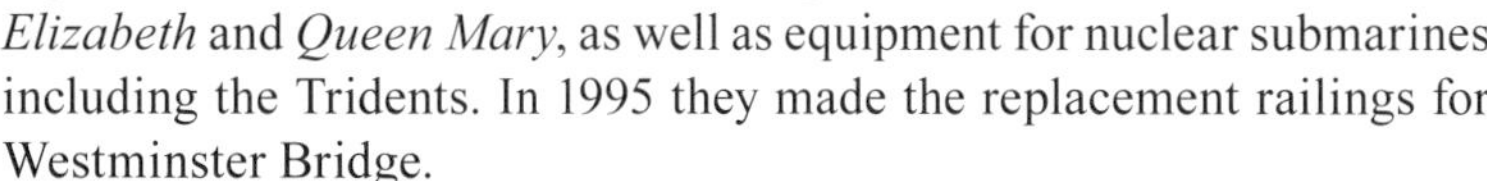

Banking and insurance has been a continually expanding field throughout the century. The Norwich Union Head Office was built in 1905 and modelled on the old Amicable House in Serjeant's Inn, Fleet Street, London. The architect was George Skipper. Pevsner wrote of being 'knocked out by the smashing Norwich Union building which, without any doubt, is one of the country's most convincing Edwardian buildings'. However, the Norfolk antiquarian G. Colman Green was not convinced, writing: 'I still detest

151 *Children watch Queen Mary, widow of King George V, at the Castle Museum, 1946.*

152 *Aerial view of the city; St Peter Mancroft is top left, with the site of the future Central Library next to it.*

the huge building which is not in accorde [*sic*] with traditional architectur [*sic*] in the Ancient English Capital and retain a sense of shock to think that the Architect perpetuates Greek style into a city with its own characteristics.' The inside is as spectacular as the outside, making use of marble originally intended for Westminster Roman Catholic Cathedral.[32]

In 1925 the Life Society acquired the shares of the Fire Office from the Phoenix, which had bought them in 1920. By 1961 the total assets of the Norwich Union Assurance group were over £250 million and in 1987 the company employed 4,500 in several office blocks in the centre of Norwich. Norwich Union merged with GCU in 2000, forming the group CGNU and later becoming the Aviva group; the Norwich Union brand was phased out from 2009. Barclays' Norwich branch at Bank Plain was one of the largest in England, employing over 80 staff in 1961; the building is now a centre for youth activities.

Norwich has declined as a port with the development of road transport, in spite of the poor quality of road links to the city. In 2011, there is still not a single mile of motorway in Norfolk. In 1961 there were 400 feet of public quay and several private wharves along the river below Foundry Bridge. The main imports were coal, grain, meal, granite chippings, paper, steel and wood, and the main export was scrap metal, but the port was not making a profit; money from shipping tolls was all used up in dredging work to maintain the channel in the river.

153a, b *Shipping on the Wensum in the 1950s and 1960s. The river is now very little used by commercial traffic.*

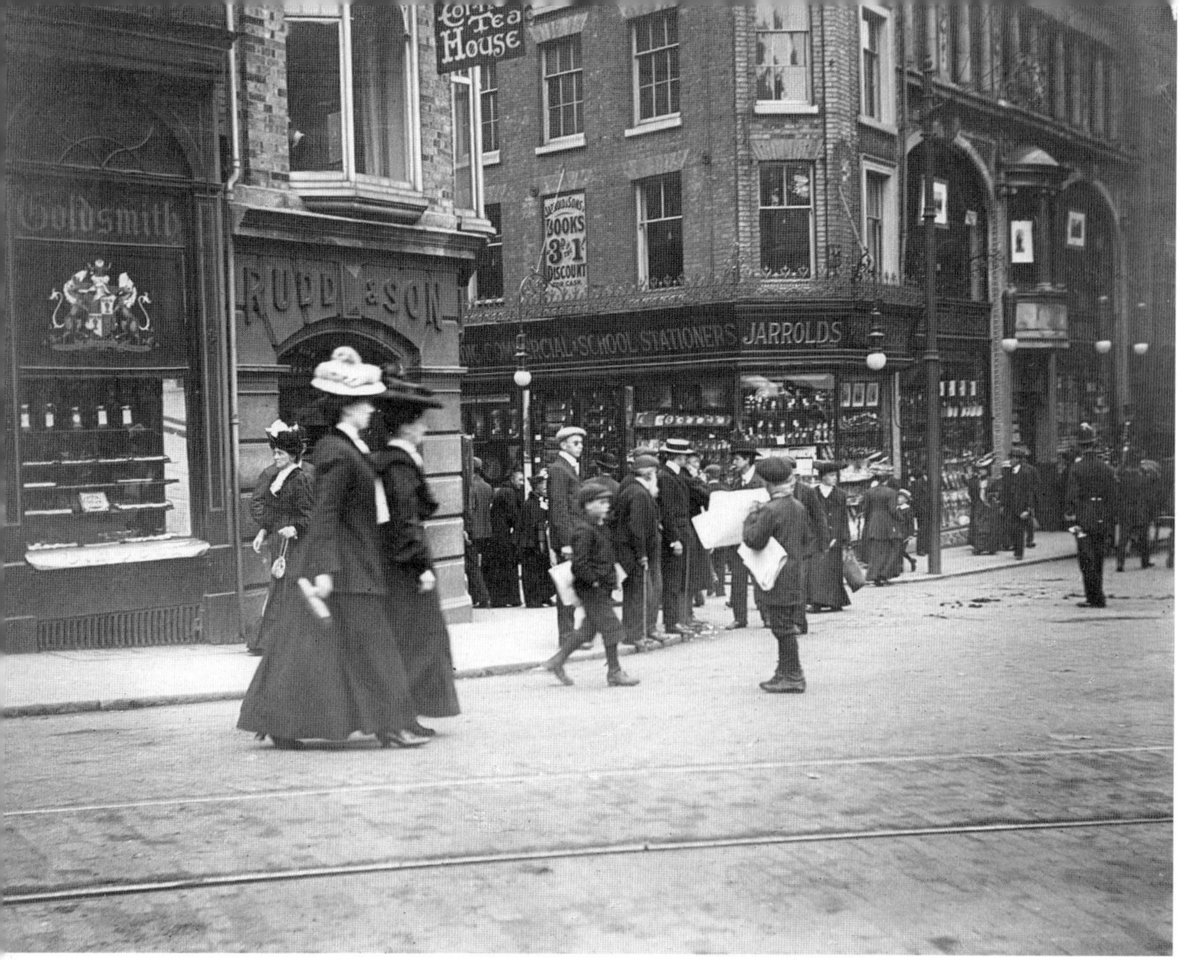

Goldsmith
RUDD & SON
BOOKS
DISCOUNT
COMMERCIAL & SCHOOL STATIONERS
JARROLDS
JARROLDS
SALE
HOUSE of JARROLDS
KODAK
JARROLD & SONS

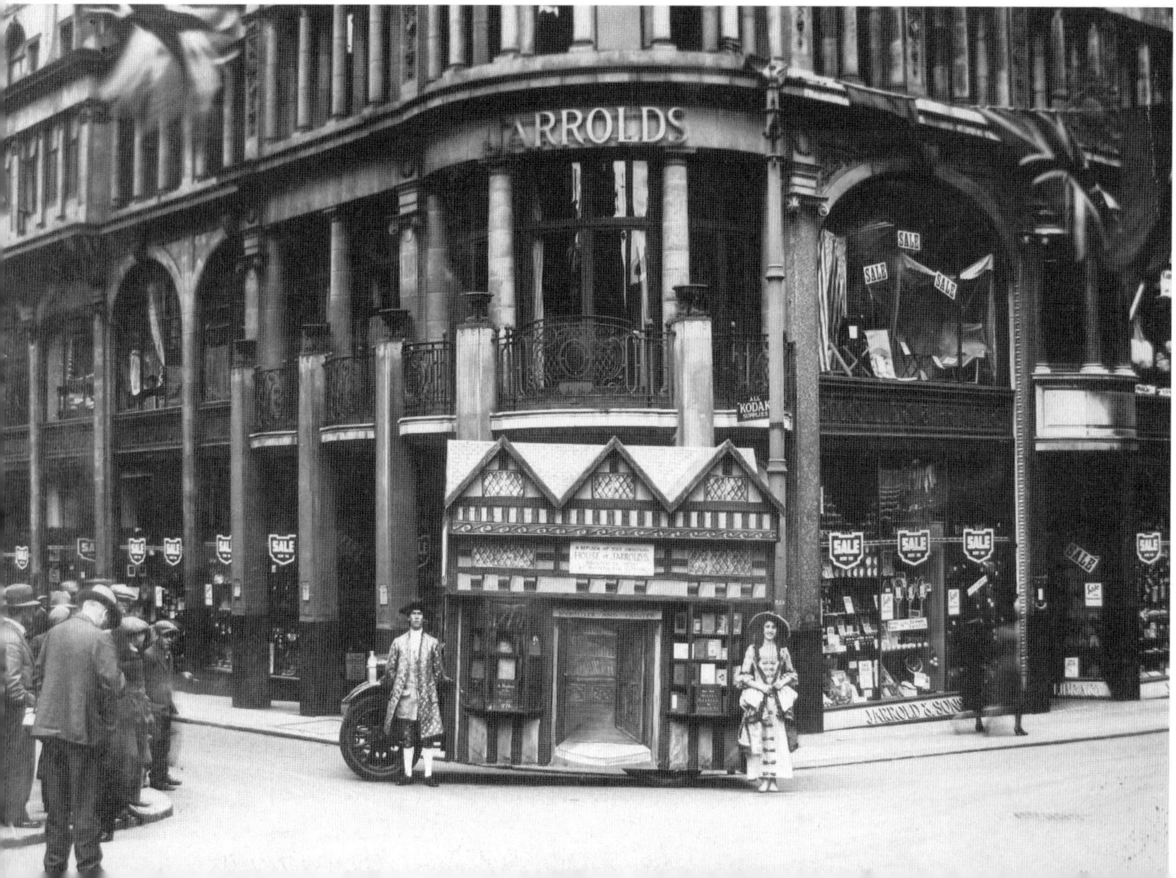

Top left: 154 *Jarrold's old front; the tramline in the street dates the picture to the first years of the 20th century.*
Below left: 155 *Jarrold's new front, with imagined image of the first store.*
Clockwise from above:
156 *Garlands fire, 1 August 1970: the Norwich 'Lanes' can create difficulties for the emergency services.*
157 *Shopping in the 1950s: Jarrold and Sons.*
158 *Shopping in the 1950s: Curl Brothers, in temporary premises after their store was destroyed in the war.*
159 *Shopping in St Stephens in the 1960s.*

Norwich markets continued to be the focus for a large part of Norfolk, and the two markets on either side of the castle were often called the lungs of the city. The sight of beasts of all kinds being driven along the city streets to the 'Cattle Market' was a common one. One resident, Irene Moore, recalled: 'We used to be terrified about the cattle going through the streets. They used to drive them on the roads and sometimes one of the cows would break loose and run away or run across the yard or something and we used to be terrified.' On one occasion in 1948, a cow being driven up Bracondale broke away and interrupted play at Lakenham cricket ground, where the Norfolk county side were playing Kent second eleven.[33]

In the second half of the 20th century, there were many changes. Before 1960 market stalls did not open on Mondays and Thursdays but after that they opened six days a week, and towards the end of the century some began opening on Sunday as well. Greengrocers and fruiterers sold an increasing proportion of foreign produce; in 1961 only 10 stall-holders grew some of their produce and only two sold just their own produce. There was a change in the character of central Norwich when the cattle market was moved to Harford, on the edge of Norwich, in the early 1960s. It was replaced by a public car park and then by the Castle Mall shopping centre, which opened in 1993; most of the mall is hidden under a park, emerging only as a 100-yard-long glasshouse. The 21st century saw a second shopping centre open at Chapelfield, on the site of the former Caley/Mackintosh chocolate factory. In 2005, the market place was redesigned by Michael Innes, with hygienic stalls and modern facilities, and remains the heart of the city. As was said at the time: 'The Market has survived plague, revolt, fires, wars and supermarkets and internet shopping.'[34]

Norwich was, and still is, the shopping centre for a large area of Norfolk and north-east Suffolk. It had a large number of department stores such as Curl Bros, Garlands, Bunting's and Bond's, but these have all disappeared or been taken over by national chains. Curl Bros was destroyed in the war and moved to temporary premises in Westlegate; a new store opened on the original site in 1956 but is now a Debenham's store. Garlands was destroyed after a disastrous chip-pan fire at 3.30 on a Saturday afternoon in August 1970; it reopened three years later but closed finally in 1984. One independent department store still flourishes and is very much part of the city's history, Jarrold and Sons; the present frontage was designed in 1904 but not completed until after the First World War.

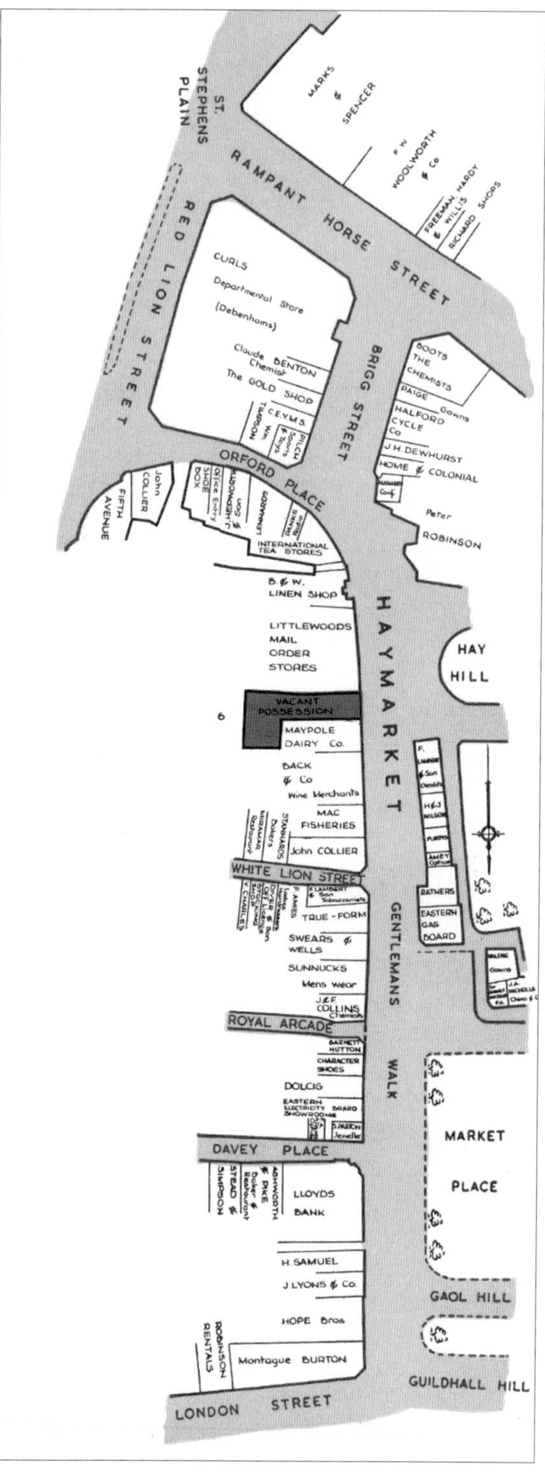

160 *Shopping map of central Norwich, 1965; which of these shops are operating today?*

Housing

Hawkins says that in the early years of the century, two-roomed tenements in yards were rented out at two shillings or two shillings and sixpence a week, with three-roomed houses at about three shillings a week: 'There are besides a number of single-roomed tenements which command rentals of from one shilling upwards. They attract an exceedingly undesirable class of tenant.' Hawkins noted that many of the yards ('except in the smaller courts – unfortunately they are rather numerous – where the houses are apt to be sunless and probably damp') were built around gardens; 'many of these are quite charming in summer when the flowers are out. Norwich, indeed is a city of gardens, and gardening, amongst popular recreations, is a formidable rival to professional football.'[35]

After the First World War the talk was of 'building homes for heroes' and Norwich led the way in the quality of its council housing in estates such as that at Mile Cross, the first estate to be built, with 769 houses. In the 1920s and 1930s standards were reduced to save costs but the later estates still provided homes of impressive quality to former dwellers of slums and yards, and the size of the gardens compared very favourably with any housing in the private sector.

There were continual disputes between local and national government about the costs of housing but by any standards the achievement was considerable. A Housing Committee report of July 1930 sums it up: since 1919 they had built 2,878 houses. There was room for a further 355 houses at North Earlham when sewers were available. The committee proposed buying land for 40 houses at Elm Grove Lane, for 400 at Mile Cross Lane and Catton Grove Road and for 500 at the Mousehold House estate.[36]

According to the *Norwich Guide* of 1935 there were about 36,000 houses in the city. The council had built a total of 4,727 houses on six main estates, with a few smaller sites on slum clearance areas closer to the city centre, and was also clearing slums, as the *Guide* explained:

> As to Slum Clearance in Norwich a good start has been made. Up to December 1933, several Clearance Areas had been declared, involved the building of over 300 houses and flats. A five-year programme to commence from 1 January 1934 was approved in September 1933 and this provided for the building of 1,400 flats and 645 houses, which it is estimated will re-house 8,099 persons … Up to the present re-housing has mainly been carried out on the Catton Grove and Mill Hill estates, but it is intended to build on the site of the Clearance Areas and this has already been done in the case of a small area in Oak Street. In particular, three-storey flats are to be built in the Barrack Street and Cowgate Area as there is a great demand for accommodation in that neighbourhood.

Facilities regarded as basic today, such as the supply of water and flush toilets, were still uncommon in the 1930s. Sheila Nursey was brought up in Ber Street:

161 *Argyle Street, with Normandie Tower.*

> My mother had to walk down two flights of stairs to get a pail of water from a pump in the yard and bring it all the way up. There was no running water, no baths, just a little bit of fire in the grate where she had to boil all the water and cook on, one saucepan at a time.

She recalled: 'the toilet outside was a wooden plank with a bucket, there was about six of us used it in the yard with a pump'. Leslie Howard remembered that their toilet was 'up the top' of the garden, with a paraffin lamp burning on the windowsill in the winter, and sacking round the pipes to try and stop them freezing up. Michael Banham used to take a candle out in a holder, and recalled the toilet paper as pieces of newspaper tied up on a piece of string.

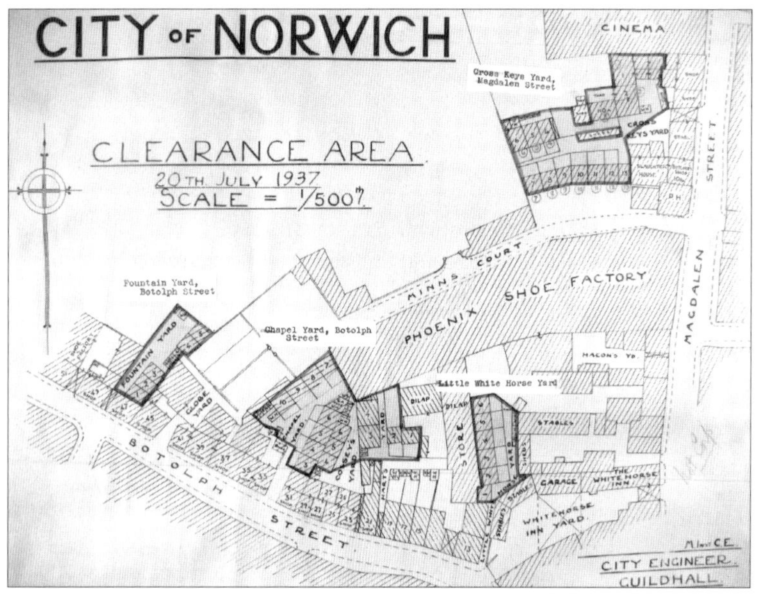

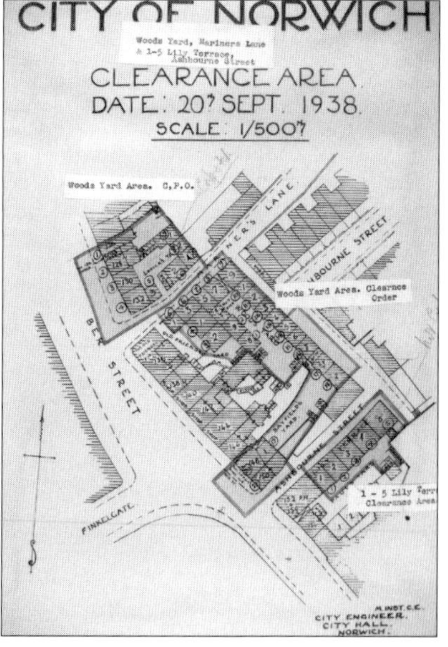

162 *Slum clearance: clearing the yards off Magdalen Street (left) ...*
163 *... and Ber Street (right).*

Electricity made a great difference. Fred Sampson remembered, 'Most of the houses had gas downstairs: one gas light in the front room, one in the living room and one in the kitchen.' A contributor to *Within Living Memory* recalled:

> Most people lived in terraced houses, streets of them, a great number of which were destroyed in the air raids in the war. The roads and streets were lit by gas lamps; these had two hanging chains 'on and off' which were operated by lamplighters on cycles at dusk and dawn each day. Houses mostly had gas for lighting and cooking but many people had oil lamps.[37]

Elizabeth Sturt, formerly Harris, recalled growing up in the Southwell Road area shortly before the Second World War:

> A bakery stood at the corner of Cheshil Place, and I remember my mother taking her Christmas cakes there to be cooked ... My mother used to obtain the cork granules in which grapes were packed in those days from the greengrocers and use them as an underlay under the floor covering ... Much of the area disappeared in a 'slum' clearance programme, many of the residents being rehoused in the new council estate between Hall Road and Mansfield Lane ... My mother would have been most upset at any suggestion that her home was a slum, although it lacked much, including any garden. We also had to share our toilet with the neighbours on one side.

Gladys Courtnell summed up the revolution brought about by the city's council houses: 'That was like living in paradise because we had a toilet of our own, a bathroom with a bath in it and a gas copper where we boiled the water for the bath.'[38]

By 1952, about 500 yards and courts had been demolished, and about 11,000 houses had been constructed since the end of the First World War, one in three of the city's housing stock. More than half of them were built by the council; Norwich's 6,000th council house was formally opened by the Lord Mayor, Arthur South, on 10 July 1956. Norwich council estates tended to be traditional in design, but tower blocks were built in the 1960s. The first plan for such blocks on Ber Street had to be abandoned as the foundations collapsed into old chalk workings, but three blocks were built on Bowers Avenue in 1964, and two central blocks are prominent features of the city landscape – Normandie Tower at Rouen Road and the Vauxhall Street tower, both of 16 storeys with 95 flats.

Council housing came to be seen as a political issue by the 1980s. A Conservative councillor wrote in 1986: 'So why does Norwich have one of the largest proportions of council housing in the country? Quite simply because what started as a generally accepted policy to meet the real need of poorer people turned into an exploitation of that situation to gain Socialist political power.' The building of council houses was effectively ended by central government policies which encouraged the sale of council houses and the work of housing associations. Whereas in 1978-9 work had begun on 528 new council houses, in 1990-1 just one new house was being built – and over 5,000 council houses had been sold under the government's 'Right to Buy' scheme.[39]

Norwich has been notably successful in rejuvenating the inner city by developing housing on the sites of closed factories. The large block of land between Coslany Street, Colegate and the river was the factory of Barnard, Bishop and Barnards from 1851. It was turned into houses and flats by the city architect, David Percival, in the 1970s and 1980s. Further east, a large area of derelict warehouses was replaced by the Friars' Quay development, erected by Feilden and Mawson in 1974; its most striking feature is the high pitch of the roofs, a style known as Norfolk Vernacular.

Argyle Street, with its Victorian terrace houses, made international headlines in the 1980s. At one time about to be bought by the UEA for student housing, 120 squatters moved in one night in December 1979, forming a co-operative in 1980 of people who may – very loosely – be described as hippies. In 1982 the city council planned to sell or lease the houses to the co-operative, but the Department of the Environment refused its permission. In 1984 the council decided to demolish the houses and replace them with sheltered housing, and the 'Alternative Republic of Argyle Street', as it was fondly known by inhabitants and their friends, came to an end after five years in 1985.

164 *Cows in King Street: a familiar sight in old Norwich.*

Historic heritage

The 20th century saw a growing interest in preserving the city's building heritage, fostered by such groups as the Norwich Society; founded in 1923, the Society played a major role in preserving Bishop's Bridge and Elm Hill. Other successes included the preservation of the *Golden Star,* the prevention of a proposed nine-storey tower at the *Maid's Head* and, at the end of the century, ensuring that the market's modernisation incorporated a new vision of the traditional stalls. Inevitably there were losses, too: the fly-over across Magdalen Street was built despite the Society's opposition, and the 16th-century *New Star* inn on Quayside was pulled down despite its historical significance, apparently because it had become a resort of prostitutes. The Norfolk Industrial Archaeology Society also does important work, preserving the industrial heritage of the city.

The end of the century saw the establishment of Norwich HEART (Heritage Economic And Regeneration Trust), under the leadership of Michael Loveday, the city's 'Heritage Tsar', with responsibility for 12 of the city's most significant buildings, from the Norman cathedral to the late 20th-century Millennium Library. HEART also promotes both historical research and tourist appreciation of the city's heritage – including a recognition of the brewing traditions of the city by promoting Norwich as Britain's first 'City of Ale'. The two societies have worked with the city council to set up the Wensum River Parkway project to re-establish Norwich as a river city.

Several old buildings in Norwich have been given to the city. Strangers' Hall was bought by Leonard Bolingbroke in 1899 to save it from destruction;

he founded what he claimed was the first 'folk-life' museum in Britain and gave it to the city, the formal handover taking place in July 1923. In the same year a local shoemaker named Henry Holmes bought the old Bridewell building and gave it to the city for use as a museum of local trades and industries. The Bridewell was completely refurbished in 2011 with the aid of lottery money, to create a museum fit for the 21st century.

Other historic buildings preserved by the goodwill of the citizens include the Assembly House, which had been used by the Norwich High School for Girls, but they moved out to Newmarket Road in 1932 and the building became a warehouse. Alan Colman, Sir Ernest White and Harry Sexton bought it before the Second World War, intending to make it a headquarters for the YMCA and YWCA. The war put paid to this scheme: later Harry Sexton spent £70,000 on restoring the building and on turning Noverre's annex into a cinema. The architect was Rowland Pierce. The cinema closed in 1992 and the roof and interior of the building were badly damaged by fire in 1995, but the building was very quickly restored to its former glory.

No survey of preservation work in Norwich is complete without a mention of Walter Rye. Born in London, he spent most of his holidays in Norfolk and retired to Norwich in 1900. He was responsible for the preservation of three buildings that would otherwise have been pulled down: the *Maid's Head* hotel, Bacon House in Colegate and the Lazar House in Sprowston Road. He was also responsible for buying and preserving many manuscripts, pamphlets, books and prints about Norwich and Norfolk, including the city's Book of Customs. This was lost for many years and restored to the city archives by Rye in 1905. The manuscripts he collected are now in the Norfolk Record Office and his books and prints are in the Norfolk Studies Library, although some of the latter were destroyed in the 1994 fire. Walter Rye died in 1929 and is buried in Lammas.

The number of medieval churches in the city centre meant that most were surplus to religious needs. Norwich led the way in finding other uses for them when St Peter Hungate became an ecclesiastical museum in 1933, the first redundant Anglican church ever to be turned to secular use. The museum closed in 1995, but a new project, Hungate Medieval Art, opened to the public in 2009. A variety of uses has been found for the others and none has been lost apart from those bombed in the war.[40]

Although religion no longer had the universal appeal of earlier periods, some churches were built, especially on the new housing estates in the city. The most prominent is probably St Catherine at Mile Cross, built in 1935 by A.D.R. Caroe and A.P. Robinson, with its exterior of purple and brown brick, and an interior described by Olive Cook: 'the design avoids actual medieval detail in an evocation of vaguely Norman massiveness'. More central is the Church of Christ Scientist on Recorder Road, by Herbert Ibberson in 1934-5, with a dramatic, almost cave-like, interior; it is currently used by the Greek Orthodox community in Norwich. Perhaps the most significant of the post-war churches is the Presbyterian church on the Unthank Road, next to the Roman Catholic cathedral, designed by Bernard Feilden in 1954-6 in a striking expressionist style.[41]

Despite a decline in traditional church-going, faith remains important to many Norwich citizens. The last decades of the 20th century saw the establishment of many new churches in the Radical tradition; according to Ted Doe there were more than 20 of these by 2011, including the King's Church, 'a Christian family of 400 worshippers'. Other faiths have also established places of worship in the city, including the Moslem, Sikh and Buddhist communities.[42]

Poverty and crime

There was great poverty in the city in the early 20th century. Hawkins speaks of a:

> vast pauper host of 11,000 … there is in Norwich a very large under-employed, and therefore semi-employable class who are always on the verge of destitution. Bad times, old age, widowhood, sickness, and any of the normal accidents of life leave them absolutely without resources … In 1907 alone over 4,000 paupers were relieved on more than one occasion. The worst of this is, that while it is easy to acquire the habit of coming to the Poor Law for assistance, it is a very difficult habit to unlearn.[43]

Dorothy Jewson, with her brother Harry and a group of supporters calling themselves 'Investigators', brought to light the conditions in which the poor in the city lived, the information being put together in a small book called *How the Destitute Live*. They found that out of the 827 cases of people on out-relief, almost 400 were living in properties where the toilet was shared with several other houses; in the most extreme cases one closet was shared with four or five, or in three cases no less than six families. The water supply was also grossly inadequate, with over 350 families sharing a tap with another family, and of these almost 100 families were sharing a single tap with six or more other families.

Jewson went on to look at the diet of the poor:

> a large number of children, while they have enough bread, with even cheap jam or margarine on it, doubtless cannot possibly be given such a diet as that on which it is possible to rear physically sound and strong citizens. White bread, jam and tea, and little else, is not a diet on which growing children can be brought up, though they may never actually suffer from hunger. Let it not be forgotten that the general amount given in out-relief in Norwich for the maintenance of children is two shillings a head per week. The mothers of these children are working, many of them, all day and late into the night, but anyone who knows anything about women's wages in Norwich will be aware that they are able to earn only just enough to pay for their own food, the rent, and firing. There is nothing left over from their earnings in most instances to help pay for the children's food, boots and clothes.

She gives the actual income and expenses of several families to show how desperately poor they were. One example was 'Mrs M', a woman with four children, who was given 10 shillings a week poor relief (shown in Table V). As Jewson concludes, 'it will be seen at a glance that this diet is altogether insufficient for children under eleven years of age'. She quotes a case of another 'Mrs M' who had children, and was deserted by her husband, so she:

> took in desperation to the streets to supplement her resources and feed her children. The children were taken and boarded out as a result, with an allowance of ten shillings a week and £1 a quarter for clothes. Why could not an adequate allowance have been given before wrecking the life of the mother in that way?[44]

The Investigators wanted a minimum hand-out of five shillings per person per week. This provoked the debate that has always been part of the controversy of poor relief: if the hand-out was as high as that, the city authorities responded, it would be as much, or almost as much, as the income of families where the husband was in work, so what would be the incentive to find a job?

Norwich children continued to be sent away to institutions. A list of 1921 records 21 boys and four girls in eight different institutions, several as far away as Lancashire. Many of these children were unloved. Dorothy Leman was born in Norwich in 1914. Her parents separated and both left the city. Dorothy attended Anguish's hospital school, but was excluded for stealing, and then took sixpence from a teacher's bag. Her parents had her taken into care; just 10 years old, she was sent to an institution in Sale in Cheshire. Ruby and Dora Shemming lived with their mother, Violet, at 10 St Lawrence Lane; their father, a carpenter, lived in Queen's Road. In 1926 Violet was sent to prison for a month for keeping a brothel, and the two girls were also sent

Table V: *A poor family's expenditure in the early 20th century.*

One woman with four children received a total of ten shillings a week from the authorities. This is how it was spent:

Rent	2s. 0d.
Coal	1s. 6d.
Oil and wood	5d.
Save for contingencies	¼d.

This leaves for food for five people, just 6s 0¾d, spent as follows:

21 loaves	3s. 11¼d.
Dripping	4d.
Cheese	1¼d.
Jam	2d.
Meat	5d.
Vegetables	4½d.
1 tin of milk	2½d.
2 ounces of tea	2d.
Half a pound of sugar	1¼d.
Pepper and salt	½ d.
Fish	2½d.
Total	6s. 0¾d.

Source: *Anonymous (Dorothy Jewson),* The destitute of Norwich and how they live *(1912)*

to Sale. Albert Smith, born 1902, was sent to the *Formidable* in March 1915, at which time his father was in the army. The boy wrote a pathetic letter to the city authorities in July 1916: 'I now have the pleasure of writing to you. I hope you are quite well. I am writing to ask you if you would go to my mother's and ask her why she do not write to me … I have not been punished yet and I am keeping myself clean and out of all mischief.' He was discharged from the school in October 1918 and our knowledge of his case ends with a short note dated November 1918: 'parents know nothing about him'.

Dealing with youth crime has been a problem for the authorities for centuries, and the 20th century was no exception. In 1912 three boys were before the Juvenile Court, George Adcock (13), Charles Colk (12) and Arthur Shropsall (10), for stealing five boxes of chocolates from the warehouse of a shop in the Royal Arcade. Adcock had climbed onto a box and put his hand through a door and they had taken the chocolates home to their mothers. They were caught when the police searched Shropsall's house on another charge. All three had committed other crimes and were sentenced to go to industrial schools until they were sixteen. Shropsall's mother ran about the court, a baby in her arms, crying out, 'I'll never let my boy go. My poor boy. May God have mercy on him.' In contrast, Colk's father was truculent, saying he would not pay the one shilling a week required for his son's maintenance; rather than do this he would desert his family, leaving the authorities with the expense of caring for them.

Several of the children made good despite their difficult circumstances. William Fultcher was born in 1889 and lived in Muspole Street in a most unsatisfactory family: 'father in asylum, mother no control over him'. He was sent to the *Formidable* in 1900, returning to the city to become a hero:

> on Wednesday afternoon [1903] two children, a boy and a girl, were playing at the bottom of Water Lane St George's Plain, when they accidentally fell into the river. They must have been drowned but for the intrepidity of a boy, fourteen years of age, who belongs to the Boy's Training ship *Formidable*, who, without hesitation, plunged into the water with all his clothes on, and rescued both of them.

Left: 165 *An early television presented to an old people's home,* c.*1953.*

166 *State of the art technology in the 1950s: telephone exchange at Barnards, in the days when every phone call needed a wire along which to run.*

167 *The first computer in the city arrives in 1957.*

Another local boy, Herbert Spilling of Heigham, born in 1891, was sent to the *Formidable* in 1903. He went on to serve on the schooner *Henrietta*, and he and his skipper were both drowned at Musselburgh trying to rescue some boys in a boating accident in 1910.[45]

Despite poverty, there had been some developments in domestic life since Bilby's marriage a century earlier (p.148); when Ethel Edwards married Dick George in 1931, they were able to buy all new furniture – 'of course we didn't have no money, so we had to get it on the mace. Five shillings down and so much a week.' They had tinned salmon and crab for the wedding meal, followed by jelly and custard, and the wedding cake was a shop-bought Christmas cake, Ethel having replaced the snowman originally on top of it.[46]

As standards improved through the century, expectations inevitably rose too. In 1970 it was said,

> Poverty is most apparent, most hurtful, where income is lower than that of friends and contemporaries – of a person's own 'community'. The deserted wife with small children is poor by comparison with her happily married sister; the young woman who has left home and is trying to support herself and perhaps a child as well on a wage which assumes that every woman is part of the household of a wage-earning man cannot keep up with a teenager living at home; a family man of below-average ability may well earn less money in a week than is deemed necessary for subsistence on Supplementary Benefit.

However, there is still real poverty in the city. In 2001, 6.4 per cent lived in overcrowded houses and 8.9 per cent of families lacked either central heating or the sole use of bath/shower and toilet – or both. Figures in 2004 described 21,300 people in the city as 'income deprived' and over 9,300 as 'employment deprived'; in August 2010, 15.7 per cent of the working age population were claiming benefits.[47]

Attitudes to punishment also changed. After centuries of executions, capital punishment was finally abolished in 1965, the last hangings in Norwich prison taking place on 19 July 1951 when two young men, Dennis Moore and Alfred Reynolds, were hanged together. Each had murdered his fiancée, Moore having killed Eileen Cullen in the city, whereas Reynolds's crime took place in Dereham. The previous hanging, that of Norman Goldthorpe on 23 November 1950, had created controversy as the hangman had bungled the job, allowing the hood to become snagged in the noose.

Health

After the war there was a pandemic of influenza in which many millions of people died. Norwich was fortunate, as the city's Medical Officer for Health recorded:

> In the early part of 1919, Influenza became markedly prevalent – and fortunately, although in the course of the year 119 deaths were attributed to it, was not so fatal a type as this disease assumed in other places. Of these deaths, 86 occurred in the first quarter of 1919, 27 in the second – and just six in the last half of the year.

In 1920 there were 11 deaths in the first quarter and just six over the rest of the year.[48]

The century saw an increasing concern with mental health. Eaton Grange was a former private school for young ladies. In 1929 the council bought it to house 'defectives' and it opened the following year for 30 female adults and seven children. As the council had not had anywhere locally to put these patients, they were in institutions as far away as Chesterfield and Bristol and they were now brought back to the city. The report quotes the case of one 34-year-old woman, who had lost her parents when young, and had been brought up in the orphanage in Chapelfield Road. In 1912 she was sent to Stoke Park Colony where she stayed for 19 years, largely forgotten one suspects. Certainly when she was moved to Eaton Grange in 1931 her improvement was rapid and she was soon able to go out in service.[49]

Fundraising for the Norfolk and Norwich Hospital was boosted in 1904 with the start of the Hospital Cup – every year Norwich City played a top national team for this trophy and the proceeds went to the hospital. In 1919 a tombola was organised which raised £13,000, but the Bishop of Norwich and many others wrote strong letters to the *Eastern Daily Press* disapproving of the gambling element in this fundraising effort. 'Egg Week' was started in 1923 and for one week every April people gave eggs for the hospital patients.

The great change in health was, of course, the introduction of the National Health Service in 1948, offering free access to doctors and hospitals for everyone. The hospital was administered by the Norwich, Lowestoft and Great Yarmouth Hospital Management Committee until 1974, when the Norfolk Area Health Authority came into being. In 1990 land for a new hospital for Norwich was bought in Colney Lane. The new Norfolk and Norwich University Hospital has almost 1,000 beds; like the old one, it was on the western edge of city of its time. The composer Sir Malcolm Arnold died at the new hospital in 2006. It includes a children's department, which replaced the Jenny Lind Hospital and is named in her honour. The old 'Norfolk and Norwich' has been converted into apartments.

Attitudes to mental health changed over the century, with much greater emphasis on home care, and so the Bethel Hospital reached the end of its long and useful life. After the war it became an annexe to Hellesdon Hospital and in 1974 an out-patient unit for disturbed children and adolescents; this has since closed. Hellesdon itself has become the much smaller David Rice Hospital, and Thorpe St Andrew Hospital has also been converted to apartments.

Two of the city's oldest charities have continued their centuries of service to the city, adapting again to changed needs and demands. The Great Hospital is both a museum piece and a state-of-the-art care home; Marietta Pallis, mentioned in Chapter Two, died here in 1963 and is buried on her eagle-headed island in Hickling. The Blind Institution has evolved into the Norfolk and Norwich Association for the Blind, offering residential care as well as support for the blind and partially sighted in the community.

Education

The city played a key role in the education of its children between 1902 and 1974. Under the 1902 Education Act the Board Schools came under the control of the city council, which became responsible for primary, secondary and technical education. The replacement of School Boards with councillors was a blow to women as they could not yet stand for the council; to get around this, women were co-opted onto the city's Education Committee.

Under an Act of 1918, all children were to stay at school until they were 14 years old. The city's education system is described in the 1935 *Official Guide*: 'Young children are admitted to Infants' schools at 4 or 5 years and for the first time in their lives become members of a community ... Formal instruction in reading and numbers is introduced by means of toys, apparatus and pictures.' At the age of seven, children moved to Primary School: 'At first the methods employed are similar to those in the Infants' School and the child gradually enters upon a more varied curriculum, in which academic and cultural subjects are included ... the curriculum includes English, Arithmetic, History, Geography, Music, Art, Handiwork, Physical Training and Hygiene.' At the age of 11 children went on to one of the various types of secondary education.

The 1944 Education Act raised the leaving age to 15, and introduced three types of secondary school – grammar, technical and modern. The city council can be proud of the speed with which it responded to the Act. In 1961 it was noted that 21 new schools had been built in Norwich since the war – nine infant, seven junior and five secondary schools. In 1974 control of schools in the city passed to Norfolk County Council. Subsequent developments saw the introduction of a comprehensive programme and in the first decade of the 21st century the establishment of academies with greater control of their finance and curriculum; the first was at Heartsease.

The University of East Anglia is one of a clutch of universities built in the early 1960s. After the war it was proposed to have the university in the centre of town on Ber Street and later the redundant Barracks on Mousehold was suggested as a possible site. The basic concept of the design and the early buildings were by Denys Lasdun and these include its best-known features – the 'teaching wall', the 'ziggurats' or students' residences, and the artificial broad, one of three in late 20th-century Norwich, the other two being on the old gravel workings at Whitlingham. The UEA motto is 'Do Different' – changed from the more Norfolk 'Du Different' by the College of Arms.

In 1973 Sir Robert and Lady Sainsbury gave their arts collection to the university, and the Sainsbury Centre for Visual Arts was built to house it at the expense of their son, David; the architect was Norman Foster. It opened in 1978, and in 1989-90 Foster added the Crescent Wing. In 2011, UEA had over 13,000 students from all over the world.

The Technical Institute became the Norwich School of Art and Design, with the painter Alfred Munnings among its pupils. The folksinger Peter Bellamy (1944-91) was a student at the college in the early 1960s; his best-known work, 'The Transports', evoked the lives of convicts of earlier ages, especially Henry Cabell, described on p.153. In 2007, it became the Norwich University College of the Arts. City College, originally founded in 1891, has been on its present site since 1953; it runs education and training courses for 14 to 16 year olds, and in 2009 won an award for its work with students with Asperger's Syndrome.

168 *The second Carrow Bridge, with early motor car.*

Transport

The great increase in population in the suburbs of Norwich together with new engineering ideas changed the face of the city. One was the introduction of a tram system. The first horse-drawn bus services had been started in 1879 by the Norwich Omnibus Company but this firm was wound up in 1899. Norwich Electric Tramways began laying rails and the first services opened on 30 April 1900, when services were run on Magdalen, Earlham, Dereham and Thorpe Roads. On the first day 25,000 passengers were carried. When the trams first appeared, 'so great was the enthusiasm that men ran out of a barber's shop, their faces still covered with lather, to see this amazing spectacle'.[50]

At its peak the firm had over 40 trams and ran services along the Dereham, Earlham, Magdalen, Thorpe, Aylsham, Newmarket and Unthank Roads and to Trowse and Mousehold. The new technology had an effect on the city landscape, including the widening of roads around Orford Hill and the road outside the present Cinema City linking Bank Plain with St Andrew's; the odd shape of Armada House is because half of it was removed to let the trams through. However, trams were destined to be a short-lived feature of city life. The first indication of decline came after 25 years when the Aylsham Road trams were replaced by buses and the number of bus services in the city steadily increased, some replacing trams and others acting as feeder services.

In 1932 the city council decided to buy the Tramways Company. In an uncommon exercise of democracy, it held a referendum on 10 January 1933; the people of Norwich voted against the purchase by 11,033 to 7,775 votes and the trams were doomed. In December of the same year the Eastern Omnibus Company took a controlling interest in Norwich Electric Tramways and over the next two years all the trams were replaced with buses, the last service to run was from Newmarket Road to the Cavalry Barracks, which ceased to operate in December 1935.

The company promised 'a large and up-to-date bus station' and this was opened in Surrey Street on 24 March 1936. It was hit by a bomb on 30 July 1940 and 16 buses were damaged. The buses were nationalised in 1948. In 1950 fares were raised for the first time in 30 years, after which fare rises became an almost annual event. The most famous memory that Norwich people have of their buses is of one that fell into a hole that suddenly appeared in the Earlham Road on 3 March 1988, a reminder of the very many chalk diggings that lie beneath the city's surface. A new bus station opened on the same site in July 2005, and now caters for 1,200 buses every day and six million passengers a year.

Other attempts at a public transport system came to nothing. In 1904/5 the Great Eastern Railway put an Act through Parliament to build a track from Norwich to Loddon and Beccles, the idea being to use trams. At the same time the Midland and Great Northern drew up plans for a branch from City Station that would tunnel under the centre of Norwich and meet up with the GER line at Lakenham. Due to the high costs involved, neither line was ever built and a bus service to Loddon was introduced instead. Victoria Station finally closed to passengers in 1916, despite a petition by local people two years earlier with 1,702 signatures. In return, the railway company gave the corporation land between Thorpe Station and the river to build a new road along the bank and also promised to issue cheap day return tickets from/to towns within 30 miles of the city on market days and during the Triennial Festival. The railway continued to be used for freight traffic, mainly coal, until the 1980s; part of the line is now the Lakenham Way, a footpath and cycleway. City Station was rebuilt after wartime bombing, but closed to passengers in 1959 and to freight 10 years later; the track is also now a footpath.[51]

The first person to fly over Norwich in an aeroplane appears to have been Bentfield Hucks on 10 August 1912. The First World War speeded up interest in air transport, and the cavalry training field on Mousehold Heath was taken over by the Royal Flying Corps in October 1914. In 1915 the first aircraft built by Boulton and Paul made its maiden flight here. In 1933 the field was opened as Norwich Airport; Crilly Airways ran daily services to Leicester, Bristol, Liverpool, Nottingham and Northampton.[52]

169 *Accident in Thorpe Road in the 1940s.*

During the Second World War the Mousehold airfield acted as a decoy site for the military airfield at Horsham and dummy planes were placed on it to deceive the Luftwaffe. There were two fatal crashes on Mousehold Heath in 1942. In February, the pilot of a bomber was killed when forced to make an emergency landing at Long Valley; the other four crew members survived. In July, a plane from Lyneham in Wiltshire attempted a forced landing and the crew were all killed. In 1990 a plaque to the memory of those killed in both crashes was erected on the Heath. The site of the airport was later used for the Heartsease housing estate and school, but some of the hangars can still be seen on the west side of Salhouse Road. In 1969 the present Norwich Airport opened on the Horsham site, funded by the city and county councils, who purchased the site from the Ministry of Defence. A new passenger turntable opened in 1988. The airport was sold by the councils in March 2004 to Omniport for £10 million.

Like most historic cities Norwich has had problems coping with the rise of the motor car. By the 1930s cars were becoming more affordable; in February 1937 second-hand cars were being advertised for as little as £50 for a five-year-old Morris Oxford saloon and £240 could buy a one-year-old Triumph Gloria saloon. The Norwich Plan envisaged an inner ring road around the centre of the city with adjacent car parks. Part of the ring road was built, including the flyover across Magdalen Street, which involved the destruction of part of the ancient street plan. The most expensive civil engineering project involved a huge viaduct across the river Wensum near Read's Mills, which would have taken the heavy traffic out of Bracondale. Funds never became available for this and the inner ring road remains incomplete.

The plan was to bring the car right into the city, hence the widening of St Stephen's and the new Duke Street Bridge, but a planned major road linking the two and running below the market place never materialised. Two decades later, attitudes had changed. Norwich led the way in pedestrianisation when London Street was closed to traffic in 1967; this was the first time in England a shopping street had been closed to traffic. The ban on traffic has spread to Gentleman's Walk and to several narrow lanes in the market place area of the city, and Westlegate will soon follow. According to the 2001 census, 35 per cent of households in the city did not have access to a car or van. More people walked or cycled to work in Norwich than in any other city in the United Kingdom.

The County Council Transport Strategy of 1997 involved creating seven 'Park and Ride' schemes in a ring around the city and aimed to

170 *Messenger boys outside City Hall in 1946*

171 *USAAF personnel outside Dodger's bicycle shop.*

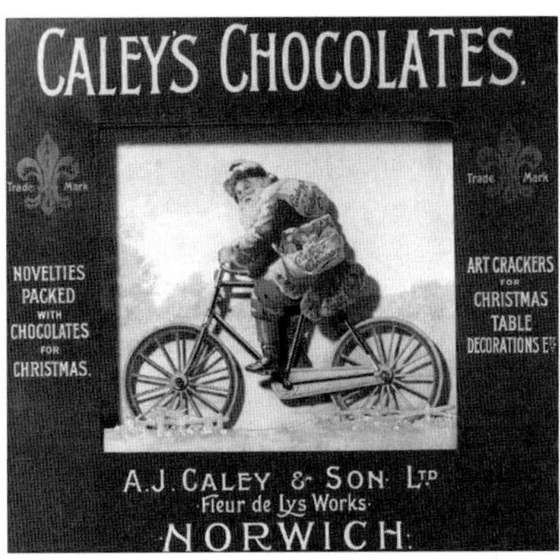

Above: 172 *Caley's advertising.*

Right: 173 *London Street, the first pedestrianised street in Britain.*

restrict parking in the city's residential streets to the people who lived in them; the plan also aimed to create a network of safe cycling routes into the city centre for commuters. In the early years of the 21st century, controversy centred on the building of a Northern Distributor Road, seen by some as providing essential relief to existing roads, by others as an outdated solution to the problems caused by the motor car.[53]

Norwich, Europe and the world

There was an Italian community centred on Ber Street from the later 19th century; Ralph Mottram recalled the striking impression they made on him, especially the women, with 'their abundant hair bound with richly coloured scarves'. Many became well known in Norwich life: the Rossi family had a jewellers on Guildhall Hill, the Valoris had six fish and chip shops and the Peruzzi family operated a scrap-metal business. Another was Antoinette Carrera, who married Jack Hannent of the *Jolly Butchers* public house; known as 'Black Anna' from the colour of her hair and dress, her jazz club was a popular venue from the Second World War to the 1970s. She died in 1976.[54]

During the war, many Polish pilots were based at Coltishall, north of Norwich, and they continued to operate from here as the Second World War turned into the Cold War. Some made the ultimate sacrifice and their graves are in the Earlham Cemetery. They include one just 20 years old, Thomas Wozniak. One of the graves is of a female, one of only two graves of Polish women air force personnel in Britain. This is Evgenia Zagajewska, 21 years old. Based in London, she was staying with a friend at Coltishall over Easter in 1946. On Easter Monday three young Poles went to Lammas for an afternoon's boating, using a plane's fuel tank; the 'boat' upset and Evgenia and a male friend were drowned. A memorial on the site of the former Thorpe Hospital cemetery, now

174a, b *The first Chinese restaurant in Norwich, exterior and interior.*

a park, honours 'the Polish community who first came to St Andrews when it was a military hospital during the Second World War 1939/1945 and whose lives centred around it long afterwards'.

Other incomers were not here by choice. As David Jones recalled,

> there were two prisoner of war camps in Norwich, one German and one Italian. I can remember the Germans playing football against some of our boys up on Duchy's [a field off Ranworth Road] … The Germans didn't speak to you much, but the Italians were allowed to go and help round the houses. We had an Italian help with our garden – he would eat with us and then go back to the camp in the evening.

They were still in the camp in the bitter winter of 1947, when they helped in clearing pavements. A few of the prisoners chose to stay in the city after the war.[55]

Since the war, more positive efforts have been made to encourage international co-operation. Norwich was twinned with Rouen in 1959, and other 'twinnings' more recently have included Koblenz and Novi Sad, explaining some recent road and bridge names in the city. Links with America have been developed primarily through the American Memorial Library, which honours the American airmen who died fighting out of bases in East Anglia. Among many other international links, Muhammed Ali visited Norwich on 19 October 1971, doing a promotional event for Ovaltine at Tesco in St Stephen's, now New Look – a plaque was put up in 2003, but has since disappeared – while the Dalai Lama bought canaries from local fancier (and ex-Canary!) Chris Goodall in the 1970s. Many incomers into the city have brought their own shops and restaurants, beginning with the first Chinese restaurant in about 1960; five years later there were already three in the Prince of Wales Road alone. The city's tradition of welcoming refugees has continued into the 21st century and resulted in formal recognition as a 'City of Refuge'.

Opposite, anti-clockwise from top:
175 *The Nest on Rosary road; the site is now used for housing.*
176a, b *Stages in the development of the Carrow Road ground.*
177 *Celebrating the return to the Premier League, 2011.*

Leisure

Norwich City football club was founded in 1902, playing originally at Newmarket Road and then for many years at the Nest on Rosary Road. This was an old chalk quarry; spectators on one side watched from the top of a cliff! It was because of this danger to the crowd that the club moved to Carrow Road in 1935. It has been there ever since, although every stand has been redeveloped, some several times, the biggest changes coming when terraces for standing watchers were replaced with seats. The players were known as the Citizens until 1907, playing in blue and white; in that year they became the Canaries and adopted the now familiar green and yellow.

The later years of the 20th century were good years for the club. They reached the semi-finals of the FA Cup for the first time in 1959, and in 1972 the club reached the top flight of the football league. It has had many successes under managers such as Ron Saunders, John Bond, Ken Brown and Dave Stringer, including victory in the League/Milk Cup Final in 1985. In 1992-3 Norwich City achieved their highest position ever, finishing third in the new Premier League under the managership of Mike – 'St Michael' – Walker. This qualified them for European competition and they became the talk of Europe when they beat the mighty Bayern Munich in Germany on 19 October 1993. Their run came to an end with two narrow defeats by Inter Milan in the following round. One star

of the team was local boy Chris Sutton. Educated at Hellesdon High School, he moved to Blackburn Rovers in 1994 for £5 million, shattering the British transfer record, and he went on to win the League Championship there. After a number of relatively poor seasons, the club has returned to the Premier League for the 2011-12 season.

Perhaps the most interesting of their many star players was Justin Fashanu. Fashanu was the son of a Nigerian barrister living in England; after his parents split up, he and his brother John went to a Barnardo's Home and then to foster parents at Shropham near Attleborough. He became an apprentice at Norwich City, turning professional in December 1978. In three years he made 90 appearances and scored 35 goals. In August 1981, he became Britain's first £1 million black footballer when he was bought for Nottingham Forest by manager Brian Clough. His career stalled at this point, supposedly because Clough disapproved of his visits to gay clubs, and he played for many lesser clubs over the following years. It was while he was playing for Torquay that he came out as gay in an interview with the *Sun* published on 22 October 1990; he featured on the cover of *Gay Times* in July 1991. He subsequently played for clubs in Scotland and America, and it was in America that a 17-year-old youth brought a charge of assault against him (which was subsequently dropped). Fashanu had already returned to England, and on the morning of 3 May 1990 he was found hanged in a garage in Shoreditch; he was 37 years old. He will be remembered as the first professional footballer to say that he was gay – and for some of the most spectacular goals ever scored by the Canaries, including one against Liverpool in 1980 that was the BBC Goal of the Season. His brother John was also a star footballer, most notably at Norwich and Wimbledon.

Motorcycle speedway was also very popular in the city, the stadium at the Firs opening in 1930. The most famous rider was the Swede Ove Fundin, who was world champion four times between 1956 and 1963 while he was at Norwich, and again in 1967. Others included Phil Clarke, who rode for Norwich from 1947 to 1959, and Billy Bales, racing between 1952 and 1964. The site of the stadium was sold for housing, the last meeting being held on 31 October 1964. Another popular venue of spectator sport was the greyhound stadium at Boundary Park, which closed in 1971; dog racing had taken place there for almost forty years.

The city's high reputation in the world of boxing continued, based around the Lads' Club, founded by the Police Constable of Norwich, John Henry Dain, in 1918 to provide an outlet for bored young men. The best-known boxer was Arthur 'Ginger' Sadd, who fought 250 times between 1932 and 1951, culminating in an unsuccessful bid for the British Middleweight Championship in May 1939 against Jack Mcavoy. The club, originally at St George's Street, moved to King Street in 1924 and was there until its final closure in 1996.

Another outlet for youngsters was the scout movement, and Norwich formed one of the earliest of all scout groups in January 1908, which is still flourishing after over a century of continuous service. One man who attributed his success in life to his time in the Norwich scouts

178 *Scouts from India on a visit to Norwich.*

was Alfred Stephenson, who was a leading explorer in the 1930s, with expeditions to the Arctic in 1930-1 and to Antarctica between 1934 and 1937; he became known as 'Alfred of the Antarctic'. Scouting has always been a truly international activity; scouts from India visited Norwich in 1929 while in England for the World Jamboree of that year, and a few years later Norwich scouts went on a visit to Poland.[56]

Before the cinema, circuses brought exotic glamour to the lives of residents. One boy's grave in the Earlham cemetery tells a tragic story:

> A little lad of about 10 years of age, one of the troupe of Japanese who about 3 weeks ago commenced a fortnight's engagement at Gilbert's Circus died early on Saturday morning from brain fever. He was taken ill early in his first week here, and his feats were thereupon performed by one of the female members of the troupe. He received the best possible treatment, Dr Burton-Fanning being placed in charge of the case, and the troupe remained in Norwich to watch over their little comrade. The interment took place early yesterday morning at the Cemetery.[57]

The boy's name was Kiyoshi Hata. He died at 27 Cattle Market Street, the house next door (downhill) to the *Shire Hall Tavern*; in 1903 this was a temperance hotel run by

179 *Graves of young incomers, Earlham Cemetery: Kiyoshi Hata and Evgenia Zagajewska.*

Mrs Anne Chapman. The circus was advertised in the local press and included, as well as the troupe of Japanese dancers, HERR CHARLES PRINZ with his 16 forest-bred Performing Lions and Giant Boarhounds, MDLLE MARCELLAS featuring her great fire dance in the den of the 16 lions, and ELLA ZULIA, 'the female Blondin'.

180 *Design for Romeo and Juliet at the Maddermarket Theatre.*

The city produced one dancer who achieved great fame in America. Vernon Blyth was born in Mill Hill Road in May 1887, the son of William and Jane Blyth; he grew up in the *Great Eastern* hotel where his father had become landlord. Blyth went to the Norwich Grammar School but left the city in 1903 and emigrated to America with his father, his sister and her husband. Blyth's father did not settle, but Vernon loved it. He changed his name to Vernon Castle, married an American girl – Irene Foote – and the pair became very well-known professional dancers. He brought Irene back to Norwich on one occasion, but she found it drab, and her dresses were laughed at in the street. Back in America, they performed before thousands of fans, culminating in a performance at the New York Hippodrome in 1915.

Vernon took part in the war, returning to England and serving in the Royal Flying Corps. He was back in America training pilots when he died in an accident in February 1918. Fred Astaire said that it was Vernon Castle who inspired him to take up dancing, and he made the film 'The Story of Vernon and Irene Castle', starring himself as Vernon and Ginger Rogers as Irene; Castle is probably the only person from Norwich about whom a Hollywood biopic has been made.

Other emigrants from Norwich to America included a group of 28 leaving for Canada in February 1912, and a builder, Ted Beane, and his wife Ethel in the same year. Ethel was born in Norwich as Ethel Clarke, and worked as a barmaid in the *Lord Nelson* on the Dereham Road. Ted was a carpenter; they married in Norwich on 7 April 1912. The only uncommon part of their experience was the ship they chose: the *Titanic*! When the ship struck an iceberg and slowly sank on the night of 14 April, Ethel was one of the ladies put into a lifeboat. Beane had to take his chance: diving into the sea he was eventually picked up by one of the lifeboats, apparently pulled out of the water by his own wife. They both spent the rest of their lives in America, Ethel dying in 1983.[58]

The century saw a great increase in leisure time and in the city's leisure facilities. The Theatre Royal flourished until 1934 when it was burnt down. It was rebuilt the following year with a faience front. David Percival remodelled it in 1970 but the faience front is said to still exist behind his brick frontage. The Hippodrome was erected in 1902-3, and some of the greatest names in entertainment trod its boards between the wars, including Charlie Chaplin, Marie Lloyd and Gracie Fields. Badly damaged by bombing, it reopened after the war and featured famous acts including the Goons. After a brief spell as a repertory theatre it finally closed in 1966 and the building was demolished. Its site is now the St Giles' car park.

Nugent Monck began producing plays in Norwich in 1910, first in his house at 6 Ninham Court, then in the Music House where there was

181 *Haymarket cinema: the interior.*

seating for just 99 people. In 1921 he paid £600 for the 18th-century Roman Catholic chapel and filled the auditorium with 200 Georgian chairs, for which he paid 1s. 6d. each. The first play Monck put on at the Maddermarket Theatre was *As You Like It* in 1921 and this was also the last play he produced before his retirement in 1952. In between he had staged all Shakespeare's plays as Shakespeare himself had intended them to be performed, the first time this had been done since the 17th century. It was W.B. Yeats who convinced Monck he was a producer not an actor, telling him, 'When I watch you produce I want you to play all the parts, but when I see you act I wonder how an intelligent man can be so bad.'[59]

In January 1897 George Gilbert introduced 'The Royal Cinematographe – The Animated Photographs – presenting with marvellous accuracy scenes of everyday life' at the Agricultural Hall in Norwich. The scenes included a pleasure boat at Yarmouth, a boxing kangaroo, and the Prince of Wales at Marlborough House. Films were also shown by travelling fairs when they visited Tombland. The first 'chain' cinema in Norwich was the Theatre de Luxe in St Andrew's Street, opened in 1910.[60]

The first purpose-built cinema in Norwich was the Cinema Palace in Magdalen Street, which opened in 1912 with 850 seats. Norwich also boasted what must have been one of the very few thatched cinemas in England, the Thatched Theatre on All Saints' Green. This was originally a restaurant and ballroom; the restaurant fronting the street had the thatched roof, with the ballroom behind having a sliding section which could be opened. It became a picture house in 1915. The proprietors exploited the roof in 1918-19, when the influenza epidemic came to Norwich: management assured customers that the sliding roof could be opened to ensure a constant supply of health-giving fresh air! The cinema showed silent movies. David Pond recalled that his mother played at the cinema, sight-reading the music to be played with the film, while his father, a cellist, played during the intervals. It flourished in the age of silent movies but it was never fitted up for sound so its demise was inevitable. It closed in 1930 and became part of Bond's store.

The Odeon chain first opened in the city in 1938 and this was replaced by a larger cinema, which in 1971 won the Quigley Award for Cinema Design. In 1923 the Regent opened in the Alexandra Mansions with 1,800

seats; the first film shown was *The Prisoner of Zenda*. It became the ABC, but its original name can still be seen at the back. In 1937 there were eight cinemas, and in 1947, after several petitions to the council, a local referendum was held on whether cinemas should open on Sundays. One of the petitions was from Dr Noel Armstrong, who suggested that people in the city 'feel that housing conditions in Norwich are such as to necessitate their opening'. The vote was held on 30 April, and those in favour of opening were in a large majority: 16,951 citizens voted for Sunday opening and just 5,051 against. Numbers of cinema-goers declined from the 1950s, and a planned Plaza cinema on Plumstead Road was never completed. With the close of the Noverre in 1992, there were only two mainstream cinemas left – the Odeon and the ABC – but a revival in cinema-going has seen several multiplex cinemas built in the city. In addition, Cinema City, in Stuart and Suckling House, has been refurbished for the 21st century and continues to show 'arthouse' and other films not shown in the main cinemas.[61]

In 1951 the Norwich Festival, part of the Festival of Britain, ran from 18 to 30 June, with its motto of 'Something for Everyone'. Princess Elizabeth visited Norwich, declaring the fortnight open from the balcony of City Hall. The Festival saw the last public appearance of Snap, now in the Castle Museum; a modern substitute has recently been brought into the lord mayor's annual procession. She also opened one permanent legacy of the Festival, the Colman Galleries in the Castle Museum, containing the painting collection bequeathed to the city by Russell Colman in 1941.

The rise in the number of television owners increased dramatically after Anglia Television opened on 27 October 1959 in a converted Agricultural Hall. There were 13,295 TV and wireless licences issued in 1955 in Norwich, and in 1959 50,788 such licences were issued. Townroe wrote: 'Being the home of Anglia Television Ltd. is a significant plus for Norwich. Not only is the company a major employer and significant income generator, but through its news and documentary programmes it also undertakes a considerable public relations function for the city and its surroundings.' The company, with its 'logo' of a silver knight on horseback, produced nationally known programmes such as 'Survival', 'Sale of the Century', 'Tales of the Unexpected' and 'About Anglia', this last programme being where David Frost began his television career. It was taken over by Meridian in 1994. At its height it occupied both Agricultural Hall and the Crown Bank; the 1982 building between the two is a reminder of its existence.[62]

The 1935 *Guide* listed 10 'Gardens and Pleasure Grounds': Eaton Park, Earlham Hall, Chapelfield, Wensum Park, Heigham

Opposite: 182 *St Augustine's Swimming Pool opened in 1961, the third largest pool in the country. It closed in 1997, due to structural defects in the building.*

Park, Mile Cross Gardens, Woodrow Pilling Park, Mousehold Heath, Hellesdon Recreation Ground and Waterloo Park. Waterloo, Eaton, Heigham and Wensum Parks were laid out by the city council partly to provide work to the unemployed during the Depression. The creation of these parks was very much the work of Arnold Sandys-Winsch, the city's Parks Superintendent for 33 years from 1919.

Other parks were generous gifts from individuals. The Woodland pleasure ground, a gift from Mrs Radford Pym, was opened in June 1904. The Woodrow Pilling Park opened in 1929, presented to the city by Mrs Mary Pilling of Withington, Lancashire, in memory of her father, Jeremiah Woodrow. She bought the site for £2,000 and gave it to the corporation, who were to maintain it forever and to name it the Jeremiah Woodrow Recreation Ground; her father, who had left Norwich in 1829, had retained fond memories of the city. The council committee report says:

> she preferred that the Gift should take the shape of a recreation and playing ground for young people of both sexes, without any limit as to age, and in particular mentioned that it should be for the benefit of young people having left school, and be available for tennis etc. The donor also hoped that it would be possible to set aside a small piece for young children and provide for sand hills for them to dig in.[63]

Opposite: 183 *The 'Anglia TV Knight', actually a Townshend family trophy. Lord Townshend was the first Chairman of Anglia TV.*

The council has gradually been developing a walk along the river through the city. The section from Bishop Bridge to Foundry Bridge was originally planned in the 1920s and finally opened in 1972; the willows planted in 1972 are now well grown.

The city has enjoyed a continuing literary tradition. Camilla Doyle, who lived in the Close, published three books of poetry in the 1920s and 1930s, some descriptive of the city. She died in 1944, leaving unpublished manuscripts, including poetry about the Norwich air raids, with the Castle Museum. Daisy Ashford (Mrs George Norman) lived in Woodland Road, Hellesdon, for the last 17 years of her life, dying there in 1972. Her most

184 *A new Chinese-style dragon in the mayor's procession reflects the multicultural city of today.*

185 *Norwich through the ages: the medieval city wall is to the left, while the 21st-century flats are built into the 19th-century industry buildings. It is this variety that makes Norwich the great city that it is.*

celebrated work, *The Young Visiters*, written in the early 1890s while she was a young child, was published in 1919. Philip Pullman, author of *His Dark Materials*, was born in Norwich in 1946, but spent most of his early life abroad as his father was in the RAF. However, all these books together could not begin to match the sales of the cookery books of Delia Smith, also a key figure in the revival of the fortunes of Norwich City football club.

Norwich features in important literary works. L.P. Hartley's *The Go-Between* includes a description of the cathedral: 'later when I left the cool gloom of the interior for the heat and sunshine outside, the domain of Tombland whose name fascinated me, I kept craning my neck to fix the point, the exact point, at which the summit pierced the sky'. The book was made into a film, directed by Joseph Losey, which received its world premiere in Norwich. Some key scenes in *The Absolutist* by John Boyne, published in 2011, are set in the city.

Norwich has another claim to literary fame, with the establishment of 'Britain's only notable university course in creative writing', under Michael Bradbury and Angus Wilson, and with students such as Ian McEwan and Kazuo Ishiguro. German-born writer W.G. Sebald was at the UEA as a lecturer from 1967, and his classic works including *The Rings of Saturn* and *Austerlitz* were written in Norfolk; he died in a car crash in 2001.

Music, too, has played a major role in the city. The jazz musician Beryl Bryden, born in Norwich in 1920, played the washboard on Lonnie Donegan's 'Rock Island Line', which sold two million copies in 1956. Guitarist Jimi Hendrix played at the Orford Cellar for a fee of £39; regarding it as the place that gave him his first break, he promised to come again and play for the same fee, but died before he could fulfil his promise. The Cellar was behind the *Orford Arms* pub, and other stars playing there included Cream, David Bowie and Deep Purple. The Beatles played at the Grosvenor on 17 May 1963; a plaque on the wall records that after the gig the band went for fish and chips at Valori's.

However, Norwich has a larger part to play in the Beatles' story in the person of Tony Sheridan, a rock guitarist often referred to by the Beatles as 'the Teacher', a term used by Paul McCartney to this day. His full name was Anthony Esmond Sheridan McGinnity; he was born in Norwich on 21 May 1940 and went to the City of Norwich School and to Norwich Art School. He moved to London in 1958, becoming a session guitarist, and met the Beatles in Hamburg when he was there with his own band, the Jets. In 1961 the Beatles made their very first recordings in a professional studio as a backing group for Sheridan. One of these, 'My Bonnie', was released in 1962; it sold well in Liverpool and was heard by Brian Epstein, who at once saw the talent of the band. The rest is history.

The Cellar was not the only music venue in the city. The Jacquard was a club originally started in the *Mischief* tavern in the late 1960s, later moving to its own premises formerly the *White Lion* in Magdalen Street. Offering jazz, blues and folk, it featured stars such as George Melly and Paul Simon, who on one occasion was not allowed to play as he had turned up too late! It found a new lease of life in 1979 as a venue for punks and later became the centre of the 'Goth' scene in the city. Its doors finally closed in 1991 and the building has been converted into flats. Later musical talents from the city have included the Farmers' Boys, Beth Orton, Cathy Dennis and the Chord.

The UEA has hosted many top bands since its foundation; the old Truman's warehouse in King Street has become the very popular Waterfront venue; and folk and other musicians play in the former church of St Swithin, the Norwich Arts Centre since 1980. The concert hall foreseen in the 'Norwich Plan' never materialised, but the triennial Norwich Festival has brought great names to the city, such as Sir Malcolm Sargeant with the London Symphony Orchestra in 1951 and Sir John Barbirolli with the Halle Orchestra in 1955. The Festival has developed into an annual arts event, the Norfolk and Norwich Festival.

George Borrow summed up the feelings of Norwich residents, whether newcomers or families who have been resident for many generations:

186 *Norwich through the ages: a young Canary fan sits in front of a 1930s Norwich lion, with the 15th-century Guildhall behind.*

187 *Truman's warehouse, now converted into the Waterfront music venue.*

> A fine old city … view it from whatever side you will; but it shows best from the east, where the ground, bold and elevated, overlooking the fair and fertile valley in which it stands … Yes, there it spreads from the north to south, with its venerable houses, its numerous gardens, its three twelve churches, its mighty mound … there is an old grey castle on top of that mighty mound; and yonder, rising three hundred feet above the soil, from among those noble forest trees, behold that old Norman masterwork, that cloud-encircled cathedral spire around which a garrulous army of rooks and choughs continually wheel their flight. Now, who can wonder that the children of that fine old city are proud of her, and offer prayers for her prosperity?

The city remembers Borrow in the words 'Norwich – A Fine City' on all the signs into the city, taken from this passage in *Lavengro* but omitting the word 'old'. Thomas Browne was more mystical, writing in Norwich one March midnight in 1658: 'All things began in order, so shall they end, and so shall they begin again; according to the ordained order and mystical mathematicks of the city of heaven.' However, I prefer to end with the words with which Edith Henderson concluded her *Child's History*:

> The past is not all, the story of the city still goes on … Each new generation must carry on the story, making Norwich a still more noble city, the fairest in all England.[64]

Notes

I *The Beginnings*

1. Brian Ayers, 'The growth of an urban landscape: recent research in early medieval Norwich' in *Early Medieval Europe* (2011), 19 (1), pp.62-90; Barbara Green and Rachel Young, *Norwich, The Growth of A City* (1981), p.7
2. Brian Ayers, *Norwich, Archaeology of a fine city* (2009), p.19; John Wymer, *The Palaeolithic Sites of East Anglia* (1985), pp.60-1
3. Rodney Castleden, *Neolithic Britain* (1992), p.142; Paul Ashbee, *The Ancient British* (1978), p.84
4. Castleden, *op. cit.*, p.141
5. A.J. Lawson, in Brian Ayers, *Digging Under the Doorstep* (1983), p.7; Ayers, *op. cit.* (2011), p.67
6. Ashbee, *op. cit.*, p.253; P. Salway, *Roman Britain* (1981), pp.113-22
7. John A. Davies, *Venta Icenorum* (2001), p.15
8. Salway, *op. cit.*, p.656
9. Brian Ayers, 'Understanding the urban environment: archaeological approaches to medieval Norwich', in C. Harper Bill (ed), *Medieval East Anglia* (2005), p.75
10. Brian Ayers, *English Heritage Book of Norwich* (1994), pp.19, 21; Malcolm Atkin, *Norwich, History and Guide* (1993), p.7
11. J.N.L. Myers, *The English Settlements* (1986), pp.96-101, Davies, *op. cit.*, p.27
12. Alan Carter, pers. comm.; K.I. Sandred and B. Lindstrom, *The Place-Names of Norwich and Norfolk – Part 1: Norwich* (1989), p.99; Tom Woolhouse with Jane Cowgill, 'An early industrial site at 12 Oak St Norwich', in *Norfolk Archaeology* XLV part 4 (2009), pp.495-507
13. Sandred and Lindstrom, *op. cit.*, p.140
14. Ayers, *op. cit.* (2011), pp.71-3
15. Sue Margeson, *The Vikings in Norfolk* (1997), p.27
16. Ayers, *op. cit.* (2005), pp.68-82; Ayers (2009), p.73
17. E.O. Blake (ed.), *Liber Elienses*, Camden Society 3rd Series, xcii, (1962), p.100
18. Edith Henderson, *The Story of Norwich* (1918), p.69; Michael Swanton, *The Anglo-Saxon Chronicle* (1996), p.134
19. R.I. Page, *Chronicle of the Vikings* (1995), p.159; Margeson, *op. cit.*, p.30
20. P. Rumble, *The Reign of Cnut* (1994), p.222; Dr J.R. Alban, pers. comm.
21. Heather Wallis, 'Excavations at Cinema City, Norwich 2003-6', in *Norfolk Archaeology*, XLV part4 (2009), pp.469-87; Brian Ayers, 'Current Archaeology', vol. 170 (2000), p.51
22. Ayers, *op. cit.* (2011), p.82; Nick Williams, *The Blue Plaques of Norwich* (2010), pp.92-3
23. Roberta Gilchrist, quoted in R. Morris, *Churches in the Landscape* (1997 edn), pp.186f
24. J. Campbell, 'The East Anglian Sees Before The Conquest', in I. Atherton, E. Fernie, C. Harper-Bill, H. Smith (eds), *Norwich Cathedral: Church, City and Diocese* (1996), pp.3-22
25. The two wills are transcribed in D Whitelock, (Ed.), *Anglo-Saxon wills* (1930)
26. Ayers, *op. cit.* (1994) p 33

II *Norwich in the Middle Ages*

1. Ralph Mottram, *If stones could speak* (1953), p.27; Lucy Marten 'The rebellion of 1075 and its impact in East Anglia', in Christopher Harper-Bill (ed.), *Medieval East Anglia* (2005), pp.168-182; Stenton, *op. cit.*, p.611
2. *Domesday Book*: 33 Norfolk (1984 edn), Chapter 1; 61, 63, 66; Chapter 21; 37
3. W. Hudson, and J.C. Tingey, *The Records of the City of Norwich* (1906, 1910), vol. 1, pp.xv, xvi
4. F. Blomefield, *The History of the City of Norwich* (1806 edn), vol. 1, p.53
5. Hudson and Tingey, *op. cit.*, vol. 1, pp.xviii, xix
6. Henderson, *op. cit.*, p.115
7. Marc Morris, *The Bigod Earls of Norfolk in the thirteenth century* (2005), p.3, n.17
8. C. Harper-Bill, 'The Cathedral and the City', in Ian Atherton and others (eds), *Norwich Cathedral: Church, City and Diocese 1096-1996* (1996), p.259
9. Barbara Dodwell, *The Charters of Norwich Cathedral* (1974), p.xii; Eric Fernie, *An Architectural History of Norwich Cathedral* (1993), p.171
10. Froissart, quoted in Blomefield, *op. cit.*, vol. 1, p.101; Blomefield, vol. 1, *op. cit.*, p.108; May McKisack, *The Fifteenth Century* (1959), p.418; John Capgrave, quoted in M. Jebb (ed.), *East Anglia, an Anthology* (1990); Herbert Eiden, 'Joint Action against "Bad" Lordship: the Peasants' Revolt in Essex and Norfolk', in *Historical Association* (1998), p.23f
11. Keith Lilley, *Urban Life in the Middle Ages* (2002), p.63, quoting from M. Weinbaum, *The Incorporation of Boroughs* (1937)
12. T. John, 'Sir Thomas Erpingham, East Anglian Society and the Dynastic Revolution of 1399', *Norfolk Archaeology*, 35 (1970), pp.96-109
13. H.F. Westlake, *The Parish Guilds of Medieval England* (1919), pp.41, 116-19, 201-6
14. E. Goulburn, and H. Symonds, *The Life and Letters of Bishop Herbert de Losinga* (1878), pp.131-5
15. M. Rose and J. Hedgecoe, *Stories in Stone: the medieval roof carvings of Norwich Cathedral* (1997), *passim*; Fernie, *op. cit.*, p.179
16. Rose and Hedgecoe, *op. cit.*, pp.84, 97

17. R. Hayes, 'The 'Private' Life of a Medieval Bishop', in *Harlaxton Medieval Studies*, vol. 4 (1994), p.5
18. Joan Greatrex, *Biographical Register of the English Cathedral Priories of the Diocese of Canterbury* (1997), p.65
19. T.A. Heslop, *Norwich Castle Keep* (1994), pp.1-13, 66
20. Ayers *op. cit.* (2009), pp.64f
21. J.T. Appleby (ed.), *The Chronicle of Richard of Devizes* (1963), p.66; NRO, NCC wills Joan Erpyngham 1404 (307-8 Harsyk)
22. V.D. Lipman, *The Jews of Medieval Norwich* (1967), *passim*
23. NRO, DCN 40/7, transcribed in Dodwell, *op. cit.*, p.241
24. James Campbell, *Essays in Anglo-Saxon History* (1986), p.226
25. Joan Foreman, *Haunted East Anglia* (1976 edn), pp.29-31
26. Marilyn Oliva, 'Aristocracy or meritocracy?', in W. J. Sheils and Diana Wood, *Women in the church* (1990) p.202; R. Gilchrist and M. Oliva, *Religious Women in Medieval East Anglia* (1993), p.57; Hudson and Tingey, *op. cit.*, vol. 1, pp.319, 320; M. Pollett, *John Skelton, poet of Tudor England*, pp.47-9
27. Helen Sutermeister, *The Norwich Blackfriars* (1977), p.2; Serena Kelly, Elizabeth Rutledge, Margot Tillyard, *Men of Property, an analysis of the Norwich enrolled deeds 1285-1311* (1983), pp.5-13; W.A. Hinnebusch, *The Early English Friars Preachers* (1951), *passim*
28. Quotation from *Catholic Encyclopedia*, and the same story is told in J.N.D. Kelly, *The Oxford Dictionary of the Popes* (1988 edn), pp.236-7; Nicholas Cheetham, *Keepers of the Keys* (1982), pp.169-70. The (19th-century) inscription on his tomb in Bologna also describes him as of Crete. However, the most recent edition of the *Catholic Encyclopedia* suggests he came from a different Candia, near Milan, and was not an orphan
29. R. Llewelyn (ed.), *Julian: Woman of Our Day* (1985), p.69; Sister Wendy, *Julian of Norwich* (not dated), p.6
30. F.I. Dunn, 'Hermits, Anchorites and Recluses', in *Julian and Her Norwich* (1973), *passim.*; NRO, NCR 4b, private deeds: St Peter Hungate, transcribed in Hudson and Tingey, *op. cit.*, vol. 2, pp.358, 359
31. Heather Wallis, 'Excavations at Cinema City, Norwich 2003-6', in *Norfolk Archaeology*, XLV part 4 (2009), pp.469-87
32. James Campbell, *op. cit.*, p.16; Nicholas Groves, *The Medieval Churches of the city of Norwich* (2010), *passim*
33. N.P. Tanner, *The Church in Late Medieval Norwich 1370-1532* (1984), pp.113-40; Ian Atherton (ed.), *op. cit.*, p.193; NRO, NCC Wills William Blackdam 1479 (230-1 Gelour)
34. Groves, *op. cit.*; *passim*
35. H.S. Bennett, *The Pastons and their England* (1968 edn), pp.197f
36. Joan Evans, *English Art 1307-1461* (1949), p.207; Francis Bond, *Gothic Architecture in England* (1906), pp.227f
37. Groves, *op cit.*, pp.131-2; Pevsner and Wilson, *op. cit.*, pp.251f
38. Hudson and Tingey, *op. cit.*, vol. 2, p.x; Francis Andrews, *The Other Friars* (2006), p.63; Norman Tanner, 'Heresy Trials in the diocese of Norwich 1428-31', *Camden Society*, fourth series, vol. 20 (1977), *passim*
39. NRO, MS 11606
40. NRO, NCR, Book of Customs, transcribed in Hudson and Tingey, *op. cit.*, vol. 2, pp.209-11
41. Men of Property, *op. cit.*, pp.13-31
42. A. Jessopp and M.R. James (eds), *Life and Miracles of St William of Norwich* (1896), p.14; James Wentworth Day, *Norwich Through the Ages* (1976), p.36; Keith Wrightson, *Earthly Necessities* (2000), p.49; David Knoop and G.P. Jones, *The Medieval Mason* (1949), p.161: Hudson and Tingey, *op. cit.*, vol. 1, p.245
43. James Masschaele, *Peasants, Merchants and Markets* (1997), p.119; Hudson and Tingey, *op. cit.*, vol. 1, p.222
44. Elizabeth Rutledge, 'Norwich before the Black Death', in Carole Rawcliffe and Richard Wilson, *Medieval Norwich* (2004), pp.178f; NRO, NCR Assembly Book 1426; N.J.M. Kerling, *Commercial Relations of Holland and Zeeland with England* (1984), *passim*
45. H.J. Hewitt, *The Organisation of war under Edward III* (1966), pp.41, 49, 81; Michael Powicke, *Military Obligation in Medieval England* (1996 edn), p.222; Hudson and Tingey, *op. cit.*, vol. 2, pp.390-413
46. James Campbell, *op. cit.*, p.16; H.S. Bennett, *The Pastons and their England* (1968 edn), p.164
47. Public Record Office, Court Rolls SC 2 (May 1275)
48. Barbara Hanawalt, 'Crime in East Anglia in the 14th century', *Norfolk Record Society*, vol. 44, p.30
49. Hanawalt, *op. cit.*, p.30, 46
50. Hudson and Tingey, vol. 1, p.xxv; L.F. Salzman, *English Industries of the Middle Ages* (1970 reprint), p.255
51. Frank Meeres, *A History of the Fens* (forthcoming)
52. Hudson and Tingey, vol. 2, pp.xxv-xxvii; Malcolm Norris, 'Later medieval monumental brasses', in Steven Bassett (ed.), *Death in Towns* (1995 edn), p.191
53. Walter Rye, Calendar of the Freemen of Norwich (1888), pp.9, 16, 148; Elizabeth Rutledge, *op. cit.*, p.183
54. Judith Bennett, *Ale, Beer and Brewsters in England* (1999 edn), pp.39-40, 79-81
55. Elizabeth Rutledge, *op. cit.*, p.175
56. Barbara Hanawalt, *The Ties that Bound* (1988 edn), p.139, citing Frances Davenport, 'The decay of villeinage in East Anglia', in E.M. Carus-Wilson (ed.), *Essays in Economic History II* (1962), pp.112-24
57. Anon., *Evidences relating to the Town Close estate*, Norwich, (1887), pp.19-24
58. C.B. Jewson, *People of Medieval Norwich* (undated), pp.89-94
59. Norwich City Council, *Norwich Walls Report* (1910), *passim*; Robert Smith and Alan Carter, Norwich Houses before 1700 (offprint from *Vernacular Architecture* Vol. 14, 1983), p.2, note 16; Brian Ayers, *Norwich, Archaeology of a fine city* (2009), p.93
60. Hudson and Tingey, *op. cit.*, vol. 2, p.218
61. Quotation from Lilley, *op. cit.*, p.174
62. Lilley, *op. cit.*, p.230; Jewson, *op. cit.*, pp.89-94
63. NRO, NCR 8a2, transcribed in Hudson and Tingey, *op. cit.*, vol. 1, pp.204, 206; Hudson (1892), *op. cit.*, pp.6, 7
64. Malcolm Atkin, *Life on a Medieval Street* (1985), *passim*
65. Brian Ayers, *Norwich, a fine city*, (2003 edn), pp.120, 137
66. NRO, NCR, 24b, transcribed in Hudson and Tingey, *op. cit.*, vol. 2, pp.360-2; B.L. Add. Roll 63207, quoted in Christopher Dyer, *Standards of Living in the late Middle Ages* (1989), p.63
67. Smith and Carter, *op. cit.*, pp.2-6
68. Blomefield, *op. cit.*, vol. 1, pp.333-4
69. NRO, NCR Assembly Roll 1380, transcribed in Hudson and Tingey, *op. cit.*, vol. 2, p.84
70. NRO, NCR Assembly Book 1453, transcribed in Hudson and Tingey, *op. cit.*, vol. 2, pp.90-1
71. Carole Rawcliffe, *The Hospitals of Medieval Norwich* (1995), *passim*
72. Carole Rawcliffe, *Medicine for the soul* (1999), p.118
73. NRO, MS 4591, manuscript of Kirkpatrick, who found the will in a register of the Dean of Norwich, apparently since lost
74. Roberta Gilchrist, 'Christian bodies and souls', in Bassett, *op. cit.*, p.115
75. NCC WILLS, Wells, Henry, 1448 (Aleyn); Greatrex, *op. cit.*, p.246
76. A. Batty Shaw, *Norfolk and Norwich Hospital, A Retrospect* (1992), p.10
77. This section is a summary of my research into the Black Death and plague in Norwich, made possible by the generous financial support of the Harry Watson bursary and Norwich HEART.
78. Penny Dunn, 'Trade', in Rawcliffe and Wilson, *op. cit.*, pp.213-34
79. Phyllis E. Pobst, *The Register of William Bateman* (1996, 2000), *passim*
80. 'The Norwich Dominicans were wiped out almost to a man': Christopher Harper-Bill, 'English Religion after the Black Death' in Ormrod and Lindley, *The Black Death in England* (1996), p.97. He cites David Knowles, *The Religious Orders in England* (1951), vol. II, pp.10-11. 'In Norwich the whole [Franciscan] community seems to have perished': Edward Hutton, *The Franciscans in England* (1926), p.177
81. R. Saunders, *The Obedientiary Rolls of Norwich Cathedral* (1930), pp.186-9
82. NRO, NCR Assembly Book 1354; Hudson and Tingey, *op. cit.*, vol. 1, p.xxv
83. W. Hudson, *The Wards of the City of Norwich* (1891), p.19
84. E. Rutledge, 'Immigration and population in early 14th century Norwich: evidence from the tithing roll', in *Urban History* 15 (1988), pp.17-18

85. James Masschaele, *Peasants, Merchants and Markets* (1997), p.129; Ayers *op. cit.* (2009), p.99
86. W. Hudson, 'Leet Jurisdiction in the City of Norwich', *Selden Society*, vol. 5 (1892), *passim*
87. Philippa Maddern, 'Order and Disorder', in Rawcliffe and Wilson, *op. cit.*, p.193
88. P.R.O. Assize roll, transcribed in Evidences, *op. cit.*, pp.10-12
89. Hanawalt, *op. cit.*, pp.28-9
90. Hanawalt, *op cit.*, pp.39-40
91. Goulburn and Symonds, *op. cit.*, pp.19-37
92. NRO, DCN 41/77
93. J.R. Greenwood, 'The Will of Thomas Salter of London 1558', *Norfolk Archaeology* 38 (1983), pp.280-95

III *Tudor and Stuart Norwich*

1. J.D. Mackie, *The Early Tudors* (1952), p.73
2. Atherton (ed.), *op. cit.*, pp.507ff
3. R. Taylor, *Index Monasticus* (1821), p.12
4. F. Russell, *Kett's Rebellion in Norfolk* (1859). This transcribes many relevant records; NRO, COL 7/1; NRO, NCR 16a, 1549
5. Blomefield, *op. cit.*, vol. 1, p.236
6. Blomefield, *op. cit.*, vol. 1, p.244; Carole Rawcliffe, *Medicine for the Soul* (1999), pp.229-33
7. Hudson and Tingey, *op. cit.*, vol. 1, p.45; Mile Cross History Research Group, *Milestones to Mile Cross* (1995), p.5
8. Charles Phythian-Adams, 'Urban Decay in late medieval England', in Philip Abrams and E.A. Wrigley, *Towns and Societies* (1979 edn), p.179, Hudson and Tingey, *op. cit.*, vol. 2, p.122f; Knoop and Jones, *op. cit.*, p.209
9. W.J.C. Moens, *The Walloons and their church at Norwich* (1887-8), pp.1-110, especially p.36. This is the basic 'source-book' for anyone with Walloon ancestry.
10. L. Forster, *Janus Gruter's English Years* (1967), pp.151-2
11. Moens, *op. cit.*, pp.220-4. The original letters were destroyed in the First World War.
12. Joan Thirsk, *Economic Policy and Projects* (1988 reprint), p.44
13. R.W. Ketton-Cremer, *Norfolk Assembly* (1957), p.126
14. Amy Charles, *The Shorter Poems of Ralph Knevet* (1966), pp.25-30
15. Blomefield, *op. cit.*, vol. 1, pp.351, 364; M. Colthorpe, 'Queen Elizabeth and Norwich Cathedral', *Norfolk Archaeology*, 40 (1989), pp.318-23; Hudson and Tingey, *op. cit.*, vol. 2, p.cxxv
16. Ronald Hutton, *The stations of the sun* (1996), p.395
17. J.T. Evans, *Seventeenth Century Norwich* (1979), pp.67-9
18. Quoted in Evans, *op. cit.*, p.94; Laud, *Works* V, p.339
19. C.B. Jewson, 'Transcript of Three Registers of Passengers from Great Yarmouth to Holland and New England 1637-9', *Norfolk Record Society*, 25 (1954)
20. Blomefield, *op. cit.*, vol. 1, p.381
21. Antonia Fraser, *The Weaker Vessel* (2002 edn), p.225; R.W. Ketton-Cremer, *Norfolk in the Civil War* (1969), pp.199-200
22. Joseph Hall, *Hard Measure* (1647)
23. NRO, DCN 107/3
24. Atherton (ed.), *op. cit.*, p.556
25. NRO, PD 58/38; NCR, Mayor's Court Book 9 March 1643/4, fo. 415r
26. NRO, NCR, 16 p.465
27. NRO, NCR 12c1. Calendared in F. Bateman and W. Rye, *The History of Bethel Hospital* (1906), pp.84-163
28. NRO, DCN 107/3
29. Ketton-Cremer, *op. cit.*, p.348
30. Andrew Hopper, 'The Civil Wars', in Rawcliffe and Wilson (eds), *Norwich since 1550* (2004), pp.89-116
31. NRO, NCR Assembly book 1658
32. R. Hill, 'Correspondence of Thomas Corie', *Norfolk Record Society*, 27 (1956), p.33
33. Dave Peacock, 'Morals Ritual and Gender: aspects of social relations in the diocese of Norwich, 1660-1703', University of York, PhD thesis, 1996
34. Thelma Morris, *Made in Norwich: 700 years of textile heritage* (2008), *passim*
35. Joan Thirsk, *The Rural Economy of England* (1984), pp.236-45
36. Baskerville is transcribed in Historical Manuscripts Commission, Portland MSS ii, 269; C. Morris (ed.), *Journeys of Celia Fiennes* (1949), p.148
37. NRO, ANW 23/5/113; Ursula Priestley, *Shops and Shopkeepers in Norwich 1660-1730* (1985), pp.19-20
38. John T. Evans, *Seventeenth-century Norwich* (1979), pp.73-6. I was alerted to Kettle's story by a talk given by Fiona Williamson of the UEA.
39. NRO, NCR Mayor's Court Book, 13, p.345. Quoted in M. Pelling, 'Healing the sick poor', *Medical History*, 29 (1985), p.131
40. NRO, NCR Mayor's Court Book, 7 January 1559, 6 December 1561, transcribed in Hudson and Tingey, *op. cit.*, vol. 2, pp.177, 179
41. Keith Wrightson, *Earthly Necessities* (2000), p.48
42. Paul Griffiths, 'Inhabitants', in Rawcliffe and Wilson (eds), *Norwich since 1550* (2004), pp.63-88
43. PRO, PCC Wills, Anguish, Thomas, 1622 (80 Savile), Tesmond, Thomas, 1626 (108 Hele)
44. NRO, NCR Mayor's Court Book 1675-6; Blomefield, *op. cit.*, vol. 2, p.60
45. NRO, NCC WILLS Doughty, Thomas, 1688 (OW 74)
46. NRO, PD 461/57; MC 500/50
47. NRO, NCR Assembly Book 1573; M. Pelling, 'Illness among the poor in an early modern English town', *Continuity and Change*, 3(2) (1988), pp.131, 282, 286; Hudson and Tingey, *op. cit.*, vol. 2, p.190
48. Ruth Hughey, 'The Correspondence of Lady Katherine Paston', *Norfolk Record Society* 14 (1941), pp.81, 126
49. Pelling (1985), *op. cit.*, pp.115-37
50. Paul Slack, *The Impact of Plague in Tudor and Stuart England* (1995), pp.128-33
51. NRO, NCR 10f; Norfolk and Norwich Remembrancer (no date), p.32; NRO, NCR Mayor's Court Book, 1666; Hill, *op. cit.*, p.20
52. Hill, *op. cit.*, p.30
53. G.R. Elton, *Reform and Reformation* (1977), p.61
54. Muriel McClendon, *The Quiet Reformation* (1999), pp.174-83; R.A. Houlbrooke, 'Church Courts and People in the Diocese of Norwich', PhD Thesis Oxford (1970), pp.354-5
55. NRO, NCR Mayor's Court Book 1578; Blomefield, *op. cit.*, vol. 2, pp.292, 3
56. F.J. Devany, *The Faithful Few: a history of Roman Catholics in Norfolk 1559-1778* (2008), pp.157-8
57. Anonymous pamphlet, 'The Old Meeting House, Norwich' (1934)
58. Atherton (ed.), *op. cit.*, pp.560-1
59. Staffordshire RO, MS 33; xerox copy NRO, MS 21489
60. NRO, NCR, Quarter Sessions Book, September 1657; Blomefield, *op. cit.*, vol. 1, p.401
61. Brian Ayers, *Norwich, a fine city* (2003 edn), p.138
62. Phythian-Adams, *op. cit.*, p.168
63. NRO, NCR Assembly Book, 18 May 1509, transcribed in Hudson and Tingey, *op. cit.*, vol. 2, p.107; Andrew Hopper, 'The Civil Wars', in Rawcliffe and Wilson, *op. cit.*, p.93
64. NRO, NCR Assembly Book, 14 April 1570, transcribed in Hudson and Tingey, *op. cit.*, vol. 2, pp.137-41
65. George Fenner, 'Mathematical Tiles', in *Norwich Industrial Archaeology Society* (March 2004), pp.9, 10. Mackerell is quoted in Colin Branford, 'Powers of Association: aspects of elite cultural and political life in Norwich 1680-1760', University of East Anglia PhD thesis, 1993, p.16
66. Alec Clifton-Taylor, *The Pattern of English Building* (1972 edn), pp.275-9
67. NRO, COL 1/114; PD 68/132; NCR 6a1/35; PD 26/133
68. NRO, NCR 16c5
69. NRO, NCR 10c
70. Blomefield, *op. cit.*, vol. 1, p.427
71. R. Houlbrooke, 'A Mousehold Abduction 1548', in *Counties And Communities: Essays on East Anglian History* (1996), pp.115-28
72. Companion, *op. cit.*, p.105; U. Priestley, *The Great Market* (1987), p.16; NRO, MC 1026; NRO, MC 500/26
73. J.R. Young, *The Inns and Taverns of Old Norwich* (1975), p.56; NRO, PD 185/3
74. T. Fuller, *The Worthies of England* (1662); De Beer (ed.), *The Diary of John Evelyn* (1959)

75. Michael and Carole Blackwell, *Norwich Theatre Royal: the first 250 years* (2007), p.4
76. NRO, NCR Mayor's Court Book, 25 February 1589, transcribed in Hudson and Tingey, vol. 2, p.195
77. Robert Greene, *A Groatsworth of Wit* (1592); *Dictionary of National Biography*
78. *Cambridge Guide to Literature in English* (1993 edn), p.249; *Dictionary of National Biography*
79. G. Stephenson, *Three Centuries of a Norfolk Library* (1917), *passim*; Clive Wilkins-Jones, 'Norwich City Library 1608-1737', *Norfolk Record Society*, 72 (for 2008)
80. Fuller, *op. cit*., vol. II, p.154
81. Hill, *op. cit*., pp.36-7
82. P. Seaman, 'Norfolk and Norwich Tax Assessment, Lady Day 1666', *Norfolk Genealogy*, 20 (no date), p.79; Baskerville, *op. cit*; De Beer, *op. cit*
83. W. Hudson, *The Ecclesiastical History of the parish of St Peter Parmentergate*, compiled and edited by Mary Rodgers (2009), pp.27-8
84. Batty Shaw, *op. cit*., p.117; A.J. Cleveland, *A History of the Norfolk and Norwich Hospital* (1948), pp.138-43

IV *Georgian Norwich*

1. *The First Report of the Municipal Corporations Commission* (1835)
2. Keith Thomas, *Man and the Natural World* (1983), p.230
3. Ronald Hutton, *The stations of the sun* (1996), p.290; E.P. Thompson, *Customs in Common* (1993 edn), pp.68-9
4. I. Gilmour, *Riots, Risings and Revolutions* (1992), p.227; Blomefield, *op. cit*., vol. 1, p.449; Thompson, *op. cit*., pp.223, 228
5. NRO, NCR 6h/1-10
6. B. Cozens-Hardy and A.E. Kent, *The Mayors of Norwich* (1938), p.130
7. C.B. Jewson, *The Jacobin City* (1975), pp.12-20; J. Steven Watson, *The Reign of George III* (1960), p.358; Penelope Corfield, *The Impact of English towns 1700-1800* (1982), p.166
8. E.P. Thompson, *The Making of the English Working Class*, pp.158-9
9. NRO, N/TC 71/2; NCR Chamberlains'accounts 1800-1
10. Jewson, *op. cit*., p.50
11. Charles Mackie, *Norfolk Annals* (1901), vol. 1, p.127, hereafter cited as *Annals*
12. E.J. Hobsbawm and George Rude, *Captain Swing* (1973 edn), p.124
13. Macauley, *History of England* (1913 edn), vol. 1, p.324; Penelope Corfield, 'A provincial capital in the later seventeenth century: the case of Norwich', in Peter Clark (ed.), *The Early Modern Town* (1976), pp.243, 245; Percy Millican, 'The Freemen of Norwich 1714-52', *Norfolk Record Society* 23 (1952)
14. Daniel Defoe, *Tour Through the Eastern Counties* (1724)
15. Cornwall Record Office, HL(20) 593
16. *Norwich Mercury*, 7 April, 28 April and 19 May 1753
17. Arthur Young, *A Farmer's Tour Through the East of England* (1771); Beatniffe, *The Norfolk Tour* (1808)
18. J.L. and Barbara Hammond, *The Skilled Labourer* (1979 edn), p.116
19. M.J. Daunton, 'Towns and economic growth in eighteenth-century England', in Philip Abrams and E.A. Wrigley (eds), *Towns in Societies* (1979 edn), p.271
20. *Norwich Mercury*, 26 November 1791
21. Pamela Clabburn, *Norwich Shawls*, Norfolk Museums Information Sheet (1977); *idem*, *The Norwich Shawl* (1995), pp.10-16; A.M.W. Stirling, *Coke of Norfolk and his friends* (undated), p.146
22. NRO, MC 26/1. All the references to Marten in this chapter come from this fascinating diary, which is being transcribed by Elizabeth Larby for publication by Poppyland Press.
23. Eric Fowler, *One hundred years in the shoe trade* (1962), not paginated
24. Anon., *The History of Norwich* (1781)
25. B. Cozens-Hardy (ed.), *The Diary of Silas Neville* (1950), p.127; Simpson, *op. cit*., p.52
26. Jewson, *op. cit*., p.7
27. *Peck's Directory* 1802
28. J. Mantle, *Norwich Union, the first 200 years* (1997). As he does not mention the luggage quotation it may be apocryphal.
29. Penelope Corfield, 'From Second City to Regional Capital', in Carole Rawcliffe and Richard Wilson, *Norwich Since 1550* (2004), pp.155-7
30. NRO, BOL 2/142/2
31. Chris Fisher, 'Building a Gas Holder in Norwich', in *Norwich Industrial Archaeological Society*, vol. 8, no 4 (2009)
32. B. Cozens-Hardy, 'Mary Hardy's Diary', *Norfolk Record Society*, 37 (1968), p.21; Parson Woodforde's Diary, 6 July 1778; D.H. Kennett, 'The pattern of coaching in early 19th century Norfolk', *Norfolk Archaeology*, 36 (1977), pp.355-72
33. Robert Malster, *Wherries and Waterways* (1971), pp.61-5; John Armstrong and David Williams, 'The "Norwich Explosion" of 1817', *Norfolk Archaeology*, 45, part 4 (2009), pp.488-94; NRO, MC 27/2
34. *Annals*, *op. cit*., vol. 1, p.145, NRO, NCR 6a/23/9-17; MC 26/1
35. George Nobbs, *Norwich, City of Centuries* (1978), p.28; J.K. Edwards, in C. Barringer (ed.), *Norwich in the Nineteenth Century* (1984), p.124
36. NRO, BOL 4/127
37. Jewson, *op. cit*., p.8
38. NCR, 5k5, 7
39. Malster, *op. cit*., pp.12-21
40. Bateman and Rye, *op. cit*., pp.1-21; M. Winston, 'The Bethel Hospital', *Medical History* (1994), pp.27-51
41. Cozens-Hardy, *op. cit*. (1968), p.25
42. A.J. Cleveland, 'The Norfolk and Norwich Hospital', *Medical Press and Circular*, 5 January 1944; Batty Shaw, *op. cit*., pp.56-9; NRO, NNH 1, 64
43. A. Batty Shaw, 'Benjamin Gooch, Eighteenth Century Norfolk Surgeon', *Medical History* (1972), 16 number 1, pp.50-60
44. Frank Meeres, *One Man's Vision* (2005), *passim*
45. David Stoker, 'The Correspondence of the Revd Francis Blomefield', *Norfolk Record Society*, 55 (1992), pp.15-22
46. White's *Directory*, 1854, p.123; Atherton (ed.), *op. cit*., p.651
47. Scarfe, *op. cit*., p.206; NRO, NCR 20e (minute books of the Guardians of the Poor)
48. The letters are transcribed in J. Crowley and A. Reid, *The Poor Law in Norfolk 1700-1800* (1983), pp.56-7
49. Robert Lee, *Unquiet Country* (2005), pp.122-3
50. NRO, NCC WILLS John Norman 1724 (p.60), printed copy NRO, MC 1213/2
51. P. Corfield, *The Early Modern Town* (1976), p.239; NRO, NCR 15c; N/S 15/1; David Souden, 'Migrants and the population structure of later seventeenth century cities and market towns' in Peter Clark (ed.), *The transformation of English provincial towns* (1985 edn), pp.133-68
52. NRO, NCR 20a/25
53. Essex Record Office, Braintree Vestry Minutes D/P264/8
54. Jewson, *op. cit*., p.123; NRO, NCR 20a Norwich Quarter Sessions records. I think the two girls to whom Jewson refers must be Anne Buttivant and Mary Gooch, tried at the August 1791 Assizes, although I cannot find the details he gives recorded in either the *Norwich Mercury* or the *Norfolk Chronicle*
55. NRO, NCR, 6a/13/31
56. W. Hudson, *History of the Parish of St Peter Parmountergate* (1889)
57. NRO, NCR 6a/7/118
58. Scarfe, *op. cit*., pp.204-5; N. Pevsner and R. Wilson, *Buildings of England Norwich and North East Norfolk* (1997), p.316
59. Pevsner and Wilson, *op. cit*., p.269; S.J. Wearing, *Georgian Norwich: its builders* (1926), pp.34-5
60. BL Add MSS 27966, xerox copy NRO, MS 554
61. NRO, MC 27/2
62. NRO, MS 579, pp.211ff
63. David Smith, 'Politics, Religion and Education', in Barringer (ed.), *op. cit*., pp.199-214
64. Cozens-Hardy, *op. cit*. (1950), pp.17, 65; Wesley, *Journals*, vol. 4, p.485
65. Atherton (ed.), *op. cit*., p.557; Simpson, *op. cit*., p.13
66. NRO, BOL 4/157; C. Jolly, *The Spreading Flame* (undated),

pp.3-30
67. NRO, FC 13/1,11; Wesley, *op. cit.*, vol. 3, p.315; Virginia Gay, 'Visit to the Octagon Chapel' in *Norwich Historic Buildings Group newsletter*, number 7 (March 2004), p.3
68. Anon., *A Great Gothic Fane* (1913), p.75
69. *Norfolk Chronicle*, 3 May 1823; E.P. Thompson, *Customs in Common* (1993 edn), pp.410, 451
70. *Annals*, *op. cit.*, vol. 1, p.58
71. *Annals*, *op. cit.*, vol. 1, pp.174, 305; NRO, PD 11/25; Robert Lee, *Unquiet Country* (2005), p.33
72. NRO, NCR 6a/29/11; *Annals*, vol. 1, p.219; Ruth Richardson, *Death, Dissection and the Destitute* (1989 edn), pp.35, 61-2
73. *Australian Dictionary of National Biography* (1967): Kable, Henry
74. NRO, NCR 12d1
75. *Norwich Mercury*, 1791, 1792
76. NRO, NCR 8i
77. J. Rose, *Elizabeth Fry* (1980), *passim*; *Dictionary of National Biography*; Dennis Bardens, *Elizabeth Fry – Britain's second lady on the five pound note* (2004), p.107; Elizabeth A. Livingstone, *Concise Oxford Dictionary of the Christian Church* (1977), p.203. There are 46 volumes of her journals, two at the NRO, the rest at the Library of the Society of Friends in London.
78. NRO, MC 1694; MS 21820 (press-cuttings and notes about the history of the Theatre Royal)
79. Jewson, *op. cit.*, p.9; NRO, NCR Sessions Book 1794-1807; Blackwell and Blackwell, *op. cit.*, p.48
80. Woodforde's Diary, 19 December 1785; Angela Dain, 'An Enlightened and Polite Society', in Rawcliffe and Wilson (eds), *Norwich since 1550* (2004), p.196
81. *Remembrancer*, *op. cit.*, p.23; *Annals*, *op. cit.*, vol. 1, p.142; *Norfolk Chronicle*, 18 and 25 January 1817
82. A.M.W. Stirling, *Coke of Norfolk and his friends* (undated), p.152
83. *Norwich Mercury*, 27 Aug., 3 Sep. 1831
84. NRO, MSS 579, p.218; BL Add MS 27966, xerox NRO, MS 554
85. T. Fawcett, 'The Norwich Pleasure Gardens', *Norfolk Archaeology* 35 (1972), pp.382-99
86. C. Elliott, *Aeronauts and Aviators* (1971), pp.15-18
87. *Annals*, *op. cit.*, vol. 1, pp.184, 214
88. Edward Hyams, *Capability Brown and Humphrey Repton* (1971), pp.118-19
89. NRO, MS 470
90. *Dictionary of National Biography*; Jewson, *op. cit.*, p.155
91. NRO, BOL 4/166
92. Jewson, *op. cit.*, p.155
93. The Brontë quotation is from the diary of Cecilia Brightwell, NRO, MS 69
94. J. Rennert, *William Crotch – Composer, Artist, Teacher* (1975), *passim*; *Norfolk Chronicle*, 25 April 1778
95. Nick Williams, *op. cit.*, pp.60-1
96. R.H. Mottram, *John Crome of Norwich* (1931), p.11

V *Victorian Norwich*

1. *Champion*, 10 November 1838, p.37
2. NRO, KIM 6/40
3. Trevor Nuthall, *Christ Church, New Catton; biography of a church* (1980), pp.4, 5
4. J.T. Ward, *Chartism* (1973), p.96; NRO N/S 2/3
5. J.R. Clynes, *Memoirs 1869-1924* (1937), p.76; *TUC Conference Report, 1894*; Caroline Benn, *Keir Hardie* (1992), p.120
6. G.M. Young, *Early Victorian England* (1934), vol. 1, p.210; *Barclay's Complete and Universal Dictionary* (1842)
7. J. Gurney-Read, *Trades and Industries of Norwich* (1988), pp.71-6
8. *Annals*, *op. cit.*, vol. 1, p.447
9. The market was regulated by the Market Committee (NRO, N/TC 8/1-18)
10. *Annals*, *op. cit.*, pp.214, 386
11. S.J. Noel Henderson (ed.), *The Goulburn Norwich diaries* (1996), p.160
12. *A Second Report of the Royal Commission for inquiring into the state of large Towns and Populous Districts* 1845. Appendix: Norwich
13. Sheila Adam, *The Plantation Garden, a history and guide* (1998), *passim*
14. NRO, MC 389/23
15. David Summers, 'George John Skipper: Norfolk Architect', in Kathryn Perry (ed.), *Powerhouses of Provincial Architecture,* (2009), pp.75-84; Nobbs, *op. cit.*, p.52
16. Pevsner and Wilson, *op. cit.*, p.279
17. Percy Lubbock, *Earlham* (1926 reprint), p.193; John Ward, *A century of electricity supply in Norwich* (1993), not paginated
18. Brian Gibson, 'Water Water Everywhere', BA Thesis (1996), copy in the Norfolk Studies Library, Norwich
19. J.F. Pound, 'Poverty and Public Health 1800-1880', in Barringer (ed.), *op. cit.*, p.61
20. Barre Funnell, 'Building the sewers of Norwich', in *Norwich Industrial Archaeological Society*, vol. 7, part 5, pp.67-76
21. R. Lambert, *Sir John Simon* (1963), p.399
22. *Norfolk Chronicle*, 2 July 1872
23. Herbert Armstrong (ed.), *A Norfolk Diary* (1949), p.23. A second volume of extracts was published in 1963 under the title *Armstrong's Norfolk Diary*
24. NRO, BR 35/2/73a, 75; BR 35/1/181
25. *Norwich Mercury*, 16 March 1850
26. Batty Shaw (1992), *op. cit.*, pp.61-4; *Annals*, *op. cit.*, *passim*
27. R. Hodgkinson, *The Origins of the National Health Service* (1963), pp.121, 185-7
28. Batty Shaw (1992), *op. cit.*, p.113
29. Quoted in *East Anglian Studies: the nineteenth century* (1984), p.19
30. *Annals*, *op. cit.*, vol. 1, p.361
31. NRO, N/S 2/1
32. NRO, N/ED 7/1
33. Lilias Rider Haggard (ed.), *I Walked by Night* (1982 edn), p.43
34. 'The 1851 Religious Census', *Norfolk Record Society*, vol. 62 (1998), pp.120ff
35. Anon., *A Great Gothic Fane* (undated), *passim*; Pevsner and Wilson, *op. cit.*, p.330
36. Lubbock, *op. cit.*, p.206
37. NRO, BOL 4/157
38. Ronald Hutton, *The stations of the sun* (1996), p.149; S.J. Noel Henderson (ed.), *op. cit.*, p.125
39. Robert Malster, *Wherries and Waterways* (1971), pp.64-7, 83-5, 118
40. *Annals*, *op. cit.*, vol. 1, p.139
41. D.I. Gordon, *A Regional History of the Railways of Great Britain* (1977 edn), *passim*; E.C. Brooks, *Sir Samuel Morton Peto* (1996), pp.168, 310
42. *Annals*, *op. cit.*, vol. 1, p.437; NRO, MS 453. Yarham's story is told in Frank Meeres, *Yarmouth Murders and Misdemeanours* (2010), pp.48-58
43. *Annals*, *op. cit.*, vol. 1, p.451
44. Alan Everitt, *Landscape and community in England* (1985), p.289; *Norfolk Chronicle*, 25 April 1845, 17 January 1846
45. E. Wood, *Historical Britain* (1995), p.443; Gordon, *op. cit.*, pp.178-9
46. R. Joby, in Longcroft and Joby (eds), *East Anglian Studies: Essays presented to Chris Barringer* (1995), p.120
47. Arthur Ransome, *Coot Club* (1934), p.1
48. Eric G. Clayton, *The first 100 years of telephones viewed from Norwich* (1980), p.23
49. Anne Digby, *Pauper Palaces* (1978), p.128
50. White's *Norfolk Directory* (1845), p.128
51. *Norwich Mercury*, 8 September 1883
52. NRO, DCN 120/2 for letters to Dean Pellew about Mousehold Heath; Oliver Rackham, *The history of the countryside* (1986), pp.299-303
53. T. Dugdale, *England and Wales delineated* (c.1845), vol. 7, p.534
54. A.D. Bayne, *A Comprehensive History of Norwich* (1869), p.61; *Dictionary of National Biography*
55. Nick Williams, *op. cit.*, pp.44,45
56. Nick Williams; *op. cit.*, pp.90,91
57. P. Hepworth and M. Alexander, *City of Norwich Libraries – History and Treasures* (1957), p.14; Kelly's *Norfolk Directory* (1883), p.409

58. David Williams, *A world of his own: the double life of George Borrow* (1982), *passim*
59. Tom Roast, *One hundred pupils of Zechariah Buck* (2010), 'Maria Brennan'

VI *Norwich in the 20th and 21st centuries*

1. Patrick Palgrave-Moore, *The Mayors and Lord Mayors of Norwich 1836-1974*, p.43
2. Charles Clarke, 'George Roberts', in Alan Haworth and Dianne Hayter, *Men who made Labour* (2006), pp.155-62
3. Patricia Hollis, *Ladies Elect* (1987), pp.445, 480
4. NRO, NCR 4g10; *Daily Mail*, 28 August 1912, a copy is in NRO, MEA 14/13
5. *The Norwich Roll of Honour of Citizens who fell in the Great War 1914-1919* (1924); Gerald Gliddon, *Norfolk and Suffolk in the Great War* (1988), *passim*. The quotation is from the article by N. Mansfield, p.27
6. Frank Meeres, *Norfolk in the First World War* (2004), pp.145-9
7. P. Kent, in Gliddon, *op. cit.*, pp.61-73
8. EDP 15/11/1969; *Sail and Steam* (Sherlock Holmes society publication) (September 2000)
9. S. Long, 'Norfolk and Norwich Hospital, Twelve Months War Service', offprint from *Eastern Daily Press*, 3, 4 August 1915; Cleveland, *op. cit.*, p.131
10. Fenner Brockway, *Inside the Left* (1942), pp.63-4
11. A.E. Clark-Kennedy, *Edith Cavell: Pioneer and Patriot* (1965), *passim*; NRO, DCN 24/12; Pevsner and Wilson, *op. cit.*, p.293
12. NRO, DCN 106/40
13. Geoff Dyer, *The Missing of the Somme* (2009 edn), p.33
14. EDP 3/12/1938
15. NRO, D/ED 23/31
16. Joan Banger, *Norwich at War* (1974), *passim*; Frank Meeres, *Norwich in the Second World War* (2006), p.123
17. E.C. Le Grice, *Norwich, the ordeal of 1942* (undated)
18. NRO, ACC 2007/242
19. NRO, MC 2299/1; Sarah Housden (ed.), *Norwich Memories* (2009), p.51
20. Le Grice, *op. cit.*
21. George Swain, *Norwich Under Fire* (undated), pp.6-7
22. Banger, *op. cit.*, p.44
23. NRO, N/ED 1/86
24. Richard Clements, *In search of Lady Jane* (1998), *passim*; NRO, MC 376/157
25. William Etherington, *A Quiet Woman's War* (2002), *passim*
26. Norfolk Federation of Women's Institutes (ed.), *op. cit.*, pp.188, 215; Housden, *op. cit.*, pp.61, 77, 180
27. Jon Sutherland and Diane Canwell, *The Holy Boys* (2010), pp.149-208; Frank Meeres, *Norfolk in the Second World War* (2006), *passim*
28. C.B. Hawkins, *Norwich, A Social Study* (1910), p.26
29. British Association, *Norwich and Its Region* (1961), p.193, hereafter cited as *Region*
30. Hawkins, *op. cit.*, pp.45, 221
31. The firm's records are now in the Norfolk Record Office, NRO BR 266, and have been ably listed by archivist Tom Townshend
32. Pevsner and Wilson, *op. cit.*, p.308; NRO, MC 322/5
33. Housden, *op. cit.*, pp.187-8; David Armstrong, *A short history of Norfolk county cricket* (1990 edn), p.35f
34. Norwich Heritage Project, *A Market for our times* (2011), p.9
35. Hawkins, *op cit.*, p.75
36. NRO, N/TC 29/6, 7
37. M. Green, *1920s Depression and Norfolk Memories* (undated), not paginated; Norfolk Federation of Women's Institutes (ed.), *op. cit.*, p.8
38. Elizabeth Sturt, *pers. comm.*; Housden, *op. cit.*, p.177
39. Miles Horsey and Stefan Muthesius, *Provincial Mixed Development: Norwich council housing, 1955-1973* (1986), *passim*
40. Alec Clifton-Taylor, *English Parish Churches as works of art* (1974), pp.17, 18
41. Edwin Smith, Graham Hutton, Olive Cook, *English Parish Churches* (1994 reprint), p.221; Pevsner and Wilson, *op. cit.*, *passim*
42. Ted Doe, *op. cit.*, p.62
43. Hawkins, *op. cit.*, pp.145-6,153
44. Anon. [Dorothy Jewson], *The Destitute of Norwich and how they live* (undated), *passim*
45. NRO, N/ED 7/1,2
46. Ethel George, *The seventeenth child* (2006), based on reminiscences now in the Norfolk Sound Archive in the NRO, an amazing resource of memories and oral history
47. D.M. Dickson, *Review of Local Charities* (1970), p.2; Norwich City Council, *Poverty in Norwich* (1991)
48. NRO, N/HE 6/1
49. NRO, N/TC 52/41; N/TC 18/2
50. Atkin (1993), *op. cit.*, p.97, adds that women appeared at their windows with their curlers still in their hair.
51. NRO, N/TC 50/29
52. Elliott, *op. cit.*, pp.146-53
53. Norfolk County Council, *Norwich Area Transport Strategy Draft Plan* (1997)
54. Ralph Mottram, *If stones could speak* (1953), p.68
55. Housden, *op.cit.*, pp.42, 191
56. NRO, SO 153/124
57. EDP 17 March 1903
58. John Balls, *Titanic: the Norfolk survivors* (1999), pp.41-4
59. NRO, SO 26
60. S. Peart, *The Picture House in East Anglia* (1980), *passim*; S. Peart, *What Happened to the Cinema near you?* (1996), pp.58-94
61. NRO, N/TC 57/33; *Region*, p.222
62. Townroe, *op. cit.*, pp.46-7
63. NRO, N/TC 52/56
64. Henderson, *op. cit.*, p.278-9

Acknowledgements

I am very grateful to the many authorities and individuals who have allowed their images to be reproduced in this book. The Norfolk Record Office's County Archivist, Dr John Alban, has supplied a large number of images, listed below with their Record Office references.

Other images have been taken from the following sources:

Norwich City Council: I, XXX
Brian Ayers: 8
Nick Arber: 18
Aviva: 30
Norwich HEART: 11, 22, 34, 35, 40, 100, 101, 147
Archives of the Roman Catholic Cathedral, archivist Dora Cowton: 93; 131a, b
Tasmanian Museum and Art Gallery: IX, X
Mr Michael Jordan: 122, 127, 129, 130, 175
Records of The American Memorial Library, now in the Norfolk Record Office: XXXII, XXXIII, 41. Mrs Marjorie Lund-Fontaine, the daughter of Ludwig Lund, has very kindly approved the use of her father's work.
Joan Banger collection: 171
Victoria Draper: 177
Jarrold & Sons Ltd, records now in the Norfolk Record Office: 154, 155, 157
Norfolk Library and Information Services: 164, 168
East Anglian Film Archive: 183
Katherine Knights, Conservation and Design Officer, Norwich City Council: 185
Nick Williams: 118
Norfolk Museums and Archaeology Service (Norwich Castle Museum and Art Gallery):XVIII, XIX, XX, 85
Norfolk Museums and Archaeology Service (Strangers' Hall Museum): XXXI (photograph by Chris Gill).

Norfolk Record Office References:

II. DCN additional
III. DCN 128/1
IV. NCR 9g
XII, XIII. DCN 128/2, 4
XIV. BR 35/2/2/32
XV. SO 50/4/8
XVI. N/AR
XXI. BR 35/2/35/7
XXV. MC 2632/1
XXVI. N/TC 49/22
XXIX. ACC 2005/60
XXXII. MC 1787/7
XXXIII. BR 110/24
3. N/AR
6. ACC 2009/161
7. Clark per Marriott 18/10/1991
10. MC 365/95
12. NCR 26a/2
13. COL 8/11
15. ACC 2004/53
16. N/AR
20. MS 20676
21, 22. N/AR
23. ACC 2004/53
25. BOL 4/5
26. Clark per Marriott 18/10/1991
28. ACC 2005/189
29. BOL 4/5
31. ACC 2009/161
36, 38. N/AR
41. NCR 24a
44. SO 50/4/8
46. ACC 1997/215
47. N/AR
49. ACC 2005/189
50. HEN 8
53. NCR 17d
60. DN/INV 53/120
61. MC 630/188
63. ACC 2010/41
72. BR 35/2/86
73. MS 177
74. a: N/AR
76. BOL 4/5
77. SO 175/39/2
78. Great Yarmouth Borough Council 4/5/1994
80. NCR 10a/749 (Towler); 755 (Taylor)
81. BOL 4/5
83. NCR 16e/14
84. MC 1787/6
86. BOL 4/5
88. N/W4/1
89. NCR 15c/1/108
90. CHC 11909
91. BR 35/2/86/4
95. NCR 16e/31
96. NCR 16e/99
97, 98. MS 4575
99. NCR 16a/37
104. BOL 4/5
105. BR 172/27/3
106. MC 2678/3
107. ACC 2005/8
108. MC 186/84/3
109, 111. MC 2678/3
110. N/EN/20/184
112. N/AR
113. MS 11303
114. MOT 116
115. a, b: MC 630/189
116. MC 2050/4
117. BR 35/2/39/7
120. MC 186/630
121. ACC 2003/210
119. MS 11351
123. BR 172/27
124, 125. MS 453
126. a: BR 220/211
128. a:MC 365/79
128 b: MC 365/88
132 a: N/LM 2/1
134, 135. MS 6237
136. BR 220/182
137. BR 266/401
138, 139, 140. BR 172/27
141. MC 371/48, USFPH 1/1
142. N/TC 60/1
148. BR 110/69, 71
149. N/LM 2/11
150. BR 110/69
151. N/TC 60/1
152. ACC 2003/210
153. a: N/LM 2/11
153 b: ACC 1997/146
154. JLD 2/30/7/2
155, 157. JLD 2/30/7/1
156. Clark per Marriott 18/10/1991
158. N/LM 2/11
159. ACC 2003/210
160. BR 184/107/2
161. N/AR
162, 163. N/EN 33/3
165. N/TC 60/1
166. BR 220/186
167. ACC 2005/170
169. PS 1/19/12
170. N/TC 60/1
172. BR 266
173. Clark per Marriott 18/10/1991
174. a, b: ACC 2007/318
176. ACC 1997/146
178. N/LM 2/13
180. SO 26/193
181. BR 241/4/580
182, 187. N/AR
186. Clark per Marriott 18/10/1991

Index

Figures in bold refer to illustration numbers.

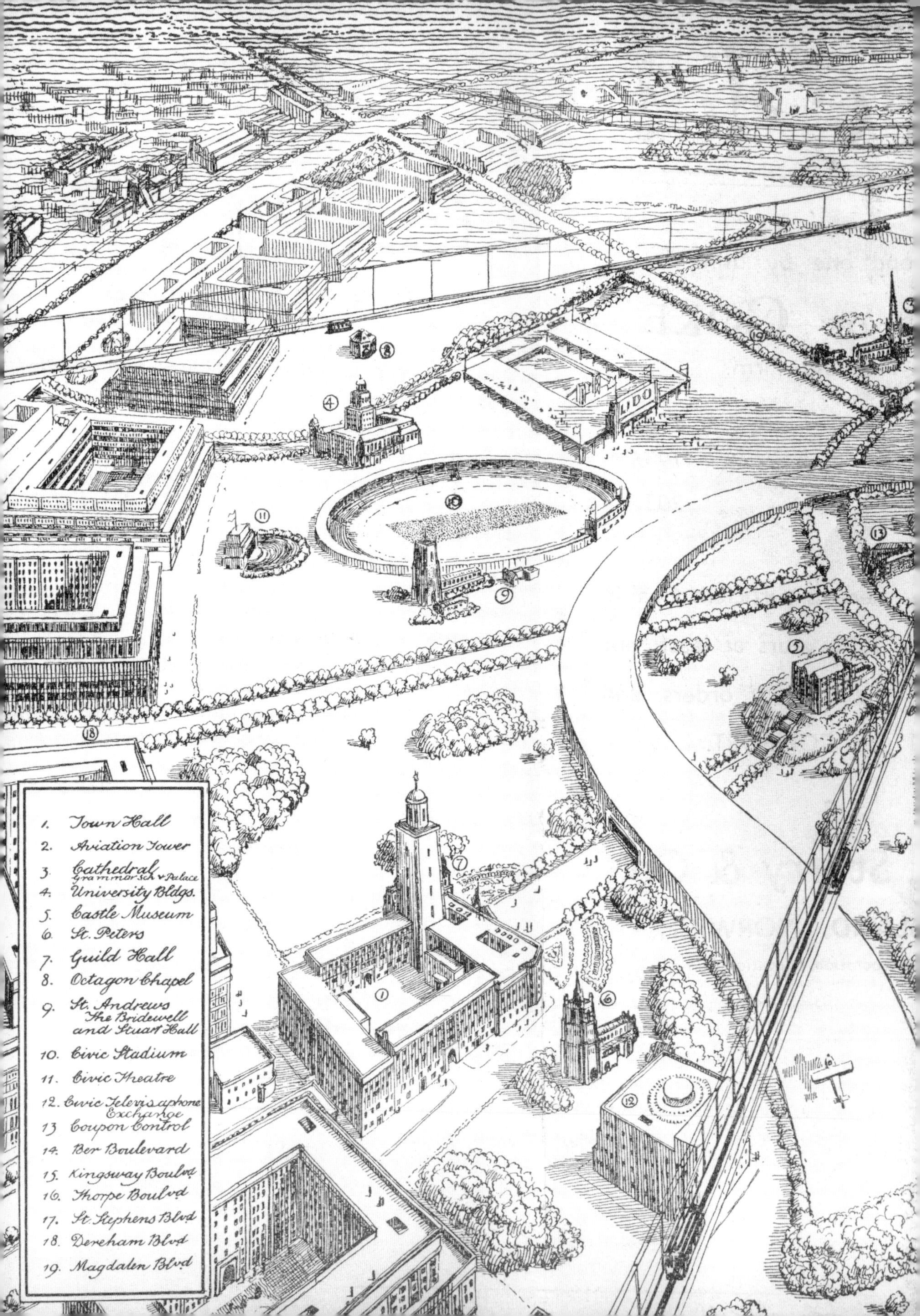

1. Town Hall
2. Aviation Tower
3. Cathedral Grammar Sch & Palace
4. University Bldgs.
5. Castle Museum
6. St. Peters
7. Guild Hall
8. Octagon Chapel
9. St. Andrews The Bridewell and Stuart Hall
10. Civic Stadium
11. Civic Theatre
12. Civic Televisaphone Exchange
13 Coupon Control
14. Ber Boulevard
15. Kingsway Boulvd
16. Thorpe Boulvd
17. St. Stephens Blvd
18. Dereham Blvd
19. Magdalen Blvd
LIDO